Ideas that Matter

Also by A. C. Grayling

The Refutation of Scepticism
Berkeley: The Central Arguments
The Long March to the Fourth of June *(as Li Xiao Jun)*
Wittgenstein
China: A Literary Companion *(with S. Whitfield)*
Moral Values
An Introduction to Philosophical Logic
Russell
The Quarrel of the Age: The Life and Times of William Hazlitt
The Meaning of Things
The Reason of Things
What is Good? The Search for the Best Way to Live
The Heart of Things
Descartes
The Form of Things
In Freedom's Name
Among the Dead Cities
On Religion *(with Mick Gordon)*
Against All Gods
Truth, Meaning and Realism
Towards the Light
The Choice of Hercules
Scepticism and the Possibility of Knowledge

As Editor
Robert Herrick: Lyrics of Love and Desire
Philosophy: A Guide Through the Subject
Philosophy: Further Through the Subject
The Continuum Encyclopedia of British Philosophy
Arthur Schopenhauer: The Art of Always Being Right

Ideas
that Matter

The Concepts that Shape
the 21st Century

A. C. Grayling

BASIC
BOOKS

A Member of the Perseus Books Group
New York

Copyright © 2010 by A. C. Grayling
Published by Basic Books,
A Member of the Perseus Books Group
Reprinted by arrangement with
Weidenfeld & Nicolson

Books published by Basic Books are available
at special discounts for bulk purchases in the
United States by corporations, institutions, and other
organizations. For more information, please contact
the Special Markets Department at the Perseus Books
Group, 2300 Chestnut Street, Suite 200, Philadelphia,
PA 19103, or call (800) 810-4145, ext. 5000, or
e-mail special.markets@perseusbooks.com.

A CIP catalog record for this book is available
from the Library of Congress.

ISBN: 978-0-465-01934-2

10 9 8 7 6 5 4 3 2 1

Contents

Introduction

First Rungs on a Ladder

In the pages to follow I offer a personal dictionary of ideas that have a bearing on an understanding of our world as the twenty-first century unfolds. Some of the ideas are contemporary, some are historical ideas which in more and less subtle ways continue to operate, or in some cases should continue to operate, in the background of the thought and institutions that shape us now. This is a necessarily limited selection, made partly according to the author's interests but chiefly for their intrinsic significance. The overriding criterion for which ideas to include turned on whether knowing about them would enhance an informed receptivity to the events, movements and possibilities of the recent past and its offspring, our time.

Another major motive for giving an overview of the ideas explained here is that the gap described by C.P. Snow in his famous Rede Lecture of 1959, *The Two Cultures*, seems to have become almost impossibly wide, making more urgent the need in today's world for a greater degree of literacy in both scientific and cultural respects. The gap of which Snow spoke is that between science and literary culture, but it should more properly and broadly be identified as a gap between the natural and social sciences, on one hand, and the humanities and literary culture on the other. As science has become increasingly more specialized and complex, so the public mind in general has become increasingly less acquainted with it, and therefore correspondingly less able to participate in informed conversations about the implications, applications, promises, possibilities – and periodic risks – of science. Moreover, attitudes to science on the part of politicians and public servants educated in the humanities have not always been as informed and responsive as the scientific community itself would like, so here too more insight is desirable.

But professionals in the sciences do well to be alert to ideas in philosophical, political and social thought too, so that the wider implications of their own work can be present to them as they do it. Of course the best scientists always are aware in this way; the example of some of the participants in the Manhattan Project during the Second World War, engaged in the construction of the atom bomb, is striking. Much more of this is desirable, and it comes from an appropriate version of the humanistic literacy that would complement and match scientific literacy.

Thus a broader view is desirable, on both sides of the intellectual divide, of the large ideas that constitute the framework of our thinking. My hope here is that a survey of some of those ideas will prove useful in this respect.

A dictionary of ideas is not an encyclopaedia but a starting-point. To illustrate this, imagine a scene: a *levée* at the eighteenth-century Parisian court, at which the assembled company includes the Cardinal de Polignac and that formidable matriarch the Marquise du Deffand. The conversation gets round to the legend of St Denis, the patron saint of Paris who was martyred by decapitation, but performed the miracle of picking up his head and walking with it under his arm for two miles from Montmartre to his abbey, preaching a sermon all the way. The Cardinal de Polignac praised the saint's feat to the king, whereupon the Marquise du Deffand, who did not think much either of the cardinal or the legend of St Denis, acidly remarked that there was nothing so great about it, for only the first step was difficult: 'La distance n'y fait rien,' she said, 'il n'y a que le premier pas qui coûte.'

In the immortal words of one of my Oxford pupils long ago, the Marquise du Deffand had put her foot on something important. She had identified the truth that although there can be no journeys without a first step, in some that first step is crucial to making their successors possible and their direction right. There are of course some journeys, like giving up smoking or losing weight, in which the first step is far the easiest. But when the first step matters, it really matters.

This is especially true when one is learning anything new, including efforts to understand the concepts and theories that shape contemporary debates or lie in the background of them. Ideas are the cogs that drive history onward, for good and ill; understanding influential beliefs, world views, scientific ideas and philosophical theories is a part of the equipment needed by engaged citizens of the world to make better sense of it. Because this is an age of expertise and specialization, in which almost all fields of learning are abstrusely technical, there is a need for concise introductions to key ideas, aimed at non-specialists. What follows in these pages is an attempt to supply that need.

The entries here are not claimed to be either exhaustive or definitive: far from it. They really are first steps of a journey merely; but in the spirit of the Marquise du Deffand's insight, they might make the rest of the journey easier. Short of writing the kind of book Jorge Luis Borges liked to contemplate, namely, one as big as a library or even the whole world itself, all endeavours, like all real art, come down to a decision about what to include and where to stop. But although there is much more that could have been included, and although the selection is a personal one, it at least mainly comes from the central cluster of ideas that matter.

Here is an important point: the perennial difficulty with books of this kind is the 'lumping and splitting' problem; that is, which ideas should have separate entries, and which should be included with closely related ideas in a single entry. Because quite a bit of lumping has taken place, readers should make frequent use of the index: they will find that many of the ideas they expect to find here are discussed under other headings. For this reason too there is inevitable overlap and repetition, but when aspects of an idea appear in more than one place, the different contexts add to an understanding of them.

To say that this is one person's take on things is to declare that attitudes to them will not be disguised, but what is description and what is attitude will always be obvious. The entries are self-standing, and occur alphabetically. But they form families: look at the Appendix (page 389) to see the structure of their relationship. In that structure the main idea is accompanied by a various entourage of associated ideas, suggesting further lines of thought. The principal groupings of ideas range from social questions and politics through philosophy, religion and science. By reading the entries grouped as the Appendix lists them, one will get an informal overview of the field of thought in question.

Readers will note the absence of references. This is deliberate. The merely pragmatic reason for their exclusion is that they would double the size of the book, for a work such as this floats on an ocean of texts and resources consulted. The main reason for their exclusion, and it is an important one, is that the entries here are a preface to the reader's own enquiries, and not a preliminary to a course of study devised by me. If it were, I would do more than select a few texts – each topic gets a brief bibliography (page 393) – as generally indicative of how one might take reading further. But apart from not wishing to prescribe what readers think – though often enough I here say what I think – there is the crucial point that a proper understanding of a topic requires doing the work of finding out about it for oneself. Listening to a lecture, for example, only yields passive knowledge – which is why, though a lecture audience might be bored if subjected to an immediate repeat of what they had just heard, they would not themselves be able to give that lecture even though its closing words still ring in their ears. To activate that knowledge, students have to go to a library or onto the Internet, and hunt for the sources, study them, discuss them, write about them, and thus make them their own. If any of the topics mentioned in the following pages inspires a reader to further interest, that interest should be all the reader's own.

Acknowledgements

My thanks go to Celia Hayley for her assiduous editorial work and her patience, which latter was considerably taxed but unfailing; she acted as midwife to the project while her own first child was on the way, and her help is warmly appreciated. So too is the invaluable help I received from Richard Dawkins, Lawrence Krauss and Kate Smith-Jones, who I may now count as tutors as well as friends. My thanks go also to Alan Samson, Florence Mackenzie, Sophie Erskine, Felice Schoenberg, Bea Hemming and Catherine Clarke, for the invaluable help they variously gave, directly and indirectly. This project started in a now somewhat remote past in a different guise under the erudite care of Richard Milbank, to whom thanks are due for its very existence. Finally no workaholic scribbler can fail to salute the tolerance and support of long-suffering loved ones who perforce shared house-room with a big and demanding book: with Horace I am moved to say, *quod peto hic est, est Ulubris.*

ABSOLUTISM

In political philosophy, 'absolutism' denotes a system of government in which the ruling power is unconstrained by constitutional, traditional, or other limitations. Alas, political absolutism still exists in the world, disguised under different names and sometimes hidden by the way it operates, but the same in its effects as absolutism always has been. The recent past is littered with the names of absolutists, some petty, some big, some malign, some more or less benign – Robert Mugabe, Idi Amin, Saddam Hussein, the imams of Iran, the royal family of Saudi Arabia, Lee Kuan Yew of Singapore – and one has only to look around the contemporary world to name some still in power, and others who have joined them.

Law in an absolutist dispensation consists in the wishes and directives of the sovereign. The views of Thomas Hobbes give the best-known statement of this thesis. Believing that life in a 'state of nature' is a brutal condition of raw conflict in which might is right, Hobbes argued that the ideal society is one in which people yield their individual sovereignty to an absolute ruler in exchange for his or its protection.

After the revolutions in North America and France in the late eighteenth century, debate about politics was frequently couched in terms of the contrast – and typically the actual conflict – between 'absolutism' and 'constitutionalism'. Liberal thinkers recognized that absolutism could take many disguises, from absolute monarchy to mob rule ('ochlocracy') masquerading as democracy. For this reason some of them found the new working-class political consciousness as troubling as the prospect of a return to absolute monarchy. They were not alone in this fear, nor indeed were they in the vanguard of it; right-wing counter-Enlightenment political thought in nineteenth-century Germany took the lead in identifying democracy with ochlocracy. It was represented by a group of writers in the *Berliner politisches Wochenblatt* during the 1830s, who argued that by replacing Christian monarchy with rationalism and conceptions of individual liberty and natural rights, the philosophers of the Enlightenment had promoted the threat of a new absolutism. It was a view that proved perennially influential, as shown by such later thinkers as Adorno and Horkheimer who adapted the argument to blame the Enlightenment for Nazism and Stalinism.

Nevertheless nineteenth-century French and British political thinkers consistently used 'absolutism' as a term of disparagement for any political tendencies that offered to concentrate power in the hands of one or a few, or conversely left minorities unprotected against unbridled majority will. This is the sense of the term that survives in discussion of totalitarianism, dictatorship, and unconstitutional forms of government in general.

In moral philosophy, absolutism is the view that certain actions are without exception wrong, whatever their consequences, and certain others are without exception obligatory, likewise whatever their consequences. Such a view is sometimes described as 'objectivism' or better still, 'strong objectivism', and its chief contrast is with relativism, the view that there are no absolute standards and that different systems of moral value, even if they contradict each other, are of equal validity.

In denying the relevance of consequences, moral absolutism also therefore and of course stands in opposition to consequentialism in ethics, which measures the rightness and wrongness of actions by their outcomes or effects. And in its strong objectivism it is close to the view that moral value is an intrinsic quality, as argued in deontology. The natural home of absolutist ethics is religion, especially of a fundamentalist or literalist stamp, in which the commands of a deity, or prescriptions laid down in texts regarded as sacred, are taken to hold absolutely.

For political absolutism see: COMMUNISM, FASCISM, POLITICS, TOTALITARIANISM
For moral absolutism see: CONSEQUENTIALISM, DEONTOLOGY, RELATIVISM

ACCOMMODATION THEORY

Accommodation theory states that when people talk to each other, they adjust their behaviour and manner of speech to take account of (to accommodate themselves to) the topic, the circumstances, and the other people engaged with them in the conversation. For two simple examples: people talk more slowly to foreigners, and use baby talk when interacting with infants. The way people communicate with each other is central to the kind of social interaction at issue. Thus, friends or lovers (and especially people in the process of becoming friends or lovers) make every effort to converge in manner, accent, tone and topic. Someone wishing to keep his distance or disagree will almost always adopt a manner of speaking expressly different from that of the other party.

These ideas matter because it is clear that the difficulties experienced by immigrants and foreigners everywhere arise in part from the difference of their speech mannerisms, and the limits to their ability to 'converge' with native speakers when trying to communicate. As the world globalizes further at an increasingly rapid pace, and as major migrations of people, especially from the southern to the northern hemisphere, continue, so the problems and too often the frictions increase: accommodation theory, for all its surface simplicity, gives insights into how miscommunication and misinterpretation happen and how matters can be improved.

Communication difficulties do not only affect immigrants and foreigners everywhere. They affect our own fellow-citizens. Social expectations and beliefs about class, intelligence and status are influenced by accent and other speech mannerisms, and therefore certain people from certain classes or regions can be disadvantaged when seeking jobs (especially away from their home localities) by the methods of communicating they learned when young.

Lack of accommodation is thus the source of problems for members of any group identified in given circumstances as an out-group of some kind.

Accommodation theory was devised in the early 1970s by Howard Giles, whose first insights into communication came while working in a medical clinic in Wales, his native country. He wrote, 'The patients I took to the physicians just had to open their mouths and speak and I could predict the manner in which the physicians were going to deal with them.' The ideas he developed have been applied by advertisers and party-political researchers in thinking about the most effective ways of getting messages across to target audiences, and by business management trainers advising clients on how to behave in foreign countries.

The limits of accommodation are illustrated by the latter. Studies found that efforts made by Western businessmen who over-accommodated in order to please potential clients or partners among Japanese businessmen were in fact counterproductive. The danger is that behaviour which appears to involve mimicry of another can look like mockery, or at very least appear condescending; in the Japanese case, the businessmen from

Japan preferred the foreigners to be foreigners – and thus, presumably, to meet their own expectations and to conform to their own planned mode of interaction.

Accommodation theory is of particular value for, among other things, thinking about ways of integrating immigrant communities into host communities, where 'integration' is a term neutral between assimilation and multiculturalism, and just means providing a way for immigrants to get along with the host community while succeeding economically. With mass immigration has come the realization that it is ineffective to expect immigrants to do all the accommodating; and that has resulted in host community adjustments to take account of linguistic and cultural factors in front-line provision of health care, education, social work, policing and legal services.

See: ADVERTISING, MULTICULTURALISM

ACTIVISM

Any form of protesting or campaigning aimed at bringing about change in the political, social, environmental, educational or other spheres of public concern is usefully described as activism, even if it involves deliberate inaction or passivity. Usually it is, as the name suggests, active, and can range from lobbying and propagandizing to street demonstrations, riots, rebellion and terrorism. It is natural to associate activism with left-wing standpoints, community causes, non-governmental organization campaigns on human rights, the environment and globalization, and similarly contested and controversial subject matters, but it can equally be associated with right-wing endeavours (for example, Nazi activism in the Weimar Republic of the 1920s) and traditionalist causes, such as demonstrations and lobbying to defend blood sports in the English countryside.

Some people are natural activists, and quickly rally to a cause they feel strongly about, prepared to put their time, energy and persons to its service, sometimes at considerable cost. Most people are understandably occupied with their private lives and individual commitments, and if they support causes they do so by donations of money or occasionally by writing letters to their Members of Parliament or Congressmen. But if they can be aroused to activism by indignation, a sense of outraged justice, or anything that seems serious and beyond the pale, they find that the shared spirit of comrades fighting a cause can be exhilarating.

There are alarming examples of activism quickly evolving into mob violence, not untypically as a response to harsh policing methods; and there are examples of mainly peaceful mass demonstrations bringing down regimes – as witnessed in the former Czechoslovakia, East Germany and Poland in 1989. These historic events were in their turn prompted by the spectacle of similar activism in China earlier that year, ending in the tragedy of Tiananmen Square in Beijing on 4 June, when army tanks rolled over the student camp that had sprung up before the gates of the Forbidden City. In the momentous events of that year in Europe the bloodiest activism was seen in Romania, when in the weeks before and around Christmas the fall of the Ceauşescu regime cost a number of lives.

Political activism resulting in regime change is a commonplace of history; revolutions in Europe in 1789, 1830, 1848 and 1919 are only some of the salient dates and more extreme examples in the last couple of centuries. But there is a quieter activism that maintains pressure for change in most societies continually, through political processes and public debates aided by the press – at least, in liberal democracies.

Or at least: there should be this latter kind of activism in liberal democracies. But a problem experienced by too many such democracies is lack of participation – that is, lack of activism – with the result that there is low turnout at elections, disillusionment with politics and politicians, and a sense of impotence resulting from a lack of real political choice given that, fundamentally, Western politics is now about small arguments between managerial parties in an age when big decisions about (especially) economies are no longer wholly in the hands of governments, but of global trends and factors.

Activism is not confined to politics. Innovation and experiment in the arts and culture generally are in significant part driven by activists in their fields. Intellectual debate, if it never flowers into action of some kind, is only an anteroom to activism; but writing is a form of activism, for as it has been well if endlessly said, the pen is mightier than the sword.

See: BLACK CONSCIOUSNESS, BLACK POWER, COMMUNISM, POLITICS, TERRORISM

ADVERTISING

Advertising has two chief functions: to inform a supplier's potential customers about the product he is offering them, and to persuade them to buy it. A third but associated function is to instil awareness of a product, brand or company identity in consumers' minds, so that they will tend to purchase accordingly.

It is impossible to escape advertising, and at the same time it is quite likely that if it were banned we would miss it. It is a key part of modern life for a variety of reasons, and though it attracts its critics, it merits defence too.

Advertising is an important aspect of marketing. Creating brand awareness, generating a desire for products, selling into target markets and informing potential customers of the products' suitability for them as determined by market research, all make key use of advertising and its techniques.

Advertising is not only important in business; it is just as important in politics at election and other times, and uses many of the same techniques of persuasion.

The first critical account of the nature and power of advertising was Vance Packard's *The Hidden Persuaders* (1957), which sold over a million copies and, despite not being a very scholarly or even accurate book, placed the question of media and advertising manipulation centre-stage. In making such claims as this: 'At one of the largest advertising agencies in America psychologists on the staff are probing sample humans in an attempt to find how to identify, and beam messages to, people of high anxiety, body consciousness, hostility, passiveness,' Packard helped to give advertising a bad name.

Doubtless advertising in part deserves a bad name, for after all it is an instrument of persuasion, and even under strict rules requiring truth-telling and accuracy, it generally succeeds in glossing facts, being tendentious and overstating its case. At the same time, much of the colour, interest, wit and amusement in life might be lost without its presence on television and billboards, and it serves the valuable purpose of letting people know what is on offer in the marketplace. In both senses, and in the sense that it sometimes helps business to flourish, the world would be poorer without it.

At its best it combines miniature narrative (everyone loves a story) with the kind of humour that arises from real perception into the human condition and its foibles. For the future historian of society, advertising's depictions of the dreams, desires and hopes (not to say fears – of acne, bad breath, social failure, looking a fool, and more) that advertising focuses on, are a treasure trove of information – as they are for anyone who cares to step back and examine what the world wants, for good or ill.

The techniques of advertising are used in propaganda or, as it is called in some liberal democracies, 'spin' to give the best gloss to what a government is doing or a political party is saying. The techniques are used by publicity agents to protect or amplify their clients' images, products, and (respectively) vices and virtues. Every individual uses some of the techniques of advertising in daily life, to find a mate, get or keep a job, and climb to or maintain a position on the social ladder. In short, advertising is a various, ubiquitous and necessary activity; one has only to be aware of it to make good use of it, which includes not being duped by it.

See: CAPITALISM, CONSUMERISM, ECONOMICS, INTERNET, PSYCHOLOGY

AESTHETICS

Aesthetics is the branch of philosophical enquiry concerned with the nature of art, beauty, and the experience of both. A yet more general characterization is that aesthetics is the study of the nature and objects of sensual appreciation, where 'sensual' has its literal meaning of 'pertaining to the senses' (the five senses of sight, hearing, smell, taste and touch). The point of describing aesthetics specifically in terms of the senses is that the term itself is a coining from the Greek word *aisthanomai*, meaning sense-perception.

The more general definition just given allows that natural objects, and nature itself, are sources of sensual delight – mountain scenery, the smell of a rose, the human form in prime condition – as much if not sometimes more than works of art. Nature is indeed far more frequently a prompt for a sense of the sublime than art, though the greatest works of music can scarcely be far behind.

The first question that besets any reflection on value, whether aesthetic or ethical, is: is value (beauty, goodness) objective or subjective? That is, does value exist in the world independently of our interests and preferences, or is it a projection onto the world of these psychological states?

In aesthetics further questions quickly follow. What is it for a work of art to express the intentions or emotions of its creator? How does the achievement of a work of art relate to the advantages and disadvantages of the medium in which it is wrought (for example: how does the excellence or otherwise of a sculpture relate to facts about marble and its workable qualities?)? In narrative arts, such as drama and the novel, what if any kind of truth can there be, and in what sense if any do fictional objects exist (think of how one would answer the question: 'Does Mr Pickwick exist?')? A symphony by Beethoven is a work of art; so is a particular performance of it by the London Symphony Orchestra on a Thursday evening; so is a performance of it on the next Saturday evening by the Boston Philharmonic; are these all the same type of work of art, or is a particular performance (a concert, a dance, the enactment of a play on a given occasion) a different kind of artwork from a single durable thing such as a statue, painting or novel?

Evidently, some aesthetic considerations are entirely general to all possible objects of aesthetic appreciation, and some are specific to particular subject matters. The importance of aesthetic experience is very great: it is impossible to imagine a good life or a good world without art, or the human ability to enjoy nature, or in general lacking aesthetic dimensions of the different kinds that feed the human spirit. Given that enquiry into aesthetics in part helps to educate just such responsiveness and appreciation, it must count as one of the central projects of humanity.

One aspect of interest in aesthetics bears the label 'aestheticism'. Aestheticism is the attitude in literature and the fine arts that art is an end in itself, and requires no external justification, least of all in requiring any practical, moral or educational use in order to be valuable.

Théophile Gautier (1811–72) provided aestheticism with its slogan '*l'art pour l'art*' ('art for art's sake'), and this idea, to which he became committed as a member of the 'Little Coterie' of artists in Paris early in the 1830s, and which he promoted vigorously as editor of the magazine *The Artist* in the 1850s, was a stimulus for the Symbolists in literature and painting in mid-nineteenth-century France and to the Aesthetic Movement inspired by Walter Pater in England in the second half of the nineteenth century. In the guise of the closely related idea that form is of greater significance than content in art, aestheticism continued in the twentieth century, and in contemporary guises survives still.

Aestheticism's theoretical roots lie in the view urged by Immanuel Kant that art is to be judged by intrinsic criteria, not by anything extrinsic. As he put it in his *Critique of Judgement* (see Introduction, VI), beautiful things are 'purposive without purpose' (or at least without *definite* purpose; sometimes this phrase is rendered as 'final without end', that is, as apparently fulfilling an aim without an aim either being given or necessary). Thus, beautiful things – and works of art in general – affect us as if they were meaningful or purposive beyond themselves while in fact not being so. Aestheticism states that this is how things *should* be in the arts.

*

If one great and hotly controversial debate in aesthetics concerns the question 'what is art?' the other great question is 'what is beauty?' This, perhaps, is the first question of aesthetics; because whatever one answers to the question 'what is art?', one has to know what one is including or excluding, showing to be essential or inessential, to its nature when the question of beauty's relation to art is mooted. Beauty is almost certainly not essential to art, but it is a common enough aim of art, and sometimes is what elevates a work to the condition of art; in all these connections we need to know what we think it is.

One effort at definition might be this: beauty is that quality (consisting in one or more of form, harmony, colour, texture, proportion, and other features) of something which excites some combination of reactions of pleasure, admiration and attraction, of a sensuous or an intellectual kind (or both), in a human observer.

The very fact that one has to attempt a definition by means of such generalities illustrates both the difficulty of defining beauty, and the difficulty of deciding whether it is an objective quality of things or a subjective projection from varying individual responses. The study of aesthetics addresses both matters.

In the tradition of antiquity there was much agreement that beauty, whether intellectual or sensuous (and here the sense is primarily that of vision), is a matter of proportion and harmony. For the ancient Greeks in general the aesthetic and moral qualities are inseparably linked; a statue of a trained athlete is as much a representation of moral as of physical beauty, because the harmonies and fitness of the figure's shape serve as a symbol for nobility of character, clearness of intellect, steadiness of purpose, and continence in appetite, as much as they display excellence of physical form.

The Pythagoreans located the harmonies in question in mathematical relations, such as exist in the Golden Section (observed when a line segment is apportioned into two parts of unequal length such that the ratio of the short length to the long length is equal to the ratio of the long length to the whole segment). The eighteenth-century philosopher Gottfried Wilhelm Leibniz also held that mathematical harmony underlies perceived beauty, without the observer being conscious of the fact (see his *Principles of Nature and Grace*, 1714).

Both Plato (in the *Philebus*) and St Thomas Aquinas (in the *Summa Theologica*, written 1265–74) define beauty in terms of proportion likewise, but without invoking unconscious recognition of mathematical underpinnings. For Aquinas as for David Hume (1711–76) much later, beauty is a form of pleasure; this differs from the view of St Augustine who argued that beauty is the cause of pleasure, not identical with it. The disagreement is a significant one because whereas St Augustine's view is consistent with thinking that beauty is an objective property, Aquinas's view makes beauty a subjective matter. With this René Descartes (1596–1650) and David Hume agreed, regarding all judgements of beauty as subjective and individual, and an expression of emotional responses.

For some eighteenth-century philosophers, Hume among them, this subjectivist account did not reduce the value of beauty but rather raised the value of the human mind, for they applauded its honourable and praiseworthy ability to see beauty in things. This was an essential part of Francis Hutcheson's argument in his *Inquiry into the Original of Our Ideas of Beauty and Virtue* (1725). Either on an objectivist or a subjectivist view, this development in eighteenth-century thinking made *taste* a central concept in aesthetics.

In characteristic vein the great Immanuel Kant defined beauty as *both* objective and subjective, or rather: he argued that the right view of it shows that it is a third thing that transcends both. He distinguished the beautiful from the sublime, arguing that the latter contains within it something that disturbs the observer because of a dissonance between reason and sensory experience, as for example when one gazes down into an awesome and profoundly deep chasm among soaring mountains and rocky crags. Beauty, by contrast, is all pleasure; and the pleasure in question is disinterested, non-conceptual, gives a satisfying sense of purpose without purposiveness, and carries with it the conviction that anyone else would share these same feelings – that is, a sense that the judgement that the object in question is beautiful would command universal agreement.

Despite Kant, the difficulty of denying that there are many and often irreconcilable differences between people – between individuals in the same culture at the same time, as well as between people in different cultures and times – in what they regard as beautiful, makes the subjectivist interpretation compelling for many. Edgar Allan Poe (1809–49) defined beauty as an effect, not a quality; George Santayana (1863–1952) agreed with Hume that beauty is what we ascribe to something on the basis of our own emotions, and that it is an interesting psychological phenomenon worthy of investigation that people should want others to agree with them when they judge something beautiful.

It is informative to look at what counts as unbeautiful, as a way of shedding light on the nature of beauty. Thus, anything ugly, grotesque, gruesome, repugnant to the stomach or the moral sense, boring, uninteresting, trivial, over-sentimental, over-decorated, sickly-sweet or nauseating, has little chance of being accounted beautiful. One notes that almost all these notions describe responses or reactions; we typically say that ugly things or situations are *repulsive*, and this literally means they makes us wish to turn away and stop seeing (or hearing or touching) them. And this gives further support to the idea that judgements of beauty are expressions of response, and say something about us (human beings) at least as much as they say something about what lies outside human heads.

A major theme in modern and contemporary art is that there is no necessary connection between art and beauty. This view has been influentially discussed by, among others, Nelson Goodman in his *The Philosophy of Art* (1966), and it directly controverts the views of an earlier aesthetician, R.G. Collingwood, who had defined art specifically as the attempt to produce beauty (see his *Outlines of a Philosophy of Art*, 1952). But if art is the vehicle for the expression of an artist's feelings, it may well be that an artist will deliberately seek to produce ugly or rebarbative, challenging or even disgusting works. (Many among contemporary artists succeed; one imagines it is considerably easier than doing the other thing.) But prevailing practice and attitude in this respect are not without their critics, as shown by the writings of the contemporary thinker Mary Mothersill, who, in decrying the detachment of beauty from art, argues that art criticism implicitly and unavoidably turns on ideas about beauty. It might be said that those who deliberately seek to produce its opposite thereby demonstrate the truth of her thesis, which has proved influential in current aesthetic debate.

Arguably, beauty is a necessity of life. It is certainly a component of anything that can be accounted a good or well-lived life. The absence of beauty from a person's experience might not make him bad, but it cannot fail to be a diminution of his possibilities of feeling and response. This is something so instinctively understood by human beings that they go to great lengths to find beauty, or make it, and almost everyone endeavours to have tokens of it present in their daily lives – the ornaments and pictures that decorate their homes, the colour they paint their walls, the vase of flowers they put on the table: these are all invocations of beauty, and testaments to its significance.

See: ENLIGHTENMENT, LOVE, METAPHYSICS, PHILOSOPHY, ROMANTICISM

AFTERLIFE

'Afterlife' denotes supposed existence in some spiritual or mental form after bodily death.

Belief in such a state is probably nearly as ancient as humankind itself, and doubtless has always recommended itself as an antidote to the terror many feel at the thought of death as extinction or nothingness. Some also or alternatively regard it as incomprehensible that so fine a thing as consciousness, intellect and feeling can be extinguished along with the death of the body. Moreover, the loss of loved ones is rendered much less painful by the hope that they will be re-encountered in a future state. And organized religions, challenged with the complaint that virtue does not appear to be consistently rewarded in this life, are pleased to invoke the idea of posthumous reward (and punishment) for individual activity in the here and now.

The lack of genuine evidence for the existence of any form of continued disembodied existence after death is compensated by dozens of different alleged and invariably anecdotal sources of evidence. Thus, 'near-death experiences', visions, legends, spiritualist seances, ghosts, visitations or messages from angels, saints, a deity, mystical intuition, tradition, scripture, religious teachings, and much besides, constitute a Babel in support of the claim that there is such a thing. None of it amounts to testable, firm, reliable evidence for it; rather the contrary.

At time of writing there were press reports that an experiment was being devised to verify reports by resuscitated patients of auto-scopic (self-viewing) out-of-body experiences during cardiac arrest. This involves placing pictures, objects or symbols on a high shelf near the ceiling, viewable only from above; so if patients report watching themselves from the ceiling being resuscitated on a gurney below, they can be asked what objects or pictures were on the shelf. This is a very poor experiment; it is open to abuse (a devout nurse who knows what is on the shelf can whisper or otherwise suggest to a semi-incompetent patient what they are), and a devout patient can say he or she did not float high enough to see them, or was too emotionally preoccupied with the efforts of the medical team and his own plight to pay attention.

In any case, well-documented neuroscientific experiment has already repeatedly induced autoscopic and 'out-of-body' experiences in subjects by electrical stimulation of the brain cortex, for example during surgery for epilepsy and in other procedures (see, for just one but comprehensive instance, the work of Olaf Blanke and associates reported in the neurological journal *Brain*, volume 127, 2004).

It is vaguely supposed that the vehicle for entry to an afterlife is a soul, spirit or mind, whose existence and functioning are taken to be independent of a body – thus, the non-corporeal entity can think without a brain, see without eyes, etc.; and despite these handicaps, can sometimes interact with corporeal reality, as when a ghost speaks to or – as it might be – attacks physical human beings, or at least somehow succeeds in making ghostly noises to frighten them.

The organized religions claim, and to some extent rely on the claims, of visitations and messages from beyond the grave, whether by saints or virgins or the deity itself; for them the existence of an afterlife is a matter of doctrine, which settles the matter; for without an afterlife the promises and threats implicit in the divine command morality associated with the major religions would lack persuasive power.

Although the idea of an afterlife is welcomed by those who fear extinction, it is a source of horror for those who believe that they merit divine wrath and punishment, and expect it. This seems a tragic cruelty, and the real oppression of mind it causes, even in the day and age in which these words are written, is a scandal.

To rational minds the 'state' of being dead is indistinguishable from the 'state' of being unborn; and as a final release from the vicissitudes of the embodied condition, complete cessation of existence seems a sweet and desirable promise. Among the Romans it was regarded as the last and greatest freedom; they were free of the fear of death therefore. Marcus Aurelius wrote, 'It is not death that men should fear, rather he should fear never beginning to live.'

The phenomenon of 'near-death experiences' is, as noted, taken by some to be an indication, if not actual evidence, for the existence of survival of bodily death. Such experiences are said to have a rather common form: the dying or temporarily clinically dead individual has the experience of passing through a tunnel towards a light, upon arrival at which a being or beings meet the individual. In a few of these accounts the being or beings are not benign; in most they are. People of different traditions are said to interpret the beings according to the traditions in question; thus Christians encounter Jesus, Native Americans encounter the Great Spirit or one of its representatives, Chinese encounter an ancestor, and so on.

The one invariable factor in these stories is that the individuals reporting them were not dead, and did not die. Trauma, physical stress, resuscitation techniques, drugs, natural or injected adrenalin, or any of a number of other causes prompting dream-like, visionary or partially conscious experiences have to be ruled out before supernatural explanations can be entertained. One would like to know how many of the would-be resurrected individuals saw a light at the end of the tunnel – sometimes described as very bright or blinding – because they were lying on a hospital gurney under an overhead theatre or emergency room lamp – and so on for some of the other phenomena they say they witnessed. Having suffered delirium in a high fever, in which lights and human figures took odd shapes and positions and fluctuated in apparent distance, I can testify to the very odd effects on consciousness produced by disease and trauma.

One of my teachers at Oxford, the philosopher A.J. Ayer, had a near-death experience in University College Hospital in London, and told me and others about it shortly after its occurrence. He claimed to have died (and to be very annoyed on being resuscitated because, he lamented, 'now I have to go through it again'), to have passed along the tunnel to a river, on the far shores of which stood the 'Captains of Space and Time', who said (as their cognates so often do to other would-be moribunds), 'You have to return to life; you are still needed in the world.' Asked whether the experience prompted him to give up his lifelong atheism, Ayer said No; he attributed the experience to the drugs and activities associated with his resuscitation. His article about it, though, fluttered the dovecotes of the clergy temporarily, for they like nothing so much as a recanting atheist.

As it happens, though I sincerely hope Freddie Ayer enjoyed the rather short time that he lived after this experience, he did not appear to do anything during it which would justify his having been sent back by the Captains of Space and Time; which somewhat calls in question not only what the superstitious would like to make of his experience, but the competence of the Captains if they exist.

See: AGNOSTICISM, ATHEISM, PSYCHOLOGY, RELIGION

AGNOSTICISM

Agnosticism is the view that one must withhold belief or disbelief on the grounds that neither is warranted by the available evidence or reasons. The term's chief use lies in the field of debate about whether or not a deity or deities or other supernatural agencies or entities exist, and the usual understanding is that an agnostic is one who does not believe there are such things, but does not feel entitled to deny their existence outright on the grounds that their non-existence cannot be proved. The strong thesis that denies the existence of such entities or agencies is atheism.

Agnosticism admits of a variety of interpretations. A typical agnostic says that because there are inherently no grounds either for asserting or denying the existence of gods, one should make no appeal to considerations about them in one's thinking and acting, and even indeed that it is irrational to do so. This is still not equivalent to atheism, because the agnostic position also claims that there is insufficient evidence for denying the existence of supernatural beings, so the possibility, however small, must be left open.

More weakly, there are those who are agnostic in a merely non-committal sense; unsure or undecided, they do not know what to think either way, because the inducements on either side appear to them equally weak or strong. This neutral stance is consistent with a lack of hostility to religion, and even to a form of religious observance, sometimes on the grounds of something like Pascal's Wager: the French mathematician Blaise Pascal (1623–62) argued that even if the probability that there is a god is extremely small, it is better to believe in its existence, and to act accordingly, because the potential benefits of doing so are far greater than those of not doing so. If there is a god, believing that there is will have earned a reward so great that it far outweighs the cost exacted by believing there is a god and being wrong.

There are also, somewhat differently, those who use 'agnostic' in a sense consistent with theism, to mean that although they believe in the existence of some sort of supernatural agency, they know nothing about its nature, and are not in a position to affirm or deny anything about it accordingly.

The term 'agnostic' was coined from the Greek *a* ('not' or 'without') and *gnosis* ('knowledge') by T.H. Huxley (1825–95), who wrote, 'In matters of the intellect, follow your reason as far as it will take you, without regard to any other consideration. And negatively: in matters of the intellect, do not pretend that conclusions are certain which are not demonstrated or demonstrable' (*Agnosticism*, 1889). As this shows, the term's originator himself took it to denote the stronger view described, namely, that there are no grounds for saying that there are supernatural agencies, and consequently no grounds for factoring them into any considerations of science or morals. On the connected matter of personal immortality he wrote, 'I neither affirm nor deny the immortality of man. I see no reason for believing it, but, on the other hand, I have no means of disproving it,' which exactly captures the agnostic attitude.

As a conscious movement, agnosticism belongs chiefly to the Victorian age, when many could no longer accept Christianity, or indeed any positive supernaturalist belief, but at the same time remained wedded to the moral outlook, and found their spiritual yearnings satisfied by scientific and romantic interest in nature. As to the moral side of the question, a light-hearted limerick sums it up: 'There was a young man from Moldavia/ Who no longer believed in the Saviour/ So he erected instead/ With himself as the head/ The religion of decorous behaviour'. 'Moldavianism' was the order of the day among the educated and scientific classes.

Although T.H. Huxley coined the term, the thinker who gave it its profoundest currency was Herbert Spencer (1820–1903) in his *First Principles* (1862), the opening work in a vast synthesis of philosophy premised on evolutionary theory. His claim was that science and religion could be reconciled – this being the vast question of the day – only if it was accepted that both rested on what is ultimately unknowable. This is agnosticism in action with a vengeance.

Agnosticism in the religious context is thought by many to be a more reasonable as well as a more conciliatory position than atheism. In fact it is not; it is a fence-sitting position premised on confusions about knowledge and rationality. Strictly speaking, if knowledge is a matter of definitive proof, then we know nothing outside mathematics and logic, and there only because we have defined the terms, axioms and operations from which the 'truths' of these formal systems follow. For consider: even so seemingly obvious a claim as that there is a laptop screen before me now as I write these words can be called in question by sceptical arguments challenging me to 'prove' that I am not asleep and dreaming, or hallucinating, or a brain in a vat only thinking it has hands whose fingers are plying a keyboard. Such doubts, in practical terms, are trivial; so in practice we give the name of knowledge to what has been repeatedly tested and verified, and which forms the basis for other things we think and do, and which is borne out in our applications of it to our actions. Thus, we take aerodynamic engineering to rest on a relevant body of knowledge whenever we take off in an aeroplane; aerodynamics is amply established as a body of knowledge by its repeated empirical success, and this despite the fact that it cannot be 'proved' to the standards of a theorem in mathematics.

But the point about the supposed reasonableness of religious agnosticism is that to think there might be supernatural beings or entities in the universe has the same rational ground as thinking that a china teapot is in orbit round the sun. This was Bertrand Russell's amusing way of pointing out the agnostic's problem: he cannot prove that there is not a china teapot flying round the sun, so by his lights he must leave open the possibility that there is such a thing, and suspend judgement either way. But obviously enough, every consideration of evidence and reason weighs so heavily against there being such a thing that to entertain the possibility that it might be so – not, note, even to go so far as to think it equally likely or unlikely – is irrational to the extent quite literally of lunacy.

All one has to do is to think very seriously about what is putatively meant by hypothesizing the existence of supernatural entities or beings – deities, fairies, gnomes, ghosts – consistently with the world as we encounter and investigate it. The gods of Olympus or the Hindu pantheon or Moses's burning bush are at one, evidentially and logically, with the tooth fairy and the flying teapot: if it is a form of lunacy to continue to believe in the tooth fairy into adult life, and to organize one's life around its existence, then it is a form of lunacy to believe in the existence of any of the other things. It only seems not to be lunacy to believe in the gods of traditional religions because doing so has such a weight of historical and social sanction, exploiting the credulity, needs and fears of children and mainly unreflective adults, though some quite intelligent adults believe (usually convolutedly sophistical versions of) such things too.

See: AGNOSTICISM, ATHEISM, ENLIGHTENMENT, RELIGION, SECULARISM

ALTRUISM

In its primary sense of putting the interests of others before one's own, the term *altruisme* was coined by Auguste Comte in 1851 from the Italian *altrui* meaning 'others'. It literally therefore means 'othersism'. The concept, if not the word, appears in most moral systems, for it is a key aspect of thinking about the good and the nature of relationships, and states that the question of what is owed to others, both in connection with particular obligations and generally, should occupy a central place.

The moral quality of altruism may be grasped through its contrast with its opposite, namely selfishness, understood as the conscious or otherwise propensity to put one's own interests before the interests of others. It is easy to imagine the range of both altruism and selfishness, from the minor to the major exercise of both, but it is the latter that most sharply brings out the essential character of each. So, the self-sacrifice of a soldier to save the lives of his comrades, and causing serious harm to others to gain an advantage for oneself, constitute focal cases of each.

On some views, an act cannot be truly altruistic if performing it brings some benefit to the actor. So if one takes pleasure or satisfaction in helping others, even if no material gain or public recognition is involved, the act can be construed as self-interested enough not to be 'genuinely' altruistic. This is a convenience for theorists whose view of human nature is such that they wish to construe as self-interested every act, however beneficial to others as well as (or even more than) to its actor. In a well-ordered moral universe one might wish that everyone would take pleasure and satisfaction in helping others or acting in their interests, and this fact would be seen as a good in itself, for thereby everyone gains.

Identifying self-interest as the true and invariable source of motivation for action is known as 'egoism' in philosophy, and as usual philosophers have identified a variety of subspecies. Psychological egoism is the view that even apparently altruistic acts always in fact conceal a self-interested motive; rational egoism is the view that the only justifiable end of action is one's own good. In guises which can be characterized as cynical or realistic depending on taste, some contributors to the revived debate about morality in the seventeenth and eighteenth centuries, such as La Rochefoucauld and Bernard Mandeville, went so far as to say that apparent altruistic acts are actually acts of vanity: 'It is not always from courage that men are courageous, or from chastity that women are chaste' is one of La Rochefoucauld's maxims.

The source of this kind of view is Aquinas, who said that love is in part a function of self-love, which he derived from what is arguably a mistaken reading of Aristotle's remark in the section on friendship in his *Nicomachean Ethics* that friendly feelings for others arise from our friendship for ourselves – the idea being (for Aristotle) that a true friend is 'another self', so that the other is comprehended in exactly the same domain of concern as oneself. There is an interpretation of this which does not entail that self-interest is the wellspring of all behaviour, obviously, but it is not the interpretation favoured by theorists of egoism.

A key area of more recent debate has concerned the possibility of altruism given a biological understanding of human development. In terms of general evolutionary theory, individual members of a species are described as behaving altruistically if what they do benefits not just other members of the species but even other organisms, and to its own individual disadvantage. Examples from across nature are legion. To explain it the notions of 'kin selection' and 'reciprocal altruism' have been mooted, the first hypothesizing that genes which cause an individual to help relatives to ensure that their shared genes have a greater overall chance of survival will proliferate in a population if the benefits of doing so outweigh the costs ('Hamilton's Rule'), and the latter is based on the observation that members of different species will act in each other's interests because the outcome of doing so is better than if each individually sought its own advantage only.

Critics have been quick to say that neither kin selection nor reciprocal altruism are 'true altruism' because of course there is an advantage to the actors themselves in both kinds of case. Among insects, plants and the rest of non-human nature it seems a little too much to expect there to be patterns of behaviour that do not have a species advantage, since the inevitable and probably fairly rapid result would be extinction. But among conscious and reflective human beings it might be expected that principles, beliefs, affections, interests and a sense of greater good might trump self-interest and even self-preservation at times – and that they often do.

See: EGOISM, EVOLUTION, POSITIVISM AND LOGICAL POSITIVISM

ANARCHISM

Anarchy literally means 'without ruler or government', and denotes a political arrangement in which there is no framework of laws or a governing authority. Anarchism is the theory that advocates anarchy in this sense; it is the theory held by those who argue for abolition of the state, defined as a body which exists to maintain a compulsory legal order. Anarchists argue that organic communities will emerge from the common sense of people opposed to living under any form of authority other than what they impose on themselves.

Colloquially 'anarchy' means riotous disorder and mess, and it is generally believed – on the basis of reasonable assumptions about human nature – that anarchy in the first, strict, sense would all too soon degenerate into anarchy in the second sense, with might quickly becoming right, and human life reverting to the 'solitary, poor, nasty, brutish and short' state described by Thomas Hobbes as pertaining to the supposed anarchic situation of mankind before government and laws, when what prevailed was a 'war of all against all'.

Anarchists reply that even if one cynically refused to accept that bonds of friendship and affection might actuate communal behaviour, even the basest self-interest dictates that free individuals would have to set up relationships of mutual assistance, so that order would spontaneously emerge in communities of self-governing people.

The claims of certain anthropologists about the Kalahari Bushmen and some others aside, there are few examples of societies that can be described as anarchies, except briefly and usually in the aftermath of war or other major disaster (for example, for periods during the French Revolution, the Spanish Civil War, and Somalia towards the end of the twentieth century). It is hard therefore to judge the validity of the psychological, sociological and political claims implicit in or optimistically assumed by anarchist theory.

Nevertheless one can canvass some probabilities to test whether an anarchic arrangement would be likely to work, as follows. Contemporary advanced societies function fairly smoothly, in general, within a framework of institutions which give assurance to most people that they can rely on arrangements they have made, contracts they have entered into, and services they depend on. This fact is overlooked by most people because of the very success of its operation; yet it is the result of its being constituted by the enforceable rule of law and well-regulated normal government – in short, the opposite of anarchy, either in the colloquial sense of disorder or in the strict sense of absence of government.

In place of what makes for such order, anarchists propose a society constituted by a sum of voluntary associations, unconstrained and unregulated by anything beyond individual good will. But the central weakness in anarchism, thus characterized, is this: individuals are to some degree self-interested, and not all self-interest is indefensible or irrational. The same applies to groups, such as families or tribes. Sympathies are limited, and so are resources; competition between individuals and groups is therefore inevitable. Competition can, and often does, lead to conflict. Therefore unless there are rules, enforceable and carrying sanctions, to ensure the regulation of competition and a just resolution of conflicts should they arise, the outcome will be that the strong will trample the weak and injustice will be general.

As this suggests, the anarchists' belief that people can live in unregulated mutual harmony is touching but naive. To this inadequate moral psychology they add generalizations about 'freedom', failing to see that the freedoms worth having require protection because of their vulnerability, and that it is precisely in pursuit of genuine liberties that humans congregate into civil society and agree enforceable laws.

The anarchist's mistake is to think that because tyranny is hateful the state should be abolished. A more rational idea is to abolish not the state but tyranny, by making the state fairer and freer, thus protecting its members from the depredations of the greedy and the vile, who are too numerous among us to make anarchism even a remotely serious option.

A close cousin to anarchism is libertarianism (not liberalism), a fact that shows how political wings bend back so far that they touch: for whereas libertarianism is typically associated with right-wing attitudes, most forms of anarchism (e.g. anarcho-communism, anarcho-syndicalism) are typically regarded as lying at the other end of the spectrum. Libertarians are apt to believe in free markets, minimal government, gun ownership and the undesirability of welfare, this latter on the ground that people have not only a right to be free and minimally governed by others, but the correlative obligation to accept the responsibilities this implies. This latter view is at least consistent, but it overlooks, rather harshly, the un-equal endowments and histories of individuals, facts which privilege the few at the expense of the many, among which latter are a further many who cannot benefit from all the opportunities that competitive societies offer. Political philosophies that place social justice and the obligations of communities to their members at or near the centre of attention are, accordingly, opposed to this aspect of libertarianism.

Libertarianism's main home is the United States; its votaries claim that Thomas Jefferson and the Founding Fathers were proponents of their view. In their preferences for economic policy they find inspiration in the writings of Milton Friedman, Friedrich Hayek and Ludwig von Mises. In Britain an apostle of this view was Mrs Thatcher, who went so far as to deny that there is such a thing as 'society', believing instead that what are misdescribed by that name are congeries of individuals busily at work furthering their own interests. For those in a good position such views are agreeable. For those concerned about people who are not in a good position, they are deeply uncongenial.

This last remark touches on an important political divide, between outlooks that differ in the relative importance they attach to social justice and individualism. Anarchism and libertarianism in fact lie on the same side of that divide, namely, on the individualist side. It is an oddity of political theorizing and activism that views so opposed in other respects as these two should in their most central impulses be so alike. The really big difference between them is this: that libertarians desire to see strong policing of those who do not profit from libertarianism, so that those who do so profit can enjoy those profits unmolested. Thus libertarianism is selective and partial in the anarchy it advocates, while anarchism is more consistent and inclusive.

See: ABSOLUTISM, DEMOCRACY, POLITICS, TERRORISM

ANIMAL RIGHTS

Human beings have used other animals for food and labour, and more latterly as subjects in scientific experimentation, without much scruple because they have standardly believed that animals are not entitled to anything like the same moral consideration as humans. Kindness to pets is expected of people who have them, and more recent history has seen many countries pass laws which criminalize cruelty to animals, and regulate their treatment by farmers, abattoir workers, hunters, zoo-keepers, circus personnel, and laboratory researchers.

This has come belatedly, and still only partially, for there has been a long history of concern for animals and their moral status. Theophrastus, a pupil of Aristotle, argued in the fourth century BCE that animals share some of the mental and emotional characteristics of humans, and urged vegetarianism and better treatment of animals therefore. His was very much a minority view, of course, and became more so during the Christian era when the biblical grant of animals to mankind's dominion was used as confirmatory justification for the universal and age-old exploitation of animals for human convenience.

Writing at the turn of the nineteenth century, Jeremy Bentham opposed this prevailing view by arguing that the key point about the moral status of animals is that they are capable of suffering, which makes a demand on us to treat them with moral respect. This insight has been the inspiration for Peter Singer, the chief contemporary proponent of animal rights, who argues that an animal's capacity for suffering (and correlatively for enjoyment) puts it into a relation of equality with all other animals having the same capacity, including humans. Language and rationality have traditionally been regarded as the demarcating features that place humans higher than other animals in the scale not just of being but (and therefore) of moral value; the Bentham–Singer view turns on the premise that it is not language and rationality but sentience which is the crucial factor.

The consequence of taking such a view is great. Questions of meat eating, the fur industry, hunting, livestock farming, dairy production, medical and cosmetics research, zoos and circuses, pet keeping, conservation, poaching and whaling, all fall within the purview of debate about animal rights and welfare. An initiative to embrace all the great apes – gorillas, chimpanzees, bonobos, orang-utans and humans – in the same sphere of moral regard, the Great Ape Project, is an important step in reshaping attitudes; for once a declaration of rights for all great apes has been secured, it will be easier to educate human sensibilities about the moral claims of other sentient creatures.

Critics of animal rights say that because animals cannot enter into social contracts with each other, in the sense of recognizing and accepting obligations and duties with respect to each other, and since they cannot make moral choices, they are not fit subjects for inclusion in the sphere of moral thought, except at best in a derivative way by making a minimal demand on humans to treat them 'humanely' when appropriate. This view rests on the mistake of thinking that only beings who can have and recognize duties can have rights. The mistake rests on treating duties and rights as the reverse and obverse of the same coin. That this is incorrect is shown by the fact that we accord rights to infants and the demented elderly even though they do not have duties, and not merely because they will have or have had duties, but because certain facts or qualities pertaining to them make us view them as proper objects of moral regard in their own right. This implies a distinction between 'moral agents' and 'moral patients'; the former are those who have and recognize moral duties and are accountable for their exercise, the latter are those entities towards whom or which some of a moral agent's duties are owed. Of course all moral agents are also moral patients, but the converse does not hold. A chicken, in virtue of being able to experience fear and suffering, is a moral patient, but obviously not a moral agent. The critic of animal rights who says that only duty-bearers are worthy of moral regard is restricting moral patienthood to moral agents. That is a stipulation, not an argument, and moreover not one based on good grounds.

And it might be mentioned, by the way, that it is moot that higher primates other than humans (monkeys, baboons, and non-human apes) do not recognize obligations to others, especially kin; primate ethology suggests that matters are quite otherwise.

It is an interesting fact that organized movements for animal welfare, and eventually animal rights more generally, began in the wake of the Enlightenment. The SPCA (Society for the Prevention of Cruelty to Animals) was founded in Britain in 1824, to be followed by similar organizations in other countries as the century advanced. Added impetus came in the 1960s when the animal rights movement as such came into being, again unsurprisingly in the context of movements against racism and sexism, which made good sense of the argument that 'speciesism' was another form of prejudice and unjustified privileging of one group (humans) over others (other animals) just as sexism and racism were prejudice and unjustified privileging of one group (males, whites) over others (females, blacks). The resonant term 'speciesism' was coined by psychologist Richard Ryder, and made famous by Peter Singer in his book *Animal Liberation* (1975).

There is a campaign for the United Nations to adopt a Universal Declaration of Animal Rights in imitation of the Universal Declaration of Human Rights (1948). It invokes the overwhelming evidence that animals can experience pain and pleasure, and emotional states of depression and anxiety (as for example when in captivity or when being herded into abattoirs), and calls for their protection from the infliction of suffering. It argues that a difference in species, as with a difference of race, is no justification for differential treatment or regard, and certainly does not justify exploitation or oppression, imprisonment, and subjection to experiment. And on the grounds of the 'evolutionary and moral kinship' of all animals it calls for animals to be accorded rights, and for their rights to be protected.

See: ANTHROPOCENTRISM, BIODIVERSITY, SOCIOBIOLOGY, VEGETARIANISM

ANTHROPIC PRINCIPLE

The 'anthropic principle' states that if the universe were different from how it is, there could be no life in it – and in particular, we would not exist to observe and study the universe. Put another way, it states that the 'constants' of nature (the values of, for example, the speed of light, the electric charge, the Planck constant) are fine-tuned for the production of life, making it appear that we occupy a preferred time and place in a preferred universe.

The implications of this view, if crudely drawn, are pleasing to those who think the universe exists so that we can exist – indeed, that it was expressly designed for that purpose. As self-centredness goes, it would be hard to find anything to beat humanity's readiness to think in these terms. This was the prevailing view for many centuries before Copernicus showed that planet Earth is not the centre of the solar system, from which it rapidly followed that the solar system was not the centre of the universe, but something relatively insignificant in the grand scheme of things – a cluster of bodies around an ordinary star, one of a very large number in one arm of a galaxy among billions of other galaxies.

But the impulse to self-congratulatory admiration of the way the universe appears to be arranged for the express purpose of producing humanity (which, remember, counts among its members Adolf Hitler and Pol Pot as well as Leonardo da Vinci, Johannes Brahms and Albert Einstein) has been given a boost by the observation that the basic constants of physics and chemistry seem to be fine-tuned to give rise to exactly a universe which can produce and sustain life (us), and which would not, because it could not, exist if the constants did not have just the values they do.

For example: if electrons and protons did not have equal and opposite charges, chemistry would be radically different, and might entail the resulting impossibility of life. Likewise there would be no water if the weak nuclear force were any weaker than it is, for then all the universe's hydrogen would turn to helium, and there can be no water without hydrogen. In any case the properties of water are miraculously suitable too: alone among molecules, because of the properties of the hydrogen atom, it is lighter in its solid than in its liquid form, meaning that ice floats. If this were not so the oceans would freeze and planet Earth would be an ice ball, inimical to life.

Equally marvellous is how carbon synthesis happens. Carbon is the key component of all organic molecules, and therefore underlies the very possibility of life – at least, of life as we understand it. If the ratio of the strong nuclear force to the electromagnetic force (which keeps electrons in nuclear 'orbit' to constitute atoms) were different, the process in the heart of stars which synthesizes carbon could not happen. Moreover the window of opportunity for carbon synthesis to happen is a very small one, requiring precise energy levels, temperatures and tiny timescales. The age of the universe is crucial too; at about 13 billion years old the universe is ripe for the production of carbon. If it were ten times younger there would not have been enough time for carbon synthesis, if it were ten times older the main sequence stars in which carbon is produced would have passed their sell-by date for the process.

So this must be what has been called 'the golden age' of the universe for life. Add to this the fact that gravity is 10^{39} times weaker than electromagnetism; were it not so much weaker, stars would be far more massive and would therefore burn up far more quickly. The value of the strong nuclear force is also crucial, for if it were even only a little stronger atoms could not form, and if it were a little weaker neither could stars.

Some – obviously enough, religious apologists foremost among them – see this as 'proving' that the universe exists expressly in order for us to exist, whereas the fact that we exist means that of course the physical constants of the universe have to be such that it is possible for us to be here, for if they were not, we would not be here to measure them. So to take the values of the constants as proving that they were fitted to produce us is to put the cart well before the horse – or better: to argue that because some of us wear spectacles, noses came specifically into existence to support them.

Moreover it is also a big assumption that the only kind of life there can be is carbon-based life, or that different universes could not produce life and even intelligence on the basis of physical arrangements different from those in the observable universe.

The term 'anthropic principle' was coined by astrophysicist Brandon Carter in his 1973 contribution to a symposium in honour of Nicolaus Copernicus. As a corrective to the view that Copernicus had shown we occupy no special place in the universe, Carter sought to show that there is a relation between the constants of nature and our existence. He defined two forms of the anthropic principle, a 'weak' one explaining the striking relations between some of the constants of nature in terms of this being a point and place in the universe's history that permits life of our kind to exist, and a 'strong' one suggesting that we can infer what the constants should be from facts about carbon-based life of our kind, or alternatively that we occupy one of a number of universes in which the constants are as we observe them to be.

In their book *The Anthropic Cosmological Principle* John Barrow and Frank Tipler provide the following somewhat different (and somewhat confusingly so) definitions:

(1) The observed values of all physical and cosmological quantities are not equally probable but they take on values restricted by the requirement that there exist sites where carbon-based life can evolve, and by the requirement that the universe be old enough for it to have already done so.

(2) The universe must have those properties that allow life to develop within it at some stage of its history because (i) there exists one possible universe 'designed' with the goal of generating and sustaining

observers; or (ii) observers are necessary to bringing the universe into existence; or (iii) an ensemble of other universes is necessary for the existence of our universe (compare the many-worlds interpretation of quantum mechanics).

(1) is their version of a 'Weak Anthropic Principle' and (2) is their version of a 'Strong Anthropic Principle'. In effect (1) can be glossed as an iteration of the point that the constants are as they are because we, made possible by them being so, now happen to observe them. (2) is more controversial under any of its three readings, one of which has it that the universe is designed (pleasing to the religious) and another having it – far more plausibly – that the universe is in fact a multiverse with the parameters differing from one universe to another, and with us occupying the one where they are suitable for life.

See: BLACK HOLES, CREATIONISM, QUANTUM MECHANICS, RELATIVITY, SCIENCE, SCIENTIFIC REVOLUTIONS, STANDARD MODEL, STRING THEORY

ANTHROPOCENTRISM

To see everything as having humankind at the centre, or as the measure, or as the chief point of interest; to conceive of the gods as human beings writ large (Xenophon said that if the horses had gods they would be horses too); to think that nothing has greater value than human beings, and that everything else can legitimately be bent to the service, use or interest of humanity, is to place humankind at the pinnacle of value in the world, and to privilege human existence over other kinds.

The contrast to anthropocentrism is 'biocentrism', the view that all life is valuable, not just human life. Biocentrism lies at the heart of environmental and ecological movements and animal rights activity. Espousers of such views blame forms of anthropocentrism that see the world as the possession, resource, playground and rubbish-bin of humanity for the harm they have done to the natural environment.

However, it is only when anthropocentrism is coupled with disregard for the rest of nature that it merits the charges laid against it by environmentalists, for one form of the latter is itself anthropocentric in arguing that the chief reason for safeguarding the natural world is that doing so protects the interests of future people. This is consistent with holding that nature is intrinsically valuable and worth protecting for its own sake, but it allows a contrast with those who think nature as a whole is more valuable than any one constituent of it, and would therefore be better off without humankind in it. This is the limiting case of a non-anthropocentric environmentalism, and is as extreme as a non-environmental anthropocentrism. Obviously enough, the right answer here is an Aristotelian mean between the two.

Debate on these matters is sometimes cast in terms of Value Assumptions, the 'Sole Value Assumption', the 'Greater Value Assumption', and the 'Equal Value Assumption'. The Sole Value Assumption says that the only thing that has value is humanity. It takes little reflection to show that this is as untenable a view as attributing sole value to plants or non-human animals, for one immediately sees that, at very least, other things can have instrumental value as subserving the interests of humanity; so, a case can be made for considering the interests of the environment and animals insofar as doing so advances the good of humanity. This in effect is the Greater Value Assumption, saying that humanity has greater value than the rest of nature, but that value can also be accorded to the latter.

A problem that now arises is that it matters what kind of value is attributable to non-human nature. If it is only instrumental value, then if any part of nature stands in the way of human interests, or some perception of what these are, it is straightforwardly dispensable. But if the value is intrinsic, then questions arise about what humanity is entitled to do, if anything, to prefer its own interests before aspects of nature. The Greater Value Assumption by its nature suggests that in a direct conflict of interests the former will always carry greater weight, and this settles the issue.

The Equal Value Assumption is what it says: humans are equal in value to other animals and the rest of nature. Very few would be inclined to accept either this or the non-anthropocentric environmentalist view mentioned above, and accordingly some thinkers, chief among them Peter Singer, have argued that a different point needs to be made, one relating not to equality of value but to equality of consideration; thus, equal consideration can be given only when interests are equal, which (for an important example) implies vegetarianism because the life of an animal is worth greater consideration than an individual human having meat for lunch. This is in essence a utilitarian argument, and as such does not rule out the claim that interests can indeed be unequal. Rather, it seeks to prevent a situation arising in which there is distortion in the consideration of competing interests by antecedent loading in favour of one side only.

See: ANIMAL RIGHTS, BIODIVERSITY, SOCIOBIOLOGY

ANTI-SEMITISM

Hostility to Jewish people, ranging from individual feelings of dislike or suspicion to organized – even by governments – persecution of Jewish individuals and communities, in every case on the principal ground of their Jewishness rather than any individual failing or character quirk, is anti-Semitism. The history of this prejudice is one of the disgraces of humankind, culminating as it does in the effort by the Nazis during the course of the Second World War to exterminate European Jewry, resulting in the industrial murder of some 6 million men, women and children, many in the gas chambers of concentration camps especially built for the purpose. This event, known as the Holocaust, is different only in degree, not in kind, from the sufferings repeatedly inflicted on Jews since they were scattered after the fall of the second Temple in Jerusalem in 70 CE.

It seems that the expression 'anti-Semitic' itself arose in one of the more disagreeable and wrong-headed arenas of nineteenth-century thought, namely debates about race and supposed 'racial purity'. The French philosopher Ernest Renan was at the forefront of racist views to the effect that the Chinese are a race of manually skilful workers, Negroes a race of agricultural labourers, and Europeans a race of masters and soldiers. He asserted that Semitic peoples (Arabs and Jews) are inferior to Aryans, and it was this remark that prompted the Austrian writer Moritz Steinschneider to coin the term 'anti-Semitic' to describe Renan's position. But it was the rabble-rousing writings of Wilhelm Marr that explicitly urged renewal of organized hostility to Jewry, even to the formation of a 'League of Anti-Semites', and this forced the label into dictionaries.

The reality of anti-Semitism did not wait for baptism with this name. It began almost as soon as the Jewish people of antiquity encountered others in the growing cosmopolitanism of the post-classical period. In the fourth and third centuries BCE Greeks and Jews came into conflict, resulting in anti-Jewish disturbances in Alexandria in the third century BCE and efforts by Greek rulers of eastern Mediterranean lands to suppress circumcision and other Jewish practices. The first recorded expulsion of a Jewish population occurred under the Emperor Tiberius in the first century CE, when Rome's Jews were made to leave the city en masse. Relations between the Roman authorities and Palestine's Jews were often uneasy, resulting in a number of rebellions, the last of which – with the destruction of the Temple in 70 CE – saw the wider dispersion of Jews into exile across Europe, the Middle East and North Africa. It is probable that the historical Jesus was executed (crucifixion was the form of execution for insurgents and rebels) for participation in subversion against Roman rule.

The record of anti-Jewish feeling and action is sketchy in the later Empire and the sequel of its fall in the West, partly no doubt because the historian Edward Gibbon is right when he characterizes this as a period of relative tolerance. But in the eleventh century CE things changed. Massacres of Jews occurred in Córdoba and Granada, and both in Spain and the Middle East synagogues were destroyed and conversion to Islam, on pain of death otherwise, was forced on many Jewish communities.

Christian countries were not far behind in anti-Semitic activity. Blaming the Jews for Jesus's death, encouraging anti-Jewish feeling with lurid stories of atrocities, including the ritual sacrifice of Christian children, and stoking resentment of Jewish commercial and financial success, the Church and Christian temporal authorities justified by these means their own pogroms and expulsions, and worst of all their Crusades against Jews. The First Crusade of 1096 saw the massacre of whole Jewish communities in the Rhine and Danube regions; the Second Crusade of 1147 saw mass murder of Jews in France. Repeats occurred in the crusades of 1251 and 1320. England expelled all its Jews in 1290; over 100,000 Jews were driven from France in 1398; in 1421 Austria drove out a large proportion of its Jewish population, and in 1492 Spain expelled all its Jews. In each case individual Jews lost almost everything they owned, and probably felt fortunate to escape with their lives.

For some centuries after the late medieval period the Jews found a welcome in eastern Europe, especially Poland, and flourished there. Elsewhere they continued to be blamed when one or another difficulty arose, and were persecuted as a result; when the Black Death swept across Europe the Jews were accused of being responsible for it by poisoning water supplies, and violence against them resulted in thousands of deaths.

By the harsh inexorability of their fate, the Jewish populations which had migrated eastward to escape the rage and hatred of Christian majorities, and which had settled in Poland, Lithuania, the Ukraine and Russia, after a while began to suffer in these regions too, not least in the horrendous period in the seventeenth century that included the pogroms enacted by Cossack leader Bohdan Khmelnytsky.

The racial theories of the nineteenth century were not needed to prepare the ground for Nazi and Stalinist atrocities against Jews in the twentieth century, but they acted as a spur nevertheless. There is a seeming paradox here, in the fact that anti-Semitism was becoming more organized in the light of these racial theories even as – particularly in German-speaking parts of Europe – many Jews were becoming assimilated, extensively blending into mainstream bourgeois and cultural life. Conversion to Christianity and intermarriage were large factors in this process, and the great success of Jewish individuals as net contributors to the flourishing of the age in music, philosophy, literature and science is undeniable. Moreover a growing opposition among some circles to anti-Semitism resulted in celebrated causes such as the Dreyfus affair in France, in which opposition to anti-Semitism was led by Emile Zola.

Yet as that affair itself shows, Jewish assimilation was only skin-deep, and may itself have been a prompt to increased hostility on the part of those predisposed to anti-Semitism. Whatever the explanation, the hideous assault on European Jewry carried out by the Nazis happened despite the apparently civilized assimilative progress of the preceding century: and it thereby serves as one climax (with the fate of Israel still pending one cannot say 'the' climax) to a deeply tragic story.

A point that requires clarification concerns whether anti-Semitism is a primarily religious hostility, or whether it is, or is also – or perhaps the question is: when did it become – a racial one too. For the Nazis it was emphatically racial; a Jew who had converted to Christianity was still a Jew, and merited extermination on that ground alone. In earlier times persecution of Jews ceased when they converted to Islam or Christianity, depending upon who was the persecutor of the day. Under Torquemada in late fifteenth-century Spain something like the Nazi suspicion led to persecution of *conversos*, though in this case a justification was offered to the effect that they might only be pretending to be Christians to save their skins. One might call this a halfway-house reason for persecuting them; the underlying reason remained the supposed stain of Jewishness itself.

The root of Christian hatred of Jews lies in several New Testament passages. One is I Thessalonians 2: 14–16: 'For you, brothers, became imitators of God's churches in Judea, which are in Christ Jesus: You suffered from your own countrymen the same things those churches suffered from the Jews, who killed the Lord Jesus and the prophets and also drove us out. They displease God and are hostile to all men in their effort to keep us from speaking to the Gentiles so that they may be saved. In this way they always heap up their sins to the limit. The wrath of God has come upon them at last.' Another is John 18: 20–2, in which Jesus is hit by a Jewish guard; this individual is the 'wandering Jew', punished for his act of *lèse* divine *majesté* by being doomed to wander the earth perpetually without promise of release by death. In Matthew 27: 24–5 Pontius Pilate explicitly places the blame for Jesus's execution on the Jews' shoulders. And in Acts 7: 51–3 St Stephen, immediately prior to his martyrdom, indicts the Jews for the betrayal and murder of Jesus, and for thereby rejecting the Holy Spirit (the unforgivable blasphemy) and God's promise.

Unsurprisingly, the Church was ever thereafter pronouncedly anti-Semitic, many of its votaries (until Vatican Two officially abandoned this view) regarding Jews as collectively responsible for the death of Jesus – which means: for the illogical crime of deicide (illogical because the deity is immortal – but such niceties do not trouble the faithful; nor are they troubled by the fact that without the Jews the alleged mission of Jesus would not have been accomplished) – and accordingly as bearers of a stigma justifying ill-treatment. It was easy for religious grounds of hostility to transpose themselves into racial form; the idea of religious inferiority and that of cultural, moral, and thence racial inferiority is a declension that unreflective hostility is bound to follow. It makes it no more excusable.

Anti-Semitism should be impossible after the Holocaust, yet alas it continues. One reason, or more often excuse, is the vexed and unhappy matter of Israel and its relations to the Palestinians and its other neighbours in the Middle East. It is frequently hard to distinguish opposition to Israeli actions in that region from anti-Semitism, and often the two are connected. They should not be: but saying this is the easy part.

See: FASCISM, JUDAISM, RACISM, TOLERANCE

ARISTOCRACY

Aristocracy is the political thesis that government should lie in the hands of those most suitably equipped by character and experience to rule. The word literally means 'rule by the best'. The best would be intelligent, informed, wise, reflective, fair-minded, humane and incorruptible people, who would have seen the world and had a good share of life's highs, lows, comforts and dangers. Given that there are so few in all history who could satisfy this prescription, aristocracy would appear to be an impossible system of government.

As a matter of historical fact, aristocracies (nobilities, ruling castes or classes) are bodies of people consisting of or descended from people who acquired wealth and power, and secured themselves and their descendants in both. The first acquisition of wealth and power has, again as a matter of historical fact, been a case largely of robbery and rapine, whether on the grand scale (as in conquest by one group of another, for example the Norman conquest of England) or on more local scales.

A self-serving thesis soon enough arose to the effect that the qualities of those who grasped wealth and power were inherited by their descendants. This helped to transform the idea of the 'best' from actual merits currently displayed by an individual, to a fiction about inherited nobility or 'blood'.

As a concept in political philosophy, aristocracy's origin lies in the reaction of Plato to the failure of Athenian democracy. 'Democracy' did not then mean what it does now; Plato defined it in the *Republic* as 'the extreme of popular liberty', in which 'slaves and women' not only have the same rights and freedoms as adult men, but the latter can actually refuse war service or other civic duties if they are disinclined to them.

What Plato meant by democracy, in short, would better be described as anarchy. He was led to this pessimistic view by what he saw as the impotence and chaos of the Athenian democracy. In his eyes it had become mob rule ('ochlocracy'). This showed, he argued, that the uneducated, ill-informed and unskilled mob cannot be expected to conduct the skilled craft of government, which requires special gifts of mind and training – and these, by definition, are possessed by few, and indeed only by the best few.

Moreover, just as the state is like a human body, in which the harmony of the humours constitutes health, and where the head rules, so the state should be harmoniously organized, with as its government a committee of 'philosopher kings' – these being men chosen in childhood for their intelligence, educated in Platonic doctrine, living collegially without wives or private property (and hence without cause, says Plato, for dissension, covetousness, greed or strife). Because they are the best for the task, and have no inducements to be corrupt or tendentious in their actions, the philosopher kings would rule disinterestedly and justly, maintaining the balance in the state to its overall benefit.

This is a far cry from what aristocracy came in fact to mean historically. In constituting a class or caste system of privilege and unequal distribution of wealth and power, it resulted in its most decayed form in the untenable and finally revolution-inspiring *ancien régime* of eighteenth-century France, in which an effete, powdered, bewigged, pointless and parasitic aristocracy, largely exempt from taxes and preying on the sweated labour of a disaffected peasantry, wasted its time in hollow formalities and pomp at the royal court.

In what is one of the most extraordinary of anachronisms even in so anachronistic a society as that of the British, with its monarchy, established Church and unwritten patchwork constitution, the entitlement of hereditary aristocrats to sit in the legislature of the state persisted into the early years of the twenty-first century.

The British aristocracy was enabled by the dazzling reach and power of the British Empire to see itself as the aristocracy of aristocracies. The Russians with their superfluity of inflated titles ('princes' and the like at two a penny), the counts and barons of then minor and more or less irrelevant places like Italy and Poland, the post-Revolution residue of France's *comtes* and *ducs* (of whom there seemed far too many for good taste) and *viscomtes*, appeared to Britain's nobility to be a tawdry lot, pimped out with meaningless decorations and self-importance but without real power in their own countries or status abroad. Some were rich – very rich – but the British aristocracy, though not in the slightest indifferent to money (rather the contrary), did not even think of it when their attention was on the blueness of blood. Impoverished noblemen were still noblemen, and still invited to house parties – these in fact were a form of outdoor relief for indigent aristocrats – and the only pecuniary consideration that ever applied to them was that daughters would not be married to them, or sons or indigent daughters if it could be helped.

The British aristocracy survived as long as it did in the real corridors of economic and political power for a variety of reasons: the British middle class's snobbery, in Thackeray's true sense of upward aspiration and emulation, whose concomitant is a completely irrational admiration for name and station; the fact that the aristocracy and the working classes, especially the rural working classes, genuinely understood and liked each other, and were therefore on each other's side; and the slow, leaden-footed, retrogressive, conservative, plodding rate of change in British society and constitutional affairs right into the last decades of the twentieth century, when – as if released by the loss of empire and the collapse towards the second division of world power – the middle classes, who so lately came to be the main managers of British affairs, embarked on a series of hare-brained and clumsy constitutional reforms whose effect is to improve little and worsen much. The thing that really kept the aristocracy and its allies in charge for so long – the old-school-tie connections, what the Chinese call *guanxi* – is untouched by the reforms, and so a version of the hidden aristocratic hand still prevails, though it is no longer truly a matter of lords and ladies, but of the new barons of hedge funds and multinational corporations. At least: until the crash of 2008.

See: ANARCHISM, CLASS, POLITICS

ARTIFICIAL INTELLIGENCE

In the words of the man who coined the expression in 1955, American computer scientist John McCarthy, 'Artificial Intelligence' denotes 'the science and engineering of making intelligent machines'. His definition, and the multidisciplinary field of research and development it has come to define, are the outcome of responses to a classic paper entitled 'Can Machines Think?' by the computer genius Alan Turing, published in 1950. With the advent of vast amounts of easily summoned computing power, the business of replicating the essential components of intelligence – the ability to learn, reason, remember, communicate information, perceive, plan, and discriminatingly act upon the environment in the furtherance of goals – as functioning features of non-animal 'agents' such as computers themselves or computer-operated machines, has come into the realm of actuality. It has done so mainly in the form of 'expert systems' directed upon states of affairs that lend themselves to analysis in statistical, pattern-recognition, or other quantifiable terms – such as medical diagnostics, logistical monitoring, operational control (for example in flying and landing aircraft), and 'data mining'.

Artificial intelligence ('AI') was effectively launched at the 1956 conference in Dartmouth, USA, for which John McCarthy coined the term in the first place. At the outset hopes were extraordinarily high that machines would be able to do everything humans could do; that machine minds, in effect, could and would be created. The founding assumption of this view is that all features of intelligence can be so precisely described that they can be replicated by a machine built for the purpose. Two of AI's founders, H.A. Simon and Allen Newell, argued that intelligence is the output of a physical system that manipulates symbols. This claim was challenged by the philosopher John Searle by means of his 'Chinese room' argument: suppose someone sits inside a room with a manual on his knee correlating Chinese symbols with each other, such that when one symbol is passed to him through the 'in' slot of the room he can select its correlate and post it through the 'out' slot – all without knowing anything whatever about what the symbols mean. He is a symbol-manipulating device, but he is not the analogue of a mind. Similarly if we looked inside a computer (a symbol-manipulating device par excellence) we would not find a 'mind' in there.

In the first heady decade of AI research, during which large research grants enabled the founding of AI laboratories at prestigious universities, remarkable progress was made in such areas as solving mathematical and logical problems, chess-playing, simple robotics, and plausible Turing-style language use. Such was the promise that the US Department of Defense channelled major sums to the AI labs, and H.A. Simon predicted with supreme confidence that 'machines will be capable, within twenty years, of doing any work a man can do'. It was a view echoed by another founding father of the field, Marvin Minsky. They said these things in the mid-1960s; by the mid-1970s the severe limitations and problems of the project had become so apparent that the funding began to dry up, and with it the hopes.

In the 1980s a more targeted and less ambitious project, that of creating 'expert systems', began to attract private money in response to its success; and on this somewhat different basis the field flourishes, enhanced by the ever-increasing availability of computing power which, as 'Moore's Law' indicates, is growing exponentially. (More accurately, Moore observed that hardware capacity doubles every two years, and his observation has held true for the last fifty years – he made the observation in 1965 as one of the co-founders of Intel. The rate of growth in processing speed and memory cannot be limitless, but it is still increasing exponentially as these words are written.)

From the outset AI has ranged widely among the sciences, social sciences and philosophy for the ideas, insights and tools it requires – not just in computing technology and systems, but in psychology, mathematics and logic, neurology, linguistics, operational research and economics, and it has major overlaps with the engineering and computing of expert systems such as those mentioned above, together with robotics and the development of security systems including face, iris, fingerprint and speech-pattern recognition. As usual, not all these applications are wholly welcome or benign; most are, so far.

Some argue that the use of the word 'intelligent' in AI is at least potentially misleading. The early desire to create non-animal agents which are to all intents and purposes as close to being human as one can get without actual skin and bone, and which 'have minds' in the same sense as human beings 'have minds', did not envisage the 'artificial' in 'artificial intelligence' as changing the meaning of 'intelligence'. But some critics (well-motivated ones; not just those frightened by sci-fi scare stories) pointed out that by definition if intelligence is artificial it cannot be intelligence as such, but a simulacrum of it, or replication of it; and a sticking point was and is the question whether a system that so closely models human intelligence as to pass the severest of updated and embellished Turing Tests could legitimately be thought to have experience and self-reflexive consciousness of the kind that distinguishes human mentation from what goes on in, say, a chess super-computer like Deep Blue.

Among the successes of the more techno-fix style of AI and robotics work which AI has become, turning away – at least for the time being – from the early heady hopes for replicating human mentation and capacity, and doing far better than humans can on the tasks for which AI is apt, are such things as spam filters for email messaging, satellite navigation traffic maps, driverless robot cars, probabilistic prediction of traffic jams, models of how cancer spreads, machine vision, and natural language analysis and employment. Some of these use very complex AI developments, some are technically simple; each fosters the other.

An element in the success of AI as thus evolved has been the use of Bayesian probability analysis in software for dealing with messy, 'noisy' (irrelevance-polluted) data. The world is just such a place, and undoubtedly the most intelligent way to approach it is to have the means for filtering out what matters from what, for the given purpose, is junk. AI seems to be considerably better than humans at getting rid of the latter.

See: GAME THEORY; MIND, PHILOSOPHY OF

ATHEISM

Someone who does not believe that there are supernatural beings in the universe of the kind, or anything like the kind, of gods and goddesses in whom votaries of history's various religions have believed, is called by these votaries 'an atheist'. As this suggests, the term is one coined and applied by theists to describe those who do not share their beliefs, and for almost all history and even to some extent today it is a pejorative term, carrying a connotation – for the great majority of people throughout history – of horror: for what might not a person do who does not believe he is watched every second of the day by an invisible policeman who when he is dead will cast him into everlasting torments for the sins, crimes, horrors, murders, rapes, atrocities and anarchies that an atheist must surely be capable of?

That sums up the appalled reaction felt by believers for most of history towards those who abjure any kind of supernaturalistic belief; for them the word 'atheist' had the connotation that nowadays (and far, far more appropriately) attaches to the words 'paedophile' or 'murderer' – words denoting people who are not notably or exclusively irreligious, and somewhat the opposite, if history and the tabloid press are ever to be relied upon.

In fact everyone is an atheist, at very least about other people's gods. Thus today's Christian is an atheist about the gods of Hinduism, the Norsemen, Greek mythology, the more degenerate and superstitious kinds of Buddhism (which in its core is a philosophy, not a religion), the Aztecs, the ancient Egyptians, and so numerously on. He eschews belief in all gods save for the somewhat ambiguous three-in-one deity of his own relatively young religion (it is only two thousand years old), having perhaps forgotten that his forerunners were themselves called atheists because they would not accept the public deities, and their public observance, which bound the Roman world into a unity. That is why they were persecuted: because they challenged the state by refusing the obligations of citizenship, asserting that their allegiance lay outside to something else.

Imagine a situation in which stamp collectors, so affronted by the refusal of non-stamp-collectors to collect stamps, coined a special term for them: 'astampers', let us say. What would this say about 'astampers'? Well: very little. It would say nothing about what hobbies they prefer, if any, to stamp collecting. To label a non-stamp-collector with a name that keeps stamp collecting in the frame is a distortion. This is why 'atheist' is a loaded term; it keeps in view the possibility that there is something for theists and atheists to discuss. But consider this: your typical atheist does not believe in fairies, goblins, sprites, water nymphs, demons, angels, ghosts or elves either. Why not call him an 'afairyist', or an 'agoblinist', or an 'anymphist', and so endlessly on? For accuracy you should call him all these things at once, conjoined by hyphens. But let us propose to call all those now called 'atheists' by one of these names – 'afairyist', say. But if not – why not? Because there is no real issue about the existence or non-existence of fairies? But that is precisely what so-called atheists think about any gods and goddesses, including the putative One True God.

Someone who rejects claims to the effect that the universe contains supernatural entities of any kind is best called a 'naturalist', not in the old-fashioned sense of one who collects butterflies and presses primrose petals between the pages of his nature-study books, but in the sense of one who takes the universe to be a natural realm exemplifying observable regularities in the way it works, regularities that are conventionally described as 'laws' and used to make empirically testable predictions.

It is customary for discussions of atheism to proceed as if it were exactly the same thing as antitheism, by rehearsing the arguments and considerations that show why belief in supernatural entities is unacceptable. Certainly, antitheism is part of atheism, especially so-called 'strong atheism' defined as active rejection of supernaturalistic outlooks on the grounds that they are false and too often harmful, with so-called 'weak atheism' consisting merely in the absence of such beliefs, perhaps for some such simple reason as that the individual 'weak atheist' has not heard of gods and the like, and has therefore never acquired any supernaturalistic beliefs. This is a distinction of limited interest, except in the sense that a 'weak atheist' (particularly of that kind) might be regarded as rather lucky in not having had to cope with a great deal of nonsense.

It is a mark of the persistence, not to say tenacity, of theistic outlooks that any such thing as antitheism remains necessary. Not much sweat or blood is shed over arguments in universities and the national press for and against the existence of Father Christmas or the tooth fairy, yet both sweat and blood have been and are still being shed over the deities of the major religions, despite the fact that the same amount and quality of evidence in favour of the actual and real existence of Father Christmas and the tooth fairy bear also in favour of the actual and real existence of the Olympian or Norse, or indeed any, gods, including the Christian and Muslim ones. Antifatherchristmasism is a function of maturity; one would have liked antitheism to be likewise. And that, in short, is the antitheist case that underlies atheism, which prefers reason, evidence, testability, and common sense as a guide to what to affirm and deny of the world, rather than (say) the beliefs of goatherds in tents 3,000 years ago.

See: AGNOSTICISM, RELIGION

AUTONOMY

Autonomy means 'self-government'; to be autonomous is to be oneself the giver of the laws one lives under. In many theories of ethics it is considered to be a central value. In some religious moralities – those requiring submission of the will to a deity – it is regarded as a sin (in Christianity it is regarded as an aspect of the sin of pride).

Self-government, independence, and possession of the right and responsibility to make decisions about one's own life, not only but especially in moral matters, are what make one an autonomous agent.

The opposite of autonomy is *heteronomy*, which means direction or government by someone or something outside oneself. It means subjection of one's own will and choices to an external authority, not untypically a deity; historically, also to a king or lord, slave-owner or master.

The conditions of social life of course mean that individuals are subject to many constraints imposed by the requirements of living in community with others, but to the extent that they can think freely for themselves, and make fundamentally important choices in the moral sphere about how to act in particular cases and what sort of person to be in general, to that extent they are autonomous.

Immanuel Kant regarded autonomy as the distinctive mark of an age of Enlightenment. In his essay 'What is Enlightenment?' he wrote, 'Enlightenment is man's emergence from his self-imposed immaturity. Immaturity is the inability to use one's understanding without guidance from another.'

Politically the notion of autonomy means self-determination of a people or group who recognize themselves as an entity with a right to govern themselves and to be free from the interference of others. As often happens in political arrangements, the term is sometimes applied in circumstances when the opposite is the case: for example, the People's Republic of China occupies the territories of a number of non-Han peoples, and calls some of them 'Autonomous Regions' because of the 'ethnic minorities' who live there; but of course the 'regions' in question are no more autonomous than a man in a prison cell. The egregious example at time of writing is Tibet, an enslaved land described in the wicked contradiction of what Orwell would call 'newspeak' as an 'autonomous region'.

See: ENLIGHTENMENT, LIBERTY, POLITICS, PRIVACY, SECULARISM

BIG BANG COSMOLOGY

The 'Big Bang' theory is the publicly best-known cosmological theory of the origin of the universe. A composite summary of it, combining the idea of an expanding universe with influential ideas about how the first moment of expansion occurred, yields a picture which has the universe coming into existence about 13 billion years ago in a 'singularity' which, from an initial immensely rapid expansion in the first infinitesimal fractions of a second of the universe's history, set the universe on the course which yields its present constitution.

The origin of the Big Bang theory lies in the observation made by astronomer Edwin Hubble (1889–1953) that the universe is expanding. This implies that at earlier points in the universe's history everything was closer together; running the clock back eventually gives us everything crunched together as a starting point. Proponents of the then rival 'Steady State' theory (which has it that the universe exists eternally, with matter spontaneously coming into existence in the vacuum of space) scathingly described this first moment of the universe as a 'Big Bang'. The name stuck. Subsequent investigations of the possibilities thus suggested have included, as a front-runner hypothesis, the idea that the first instant of the universe's existence consisted of a singularity which extremely quickly – in just tiny fractions of the first second – 'inflated' into the universe's earliest primordial state, from which it has continued to expand and develop. This is the idea sketched in the first paragraph above.

At the very beginning of the universe's history, says the theory, what had a moment before been a vacuum was an enormously hot plasma which, as it cooled, at about 10^{-43} seconds old, came to consist of equal numbers of matter and antimatter particles annihilating each other as they collided. Because of an asymmetry in favour of matter, to the initial order of about one part per billion, the dominance of matter over antimatter increased as the universe matured, so that matter particles could interact and decay in the way our current theories of the structure of matter describe. As the initial 'quark soup' cooled to about 3,000 billion degrees Kelvin a 'phase transition' led to the formation of the heavy particles (protons and neutrons) and then the lighter particles (photons, electrons and neutrinos). A more familiar example of a 'phase transition' is the transformation of water into ice when the temperature of the water reaches zero degrees Celsius.

Between one and three minutes into the universe's history the formation of hydrogen and helium began, these being the commonest elements in the universe, in a ratio of about one helium atom to every ten hydrogen atoms. Another element formed in the early process of nucleosynthesis is lithium.

As the universe continued to expand, gravity operated on the matter present in it to begin the process of star and galaxy formation. An essential assumption needed to explain how this happened is that the earliest phases of the universe's expansion happened extremely quickly; this is the reason for the name 'inflationary model'.

As noted, the hypothesis that the universe began in a Big Bang was put forward to account for Hubble's observations regarding the expansion of the universe. He saw that in every direction one looks in the sky, every galaxy is travelling away from us, and that the rate at which they are receding is proportional to their distance from us (Hubble's Law): the further away they are, the faster they are receding.

To understand this, imagine that our galaxy is a raisin in a lump of dough swelling up in a hot oven; from the point of view of our raisin, all the other raisins will be seen to be getting further and further away as the dough expands in all directions, and the further away they are the faster they will be receding, just as Hubble's Law states.

The speed and distance of galaxies can be calculated by measuring the degree to which the light emanating from them is shifted to the red end of the colour spectrum. Light behaves in a way analogous to the 'Doppler effect' in sound. This latter is familiarly illustrated by the way the noise of a car drops in pitch as it moves away from us. In a similar way, as a source of light moves away from us, so the light streaming from it increasingly displays 'red-shift', that is, has a colour closer to the red end of the spectrum. (If a light source is coming towards us, its light is shifted towards the blue end of the spectrum.) The greater the red-shift, therefore, the faster the source of light is moving away, and the further away it is.

The Big Bang theory received powerful support from observations of cosmic background microwave radiation, left over from the universe's earliest history. This observation won the 1978 Nobel Prize for physics for the two astronomers who made it, Arno Penzias and Robert Wilson. It is also supported by the observation that the most abundant elements in the universe are helium and hydrogen, just as the Big Bang model predicts.

The standard version of the Big Bang theory requires a consistent mathematical description of the universe's large-scale properties, and the foundation of such a description is the law of gravity, describing the basic force by which large structures in the universe interact. The standard theory of gravity is Einstein's general relativity, which gives a description of the curved geometry of space–time, supplies equations describing how gravity works, and gives an account of the large-scale properties of matter. The standard model premises that the universe is homogeneous and isotropic, meaning that the same laws operate everywhere and that we (the observers) do not occupy a special spatial location in it – which entails that the universe looks the same to observers anywhere in it.

These assumptions, jointly known as the 'cosmological principle', are just that: assumptions, and are of course challengeable – and there are indeed questions about them, not least one that asks how the universe's properties had sufficient time to evolve (especially in the very early history of the universe) to be as they now are. This is known as the 'horizon problem'. A persuasive answer to it is indeed the 'inflationary theory' which hypothesizes a much smaller starting point for the universe, and a much more rapid expansion from that point, allowing known laws of physics to explain how the universe's properties arose. There are other less conservative answers, some requiring adjustment to Einstein's equations, or more generally requiring acceptance of the idea that the values of what we now think of as the constants of nature (such as the speed of light) might have been different in the early universe.

One puzzle concerns whether the universe will continue to expand for ever, or whether gravity will eventually slow down its expansion and then pull it back into an eventual 'Big Crunch' – which perhaps, if the cycle repeats itself endlessly, will be a new Big Bang starting everything over again. The answer depends on the density of the universe. This is estimated by working out the density of our own and nearby galaxies, and extrapolating the figure to the whole universe – which involves the assumption that the universe is everywhere homogeneous, something we have reason to doubt. This is the 'observed density'. The ratio of this density to the 'critical density' – the density of the universe which, so we can calculate, would eventually stop it expanding – is known as ω (omega). If ω is less than or equal to 1 then the universe will expand until it cools to the point of extinction (a 'cold death'). If it is greater than 1 it will stop expanding and begin to contract, suffering a catastrophically explosive death in a Big Crunch.

For reasons of theoretical convenience, ω is assigned the value 1. Measurements achieved by observation suggest that it is about 0.1, which if right predicts the continual expansion to a cold death scenario.

Although the Big Bang theory is the one most widely held by cosmologists, it leaves many questions unanswered, so that research into the origins of the universe remains a highly active field, and neither the theory itself nor the various supplementations and emendations of it are uncontroversial.

One historical rival to it, mentioned above, is the 'steady state' concept put forward by Fred Hoyle, Hermann Bondi and others, which hypothesizes that the universe exists infinitely in the same average density, with new matter being spontaneously generated in galaxies at a rate which equals the rate at which distant objects become unobservable at the edge of the expanding universe. (Hoyle and Bondi accepted that the universe must be expanding because in a static universe stellar energy could not be dispersed, and would heat up, eventually destroying the universe.) The rate of appearance of new matter required for the steady state need only be very small – just one nucleon per cubic kilometre per year.

Apart from the discovery of the cosmic background radiation, which powerfully supports the Big Bang model, another reason for scepticism about the steady state theory is that its assumption that the universe does not change appears to be refuted by the existence of quasars (quasi-stellar objects) and radio galaxies only in distant regions of the universe, showing that the earlier universe was different from how it is today (distance in space is equal to remoteness in past time; to look at far objects in space is to see into the history of the universe).

There are a number of other rivals to the Big Bang theory, in the form of alternative models: the symmetric theory, plasma cosmology, the 'ekpyrotic model', the 'meta model', 'subquantum kinetics cosmology', and others. These proposed alternatives have different degrees of plausibility.

Plasma cosmology was mooted in the 1960s by the physicist Hannes Alfvén, who won the Nobel Prize for his work on plasmas. He suggested that electromagnetism is as important as gravity at cosmological scales, and that galaxies are formed by its effect on plasmas.

The ekpyrotic (from Greek, 'out of fire') model is suggested by string theory and supports the idea of an endlessly cyclical universe; it hypothesizes that the original hot expansive beginning of the universe was caused by the collision of two three-dimensional precursor universes propagating along an additional dimension. The two universes mingle, their energy converting to the particles (quarks and leptons) of the three-dimensional present universe. The two precursor universes collide at every point almost simultaneously, but the occasional point of non-simultaneity gives rise to the temperature variations in the background microwave radiation and the formation of galaxies.

'Subquantum kinetics cosmology' offers a unified field theory drawn from the way non-equilibrium reaction systems generate self-organizing wave patterns, hypothesized as giving rise to matter continuously in the universe.

And so on – some of these ideas are as exotic as they are imaginative.

These competitors of the Big Bang theory are motivated by the fact, already noted, that the theory has many problems. Among the criticisms it faces are these. It has to adjust parameters, such as the cosmic deceleration parameter or those that relate to the relative abundance of elements in the universe, to conform to observation. It has to explain why the cosmic microwave background temperature is the residuum of the heat of the Big Bang rather than the warming of space effected by radiation from stars. It has to account for the fact that the universe has too much large-scale structure to have formed in just 12–15 billion years, thus needing the 'inflationary' hypothesis to render consistent, ad hoc and untestably, the apparent age of the universe and the greater age needed for the formation of its structures. A particular example is that the age of some globular clusters appears to be greater than the calculated age of the universe. Some observers claim that the most distant – and by hypothesis therefore the oldest – galaxies in the universe, those in the 'Hubble Deep Field', show a level of evolution discrepant with their supposed age. And perhaps most puzzling of all, the Big Bang theory requires that we accept that we know nothing about 80 per cent of the universe, which has to take the form of 'dark matter' to explain the distribution and relationships of observed galaxies and galaxy clusters, and moreover with another mysterious ingredient – 'dark energy' – pushing the universe apart.

Cosmology is a field that offers ample room for speculation, and science is as creative and imaginative an enterprise as any other, if not more so. The Big Bang theory itself undergoes modification and adjustment constantly as new discoveries are made, new challenges and criticisms offered, and new hypotheses advanced in physics at both the cosmological and quantum scales. Whether it or one of its competitors – or perhaps a theory yet unborn – is right, cosmology itself is a never-failing source of intense interest. In the coming years and decades there are sure to be remarkable new discoveries about the universe and new proposals concerning its history; it is well to be informed about the current state of both knowledge and doubt in order to appreciate them.

See: ANTHROPIC PRINCIPLE, BLACK HOLES, CREATIONISM, QUANTUM MECHANICS, RELATIVITY, SCIENCE, SCIENTIFIC REVOLUTIONS, STANDARD MODEL, STRING THEORY

BIODIVERSITY

'Biodiversity' is a contraction of the two words 'biological diversity' into one, and refers to the wide variety of living things and systems on planet

Earth, ranging from microbes and viruses all the way up (in scale) to entire ecosystems.

The term was coined during the planning for a conference arranged in 1986 by the biologist E.O. Wilson, and appeared as the title of the book he edited from the conference papers, *BioDiversity*. Prior to this date there had been relatively little discussion of the diversity of life forms and systems on the planet; since then the topic has become a major area of interest.

The foremost practical concern associated with the concept is expressible in the question: how can biodiversity be preserved consistently with the needs of human society? A now familiar, recurring and contentious point of debate is the conflict between conservation of the natural environment and urban, agricultural and industrial development.

For biologists such as Wilson the concept of biodiversity signals a more holistic approach to the natural world, where traditionally there had been what he called a 'bits and pieces' approach. This is a corollary of the preceding rise of ecology as a major development in biological science, but it also registers the concern felt by many that biological diversity is being reduced, mainly by the activities of mankind, and that this reduction threatens to upset sensitive ecological balances which could eventually result in great and yet more serious harm to the environment, and therefore to mankind itself.

Organized campaigning and lobbying in political and media arenas on behalf of protecting biodiversity and special ecological systems such as wilderness, wetlands, rainforests, and others, is known as environmentalism. This broad movement encompasses 'Greens' and conservationists across a wide political and social spectrum, including formally organized political parties who campaign for major changes in patterns of production and consumption and more sustainable lifestyles, to activists in non-governmental organizations concerned with particular aspects of the environment or animal kingdom.

The principles that underlie environmentalism include either or both of the ideas that the natural world is valuable in itself and merits our respect, concern and attention for that reason, or that the natural world is instrumentally important for future generations, to whom we owe a duty of care. The principles are mutually consistent; if the first does not recommend itself to those with harder noses than most, the second by itself is enough to entail that our behaviour towards the environment should be responsible.

Because the nature and degree of possible harm that might flow from reduced biodiversity is not known, an important concept in discussion of it is 'option value', which refers to the possibility that this or that aspect of life in the natural world will have significance to humanity in the future, as a new source of foods, pharmaceuticals, and much besides. Given this possibility, it is important to preserve as many gene pools as possible so that future options can be kept open.

Option value is obviously not the only value that biodiversity has for mankind; at least equally valuable is what it means in aesthetic and recreational terms. Biodiversity's greatest value, though, is itself.

See: ANTHROPOCENTRISM, SOCIOBIOLOGY

BIOETHICS

As the name suggests, bioethics is the study of ethical questions raised by the rapid advance of the biological sciences. It also and very importantly comprehends medical ethics too. In the non-medical biological sphere such matters as genetics and the various and often unforeseeable implications of genome mapping, genetic modification of crops, cloning, animal rights, and aspects of controversy over evolutionary theory, are much and often heatedly debated. In medical ethics the controversial topics include abortion, euthanasia, end-of-life care, paternalism and informed consent, patient rights, sensitive questions related to fertilization and embryology including sex selection of embryos and genetic enhancement, psychiatric treatments, stem-cell research, human cloning both therapeutic and reproductive, and much more.

Although the non-medical bioethical debates are important ones, most uses of the term 'bioethics' tend to apply to medical ethics. For example, the academic journal *Bioethics* begins the official statement of its aims thus: 'As medical technology continues to develop, the subject of bioethics has an ever increasing practical relevance for all those working in philosophy, medicine, law, sociology, public policy, education and related fields.' The reason is not far to seek: medical ethics addresses questions, often very pressing ones, of great moment to the well-being of individuals, and even in an age where the rights and interests of animals and the wider environment prompt ethical concern too, the place of humanity in ethical concerns remains central.

Until quite recently medical people lived by two principal ethical injunctions: do not advertise, and do not engage in sexual relations with patients. There was also an at least implicit adherence to the professional code formulated by Hippocrates (c.460–370 BCE), 'the father of medicine', enjoining strict confidentiality and requiring the practitioner to cure if possible but at very least to avoid doing harm. In the Hippocratic ideal the primary focus is on the relationship between a practitioner and his patient, and this remains the case in the much more extensive set of considerations addressed by contemporary medical ethics.

Questions about the relationship between practitioners and patients are complex and diverse. They concern patients' rights, their consent to treatment, the practitioner's duty to tell them the truth, the degree to which paternalism is justified, and how the practitioner is to decide in cases of divided loyalties – for example, as when a patient presents a wider public health risk because he has an infectious disease, or when a patient would be very suitable as an experimental subject in testing an important new treatment. From life's beginning to its end – from the dilemmas of abortion and whether to withhold treatment from severely deformed neonates, to problems about keeping the aged on life-sustaining treatment, and on to euthanasia itself – ethical questions multiply and press.

The ethical problems surrounding contemporary technologized medicine began to rear their heads with a vengeance when life-support systems and kidney dialysis machines first became available, in the small numbers that made rationing access to them a severely testing matter. Committees were established to choose who would be offered treatment, and studies soon showed that they were granting treatment to patients who tended to be rather like themselves in social and educational profile. This reflected the way selection biases operate in all walks of life, consciously and otherwise; it was the unconscious bias here involved that gave such pause for thought.

Life-support technology gave rise to the vexing problem all too familiar from news reports about families and doctors debating whether life support should be continued or ended for patients in persistent vegetative states. Who should decide? Who has the right to decide? People hope that medical advances might eventually bring the comatose patient back to consciousness: hope springs eternal; the thought of switching off the one tenuous spring of hope is an agonizing one. Sometimes these profoundly difficult and tragic cases have to be settled on their individual merits in a court of law.

Medical practitioners in such fields as paediatrics, neurology and psychiatry have to deal with patients who quite often are not competent to take part in making decisions about their own treatment. In reproductive medicine difficult choices have to be made about fertility, surrogacy, parenthood, and the fate and rights of possible future persons.

In every general practitioner's surgery, the hard fact that resources are limited means that there has to be rationing. Doctors are obliged to choose who will get treatment, who not. It is sometimes difficult for busy GPs to make these decisions; it is more difficult still for patients, whose chances of health, even of life, thereby hang in the balance.

Everything so far mentioned is drawn from real-life difficulties which are familiar, even commonplace, aspects of life in contemporary medicine. But behind them there are other more general questions, which might seem abstractly philosophical, but are in fact both central and essential to thinking about these problems. Some of them might seem to be squarely practical problems at first glance, until a little reflection shows that they concern deep matters of principle. A representative list is as follows. What is a person? What is meant by 'rights' when we say that persons have rights? Is a foetus a person? If not, does a foetus have rights anyway? Is a frozen embryo a person? When does life begin? When does it end? How does one define 'benefit' and 'harm' in the context of medical treatment? What exactly is a 'treatment' anyway? Are doctors always obliged to help their patients? Must doctors always save life? Is it not sometimes justified and humane for them to end life rather than to try to prolong it? Are young people more valuable – more entitled to treatment – than old or older people? What is the definition of a 'worthwhile life'? Is a person with a family for whom he or she is responsible more valuable than a person who does not have a family? Is it permissible to experiment on embryos, or should one never do so? Does a woman have an exclusive and total right to determine what happens in and to her body, including the right to choose to terminate a pregnancy? If a treatment for a given condition exists, does everyone with that condition have a right to that treatment? Who decides what treatment shall be given to individuals (such as those with dementia) who are without representatives or competence to share in decision-making?

This list could be much extended, but the implication of these very tough questions should be clear enough. In the intimate and unequal relationship between the knowledge- and technology-possessing doctor and the vulnerable, perhaps afraid, and almost always less knowledgeable patient, there are many areas where these questions obtrude. Medicine is accordingly one of the main arenas where ethical dilemmas arise, and in acute form.

There are a number of clear general principles of ethical medical practice which any professional body of practitioners would accept as a minimum. They are that practitioners should always seek to act in their patients' best interests, and at least – as Hippocrates required – do them no harm; that they should respect the patient's right to refuse treatment or to have a say in his or her treatment, and that the patient's dignity and autonomy will always be respected; that when resources are scarce they will be rationed fairly; and that patients will always be told the truth and treated with honesty.

A crucial concept underlying much of this is 'informed consent'. Medicine can be a highly complicated proceeding with risks and uncertain outcomes, and some procedures can commit the patient to suffering unpleasant experiences. Ensuring that patients understand what is involved in prospective treatments, so that they can choose whether or not to undergo them with good understanding of what their choice means, is essential. A key to this, in turn, is good communication; in contemporary medical education a training in communication skills is more significantly required than ever, because there is so much more, and more of a complex kind, to explain.

The reason why informed consent matters is that if someone consents to something (or refuses something) that they do not understand, their choice is likely not to reflect what they would choose if they did understand; it is likely not to reflect their values or true desires. In cases where a patient is not competent to make decisions, by virtue of age or incapacity, the next of kin are usually deemed the appropriate decision-makers, provided they too properly understand the options. In the absence of any obviously responsible agent in the case, as in emergency situations where there is no time or next of kin cannot be contacted, medical practitioners themselves are obliged to do what they think is in the patient's best interests at that moment.

A concept that plays a large part in medical practice is that of 'double effect'. Some treatments that do good to a patient, and are intended to do good, can also at the same time do harm. The classic example is the administration of morphine to alleviate pain; it does this, but in large enough doses can also kill the patient. Terminally ill patients requiring ever larger doses of morphine have their lives shortened by it; this is the double effect. The 'doctrine of double effect' states that in such a case the successful intention to do good in one respect exonerates the practitioner from the other consequence of the treatment – in the case of the increasing morphine doses, the death of the patient.

The doctrine of double effect was first articulated by St Thomas

Aquinas in his *Summa Theologica* in connection with self-defence; if in the process of protecting oneself against an assailant one kills him without intending to, Aquinas said, one is not culpable for his death. In this case the self-defender is not even anticipating or envisioning the assailant's death, but in the medical case the second effect of a treatment can be well known but still acceptable, so the doctrine in fact goes further than Aquinas's first statement of it: the practitioner cannot achieve the good effect without the bad effect attending, so in willing and seeking the former he is in effect permitted to bring about the latter even though he knows it will happen. But the good effect must be of sufficient value to justify acceptance of the bad effect. It might also be a requirement that, when possible, the harmful side effects of something done to produce good should be minimized as far as possible; this is surely a tacit assumption of the application of the doctrine in any case.

And there is more that practitioners and society have to take into account on the ethical aspects of medicine. For example, conflicts of interest that might arise in cases as various as practitioners receiving pharmaceutical research grants, or treating members of the same family with competing interests; the question of when treatment is futile, or is likely to prolong suffering or to increase it; the validity of 'living wills' and their relationship to the wishes of kin or to best medical advice; whether, and if so when, euthanasia and physician-assisted suicide might be regarded as acceptable; and much more.

It is no surprise that medicine should be an arena of such rich and multiple ethical concern, for it is about relationships between people – carers and sufferers – in very intimate, vulnerable, life-sensitive circumstances, with great imbalances of knowledge and power in play, and often much at stake: quality of life, and life and death themselves. It is a happy fact, given these considerations, that the majority of people who feel a vocation to medical practice are, by the very fact of that vocation, among the most likely people to think about these questions with intelligence, generosity, and compassion.

See: CLONING, EUTHANASIA

BIOLOGY

Biology is the science of life. It is currently the most important of the sciences, in the sense that some of its subdivisions and offshoots – not least genetics, the theory of evolution, and sociobiology and evolutionary psychology – are at the forefront of changes in medicine and in human self-understanding, and some of these developments in turn present new ethical and social challenges of great significance.

Biology is an enormously wide subject with many major subdivisions, reflecting the variety and complexity of life itself. The single unifying concept in biology is evolution; as the Russian geneticist Theodosius Dobzhansky said in a widely quoted remark: 'Nothing in biology makes sense except in the light of evolution.'

The roots of biology lie in 'natural history', which received its first organization as an area of study in the work of Aristotle (384–322 BCE) and his pupil and successor Theophrastus (died 287 BCE). They engaged in direct and comparative research in zoology and botany, and were among the first to introduce system into ecology and taxonomy, this latter being the classification of plants and animals into rational arrangements.

Another source of biological science was medicine, not just in research into anatomy and physiology as first systematically conducted by Hippocrates (b.460 BCE) and Galen (c.130–200 CE), but into herbs and other plants investigated for medicinal properties. For this latter reason, together with agriculture, botanical knowledge was advanced in many specifics long before the classificatory work of Carl Linnaeus (1707–78). Large and detailed herbals existed in medieval times, and today over 70 per cent of medicines are derived from substances known to herbal or traditional medicine.

Modern biology began in the eighteenth century. The invention and continuing improvement of microscopes were crucial to development in the study of cells (cytology) and tissues (histology), which in turn was the foundation for the rapid advance in biology thereafter made – not least in embryology, heredity, and evolutionary theory itself.

Among the major advances in biology in the twentieth century, including the identification of viruses and the first application to evolutionary theory of genetics (the significance of Gregor Mendel's work in the nineteenth century was at first only fully appreciated in 1905), clearly the chief is the discovery of the structure of DNA by Rosalind Franklin, Maurice Wilkins, Francis Crick and James Watson in 1953.

The revolutionary impact of this discovery cannot be underestimated; within half a century it had resulted in the mapping of the human genome, and with it immense prospects for a giant leap forward in medicine and much besides, including new understandings of the history of mankind.

The sheer scale and rapidity of developments in biology explain the intense debate in the contemporary world over the questions of biodiversity and environmentalism, bioethics including medical ethics, and sociobiology as an account of the nature of humankind – all of them discussed in other pages here. The naturalists of yesteryear with their binoculars and butterfly nets could not have imagined how controversial and exciting the descendants of their pursuit would be – until, that is, Darwin. For some of the most assiduous students of nature and its wonders, which seemed to bespeak the wise and bountiful providence of a deity, Darwin's ideas seemed like blasphemy. And yet when they reflected on the evidence of their own eyes, they could see what a challenge Darwinism posed to the tidy certainties of previous thinking.

One of the most poignant accounts of the conflict between the old and new outlooks in biology (and geology) occurs in Edmund Gosse's memoir of his father Philip Gosse, entitled *Father and Son*. The elder Gosse attempted to oppose Darwinian views with a creationist account of nature, in which all the biological and geological phenomena adduced by Darwin in support of his evolutionary theory were explained as having been laid down, just as they appear, in the six days of creation. He was ridiculed in the press (jokes were made about God having concealed fossils in rocks to tempt scientists to unfaithfulness), so he exiled himself from London and its scientific community as a result. Edmund Gosse says that he sincerely believed his book opposing Darwin, entitled *Omphalos*, would reconcile Genesis and the fossil record; its comprehensive failure settled matters on the eastern side of the Atlantic, but has yet to do so on the western side, where creationism and its disguised version called 'Intelligent Design theory' thrive on the large funds provided by fundamentalist Christians.

See: BIODIVERSITY, CREATIONISM, EVOLUTION, SOCIOBIOLOGY

BIOPOIESIS

Biopoiesis is the process by which life emerged from non-living matter in the early history of planet Earth. This is taken to have happened over 3 billion years ago, about a billion years, or perhaps less, after the formation of the planet. The word 'biopoiesis' is derived from a Greek term meaning 'making life'.

The idea that life arose from inorganic matter in the dramatic conditions of the Earth's early history was mooted in the 1920s by the British scientist J.B.S. Haldane and the Russian scientist A.I. Oparin. The idea is that under the climatic and other environmental conditions prevailing in the early Earth, with high levels of incident ultraviolet light and massive electrical storms to add to other natural catalysers, complex carbon-containing (organic) molecules could have formed in random interactions between inorganic molecules, with thereafter the organic molecules in turn interacting in ways that gave rise to a pre-life or early life form (named 'eobiont'; the term derives from the Greek for 'dawn life'), from which, in turn again, the life forms of today emerged by the processes of biogenesis and evolution.

These ideas received support from experiments done in the 1950s showing in the laboratory that organic compounds form quickly in the 'primordial soup' of inorganic chemicals characteristic of the early Earth when subjected to electrical discharges or irradiation by ultraviolet light.

The results of these and later experiments undermine support for the alternative view, known as 'panspermia' or 'exogenesis', that life was brought to the planet, for example in the tails of comets, from elsewhere in the universe. This view has had some distinguished proponents, including Sir Fred Hoyle and Chandra Wickramasinghe, but remains a minority view among students of the origins of life. But the idea that some of the necessary building blocks for life – amino acids and nitrogen-containing bases – might have arrived on Earth in meteors, or in comet tails or cosmic dust, is considered by some as a possible alternative, given that knowledge of the constituents of the prebiotic 'soup' of the Earth's early environment is still slender.

A little more detail explains the intricacies and difficulties of research in this field. The 1950s experiments mentioned above, conducted by Stanley Miller (the Miller–Urey experiment), demonstrated that amino acids arise spontaneously when a mixture of methane, hydrogen, and ammonia in water is subjected to electrical discharges mimicking lightning. The composition of this 'reducing atmosphere' was inferred from observations of the gases of Jupiter and Saturn, which led to the belief that ammonia, methane and hydrogen, as residue of the solar nebula, had been captured in their atmospheres and those of the other planets including Earth. It mattered that the early atmosphere should be a reducing atmosphere because otherwise the right quantities of organic molecules would not be produced.

The key question of the nature of the Earth's early atmosphere has been much discussed, with some research suggesting that it was not reducing but neutral, and other research suggesting the reverse. The consensus is now that it was indeed a reducing atmosphere, and that the three key gases required for it to be such were probably produced by escape from chondritic material subjected to the high temperatures and pressures characteristic of early Earth history.

Some argue that the 'prebiotic soup' would have been too dilute for organic molecules to exist in sufficient concentrations to interact; others reply that local concentrations would have been enough in the first instance, caused by accumulation in tidal pools or evaporation during climatic cycles.

One thing almost all researches agree upon is that the DNA/protein system was not present at the beginning of life, but evolved at a later stage. Since there is no question of protein and DNA existing without each other, and little question of their spontaneously appearing at the same time, it has been alternatively suggested that RNA was the precursor to both, given that it can play the roles both of catalyst as protein enzymes do, and as a store of genetic information like DNA because, like DNA, it is a polynucleotide. But the idea of an 'RNA world' has itself been extensively criticized, suggesting that although RNA might indeed have preceded DNA and proteins, it could not itself have been the first product of activities in the prebiotic soup; and so the search continues, with intriguing possibilities such as the hypothesized 'PAH world' – in which polynuclear aromatic compounds provide the scaffolding for the emergence of an RNA world – being offered and investigated, and much to play for.

See: CREATIONISM, EVOLUTION

BLACK CONSCIOUSNESS

'Black Consciousness' refers to the political movement in South Africa led by Stephen Biko that arose in the 1960s and 1970s in the context of the anti-apartheid struggle in that country. Its chief tenet was that black South Africans should be self-reliant in their effort to bring apartheid to an end. Existing black political movements in South Africa such as the African National Congress (ANC) had been driven either into exile or underground by the white apartheid regime, and their leaders, most notable among them Nelson Mandela, were either in prison (as he was) or abroad. Hence the reason for the new initiative, which took inspiration from the Black Power movement in the United States.

The death in police custody of Stephen Biko in 1977 drove many of his fellows and followers into exile, where they joined the ANC and the armed struggle from outside the apartheid regime's borders. But the international status accorded to Biko's name by this event was a factor in making the collapse of the apartheid regime inevitable.

A black consciousness movement that began in Paris in the 1930s and has since had much influence in the growth of literature and art among black peoples was known as 'Negritude'. It resulted from the discussions of a number of black students who had gone from their French colonies to study in Paris, and who met regularly to exchange ideas. Chief among them were Aimé Césaire from Martinique, and Léopold Sédar Senghor from Senegal.

Césaire and Senghor not only became significant writers, but they had major political careers in their respective homelands: Senghor was the first president of independent Senegal, and Césaire was a member of the French parliament for Martinique for nearly half a century. (He was also the mayor of Martinique's capital, Fort-de-France.)

Aspects of modernist French culture were an important influence on the thinking of Césaire, Senghor and their fellows, especially Surrealism in poetry, which allowed forms of expression alternative to traditional French conservative rationalism. But the Negritude movement premised itself on the idea that black experience is wholly different from white experience, because black affinities for emotion, intuition and rhythm set it apart from the white Western affinity for logic and order.

If Negritude has a founding text it is Césaire's long poem 'Cahier d'un retour au pays natal' ('Record of a return to my native land'), which affirms what is now called black pride by means of lyrical autobiography.

See: ACTIVISM, BLACK POWER, RACISM

BLACK HOLES

Black holes are astronomical entities whose gravitational field is so strong that nothing, not even light (hence their blackness), can escape from them. Their existence is predicted by Einstein's General Theory of Relativity, which describes space–time as curved, and which accordingly implies that when space–time is curved round upon itself tightly the result will be so compact that nothing can escape the strength of gravity thus generated.

In fact the existence of black holes was anticipated as early as 1795 on the basis of Newton's account of gravity. Pierre-Simon Laplace worked out that if an object were compacted into a small enough radius, its 'escape velocity' (the velocity required to overcome the gravitational force it 'feels') would have to be greater than the speed of light – which is impossible.

The standard account in contemporary astrophysics locates the origin of black holes in the death of stars (specifically, stars at least four times larger than our own sun). Stars are gigantic fusion reactors which exist as long as the forces fuelling them outweigh the large gravitational forces their size generates. When a star of the appropriate size begins to exhaust its fuel, gravity compels it to collapse inwards upon itself. At a certain point the degree of compression of its core, and the heat thus generated, become too great, and the star explodes in a supernova. What remains is a highly dense remnant, whose gravitational field is so great that nothing can attain an escape velocity sufficient to leave it.

The first person to recognize the implication of Einstein's account of gravity in this connection was Karl Schwarzschild (1873–1916), who worked it out while serving on the Russian front in the First World War, just months before his death. He gave a description of the geometry of space–time around a spherical mass, showing that for any such mass there is a critical radius within which any matter would be compacted to such a degree that it would in effect seal itself off from the rest of the universe. He sent his paper with these calculations to Einstein, who presented it to the Prussian Academy of Sciences in 1916. That critical radius is now called the Schwarzschild radius.

What the Schwarzschild radius measures is the 'event horizon' of a black hole, that is, the demarcation line from inside which nothing can escape. At the centre of a black hole is a 'singularity', the name physicists give an entity to which the standard laws of physics do not apply.

There are two types of black holes, distinguished by whether or not they are rotating. The non-rotating kind are called Schwarzschild black holes, with just a singularity as their core and an event horizon. If the core is rotating – and most black holes will be of this type because the stars from which they formed rotated – there will be two further features. One is an 'ergosphere', an egg-shaped region of space outside the event horizon, so shaped because it has been distorted by the black hole's gravity dragging on space–time in the neighbourhood. The second additional feature is the 'static limit', the boundary between the ergosphere and normal space. If by mistake one flew one's spacecraft into the ergosphere, there would still be a chance of escaping across the static limit by exploiting the energy of the black hole's rotation. But once across the event horizon there would be no going back.

Although nothing is known about the singularity which lies at the core of a black hole, its mass, electric charge and angular momentum (rate of rotation) can be calculated. This is not done directly but by means of the behaviour of objects in the black hole's vicinity – the wobbling or spinning of a nearby star; 'gravity lensing' effects, which occur when light is bent by the black hole's gravity as predicted in the General Theory of Relativity; X-ray emissions caused by a black hole drawing material from a neighbouring star and heating it up so greatly by compressing it in its gravitational field ('superheating' it) that the material emits X-rays; and more. It is also hypothesized that supermassive black holes (those with masses billions of times greater than that of our own sun) can throw off high-speed jets of matter, presumably from the ergosphere, and emit powerful radio signals.

Black holes are such exotic entities that they suggest other ideas. One was put forward by the mathematician Roy Kerr in 1963, who suggested a way that black holes might be formed without a singularity at their cores, and if so, flying into one would not result in being crushed to an infinitesimal point, but might result in being spewed out on the other side into a different time or even universe, through a 'white hole' – the reverse or other side of a black hole, which ejects matter rather than sucking it in.

This was one suggestion for time-travel or (if there is more than one universe existing in parallel or honeycomb fashion) for visiting other universes. Other suggestions (for example the existence of 'wormholes' in the fabric of curved space–time that would allow one to shortcut through time) do not hypothesize the absence of singularities at the core of black holes.

See: BIG BANG COSMOLOGY, QUANTUM MECHANICS, RELATIVITY, SCIENCE, SCIENTIFIC REVOLUTIONS, STANDARD MODEL, STRING THEORY

BLACK POWER

'Black Power' refers to a political movement that arose in the United States in the 1960s to assert and defend the rights and interests of black Americans. It was an outgrowth of the civil rights movement, but was less directed at integration than at building African American self-reliance and dignity. As the musician James Brown put it, 'Say it loud: I'm black and proud!'

One of the most eloquent and charismatic leaders of the movement was Malcolm X, but its early theoreticians were Robert Williams and Stokely Carmichael (now called Kwame Ture). Its vanguard was provided by the 'Black Panthers' ('The Black Panther Party for Self Defense' founded by Richard Aoki and others). As the concept of black consciousness and pride flourished, so it encouraged African American debate about the arts and literature, and the themes of black history and aesthetics have since become established focuses of discussion.

The radical outlook of the Black Panthers soon began to trouble not only allied white groups in the civil liberties movement but also other African Americans, because it seemed to risk appearing separatist and anti-white. The Black Panthers were not sympathetic to the non-violent campaign urged by Martin Luther King, and when the black American athletes Tommie Smith and John Carlos gave Black Power salutes on the medallists' podium at the 1968 Olympics, great controversy ensued.

Some of the violence involving Black Panthers was doubtless instigated by police attacks, and it has been alleged on good grounds that the party's collapse in the early 1970s had much to do with covert FBI operations against it. But by then the Black Power movement had established the grounds for a legacy which has in many ways borne great fruit; the situation of African Americans in US society by the beginning of the twenty-first century was unrecognizably different from the mid-twentieth century.

More generally, the concept of 'black power' can be applied to aspirations of black people everywhere, not least in Africa, for recognition, progress, empowerment and development. It ranges from the call for an independent black nation in the southern part of North America (in effect, carved from the region of the USA where the majority of the population is black) to movements in Africa such as Pan-Africanism.

See: ACTIVISM, BLACK CONSCIOUSNESS, RACISM

BUDDHISM

In its original meaning, Buddhism is the philosophy expounded by Prince Siddhartha Gautama of the Sakya tribe in Nepal in the mid-sixth century BCE. In the many centuries that have elapsed since then it has been transformed into various forms, almost all of them replete with imported religious and supernaturalistic elements; Tibetan Buddhism is a salient case in point. That the core of Buddhism is a philosophy and not a religion, in the all-important sense that it is free from belief in deities or supernatural beings, is a significant fact about it.

The central tenets of Buddhist philosophy are expressed in 'the Four Noble Truths', namely, that life is suffering; that suffering is due to attachment; that attachment can be overcome; and that there exists a sure method, if properly applied, for overcoming attachment. Liberation from suffering is thus the arch-goal of Buddhism. Neither the First Noble Truth nor this goal is unchallengeable; indeed, they are both arguably mistaken; but as often happens with theories that start and end in the wrong place, there is much of interest and beauty in Buddhism nevertheless.

The Sanskrit word translated as 'suffering' is *duhka*, which can also mean stress, anguish or imperfection. According to the Buddha what gives rise to suffering is the realization that all things are transient (*anitya*). The word usually translated as 'attachment', *trishna*, also means thirst, desire, craving, and even lust. Because we are all impermanent, dependent beings we are constantly craving or clinging to things, and because our craving is unsatisfied we often feel anger or hatred (*dvesha*). But we do not see what our plight is; we are ignorant; perhaps we are wilfully ignorant (*avidya*).

Once we cease to be ignorant of our plight, we require a path (*dharma*) to help us live aright, and thus to overcome attachment. The dharma consists of eight aspects, and is known as the 'Eightfold Path'. Right View consists in grasping the Four Noble Truths, Right Aspiration consists in desiring to free oneself from ignorance, hatred and attachment, Right Speech consists in never lying, gossiping or speaking maliciously, Right Action consists in never stealing, killing, or indulging sexual appetites, Right Livelihood consists in earning one's crust honourably and without doing harm, Right Effort consists in mastering one's bad qualities and fostering the good ones, Right Mindfulness consists in enhancing one's self-awareness to free oneself from attachment, Right Concentration consists in progressing towards freedom from attachment through meditation. In fact these last three are *samadhi* or meditation aspects of the path; the first two are *prajna* or wisdom, and the next three are *shila* or morality.

This world is *Samsara*, the realm of suffering. The law of *karma* applies to all its inhabitants; what they intend or do, think or say, has consequences (*vipaka* – fruit), and is passed on – not necessarily through reincarnation, although some Buddhists believe in it, but through action and effects on others.

In addition to the *shila* or moral precepts already mentioned, followers of the path are enjoined to aim at achieving all ten of the following virtues: generosity, morality, patience, wisdom, energy, renunciation, truthfulness, determination, kindness, and equanimity.

From this sketch it can readily be seen that there is much in common with aspects of the teachings of ancient Greek ethical schools; the cultivation of virtues reminds one of Aristotle, the exercise of self-mastery reminds one of the Stoics, the idea of an honourable life, of continence, of a duty to combat one's ignorance and negative qualities – all these are common ground between Buddhism and the rich tradition of classical and Hellenic thought. Renunciation and simplicity, especially enjoined on Buddhist monks and nuns, were sought by the Cynics, and for lay Buddhists the prescriptions of the ancient Epicureans would seem very familiar, in their recommendation of frugality and sobriety. These injunctions of the Greeks were aimed at the attainment of self-control and *ataraxia* – loosely: peace of mind, tranquillity, self-possession – which in effect is what the Buddha directed himself and his disciples towards too. So there are marked resonances.

The chief difference is that the Buddha taught that individuality is an illusion and a harmful one, since it underlies the attachments that bring suffering. By contrast the Greeks assumed that we are individuals, and as such are ethical agents responsible for ourselves and what we do. They had a concept of the *great* individual – the hero, the outstanding person, the *megalopsychos* – which is a conception alien to the Buddhist view. Major strands of Buddhism have the notion of a *Bodhisattva*, a Buddhist saint who helps others attain nirvana before he does so himself, never for a moment thinking that any credit redounds to him because he does so; but this is not at all the same thing as the 'great man' idea, indeed it is opposed to it. The Greeks exported the idea of the outstanding individual from the days of warrior virtues to the new ethics of civic, intellectual and moral virtue, wonderfully recorded in allegorical form in the third of Aeschylus's *Oresteia* trilogy (the *Eumenides*). The idea of submerging individuality in the mass, or in the universe, or of losing a sense of self (Aristotle was dubious about sexual pleasure for precisely this reason) would have been exceedingly unGreek.

One might be with the Greeks on some of these points, but without question there is a good deal to admire in Buddhism in its pure form, before the human inclination to apotheose, mystify and mythologize got hold of it in its travels across Asia. It comes as an unpleasant jolt, but not alas a surprise, to learn that Buddhist monks (for example in Japan) have had occasion to make war on each other because of rivalries between monasteries – such stories abound in Kyoto, where hundreds of monasteries abut one another – and when one sees Tibetan Buddhist monks battling Chinese policemen in the streets of Lhasa one's sympathy is so far with them that one forgets they are meant to be committed to peace and wisdom, forgoing the attachments and hatreds all too evident in their – otherwise perfectly understandable and human – behaviour. Such is life; as Kurt Vonnegut was wont to say – so it goes.

Nevertheless as one wanders along the Philosopher's Path in Kyoto – the *tetsugaki no michi* that follows the foot of the wooded Eastern Hills from the Silver Pavilion in the city's north-east down to the suburb where the big rich temples are situated, one cannot but think of the best things about Buddhism, and meditate on some of what it manifests: the tranquil stone gardens, the ponds and paths of the temple precincts, the beauty of the halls and verandas, the stone lanterns and quiet trees everywhere.

See: DAOISM (TAOISM), PHILOSOPHY, RELIGION

BUSINESS ETHICS

As the name suggests, business ethics is the project of applying ethical principles and concepts to an area of human activity in which aims, motives and methods are not notable for their ethical nature. Indeed appearances seem rather to the contrary, for business is about making money, turning a profit, buying for the least and selling for the most, beating the competition, enticing people to buy one's goods and services with blandishments, promises, psychological techniques of suggestion – and other things besides that do not immediately smack of altruism, the milk of human kindness, or even honesty.

But a moment's reflection shows two things: that there is nothing wrong per se with doing business and making money, provided it is done with probity; and there is no reason why ethical standards should not apply to business activities just as they do in every other walk of life. Given the particular nature of business practices and their aims, business ethics – as a branch of applied ethics in general – is the endeavour to show how those aims can be achieved consistently with good standards.

From ancient until modern times business was always looked down upon as something third-rate, because it appeared to engage some of mankind's worst and most self-interested appetites. Aristocratic disdain for 'trade' is a commonplace of literature, the latter regarded as tainted by the low and banausic nature of what it involves. Aristotle attacked business and trade as occupations wholly devoid of virtue, and described people who engaged in it as parasites. Christian ethics demonized usurers (among them Jews prevented from engaging in occupations other than banking and brokerage) until in the sixteenth and seventeenth centuries Protestants came to apply the virtues of thrift, self-sufficiency and enterprise to trade and business too. This was not an entirely novel development; in the centuries beforehand, and very gradually, the medieval guilds had increased the respectability of business, and in any case even aristocrats were not above sinking mines, cutting timber, building mills and manufacturing commodities on their estates. This did not stop them looking down their noses at the people who sold their coal or timber on their behalf, nor did it stop their younger sons, occupying sinecures in the Church, from preaching sermons about the wickedness of the profit motive. But with the inexorable rise into wealth and therefore power of the middle classes, for whom business became as respectable as the professional activities of law and medicine, this lofty view was not permanently sustainable, and has now vanished.

Attitudes to business tend to involve caricature. The profit motive is thought to override every other consideration, so that the idea of a business seeking to serve its customers well with good-quality products, and to fit into the community as a responsible player, is frequently greeted with a horse-laugh; and yet unfairly so, for although unscrupulous business activities certainly occur, they are not the norm, for rational businessmen recognize the self-defeating nature of dishonesty. But it is true that businesses' responsibility is to shareholders, and thus to the 'bottom line' on the balance sheet; they exist to make a profit and to pay dividends, which is the reward for the risk taken by investors; but – to repeat – there is no reason why this cannot be done within the parameters of responsible and accountable behaviour. Which means, of course, not merely within the law, for the boundaries of legal permission in all capitalist economies lie outside those of moral acceptability.

The agents recognized in business ethics are corporations (that is, business entities recognized as legal persons) and human beings, especially those who hold senior office in corporations with final responsibility for decisions on all matters relating to the conduct of the business including governance and policy. Governments, by extension, also have a role in business ethics, in relation to what they enact in the way of laws and regulations affecting the treatment by businesses of their stakeholders. These latter are the shareholders, employees, clients, suppliers, the community at large, and even competitors – though obviously there is a ranking among these, with competitors last; the point about competitors is that businesses have to treat them with fairness and honesty, for example, not running false and injurious advertisements about their goods and services. The obligations of business entities to the community are known as 'corporate social responsibility', and are clearly much wider than just their obligation to abide by the law.

Almost all businesses have codes of ethics for themselves, and these together with society's endeavours, especially as expressed through government action in regulating and overseeing the business world, bear on the range of questions that can arise. These include 'creative' or plainly dishonest accounting, insider trading, fraud, tax evasion, excessive executive compensation, legal compliance, corruption and bribery (including backhanders, kickbacks, 'facilitation payments', inducements in kind), price fixing, cartel and monopoly arrangements, spying on competitors, copyright and patent breaches, piracy of products, poaching of employees, employment discrimination in respect of sex, age, race and creed, harassment including sexual harassment, invasion of privacy and surveillance of employees, hiring and firing practices, union relations, child labour and labour employed abroad in developing countries, health and safety obligations, environmental impact, honest advertising and marketing, targeting unsuitable products at children (alcohol, tobacco products), supplying dangerous or defective products, producing ethically questionable products such as guns and anti-personnel mines, use of animals in product testing – the list is long, illustrating how many areas there are for discussion and analysis in pursuit of good practice and ethical behaviour.

All companies should have an 'ethicist' (a clumsy term now commonplace in the United States) on their boards; some of the best already do. The banking debacle of 2008 makes this even more urgent.

See: ADVERTISING, CAPITALISM, CONSUMERISM, VIRTUE ETHICS

CAPITALISM

Capitalism is an economic system in which the means of production are privately owned, the motive for economic endeavour is profit, and workers are paid wages for their labour. By 'capital' is meant everything required for the production of goods and services, from buildings and machinery to money.

The ethical basis of capitalism is the principle that it is acceptable for individuals to own capital (as just defined) and to accumulate wealth. Private property is accordingly the central institution of a capitalist economy. Free enterprise, conducted in open markets which determine the prices of goods and services according to the relationship between supply and demand, is crucial to the success of capitalist activity, and therefore a political system favourable to capitalism is not only desired by capitalists but actively worked for by them, not least in the form of donations to friendly political parties and other direct support for their success. In major capitalist countries such as the United States it is not possible so much as to enter the political arena without substantial backing from wealthy supporters, including businesses. This is one way that continuation of the capitalist system in those countries is ensured.

The traditional contrast to capitalism is socialism, in which there is public or common ownership of the means of production. Among socialism's objections to capitalism is its class divisiveness – wealth accumulates in a few hands while the many have to sell their labour to survive; since wealth equates to political power and social influence, the capitalist class benefits at the expense of the labourers, whether by hand or brain, whom they employ to do their bidding. Economic activity under capitalism is geared towards the making of profits, not the satisfaction of people's needs, for even though products have to find buyers, the primary aim is not their interests but the profit to be had from doing enough to entice them to buy. At the root of socialist objections to capitalism, then, are the evils seen to arise from class divisions and the profit motive. Most socialist analyses of capitalism regard wage-labour as a form of exploitation, because the labourer does not receive the value of the labour he has put into making a product, and because the capitalist pockets the difference between the cost of labour and the price of the commodities when sold. This way of putting matters rather crudely overlooks the other costs involved in production (raw materials, equipment, power, transport, property rental or purchase, insurance, taxes, research and development, marketing, reinvestment, and more) and the compensation merited by the risk taken by investors in putting up money for the enterprise to commence and operate.

Capitalism took its current mature form in the Industrial Revolution of the late eighteenth and nineteenth centuries, but its roots lay in the mercantilist system of trade and commercial enterprise that displaced feudalism in the centuries before the Industrial Revolution began. Some see the origins of capitalist individualism in Protestant attitudes to work and saving. Part of the story must involve the increasing displacement of peasants from the land as enclosures took place from the sixteenth to the eighteenth centuries in England, thus forming a wage-labouring class. At the same time capital accumulation from the increased profits of agriculture and trade provided the funds for investment in industrial activity.

Theoretical justification for nascent capitalism was supplied by Adam Smith and the French theorists called 'Physiocrats' in the eighteenth century; they claimed that private ownership, division of labour in manufacturing, and laissez-faire trading policies, would be the most efficient and profitable course, benefiting everyone (even the poor, by the 'trickle down' effect).

As the foregoing words were written, the effects of the autumn 2008 meltdown in global financial markets were still rolling out across the stock exchanges and economies of the world. With the threat or actuality of recession looming in many of the latter, the extent of the turmoil's effects on individuals and developing countries ('emerging markets') was still unknown – except that individuals were already losing homes and jobs, and developing economies were least able to insure themselves against the turmoil's worst consequences: the spectre of the 1929 crash and the ensuing Great Depression that lasted well into the 1930s loomed.

At the same time the world was being treated to the educative spectacle of the hitherto more robustly capitalist Western economies – above all, the United States – pouring public money into banks and other large financial institutions, in a form of nationalization inconceivable a few months before the necessity for it became pressing. The autumn of 2008 seemed to be a vindication for what capitalists abhor: state intervention, state regulation, state ownership. Thus, in the view of some, the avariciousness of banks and financiers in an insufficiently regulated marketplace for money, the ultimate expression of capitalist excess, has brought socialist remedies crashing down on their heads, as if they were blind Samsons wrecking the pillars of their own temple of Mammon.

To give some idea of how financial novelties in an insufficiently regulated marketplace exploded in number and – until the crash – value, consider that the first 'hedge fund' was created in the 1940s, and in 1990 there were just over six hundred of them. By 2008 there were over 10,000 hedge funds managing more than $2.65 trillion. But this is just part of the story. With other innovations the value of the assets created and traded on stock, bond and derivatives markets far exceeded the economic output of the entire world. In 2006 the latter was measured at $47 trillion; by contrast the total capitalization of the world's stock markets was $51 trillion, the total value of all traded bonds was $68 trillion, and outstanding derivatives were valued at a staggering $473 trillion, ten times the value of the world's overall economic output.

Whether or not these figures make any sense, they certainly give the impression of a teetering inverted pyramid waiting for a little adverse puff of air to blow it over. This came in the form of deregulation or insufficient regulation of the complicated and fast-moving financial markets, together with a dangerous virus infecting them in the form of bad debts – specifically, the sub-prime mortgages issued in the United States from the 1990s onward.

The story went somewhat as follows. No-deposit mortgages were offered at attractive initial 'teaser' rates to people who were not in a wholly reliable position to sustain the repayments, especially when the teaser rates ended and the interest went up. Property values had been increasing steadily for some time and everyone, lenders included, thought that with an appreciating asset such as a house to back the loans thus given, there could be little risk. But the rate of defaults on mortgage repayments in the US increased by 79 per cent in 2007 as against 2006, an enormous jump, accompanied by a decline in property values. Meanwhile these risky mortgages had already been packaged up – 'securitized' – and sold to investors. Adding other securitized debts, and trade in derivatives in the form of credit default and interest-rate swaps, the total assumed value of this market lay in the region of trillions of dollars by the end of 2007, having not even existed in the 1980s.

When it became apparent how much bad debt existed in the system, and banks began to write off huge sums because of it, fear crept into the markets – and the markets operate on sentiment. When the share value of certain banks began to plummet because of anxieties that they were carrying too much bad debt, the entire money machine started to seize up: for banks have to be able to borrow to manage their day-to-day commitments, and if banks cannot borrow – if a 'credit crunch' occurs – and liquidity vanishes, the consequences are catastrophic. That is why central banks and governments had to intervene to provide liquidity and, as the extent of the crisis became apparent, recapitalization and guarantees too, so that institutions could trust each other enough to lend each other money.

The unavailability of money was a function of a general and not just an interbank freeze. For a chief example of another factor in this equation, hedge funds had been big purchasers of collateralized debt obligations ('CDOs') because they offered such high returns. As soon as they along with other investors began avoiding CDOs because of their infection by sub-prime debt, their reluctance added to the cash drought.

Stock markets proved to be dangerously volatile in the meltdown. Greed and fear seemed to be the dominating passions respectively before and during the crisis, as share prices plummeted in an orgy of flight from the consequences of years of unconstrained activity. Major financial institutions collapsed or had to be bailed out on both sides of the Atlantic, with entire countries – the smaller and poorer ones of course – facing bankruptcy. It soon became evident that some of the players in this disaster had known for some time that trouble loomed, but the madness had continued partly because of the 'IBG-YBG' factor: 'I'll Be Gone and You'll Be Gone before the chickens come home to roost' – the chickens being the toxic debts and the opaque financial instruments poisoned by them that the banks and other financial institutions which had bought them falsely thought were assets. If there was one thing that horrified observers of this situation wished, it was that those responsible should be brought to book for plunging the world into a mess.

As a morality tale for capitalism's excess, which by its nature it always pursues unless sensibly constrained, one could not improve upon the crash of 2008. Yet it is not a matter for gloating by capitalism's critics, for the cost was borne in real human terms – a reason why the more socially considerate (and therefore less wealth-producing) form of capitalism in Europe is preferable to the raw Anglo-American model of which the 2008 crash must forever stand as an indictment.

See: BUSINESS ETHICS, COMMUNISM, CONSUMERISM, GLOBALIZATION, SOCIALISM

CATHOLICISM

'Catholicism' is the short name for the brand of Christianity preached and practised by the Roman Catholic Church, whose head is the Pope and whose headquarters is the Vatican in Rome, Italy.

'Catholic' means 'universal', and the phrase 'Roman Catholic' might therefore seem to be oxymoronic in so highly localizing what, by means of the very next word, is claimed to be universal. But the 'catholic' in 'Roman Catholic' is intended to convey the claim of that Church to be the true and universal Christian Church, and the keeper of the correct form of Christianity, from which the forms of Christianity of all the many other Churches (Orthodox, Anglican, Nestorian, various Protestant) are aberrations.

The Roman Catholic Church is the largest of the Christian

denominations, and until late in the first decade of the twenty-first century had more adherents than all the sects of Islam put together. At time of writing this had ceased to be true, with Islamic sects jointly claiming over 19 per cent of the world's population, and Roman Catholicism just over 17 per cent. Traditionally Roman Catholicism has been a high-birthrate religion because of its prohibition against artificial contraception, permitting only abstinence and 'natural' methods.

Its differences from the Protestant sects of Christianity are so great in so many respects that it is sometimes tempting to think of Roman Catholicism as a different religion altogether. Central to its observance is the Mass, the ritual in which the Last Supper is re-enacted, with wine and bread transubstantiating – changing its substance – into the body and blood of Christ, sacrificed for our redemption. (In other denominations the wine and bread represent but do not actually become the body and blood, though in some denominations 'consubstantiation' is said to occur: the bread is still bread and the wine is still wine, but the body and blood of Christ are there along with them.)

The Virgin Mary occupies a tremendously significant and central place in Catholic observance, as Mother of God and (a relatively late doctrine) co-redemptrix with Christ in virtue of her sufferings at seeing the passion and death of her son. It is quite typical in a Roman Catholic Church to see the figure of the Virgin Mary occupy the central iconic place above the altar, and to be the object of much devotion and petition in side chapels, to a greater extent than Christ himself. To critics of Roman Catholicism, worship of the Virgin Mary is described as Mariolatry, and is regarded as a serious deviation from the purity of the Christian faith.

The many saints of the Church calendar are active objects of devotion and petition also, and Catholic practice includes much devotion of holy relics, saints' bones and graves, sites of miracles and visions such as Lourdes, and all of this gives critics further ammunition against its superstitious and credulous character. For example, the late Pope John Paul II described Loreto as the holiest place in Christendom: Loreto is a small town in Italy near Ancona in which there is an ancient cottage said to have been the home in Nazareth of the Holy Family, and further said to have been flown to Italy by angels via Tersato in Illyria at the end of the thirteenth century. To believe this requires a degree of faith that is, to put the matter in its frankest terms, pathological: and yet it is characteristic.

The Catholic Church regards itself as the true Church, its Popes having descended by apostolic succession (and sometimes, undoctrinally, normal biological succession) from St Peter, to whom Jesus gave the keys to the kingdom of heaven, thereby consecrating him as first Pope. The Church regards itself as immune from doctrinal error, protected from committing it by the Holy Spirit. The Catholic faith is expressed in the Nicene Creed, and all Catholics have to learn the Catechism which sums up and fixes the details of what is to be believed, which includes a Trinitarian commitment (God in three persons), the virgin birth of Jesus, his suffering and death in atonement for the sins of mankind, his resurrection from the dead, and the promise of everlasting life for those who believe in him and follow his teachings. Whereas in the more stringent Protestant sects faith alone is the determinant of salvation, in Catholicism justification comes by 'works'. The souls of the dead go to Purgatory (if they escape Hell) to purge away their sins over time; the intercessionary prayers of the living can help them there. Souls appear before the throne of God at the moment of death, and are assigned their deserts there and then.

A major difference between the Catholic Church and Protestant sects is that in the former priests have a special power conferred on them by consecration to administer the sacraments of baptism, confirmation, matrimony, the Eucharist, penance, and anointing of the sick. Even if they fall into sin and error, their consecration as priests still makes their administration of sacraments effective. So a whisky priest living with a native woman in the jungle can still give you final unction at the point of death, quite safely and legitimately. In Protestantism each individual is his or her own priest before God, no intervening layer of specially sanctified personnel being necessary – or desirable.

Although it is not the most reactionary and backward-looking of the Christian sects, the Catholic Church is a profoundly conservative institution, and in some of its policies stands against much that is accepted in the contemporary world regarding sex, sexuality, and control of reproduction by means of contraception and pregnancy termination. Its opposition to contraception has meant that it has undermined efforts to control the Aids epidemic by discouraging use of condoms; some of its high clergy have irresponsibly expressed the view that condoms give no protection against the virus that causes Aids.

The history of the Catholic Church is never complete without mention of the Inquisition, the Index of Forbidden Books (on which every book of any merit has at one time or another been listed), the Reformation and Counter-Reformation in which the Church struggled with much bloodletting to regain its grip over Europe and the world so far conquered by Europe, and the many periods in its history when its Popes and hierarchy were merely venal princes as given to whoring, drinking and the accumulation of ill-gotten gains as anyone else offered the opportunity to do likewise. At crucial times in the development of the modern world, such as the rise of science in the sixteenth and seventeenth centuries, it sought to stand in the way of those developments, and persecuted those who championed the cause of scientific enquiry, most notably Galileo Galilei. In recent times it has suffered scandals over sex, including child sex abuse, prompted in part by the celibacy of the priesthood – scandals which it has even more scandalously sought to hush up, and which throughout its past it most certainly mainly succeeded in doing.

Nor is the Roman Catholic Church's history complete without mention of its missionary activity around the world, its charitable work, and its zeal in proselytizing the young of its own members ('give me the child until age seven and I will give you the man'). For a thousand years it stood at the centre of European history, for good and ill both; but in the judgement of this writer, mostly the latter.

See: CHRISTIANITY, PROTESTANTISM, RELIGION

CHRISTIANITY

Christianity is the name of the religion invented by St Paul of Tarsus and other followers of a possibly genuine historical figure called Jesus, said to be a native of Nazareth in ancient Palestine. This Jesus was executed by the Roman authorities in Palestine about 30–35 CE by means of crucifixion, a form of capital punishment reserved for terrorists, insurgents and political insurrectionaries. In the view of some historians, this makes it probable that Jesus was a leading member of a group of Palestinian rebels against Roman occupation, although if some of the teachings attributed to him in the canonical 'Gospels' (the four works chosen by a succession of Church councils and ratified by Pope Innocent I in the early fifth century CE – chosen, that is, from among a number of others purporting to record Jesus's life and teachings) are correctly described, he was more a Gandhi-like figure than a Spartacus-like one. Such at least was the impression that the Church fathers, so long after the events, wished to leave upon readers' minds, despite Jesus's involvement in incidents such as attacking traders in the Temple precincts in Jerusalem, and his remarks about his teachings promising strife and division rather than ease. In this, at least, he was prescient.

Christianity began as a predominantly Middle Eastern and eastern Mediterranean religious movement, syncretistically manufactured out of

Judaism with bits of Zoroastrianism, Orphism and other Greek themes both philosophical and mythological increasingly added in. At first it was a secretive minor cult, which survived by insinuating itself among slaves and women in the Roman world. The myth of a dying and resurrecting hero or god is very widespread in the east-Mediterranean religions of antiquity, from very ancient Egyptian vegetation myths to stories of heroes who went down to and returned from the underworld, some (like Hercules) later achieving apotheosis (elevation to divine status) for their achievements. One among a number of commonplaces of such stories was that the heroic figure in question was the result of a god having impregnated a mortal woman; Zeus, for example, had many such offspring, Hercules among them. The Jesus story borrows from these traditions. Stories about descent into the underworld include that of Orpheus, origin of a mystery cult involving rituals of initiation and illumination not unlike later Christian practices.

The attractions of Christianity to slaves and women lay in the promise of Hercules-like apotheosis through faith, freeing them (if only posthumously) from their enchained condition, and rewarding them for patience and suffering. Friedrich Nietzsche much later pointed out how this valorization of the enslaved condition differed from the Greek view of an ethics of action and achievement.

Early Christianity was periodically persecuted in the Roman empire, because its votaries refused to observe the empire's public religion, which was a responsibility of citizenship. They were therefore thought to be subversives, whose loyalties were such that they refused to participate in the state's observances of civic cohesion; and because they refused to believe in the gods, they were dubbed atheists.

For some centuries after the Emperor Constantine made Christianity the official religion of the Roman empire in 312 CE, votaries of the faith were preoccupied with forging and enforcing a unitary orthodoxy against many 'heresies' – that is, different versions of their view. A naturally fissiparous and internally quarrelsome movement, Christianity soon suffered its first major schism when the Roman and Byzantine versions parted company in the eighth century. A second and in many ways more consequential schism occurred in the sixteenth century, the so-called 'Reformation' initiated by Martin Luther's nailing of theses to the church door in Wittenberg in 1517 in protest against the practice of selling indulgences (one could ensure a remission of thousands of years in purgatory, this being the posthumous location where one's soul is to be purged of its sins, by paying a sum of money). The protesting (hence Protestant) communities of Christians themselves split into two main communities, Lutheran and – a much stricter sect – Calvinist; and these in turn have since spawned a multitude of further sects, now said to number over 20,000 in the United States alone.

The Reformation caused more than a century of terrible and destructive warfare in Europe (the Thirty Years War between 1618 and 1648 alone caused the death of one in every three of the German-speaking peoples of the continent), and spurred the exodus of Christian groups to America and elsewhere, seeking freedom for their own preferred form of worship.

The majority of Christians in the contemporary world live in Africa and Central and South America, and have combined their own local animism and other superstitions with it, making it a lively if approximate version of the original. In most of the more mature and educated parts of the world, from Europe to the east coast of the United States, it is a minority and diminishing avocation, despite the vigorous efforts of evangelicals and fundamentalists to impose themselves on society and to influence the laws and morals of the communities in which they are minorities.

As a religion Christianity is focused on a core set of beliefs: the first (obviously enough) is that there is a God (traditionally referred to as 'he' for reasons as much grammatical as sexist); that he 'sent' his son to be born a human being in Palestine, this being Jesus; that Jesus is the promised Messiah of the Jews; that he iterated a Jewish teaching to the effect that one's duty is to love God and one's neighbour; and that anyone who 'believed in' him (i.e. Jesus) – presumably: believed that he is indeed the son of God – would be 'saved', that is, would not die, or at any rate would not go to hell upon dying. Although assertions to this effect are to be found in the canonical Gospels, the importance of faith in the divinity of Jesus as the Christ (this term meaning 'the anointed one', allegedly proved by his performance of miracles and his resurrection from the dead) is chiefly asserted by St Paul, for whose original and philosophical mind the story of Jesus's mission, death and resurrection meant that the old Jewish laws had been superseded by a new 'covenant' between God and man, this being that if one 'believes in' (and of course obeys the teachings of) Jesus as the Christ, one will be 'saved'.

Because Christianity's first official form was Roman, it adopted much of the administrative techniques and hierarchy of the Roman state, took over and Christianized many of the pagan feasts and festivals, and incorporated, as saints, many of the favourite deities of the peoples of the empire, most notably exploiting the widespread and fervent worship of the virgin goddess Diana by offering worship of the Virgin Mary ('mother of God') in its place. In the Roman Catholic version of Christianity, Mariolatry and the cult of saints constitute one of the most important features – and are much despised by the austerer Protestants, the well-springs of whose version of Christianity rose at the distance of many centuries from the problem encountered by the early Roman Church in competing with the great attractions of local superstitions.

Whereas one side of Christianity, notably the Roman, emphasizes 'justification through works', another – notably the Protestant – emphasizes 'justification through faith'. The latter is closer to the doctrine of St Paul, the real founder of Christianity, whereas the former retains many features of pre-Christian moral thinking, in which what you do and what you are are the key, rather than what you believe.

Christianity began as a movement imminently expecting the end of the world, and in its early centuries was disappointed in that expectation. It therefore needed to import ideas both in ethics and metaphysics to flesh out what was a somewhat thin philosophical basis in both respects. The impractical ethics of the New Testament (give everything away, repudiate your family if they do not do likewise, passively accept all suffering, plan nothing and give no thought to the morrow, live ascetically, love everyone indiscriminately including your enemies and those who persecute you) was only ever possible for monks, nuns and anchorites who could in effect leave the world while still alive. Ethics was imported largely from Stoicism; the required metaphysics came largely from Neoplatonism.

Neoplatonism is the name given by historians of philosophy to the final phase of Greek philosophy that flourished between the third and sixth centuries CE, which is to say from Plotinus (205–270) to the closing of the Greek philosophical schools in the year 529 by the pious Emperor Justinian, who disapproved of their paganism, scepticism, rationality, and learning.

With eclectic roots in Hellenistic philosophy, and influenced by Christianity, Gnosticism, and Jewish scriptures in Greek translation (the *Septuagint*), Neoplatonism went through several phases of development. Plotinus's great work, the *Enneads*, is in effect the result of long meditation and debate upon both the creation story of Genesis and Plato's cosmological dialogue the *Timaeus*. Cosmology is one central theme in Neoplatonism, although Plotinus's successors, Porphyry (233–305) and Iamblichus (d.c.330), did not produce a systematic treatise of the dimension and ambition of the *Enneads*. Nothing so bold was forthcoming until the work of Proclus (410–485).

Late in the development of Neoplatonism came the completion of the marriage of its thought with Christianity in the work of the thinker known as the Pseudo-Dionysus (dates unknown, but active in the late fifth century). This overarching synthesis retained immense influence in Christianity for the next thousand years.

The synthesis of Christianity, Gnosticism and Platonic philosophy begun by Plotinus turned on his attempt to solve the problem of how the perfect mind of God could be responsible for the creation of so imperfect a thing as the cosmos. He argued that objective reality is the outward expression of the inward contemplation of the 'ineffable and transcendent' One (The One, *to hen*, sometimes The Good, *to kalon*), and the fact that this outward expression in its temporal concrete form is far less perfect than the idea of it in the divine mind is only a transitory feature, albeit a necessary one, of The One's complete expression of itself. This is not the first of many futile attempts to square the supposed goodness, omniscience and omnipotence of a supposed deity with the manifest horrors of nature (disease, tsunamis, etc.) and the wickedness of man (the Inquisition, the Holocaust, etc.).

The writings of Porphyry (which include an exposition of his teacher Plotinus's thought), Iamblichus and – more systematic and finished – Proclus variously extend and modify the themes initiated by Plotinus. But as noted it is the work of Pseudo-Dionysus that had most impact on subsequent Christian thinking.

Pseudo-Dionysus is so called because he was once improbably identified with a very early figure, Dionysus the companion of St Paul. The real Pseudo-Dionysus lived at a time when the full flood of Neoplatonism had passed, and his heroic concern was to make it and Christian thought consistent – rather as, many centuries later, Aquinas sought to effect a synthesis of Aristotelian thought and Christianity. The central claim of Pseudo-Dionysus's thought is that God is beyond all knowledge and description – easily the most convenient solution to the problem Pseudo-Dionysus set himself to solve – and that all human striving is aimed at uniting with him.

It is or should be a cause for amazement in the twenty-first century that tens of millions are expected to – or, indeed, do – believe such things as this: that 'the Father, the Son and the Holy Spirit are one God in three persons, sharing one essence, consubstantial, eternal, existing beyond and before time but acting within time; the Son is begotten of the Father and the Holy Spirit proceeds from the Father; to try to understand this, says Gregory the Theologian, leads to insanity, so the Church approaches God in divine mystery, apophatically, being content to encounter God personally and yet realize the inadequacy of the mind to comprehend him.' This is a paraphrase from a Church statement of faith; the only things in it that approach comprehensibility are the bits about insanity (which is the only bit that is true) and the standard fudge about it all being too difficult to understand which is why it only looks like nonsense. This text ends with the emetic claim that 'worship of God is the highest calling of mankind, to fall down at the feet of the Almighty God, the Holy Trinity, and to be given over entirely to him, becoming united mystically with him in the holy mysteries. To worship God is to fulfil the purpose for which we were created.'

That such things can still be seriously stated, let alone believed, explains David Hume's wry remark that it is not true that miracles died out with the first army of the faithful; for this is miracle enough.

It is worth mentioning, in conclusion and apropos this last comment, the phenomenon of Millenarianism, given the earliest disappointment experienced by Christians in the failure of the Parousia, the Second Coming, to materialize, which they thought had been promised for an early date. Millenarianism is a substitute for it in the minds of some. It is a cultic belief relating to the coming of the Day of Judgement. The Book of Revelations has a passage (chapter 20 verses 2–8) appearing to imply that when Satan has been imprisoned for a thousand years, the martyrs who have 'reigned with Christ' will come back to life. Millenarian expectations were very high towards the end of Christianity's first thousand years; portents and prodigies were reported, and a frenzy – partly of joyful expectation, partly of fear and repentance – gripped Christendom as the fateful date drew nigh.

Millenarian expectation was much less vivid at the close of the second thousand years, at the end of 1999, if just as frenzied in certain (diminished) quarters. The outcome was the same. Mathematics had somehow deteriorated between the two surges of millenarian fervour; the last year of the second thousand years was 2000, not 1999, so the Millenarians were a year out anyway, and had they been right in principle would have been caught napping a year after thinking they had been disappointed again – and so would have been like the foolish virgins after all.

Various sects calculate the millennium differently, and therefore the end of the world has been often predicted and expected, and so far has invariably proved a disappointment, a relief, or an irrelevance, according to view.

See: CATHOLICISM, ORTHODOX CHRISTIANITY, PROTESTANTISM, RELIGION

CIVILIZATION

Civilization is the condition of a people who have attained a relatively high level of development in culture, technology and organization. It is a positive notion, as shown by such associated expressions as 'civilized' which means educated, cultured and sociable, and 'civil' which means polite and decent. The term derives from the Latin *civis* which denoted a Roman citizen, that is, a fully enfranchised member of the Roman polity.

It is instructive to contrast the concept of civilization with that of its opposite, barbarism. This latter term is derived from the Greek *barbaros* to denote a non-Greek speaker, that is, someone whose speech sounded to Greeks as an unintelligible 'bar-bar-bar' noise. From the outset therefore it was a negative term; the Greeks thought that the natural destiny of barbarians was to be slaves. With the development of historical anthropology in the nineteenth century the term was applied to early stages of mankind's development; for example, Friedrich Engels described barbarism as the period during which man learned to domesticate animals and practise agriculture, whereas civilization is the period of industry and art that came afterwards.

Looser uses of the term 'civilization' make it practically synonymous with 'culture' in the anthropological sense of the practices, lifestyles, beliefs, and material artefacts and equipment of an identifiable group (and thus one might speak of the 'civilization' or 'culture' of a remote jungle tribe living in stone-age conditions) or 'human society', as when one says 'nuclear war could destroy civilization'.

But if the term is to have real use, it should properly be restricted in denotation to those societies exhibiting at least most of the following characteristics: organized systems of production of food supplies and goods, markets for their exchange with a currency to facilitate transactions, social and political organization with a recognized leadership and organs of administration and justice, organized systems of education, civil society activity, defence and external relations, all with a largely urban basis requiring division of labour, training in expert skills, methods of taking and keeping records, and therefore literacy and writing – and the leisure, wealth and interest to promote and support the various arts.

Historians list a number of ancient civilizations, which in roughly chronological order starting with the earliest are the Mesopotamian or Sumerian, the Indus Valley civilization, Ancient Egypt, the Helladic civilization of Greece, the Minoan, the pre-Han Chinese civilization, Persia, Rome, and others. Han and Tang China and the successor dynasties there, Christendom, and the various manifestations of Islamic civilization exemplified by such as the Andalusian and the Mughal, are the more immediate precursors of modern civilizations. Since the sixteenth century 'Greater European' civilization ('Greater Europe' is a term coined to include North America, Australasia and other parts still recognizably the product of European colonization) has been dominant because of its science and industrial power. If some of the assumptions and implications of Samuel Huntington's 'clash of civilizations' thesis are right – envisioning tensions and conflicts among what he identifies as the eight contemporary civilizations – the Western, Latin American, Islamic, Chinese, Indian, Orthodox, Japanese and African – then this dominance will not last, and the age-old struggle for supremacy between powers, not least between a waning and a waxing power (such as the West and China respectively?) or between waning powers (the West and Islam?) or between waxing powers (China and India?), will reprise a story far older than that of Persia and Greece in the days of Marathon.

See: EVOLUTION, LAW

CLASS

Stratification of societies into classes is an almost universal phenomenon, although in some the divisions are informal, in others institutionalized. In some societies movement between the classes is very difficult, in others there is greater fluidity, although it is generally easier for people to slip downwards in the hierarchy of social distinctions than to rise.

European society had, and in Britain residually still retains, a class system marked at its upper end by titles and formal ranks, and lower down by often jealously observed distinctions. In Britain the aristocracy was taken to be socially superior to the gentry, the gentry to the middle classes (professionals in the upper middle class, merchants and business-men in the middle class, traders in the lower middle class), and the middle classes to the lower classes, the latter consisting of working people such as servants, factory hands and agricultural labourers, but with stratifying distinctions even among them, as for example between skilled workers and unskilled workers, between butlers and housekeepers, cooks, grooms, gamekeepers and maids.

In the British aristocracy the ranks of nobility below royalty were ordered as follows: dukes, marquises, earls, viscounts, barons. Below these last in order of precedence came baronets (hereditary knights), and after them the various orders of knights, and then untitled gentlemen. Without a coat of arms no one could strictly be entitled to be described as a 'gentleman' of any of these ranks. The offspring of noblemen had courtesy titles and a place in the ranks of precedence dictated by their fathers' position. In the case of noblemen of the rank of earls and above the courtesy title of the eldest son was the nobleman's next title.

The British nobility were apt to look down their noses at the nobilities of other countries, especially despising the fact that they did not observe proprieties of distinction. For example, in Russia the title of the father was enjoyed also by his sons – so the sons of a Russian prince (not invariably a royal designation there) were princes also, and his daughters princesses; and the sons of a count were counts too, and their daughters all countesses.

A class system is most invidious among those whose position in it is neither the highest nor lowest, but hovers with some ambiguity in the intermediate ranks. Jealousy and snobbery, emulation and gossip, scrutiny of the lifestyles, possessions and pretensions of others, are commonplaces of the satire directed at such systems. 'Snobbery' once meant ingratiating emulation of those a little higher in the pecking order; this nineteenth-century sense (employed as such by Thackeray in his telling satires on the agonies and quarrels of social nuance) has been lost, and now describes the attitude of those who look down on those they take to be 'below' them.

Class hierarchies once encapsulated genuine differences of power, privilege, opportunity and (usually) wealth also. Almost all the most ancient aristocratic lines were founded by the most vigorous and least scrupulous of the strong-arm men around at the time, who could dominate their fellows and grasp land and resources which they passed on to their heirs, and which gave them and their heirs access to the centre of power in the society – the monarch, typically – so that when distinctions of place and status were fixed by title, they naturally were the ones who benefited. Later other kinds of service, military or political, and even distinction in the various arts, came to be a reason for the award of titles and honours. In France, Louis XIV solved some of his financial problems by increasing the numbers of the 'nobles of the robe', whose families had earned their titles by government service (unlike the 'nobles of the sword' whose honours came from military service), much to the annoyance of this latter branch of the Second Estate, who at the time were seeking to close access to their order of nobility to preserve its exclusive status.

In contemporary Western societies distinctions of class remain, now mainly functions of income or wealth but also of education, family background, and occupation. The outward marks of status tend to be the quality of clothing and accessories such as watches and designer shoes, the kind of motor car, the size and location of house, the type and location of holidays, and other money-dependent signs. Manners and speech also mark class differences, and are a function of education and home environment.

Historically the most important and interesting of the classes is the middle class, not least because its emergence between the landowning and land-working classes – hitherto the only two – marked a major change in economic and social structure. The Western liberal democracies are in effect the creation of the middle class, whose place in the industrial-commercial order, and therefore whose eventual control of the political order, helped to shape the kind of society that has developed out of its growing dominance.

The history of the middle class is accordingly the history of modern times. Of course there is a complicated transition from feudalism through the many struggles of many kinds that fashioned the economic and political systems associated with the growth of the middle class, but in essentials all this change – including changes in religion and international relations from the sixteenth century onwards – is undetachable from the inexorable rise of the middle class. The business-mindedness of the middle class and the emergence of capitalism have famously been associated with the rise of Protestantism by the historian R.H. Tawney and the sociologist Max Weber.

A class system is significantly different from a *caste* system. The latter is a social arrangement which divides groups of people into a strictly defined and, in its paradigm instance in the Hindu tradition of India, rigid social hierarchy. Class systems, properly speaking, are not rigid; people can move up and down the social ladder by such means as gaining or losing wealth, making good or bad marriages, earning or losing the title and status of nobility through political, military, or other notable action. But the Indian caste system is one in which only birth can admit one to a given caste, and only death can release from it.

The four principal *varnas* (the word literally means 'colours') of India's caste hierarchy are – from top to bottom – Brahmins (priests and scholars), Kshatriyas (rulers and warriors), Vaishyas (farmers and merchants), and Shudras (servants and peasants). Scarcely included in the hierarchy in consequence of being too low for it are the Panchamas (the word means 'fifth division'), otherwise known as 'Untouchables'. These outcastes are so unclean that it is polluting to be touched even by their shadows. They undertake taboo work as barbers, road-sweepers, leather-workers, and anything else polluting to the higher castes.

A myth underlies the formation of the castes; it is that the god Purusha was dismembered, and his mouth became the Brahmins, his arms the Kshatriyas, his thighs the Vaishyas, and his feet the Shudras.

Several thousand fine gradations of subcaste, determined by occupation and the degree of 'purity' it allows, determine position in society with many consequences, not least among them what counts as permissible social relations, ranging from dining to marriage. At various points in Indian history major revolts against this oppressive system have produced whole new casteless movements, among them Buddhism and Sikhism. The most recent was the result of Mahatma Gandhi's refusal to countenance the treatment of Untouchables. (he called them *Harijans*, 'children of God'; they are now often called *dalits*, or, officially, 'scheduled castes'). In contemporary India the law rules out untouchability, although unofficially the divisions of the caste system, and the pariah status of Untouchables, remain. Certain marks distinguish the castes, as for example the thread worn round the shoulder of a Brahmin; they can be seen to this day.

See: ARISTOCRACY, HINDUISM AND BRAHMANISM

CLONING

Cloning is the replication of biological material. There are three kinds of cloning: reproductive cloning, therapeutic cloning, and recombinant DNA cloning. The first two generate most interest, for obvious reasons; the third has been common practice in molecular biology laboratories for decades.

Recombinant DNA cloning is the transfer of selected portions of DNA from one organism to a host cell of another, in a vehicle (called a 'cloning vector') such as a bacterial plasmid or similar self-replicating genetic element. Applications of the technique include the production of synthetic insulin for treating diabetes, and delivering gene therapies.

Reproductive cloning is the process of producing an animal with the same nuclear DNA as an existing animal – the first such case was Dolly the sheep, produced by somatic cell nuclear transfer in 1996. Therapeutic cloning uses stem cells to produce replacement cells for treatment of serious diseases, including whole organs grown from stem cells to substitute for diseased or damaged organs.

Therapeutic cloning promises hope for the treatment of a number of distressing conditions, among them Alzheimer's disease and Parkinsonism. It might, and probably will, come to replace transplant surgery by allowing healthy organs to be regrown from a patient's own cells. It might heal damaged hearts and brains, and allow the paralysed to walk again by nerve regeneration. If the promise of therapeutic cloning were fulfilled it would have a huge impact by reducing the amount of suffering in humankind, and enhancing quality of life for many, from elderly arthritis sufferers to children living under the death sentence of cystic fibrosis. It is justifiably tempting to say that therapeutic cloning promises the greatest single advance ever made in medicine, and thus one of the greatest promises for the good of humanity.

And yet it generates heated ethical debate. The questions of principle have to be separated from objections based on practical difficulties of technique and technology. First there is the matter of 'harvesting' stem cells from human embryos. Religiously motivated objectors regard human embryos as fully human already, and do not regard their use as sources of stem cells to be justified by the prospect of alleviating suffering among those who have already been born. They argue that using embryos to provide stem cells for research or therapies is a violation of divine prerogatives.

Objectors fear too that cloning research will lead inevitably to reproductive cloning, producing children who will be identical twins of the people they are cloned from. Some who are in favour of therapeutic cloning feel uneasy about reproductive cloning.

Since arguments about cloning begin from considerations about the status of stem cells, it is first necessary to be clear about their nature. Stem cells are taken from an embryo when it is still a blastocyst, that is, a small collection of unspecialized cells ready to take on any of the different forms of cells required in the body. Huge numbers of blastocysts are formed in the course of human sexual relations which never implant in a womb, or which, once implanted, are soon after expelled in naturally occurring or 'spontaneous' abortions. As regards their potential to grow into human beings if the right circumstances prevail, blastocysts are no different from unfertilized eggs or unfertilizing sperm, both of which are produced in superabundance and never develop into foetuses and children. Blastocysts are primitive clusters of human cells, not people; and their use in helping to reduce suffering in humanity should far outweigh scruples about their status. The right comparison to make is between the pluripotent cells in a blastocyst and an organ that could be used in transplant surgery to save a life.

The question of practicalities is easy to answer. In any form of medical research, when there are problems about effectiveness of new techniques, it is wrong to go too far too fast. The same assuredly applies to cloning. In reproductive cloning especially there is at time of writing no guarantee of safety and reliability; on the contrary, the health problems of the world's first cloned mammal, Dolly the sheep, suggest that clones might suffer premature ageing and a variety of genetic disorders. While unknowns surround reproductive cloning, it cannot be right to try it. Therapeutic cloning is an entirely different matter.

If the technique of reproductive cloning is ever made safe and secure, the ethical problem becomes entirely different, and objections to it all but vanish. For a clone is nothing other than an identical twin, and identical twins present no ethical difficulties as such. A person unable to have children either by normal means or by other fertilization techniques would have the chance of family life by way of cloning; they would in effect be bringing into the world their own or their spouse's twin, and raising them in the ordinary way of family ties. They would in a strict sense be siblings rather than parent and child, though functionally the latter; but in any case there is nothing unnatural about sibling relationships of love and care; and therefore there is nothing to object to in the thought of a clone and its relationship with its family.

Some who are untroubled by the idea of twins and sibling relationships might yet object to the use of reproductive technology in general. So they should object to in vitro fertilization also, and donor insemination, for both these techniques are aimed, as reproductive cloning would be, at helping women who cannot conceive normally, and who would otherwise be denied motherhood.

As soon as we see that reproductive technologies in medicine are aimed at helping people to have children – people who so want to have children that they submit to the expense and difficulty of the process, and who therefore would most likely be highly committed parents – objections vanish. Such objections as remain tend to be prompted by religious views that nothing must interfere with natural reproduction, a process to be left to chance (or as some say, 'providence').

If they were consistent, those who hold such a view should oppose antenatal classes, foetal monitoring, treatment for such conditions as eclampsia, amniocentesis to check for genetic disorders, epidural anaesthesia, Caesarean section, and other obstetric aids, since these too are technological interventions in the reproductive process. The result of the absence of such aids are easy to see in the Third World, measured in human suffering and death; withholding these aids is not ethical behaviour. Logically, the point embraces all reproductive technologies.

Cloning is the result of human intelligence. Human intelligence is itself a product of nature. So there is nothing unnatural about the achievements of intelligence, which can be used for good or ill, as everything human can be. As with everything else it deals with, society can do its best to minimize abuses while reaping the benefit of scientific advances, especially those that can make the world a better place. Rightly used, cloning is one such.

See: BIOETHICS, EVOLUTION

COGNITIVE SCIENCE

Cognitive science is the study of mind and intelligence. It is an interdisciplinary science, drawing on contributions from neurophysiology, philosophy, psychology, logic, artificial intelligence, linguistics and anthropology.

Although enquiry into the nature of mind goes back at least to the ancient Greeks, the first scientific efforts to study mental functioning date to the work of Wilhelm Wundt (1832–1920) in his psychological laboratory, the first ever, at the University of Leipzig, where he experimented on sensory perception.

Within a short time the study of mind had fallen under the influence of behaviourism, which demanded that all mental life should be understood reductively in terms of stimuli and behavioural responses to them, excluding all reference to inner psychological processes and states. But the dominance of behaviourism was ended in the 1950s by three developments: advances in the study of memory, the work of Noam Chomsky on language acquisition, and the development of computer technology suggesting the possibility of artificial intelligence.

The chief presupposition of cognitive science is that the most fruitful way to understand mental activity is to premise two basic ideas: first, that the contents of mental states are 'representations', on analogy with the data structures in computers, and secondly that the mind operates on and with these representations computationally, that is, on analogy with the way a computer operates (computation – to put matters more accurately – is what mathematically idealized computers called 'Turing machines' do). In this latter regard the most powerful and natural hypothesis about the way the brain functions in processing representations is to use the 'neural-network' or connectionist model suggested by the brain itself.

Mental representations are such things as propositions, rules, concepts and images. The computations performed on and with them include inference, comparison and retrieval. These remarks alone suggest the reason for the widely thrown net of cognitive science in its interdisciplinary reach. Each of logic, psychology, philosophy and neurophysiology offers much to an understanding of both mental content and the mind's operations upon it, while linguistics and anthropology bring comparative data to bear. The significant point is the convergence thus achieved; cognitive science is not the mere juxtaposition of these disciplines, but the synthesis of their contributions.

Cognitive science is not without its critics, who point out that it leaves emotions and consciousness out of the picture, says nothing about the relation of mental content and functioning to the physical and social environments in which the mind exists, and pays too little attention to the intimate connection between mental life and the fact that it takes place in and through a body.

These challenges ask cognitive science to take important additional factors into account. Very different challenges come from critics who think that the fundamental assumptions of cognitive science are mistaken: that mental activity cannot be computational, for either or both mathematical and functional reasons. For example, Roger Penrose in *The Emperor's New Mind* (1989) argues that thinking is not and cannot be computational. His argument, if correct, undercuts not only cognitive science but the project known as 'strong AI', that is, the project of creating genuine artificial intelligence (the phrase only appears oxymoronic), espoused by such as Stephen Pinker and others, and fiercely contested by John Searle and Penrose himself.

Penrose's argument is as follows. Suppose the brain is indeed a computer. Then, as Alan Turing and Kurt Gödel showed, it is constrained by limits that apply to all computation. Turing's point is that every me-chanical computation can be specified by an algorithm, that is, a descrip-tion of the simple steps constituting the computation. In his famous 'Incompleteness Theorem' Gödel showed that no algorithm can prove all the truths obtainable in a formal system. Penrose claims that there are truths that minds can intuit – for a prime instance, mathematical ones; perhaps Goldbach's Conjecture is a case in point – that cannot be generated by a computer. If true, this together with the Turing and Gödel points shows that mental operations cannot be computational ones.

The explanation Penrose offers for this turns on the fact of conscious-ness. He argues that consciousness, which computers lack, adds a dimen-sion to thought that computers can therefore never have, namely, that of providing a non-algorithmic way of arriving at conclusions from a 'morass of data' for which no clear or practical algorithm process of selec-tion exists. Possibly, though (so Penrose concedes), this might be done if the brain is a 'quantum computer', that is, one that uses a massive superposition of computational states to search a huge range of possi-bilities, with the one that collapses the wave-function being the answer. But whatever explanation ultimately proves satisfactory, it remains for Penrose that minds trespass beyond the Turing–Gödel boundaries of what is actually possible in computation, and this is the central point of his disagreement with cognitive science.

See: ARTIFICIAL INTELLIGENCE; MIND, PHILOSOPHY OF

COGNITIVE THERAPY

Cognitive therapy and 'cognitive behaviour therapy' together denote a well-established and efficacious technique of psychotherapy aimed at helping people suffering from such conditions as anxiety, depression, obsessions, compulsions, shyness, phobias, stress, eating disorders, insomnia, relationship difficulties, addiction, inhibition, anger, poor self-esteem, passivity, lack of motivation, panic attacks, post-traumatic stress, and more.

Cognitive therapy as such is aimed at helping sufferers to recognize and change the patterns of thought that give rise to their conditions.

Cognitive behaviour therapy provides tools, techniques and strategies for short-circuiting both maladaptive thinking and the behaviour that arises from it, in order to help sufferers think and act in more positive ways, and correlatively to establish the positive attitudes that will first solve and then avoid the problems that sufferers have created for themselves.

As this shows, CT and CBT are not just 'listening cures' as in the case of certain other psychotherapies, notably psychoanalysis (Freudian practice), but active techniques in which therapists take a strong role, especially in the process's early phase, to help break problem patterns. As a present- and forward-looking activity rather than dwelling on the past, CT and CBT prove highly effective. That effectiveness, obvious in relatively short periods of time, makes this an approach of choice for many of the problems listed above.

Judith Beck writes in the introduction to her *Cognitive Therapy: Basics and Beyond* (1995) about her husband's work, 'Cognitive therapy was developed by Aaron T. Beck in the early 1960s at the University of Pennsylvania as a structured, short-term, present-oriented psychotherapy for depression, directed towards solving current problems and modifying dysfunctional thinking and behaviour.' Beck was not the only psychologist to see the value of such an approach, and the movement might claim other founders. But it certainly has had many other contributors, and a substantial body of empirical work underpinning it as practice. As a result it has since become a major psychotherapeutic resource with applications far beyond depression alone.

See: PSYCHOANALYSIS

COMMUNISM

As a modern theory communism owes much to Marxism. In practice, as in the regimes of the late Soviet bloc and China, communism is a totalitarian one-party system in which arbitrary power is exercised by 'the Party', which in effect means those who control the Party.

Communism is an ancient doctrine, and was perhaps unconsciously applied in the very first proto-human and early human groups. Legends in antiquity of a 'Golden Age' might conceivably refer to circumstances where sufficiencies of resources meant that there was no competition – and hence no conflict – over them, and no motive to accumulate them (this being the origin of property, thence of wealth and its consequent social disparities of power and status). Primitive Christianity was communist; it preached the sharing of all resources, each giving according to his ability and taking according to his needs.

Many if not most eutopias ('eutopia', *sic*, meaning 'a good place';

the more familiar word 'utopia' strictly just means 'nowhere') envisage forms of communism for precisely the reason that the evils of society seemed to eutopiasts to be the result of differences of wealth and the greed, injustice, strife and conflict thus engendered. Periodically political movements have arisen urging just such eutopian claims; England's seventeenth-century 'Levellers' were in effect communists, and like all their kind received short shrift from property- and wealth-holding classes.

The communism envisaged as the final state of the Marxist dialectic of history, in which the state withers away leaving a benevolent anarchy made possible by the lack of competition for resources (as in the Golden Age), is not state or public ownership of the means of production – this is the socialist, penultimate historical stage – but common ownership of everything. For Marx and Engels, disparities in wealth rested on exploitation of workers, so communism as the end state of the dialectic of history means the abolition of the conditions in which workers are exploited.

The command economics of communist states as, allegedly, they passed through the socialistic stage, proved a disastrous failure. The eutopian idea that the means of production should lie in the people's hands and be used for their benefit, without profit to a few at the expense of the many, is a commendable one; its failure prompted some to claim that there should be no control of the market mechanism. Critics of this latter view observe that an unbridled or unregulated market is as unforgiving in different ways.

In practice, all too familiarly, communist states have proved to be nothing other than versions of the monolithic ideologies that all totalitarianisms, including theocracies, by nature are. Their defining feature is that they have One Big Idea or Truth, to which everyone must be loyal and subservient on pain of punishment even to death; and therefore free speech, individual liberty and democratic practices are outlawed as threatening the monolith's control.

China is the only country to try the experiment of a capitalist economy with a communist-style unelected central party command government. Despite that party being called the Communist Party of China, it is in almost all functional respects a mere reprise of the authoritarian imperial government commonplace throughout China's history. In this it is paradigmatic of what communism has been wherever it has been put into effect in the modern world; most of the experiments in this regard have failed in what, in historical terms, is the blink of an eye.

See: CAPITALISM, MARXISM, POLITICS, SOCIALISM, TOTALITARIANISM

CONSEQUENTIALISM

Consequentialism is the ethical theory or family of theories based on the idea that what is right is what brings about good results. The primary focus of consequentialism is what agents do – their acts – and it evaluates acts by taking the goodness or badness of their consequences as the measure of their respective rightness or wrongness. It thus provides what on the face of it looks like a straightforward criterion of moral evaluation. But this presupposes that we know what the 'good' is so that we can recognize good consequences as such if they are indeed such. Are 'good consequences' those that maximize happiness for the majority, or produce most pleasure all round, or conform to some other definition of 'the good'? Unless we know what we mean by 'good' we will be at a loss to know whether an act that has produced a given consequence was right or not.

Consequentialism stands in contrast to deontological ethical theories, which state that the rightness or wrongness of an action is intrinsic to the action itself, and is quite independent of whatever consequences follow from its performance.

The principal example of a consequentialist ethics is utilitarianism. This famous theory comes in many forms, but in essence states that right acts are those that maximize happiness, 'utility' or benefit as somehow specified, wrong acts are those that diminish (note: not necessarily 'minimize') happiness, utility or benefit. But there are in fact a number of qualifications and distinctions that need to be drawn even at this level of generality. It is insufficient to stop short at saying that an act's consequences determine its moral worth; one needs to say whether it is the act's actual consequences that count, or whether one has to take into account what was intended by way of consequences, or what consequences were foreseen or could be foreseen or expected. Suppose someone acted with the intention of doing evil, but by accident a quantum of good resulted; does this make his act right? Does it make him a good person? One also needs to say whether an act is right only if it produces the best possible result, or can be allowed to be right if it merely improves things somewhat. What if it benefits only some people and not everyone? What if only parts of the consequences can be described as good, utile or beneficial, while others are neutral or even bad? Is there invariably a way of adding up the good and bad consequences to see which outweigh the others? And for whom are the consequences good or bad – for the agent, or for those affected by his action, or both? Some argue that acts have to be evaluated independently of the agent's motives, whether or not these were disinterested, that is, not aimed at the realization of certain personal ends; others argue that the agent's motives are germane to the evaluation, and his own good can or even must enter into the account.

One can ask a number of such questions about what has to be the case before the consequences can be taken to confer rightness on the action that produced them – and these are questions quite different from any about the definition of 'good' itself. Here the debate is different. Candidates for what is good range from such psychological states as happiness and pleasure to less subjective goods such as political equality, liberty, wealth or material benefit. Obviously enough, determining whether an act was right will depend on what one takes the good to be, for it is easy to see how the same act can be right for certain conceptions of good and wrong for others.

Given the difficulty of being able to foresee all the consequences of an act, and mindful that acting with the best of intentions might nevertheless produce harmful outcomes, some consequentialists argue for 'rule-consequentialism', which states that right action is whatever conforms to a rule which generally promotes the good if obeyed. This takes the guesswork out of individual action on a case-by-case basis, and also achieves something of a compromise with deontological views of ethics. Generally speaking, consequentialists who favour the idea of rules do so as a supplement to individual decision, as 'side-constraints' or aids, understanding them as non-absolute and as dispensable if applying the rule too vigorously could lead to undesirable outcomes.

Some critics of consequentialism say that it fails to recognize the claim that certain acts are intrinsically right or wrong independently of any other consideration (these are the deontologists); other critics say that it denies significance to the personal character of moral experience and the decisions constituting it, in which the agent's concerns, projects and goals are intimately connected with his acts and practices. If all that matters to the evaluation of what he does is the consequences of what he does – especially if these are the actual consequences as opposed to what he intended or desired, and especially also if the agent's own good is not taken to be a factor – then too much distance has been placed between agents and the morality of what they do. This is a criticism made by the philosopher Bernard Williams.

See: DEONTOLOGY; METAPHYSICS; MIND, PHILOSOPHY OF

CONSUMERISM

A society in which significant importance is attached by significant numbers of people to shopping for goods and services, to owning things that manifest their wealth, taste and status, to achieving satisfaction or happiness through things that can be bought, and which in general enjoys and even celebrates the processes of shopping, buying and owning, is said to be a consumerist society.

The joke phrase 'retail therapy' used to denote the restoration of good spirits that a shopping expedition induces – usually the forage among brand-name goods in a variety of shops, with a few triumphantly found bargains or exactly suitable items – is in fact an accurately descriptive phrase. More to the point, the word 'forage' used in the preceding sentence is also speakingly accurate: if anthropological models of hunter-gatherer societies are correct, foraging among bushes and roots for edibles was an important task for women while their menfolk were away on (probably often unsuccessful) hunting expeditions. Observing a keen-eyed, highly choosy shopper at work among the hanging rails in Sachs on Fifth Avenue is to see the early nutritional history of mankind replayed in metaphor.

The fashionable moralistic stance is to deprecate consumerism as shallow and materialistic, and so indeed it can be when people take too seriously the idea that what they own is the measure of their value as human beings. But as is suggested by the anthropological hint just given, there are also deeper impulses at work, and something worth reflecting on is this: that consumerism would not exist if there were not genuine satisfactions involved, and if there were not at least some correlation between things owned, the money that buys them, the work or talent that earns the money, and the qualities of the person who does that work or has that talent. In short, consumerism is not merely empty and point-less, except when it exaggerates itself into becoming so. This seeming truism has the virtue of being a truth.

Critics of consumerism also blame the profit-driven manipulations of the public by advertisers and marketing men, whom some see as sinister Machiavellians practising on a helpless, feeble, malleable, child-minded, gullible, hypnotizable herd of human sheep. Well: this picture is not without its truth either, though as a corrective one need only bring to mind that keen-eyed shopper in Sachs.

There are however serious points to be made about consumption, which consumerism drives to excess in the richer economies of the world. The chief ills it causes are environmental harm, exploitation of human beings, especially in poorer countries, but also among workforces in rich ones, and inequalities everywhere – not just in wealth, but in what 'inequality of wealth' really means: which, for those at the bottom end, is lack of opportunities, lack of education, lack of adequate housing, lack of health care, lack of justice. It can also mean envy, resentment, and conflict.

Actually, it is not just consumption itself – excessive, conspicuous, environment-polluting consumption – but its global pattern that is the problem. Consider: in 1998 the UN Human Development Report focused on consumption, and found astonishing inequalities; the report stated that the richest 20 per cent of the world's population accounted for 86 per cent of total private expenditure on consumption, while the poorest 20 per cent of the world's population accounted for 1.3 per cent of such expenditure. All indicators suggest that this gap has widened, scarcely possible though that seems.

The despoliation of natural resources that goes to feed the ever-growing desire for consumer items and services has been a justifiable target for 'Green' activism. Another activist sphere is the campaign for fair trade arrangements with producers in developing countries who are profoundly discriminated against by the muscle of corporations and the protectionism practised by governments in powerful economies. Green policies and fair trade policies are, however, not always consistent, given that some production activities in developing countries (for example, those that involve clearing forests to create agricultural land) are anything but green. But generally speaking, traditional methods of production are by their nature ecologically friendly, so the synergy between green and fair trade politics should be an effective one.

Karl Marx and Thorstein Veblen are salient modern critics of consumerism and the capitalism that fosters it, and which desires ever-more consumption to fuel ever-more growth. But hostility to consumerism has much deeper roots. From ancient until recent times there existed 'sumptuary laws' designed to restrain luxury and extravagance, aimed especially (as *Black's Law Dictionary* reports) 'against inordinate expenditures in the matter of apparel, food, furniture, etc.'. The Locrian code in ancient Greece forbade free women to be followed by more than one maid 'unless she was drunk', or to wear embroidered robes 'unless she was a professed and public prostitute'. As it happens, although in Rome's austere Republican times show and flamboyance were generally disapproved of, so that the *sumptuariae leges* applied to everyone, later in imperial Rome and in the medieval period sumptuary laws were aimed at maintaining clearly visible differences of social hierarchy. Purple and scarlet were only allowed to royalty and nobility respectively, and silks and furs were reserved to them; manifestations of social rank were not to be blurred by commoners and rich bourgeois aping their betters.

In the reign of Elizabeth I of England sumptuary regulations had the twofold aim of preventing money going out of the kingdom to purchase rich and fancy apparel made abroad, especially in Italy, and to stop young men 'otherwise serviceable' from foppishness and effeminacy and wasting their money on becoming so. But they also aimed at maintaining 'a difference of estates known by their apparel after the commendable custom in times past'.

Sumptuary laws must be distinguished from laws regulating what certain groups in society must wear in order to be recognizable for what they are. In early Muslim lands Jews, Christians and other non-Muslims had to wear signs proclaiming their status; Jews and prostitutes everywhere had to advertise what they were with special clothing or badges, as for example the conical hat in Islamic countries and the yellow star in medieval Christendom and later in Nazi Germany, and the striped hoods or shoulder tassels of prostitutes.

See: ADVERTISING, CAPITALISM, GLOBALIZATION, WEALTH

CREATIONISM

Creationism is the theory held by religious people that the world was created by a deity. In the book of Genesis, regarded by both Jews and Christians as a holy text, there are two accounts of the creation of the universe by God, taking six days. Despite overwhelming proof that this account is mere fancy – evidence from geology and evolutionary biology, to say nothing of its conflict with many other different accounts in the world's many other religious traditions, settles the matter – numbers of religious people, and chiefly fundamentalists, continue to profess belief in it.

As a result of constitutional provisions in the United States establishing secularism (separation of state and religion) in the public domain, creationism cannot be taught in the country's schools. Accordingly the country's well-organized and well-funded 'Bible-believing' Christians have promoted an alternative method of arguing for creationism, which makes no explicit mention of God or indeed the act of creation itself, but adopts a would-be scientific guise and calls itself 'Intelligent Design

Theory' (ID). Efforts to have ID taught in school biology classes, and simultaneously to have evolutionary theory downgraded to a 'mere hypothesis' because of the risk it poses to the children of the faithful, who might be dissuaded from their beliefs about creation by it, have so far not met with success in the United States, the main location of these developments and efforts.

Neither creationism nor 'ID' is of scientific value, but they have sociological interest because they constitute the last salvoes in the war between science and religion which started in the sixteenth century and had one of its greatest battles in the nineteenth century after the publication of Darwin's theory of evolution by natural selection. In the United States the first shock of the science–religion war was the Scopes trial in Tennessee in 1925.

The Scopes case involved a biology teacher, John Scopes, who defied the laws of Tennessee prohibiting the teaching of evolutionary theory in schools. (Florida, Mississippi, Louisiana and Arkansas had also banned it.) The American Civil Liberties Union sent Clarence Darrow to defend Scopes's First Amendment rights, while former presidential candidate William Jennings Bryan defended Tennessee – and with it religion. It was an epic confrontation, but not much of a battle, for Darrow was a brilliant advocate with a strong case, and Bryan's best argument was that the people of Tennessee had a right to defend themselves against the 'untested hypothesis' of evolutionary theory, given (as he and the people of Tennessee claimed) its danger to morality. Both legs of this argument were easily cut away by Darrow, who went on to force Bryan onto the witness stand, where he was cross-examined and, in short, humiliated. He died a few days after the trial, having confessed that he had neither studied other religions nor made a critical evaluation of the Christian religion, and showing under examination (despite having written a Christian refutation of Darwin) that his understanding of evolutionary theory was extremely weak.

Despite the demolition of Bryan's case, no Tennessee jury was likely to find in Scopes's favour, so he was duly convicted. But though Scopes lost, science had won; the rest of the nation poured scorn on the Tennessee hicks, whom H.L. Mencken called 'the gaping primates of the upland valleys', and the cause of religious fundamentalism seemed doomed.

But the religious lobby in the United States is a powerful entity, and although it took a long time to recover from its defeat in Tennessee, by the 1990s it was resurgent, well funded, equipped with television and radio stations, and even a museum showing the children of Adam and

Eve playing with *Tyrannosaurus rex* babies (which in Eden, of course, were vegetarian).

Creationists explain the apparent antiquity of the Earth and its fossil record by appeal to the Flood, which they say laid down the Earth's geological sediments, in an instant crushing and burying in them all antediluvian life. But their principal argument is that the world exemplifies design, and could only be as intricate, various, beautiful and wonderfully organized as it is if made by a deity. This argument – called the 'argument from design' – is one that first-year students at university easily learn to refute. They do so as follows.

First, the appearance of order in some complex phenomena can be explained by one of two things: either as the result of the human propensity to impose an appearance of order on complexes, or as a function of some objective order in the complex itself. It is a feature of the human mind naturally to interpret complexes as manifesting patterns even when they are not intrinsically there, as exemplified by our reaction to Rorschach blots. We are likewise over-apt to interpret symmetries and coincidences as evidence of purpose – for obviously advantageous evolutionary reasons. This is merely a cautionary point; but physics teaches that the universe is entropic, that is, is constantly moving in the direction of disorder, and that local reversals of entropy (as in biological phenomena) take a great deal of energy to start and maintain them. So order, as something static and inertial, is not a physical norm. Despite that, it is something we humans almost invariably manage to project onto things, because our minds naturally dislike unstructured or incoherent appearances.

Secondly, evolutionary theory explains the emergence of pattern and structure very well without any supplementary premises. If life forms give the appearance of design, it is because they have evolved that way under selective pressures, survival of the species ensuring that anything unfitted to survive will die out of the record. So the butterfly wing's pattern of eyes, making it look like a larger and fiercer creature to frighten away predators, is economically explained by hypothesizing that those of its ancestors which survived to pass on their genes had an adaptation which conferred survival value in this way, an adaptation preserved and perhaps improved over the course of the species' genetic history. On classical Darwinian views this would happen by random mutations proving reproductively advantageous. According to other versions of evolutionary theory, adaptation in response to environmental pressures might happen more swiftly and directly, with evolutionary change taking place in spasms punctuated by periods of equilibrium ('punctuated equilibrium' is the name given by Stephen Jay Gould and his colleagues to just such a process).

Thirdly, if there is indeed conscious design in the universe, the most that its presence entails is a designer or designers; it tells us nothing about how many, who or what they were, and certainly not that it or they fit the notions of a particular religious tradition. Moreover, since suffering and death, the preying of animal upon animal, natural disasters, diseases and plagues, deformities, pain and anguish seem to be part of the design, it is not as good as it might be, so if there were indeed a designer, it's clear he could have done with more practice – unless the natural and moral evils built into the design are there on purpose, which by parity of reasoning (if beauty implies a good designer) implies malice or evil on the designer's part.

In short, the argument is a bad one, and it is surprising to find educated people still invoking it.

Among the many puzzling things about literal believers in the contents of the Bible is the fact that they do not appear to ask the simple questions about those elements which make the collection of writings – its poetry, history, sex and humour aside – so implausible as an alleged account of the activities of a deity. Why, if the deity it portrays is omnipotent, did it take it six days to create heaven and earth, and why did it need a rest afterwards? Why is a 'day' for this God and the universe twenty-four hours long, when that merely happens to be the period of rotation on its axis of our planet? Why do hours and days apply to deities anyway, since they are supposed to be eternal, which means 'outside time'? If there is a deity and it knows everything and is wholly good, why did it repent of having created humans, and proceed to murder all but a very few of them in a flood? Obviously this deity is not as advertised; it makes bad mistakes and gets into genocidal rages. Why therefore do those who believe in the literal truth of the Old Testament not blench at the portrait it gives of a despotic, jealous, violent, temperamental, petty and murderous being?

And as to the New Testament's supposedly more avuncular deity, how can they tolerate a God who makes an unmarried teenage girl pregnant and then arranges for the resulting offspring to be tortured to death? Theologians would doubtless respond that it is a mistake to read the Bible literally, and that some or all of these things are to be understood metaphorically, symbolically, mystically, or all three. A different set of questions therefore arises. Which bits are to be taken literally, and which figuratively? Whose interpretations of the latter are the authoritative ones – and why are they so? How does one know which of competing interpretations to accept? At this point one does well to remember Karl Popper's dictum that 'a theory that explains everything explains nothing', for that is what explaining everything by means of selective interpretation does.

See: BIOPOIESIS, CHRISTIANITY, EVOLUTION, RELIGION

DAOISM (TAOISM)

Daoism is often described as the second great philosophical tradition of China after Confucianism, although its roots are older than Confucianism, and its central concepts find a place both in it and in later movements of Chinese thought, this being especially true of its chief concept of 'the Way'. Its founder is said to be Laozi, but since this simply means 'Old Master' it is likely that this is a mere personification of more than one reflective personality who contributed to its earliest development.

The first named historical figure to whom contributions to Daoist thought are attributed is Zhuangzi, who lived in the fourth century BCE and is the author of the book that carries his name. That book, and the more ancient *Dao De Jing*, are in fact compilation texts put together from different sources over long periods.

It is possible that the idea of a 'school of thought' of which these classics are defining or authoritative texts is the creation of the ancient historians Sima Tan and his son Sima Qian (first century BCE). In the somewhat characteristic Chinese way of organizing everything into neatly numbered orders, Sima Tan defined six schools of philosophy, with Daoism as one. They are the Yin-Yang, Confucian, Mohist, Legalist, School of Names, and Daoist schools, and this neatness suggests a post-facto imposition of differences where fewer (or more) might have existed in reality. Nevertheless the classification stuck, and the texts and traditions attributed to Daoism have a distinctive enough shared character for the classification to have merit. Certainly, in the remainder of Chinese history Daoism was recognized as a unitary movement, and in time came to have its monks and monasteries, teachers and masters, and they attained great influence.

The *Zhuangzi* and the *Dao De Jing* are very different in character. The latter is vatic, poetic, enigmatic and pithy. The former is diffuse, funny, and often fantastical, but no less enigmatic in places. Both consist of reflections, meditations and observations on questions relating to 'the Way' (*Dao*), and are deliberately unsystematic.

Daoism in what one takes to be its original form is something of a hippie philosophy, opposed to authority and compulsion, and in favour of spontaneity, nature and unreflective inspiration. When Buddhism began to spread in China from the second century CE onwards many who were influenced by Daoism were drawn to it, as congenial to its outlook; from among these came some of the most influential schools of martial arts.

In the expression *Dao De Jing* the word *Dao* means 'way' and *De* means 'virtue'. The eighty-one chapters of the book divide roughly into two halves, the first on *Dao* and the second on *De*. The concept of the Way is multiple, ambiguous, capacious and fundamental. Roughly it means reality in all its variety and constant flux, not conceivable as a single thing such as 'the World' as Western thought has it, but as variety: it is *wanwu*, 'ten thousand things'. It is not something that can be grasped in thought, stated or described; rather, a person might succeed in becoming one with it. The method for doing this centrally includes the 'effortless, natural, non-willed action' that is conformity with the Way. The term here used is *wu wei*, sometimes interpreted as 'do-nothing' or 'empti-ness'; in fact the concept is much closer to the idea of Zen in Buddhism (and it has been claimed that Zen – in China *Chan* – was an import into Buddhism from Daoism during the period of mutual influence in China's Tang Dynasty, 618–906 CE).

The Way is a flow, and the Daoist sage is one who knows how to flow with it. The stories and fables in the *Zhuangzi* illustrate this to perfec-tion, perhaps the most famous among them being the discourse of Ding the butcher, who explained his extraordinary skill at cutting up oxen by saying, 'I follow the Dao, which is something beyond mere skill. When I started I could see only the ox. After three years I ceased to see the whole ox, no longer looking with my eyes, because Dao is beyond perception and understanding. I follow the natural form, never touching a ligament or tendon, however small, and still less a bone or joint. An expert cook buys a new knife every year, because he cuts. An inexpert cook buys a new knife every month, because he hacks. I have had this knife for nineteen years and it is as good as if it had just been on the grindstone. It is as if it has no thickness, but finds the spaces in the joints; I move the knife subtly, and suddenly the ox falls like a clod of earth, flopping apart and falling without effort.'

China has had such a long and various history that naturally its trad-itions of thought mutated and developed over time. For Daoism the most significant such development was its receptiveness to Buddhism, a kindred outlook. Even when the two outlooks did not assimilate, they were so to speak fraternal. The most flourishing epoch of Daoism, though, was that glorious period of Chinese history, the Tang Dynasty, whose imperial family claimed descent from Laozi, and favoured the movement's teachers and practitioners, giving them a place at court and funding major monasteries. By this time Daoism had come to be a more fully articulated philosophy of life, teaching compassion, integrity, humility and moderation, maintaining the idea of achieving oneness with the Dao through *wu wei*, and no longer rejecting authority or rule but offering advice on how government could best be conducted. The foundation of monasteries and the status to which Daoist masters were raised in the Tang ensured that for centuries thereafter the outlook's ideas retained a major place in Chinese thought. That changed with the advent of communism in China in 1949, for then, and especially during the Cultural Revolution (1966–76), a concerted effort was made to stamp it out.

See: BUDDHISM, COMMUNISM

DEMOCRACY

'Democracy' is a word with positive connotations in Western liberal societies; it is what the West stands for, and even claims to go to war to defend or promote. Its flaws and weaknesses are recognized, and constitutional efforts to adjust for them are standardly made; but the consensus is that democracy is the least bad of all political systems, because it most reflects the will of the governed in their own government, and thus confers the greatest possible degree of consent and legitimacy on the political process. Few would dream of saying, at least aloud, that oligarchy, plutocracy or dictatorship are preferable alternatives.

The basic idea of democracy is that it consists in 'majority rule', though in fact the need to protect minority interests makes this phrase something of a *façon de parler*. It would apply in the case of 'direct democracy', and decision by referendum; but most democracies are 'representative democracies' in which members of a legislature are elected by constituencies and thereby in effect deputized to take decisions, hold office, and generally consider what is best on their electors' behalf.

The feel-good meaning of 'democracy' as understood in liberal Western states comprehends not just the system by which legislatures and governments are elected, but a whole package of concepts besides, centrally including the following: the rule of law characterized by due process; respect and protection for civil liberties and human rights; and the freedom for civil society organizations to exist, representing interests and meeting needs across a wide spectrum.

But democracy has not always had such a good press. Rather the contrary, for Western civilization has in fact been profoundly anti-democratic for most of its history, with democracy regarded as nothing better than the despotism of ignorant and venal majorities. Since most of those who have been literate enough to record their opinion of matters political belonged to the classes of people apt to suffer under mob rule, history is filled with condemnations of democracy.

When classical Athens was a democracy it was not a democracy in the sense that we would now accept. Women, foreigners and slaves (between them constituting the majority of the population) had no say, and freeborn male citizens only reached official adulthood at the age of thirty. Yet at its height under Pericles, Athenian democracy produced art, architecture, literature and philosophy of such excellence and power that they continue to shape Western civilization to this day.

Athenian democracy, despite not really being one, had vigorous opponents. The aristocratic Plato blamed it for making the citizenry 'idle, cowardly, loquacious and greedy' and for devouring those – Pericles, Miltiades, Themistocles – who had given it to them in the first place. Control of the state had, he said, been put into the hands of the ignorant, feckless and greedy mob.

With Plato and after him Aristotle against it, democracy had small chance with later thinkers. Renaissance thinkers assumed that democracy promised nothing but unlimited turmoil. Enlightenment thinkers saw it as a threat to virtue. The founding fathers of the United States believed it would lead to a dangerous equalization of property. And as the much grudged change towards today's simulacrum of democracy began in Britain in 1832, its opponents lamented that they were being sold to the mob, because for them democracy meant only the terrors of ochlocracy as experienced in the French Revolution.

What at last made democracy not merely respectable but something worth fighting wars to protect (and even to disseminate among unfortunates who do not possess it) is the achievement of nineteenth-century historians in rescuing Athenian democracy from the opprobrium bestowed on it by Plato and many intervening centuries of historians. They did it by linking the ideals of democracy with the glories of Periclean Athens and the fertility of the Athenian mind at that period. The new perspective has proved irresistible.

Still, democracy is only truly respectable when it can be made to work both effectively and, even more importantly, fairly. It needs a method of representation that yields stable government while respecting, and to the extent possible accommodating, minority and individual interests, including those that are sometimes not directly conformable to majority interests. Most of the major Western democracies are very imperfect, and rely on the population's general acceptance of their imperfections in return for more or less satisfactory performance otherwise. The imperfections in question include always producing governments elected by an absolute minority of voters, as in the United Kingdom with its first-past-the-post system; the supposed virtue of this is that strong government results, whereas electoral systems that are too accurately proportional to voters' wishes tend to produce weak and unstable coalition governments (Italy is an example), or governments that are at the mercy of tiny minority parties which hold the balance (Israel is an example).

A condition of genuine and effective democracy is a thoughtful and informed electorate, and one that actually bothers to vote. Some argue that voting, as in Australia, should be compulsory, making it a civic duty like paying taxes and abiding by the law generally. 'Voter apathy' is standardly blamed on politicians, who may indeed merit some of the blame; but it is much more the fault of lazy, indifferent, complacent or ignorant citizens who do not make use of their important right to vote – a right for which people elsewhere have fought and died.

Democratic structures and procedures can and often do exist at the sub-state level too, in organizations such as clubs or boardrooms, educational institutions, even families. The strengths and especially the weaknesses of democracy are particularly marked in such settings, most of which seem to work better under some form of benign dictatorship. At very least, under benign dictatorship meetings tend to be shorter. In a household with children this seems to be the best system of governance, although when the children become teenagers the dictatorship, now exercised by these latter, tends to turn malign.

To Abraham Lincoln is owed the resounding remark that 'Democracy is government of the people, by the people and for the people', and this certainly sums up the best aspiration of the least bad basis for political and governmental authority so far known to mankind. But it is salutary to remember the acidulous but all too speaking comment made by Winston Churchill on the other side of the subject: 'The strongest argument against democracy', he said, 'is a five minute discussion with the average voter.'

See: ANARCHY, ARISTOCRACY, COMMUNISM, FASCISM, POLITICS

DEONTOLOGY

A deontological ethical theory is one that says there are kinds of acts which are intrinsically wrong no matter what, even if the consequences of performing them are good, indeed even if the consequences of performing them are morally obligatory. The word comes from Greek *deon* meaning 'duty', and the concept of duty accordingly plays a central role in the formulation of deontological ethics.

The contrasting ethical outlook is consequentialist or 'teleological' (*telos* is Greek for 'end' or 'goal'). Such a theory holds that what makes an act good is that it brings about something good. On this view, to judge the moral worth of an action one must look at the consequences of its being performed. It is standardly taken that deontological and teleological theories of ethics divide the field between them.

For the deontologist, ethical decisions about what to do turn wholly on the duties or obligations of the agent, or the rights of the patient (understanding 'patient' as the recipient or 'sufferer' of the agent's actions). When anyone performs an act good in itself which exceeds his obligation to perform it, or gives more than a patient has a right to expect, his act is described as 'supererogatory' – as the phrase has it, it is 'beyond the call of duty'.

Whether the theory is agent-centred or patient-centred, the principle acted upon is such that it is acted on for its own sake, because of what it requires or enjoins in itself. It is never instrumental or subordinate to something beyond itself, but has what is sometimes called a 'categorical' status to contrast it with merely 'hypothetical' principles which say 'if you want such-and-such, then do so-and-so', implying that if you do not want such-and-such, then you do not have to do so-and-so. A categorical principle, by sharp contrast, just bluntly says, 'do so-and-so', no ifs or buts.

Deontological theory can easily be made to seem counterintuitive. Thus suppose you have been asked by a friend to look after a loaded pistol, and you promise to return it when he asks for it. He comes and asks for it when in a state of rage towards someone he feels has done him serious harm. It would appear that according to the theory, the promise must be honoured irrespective of any consequences that might be foreseen in the case.

Arguably, though, such examples are too crude. For a more reflective deontologist might easily find a principle stating a higher duty in the case – it is not difficult to imagine what that could be – and by that means avoid a tragedy.

An interesting way of drawing the contrast between deontological and teleological views, and one that throws much light on both, was offered by John Rawls. Given that the two main concepts of ethics are *right* and *good*, the two fundamental types of ethical theory can be defined by their view of the connection between them. The simplest is the teleological way, for it says that 'good' is defined independently of 'right', and 'right' is defined as what brings about the good. By contrast, a deontologist either does not define the good independently of the right, or does not define the right as what brings about the good. So the goodness of the consequences that flow from some action has nothing to do with the rightness or wrongness of the action itself, but the two matters are quite distinct, and correlatively therefore we have to say that questions about the rightness of an action are prior to, not posterior to, the goodness or otherwise of what results from it.

The chief proponent of a deontological ethics was Immanuel Kant (1724–1804). He argued that a good person is one who wills himself to act in accordance with the moral law, out of respect for that law and for no other reason. To obey the moral law is conceived of as a duty, and doing one's duty is conceived of as something that no other consideration – one's desires, fears, self-interest, possible gain, worldly ends, even sympathy for others or love of one's family – can trump. The only morally acceptable motive for action is the performance of one's duty; and knowing one's duty in any given case is a matter of rational recognition that the act to be performed in that case is one that anyone and everyone should perform if so placed. This is the idea of the universality of the moral law, which underwrites the categorical nature of the moral imperative involved: 'do so-and-so!' (not: 'if you want such-and-such do so-and-so'). Kant described the categorical imperative – the command that enjoins one's duty – as the instruction to 'act only in accordance with that maxim through which you can at the same time will that it become a universal law'.

One of the unintuitive consequences of Kant's theory is that it is only morally good to read to your children if it is a duty to do so, but not if you do so because you enjoy it. Indeed a more general objection to deontological ethics is that it would seem to entail that it is morally right to do things that can cause harm or make the world a worse place. An example of this is refraining from torturing – because torture is wrong – an individual who knows where the terrorist nuclear bomb is that will kill millions. Here it might be argued that a higher duty has to be observed; but this introduces a requirement for deontologists to provide an account of how to resolve conflicts between duties when these arise. Kant boldly asserted that such conflicts of duty never happen, but it is not hard to think of cases where they do. And if conflicts arise, and are resolved by recognizing the superior claim of one duty over another (as envisioned in the loaded pistol or even torture cases above), then the peculiar result is that some duties are not absolute, and in specifiable circumstances do not have to be (and in conflict cases cannot be) carried out.

These difficulties for deontological ethics all relate to the main difficulty, which is stating the absolute principles, the binding duties, the categorical obligations, that have to be observed. There are surprisingly few candidates for absolute prescriptions which do not require qualification and subclauses describing circumstances in which they do not apply or can or must be trumped by something else. One could try to construe an ethics such as religions enjoin on their votaries – an ethics of divine command – as deontological, but in fact even divine commands are hidden hypotheticals: the protasis (the 'if' part) says something like 'if you wish to get to heaven' (or, since it puts a better complexion on things to say 'if you love God' than to say or imply 'if you do not wish to go to hell') then 'you must do so-and-so'. It is the putative unbendingness of deontological principles that makes this kind of ethics seem implausible and unworkable. A much more plausible domain for deontological principles is the law: but that is another debate.

See: CONSEQUENTIALISM, ETHICS

ECONOMICS

In the conjunction of ancient Greek words from which 'economics' derives – *oikos* meaning 'house' and *nomos* meaning 'law' or 'rule' – there is a certain cosiness, connoting household management and homely arrangements. But as arguably the most influential of the social sciences – because it is not only a theoretical but an applied discipline which, through its applications, affects the individual lives of billions of human beings, and moreover not very reliably to their benefit – economics is a good deal less cosy than the etymology of its name suggests. It is sometimes characterized as 'the dismal science', some think because of its dry subject matter, others because of the dismal things done in its name.

Economics is the study of how goods and services are produced, distributed, valued, and consumed. It is both the empirical study of how economies – as systems of supply, demand, markets and means of exchange – work, and the normative science of how to make them work well (depending on what 'well' means: to maximize wealth? To ensure just distributions? These questions raise the political angle).

Adam Smith, author of *The Wealth of Nations* (1776), is conventionally regarded as the father of economics as a genuine social science. He called it 'political economy' (doubtless mindful of its household etymology and therefore qualifying it to the *polis* or state, very educatedly), and described it as the science by whose application legislators could enrich both the private individual and the state. The great names in early economic theory after Adam Smith include David Ricardo, the first to state a labour theory of value, and Thomas Malthus, who was against helping the poor on the grounds that they would only have more children and make themselves poor all over again. The theory that people will thus keep themselves at subsistence levels by increasing the number of their offspring whenever they have a little extra income seems not to have been grasped or, more to the point, applied by his own father, who had eight children and was prosperous.

Economists reflect on the principles governing such questions as what should be produced, how and for whom, at what cost, and with what efficiencies to ensure that the difference between the cost of supply and the price commanded will return a profit. The question of efficiencies further subdivides into the advantages of specialization, division of labour, and economies of scale. Economists also examine the interesting subject of money, considered as the token of exchange and therefore 'means of final payment' and unit of account. Money is a brilliant invention; it beats taking a cow to pay your dentist; but very few of us believe ourselves to have enough of it.

Two of the principal divisions of economics are 'microeconomics', devoted to the study of the economic behaviour of individual agents (this includes businesses) and their relationships in the marketplace, and 'macroeconomics' which studies the economy as a whole, concerning itself with national production and income, employment and unemployment, taxation and money supply policies, and public borrowing.

One of the reasons for scepticism about economics, especially when applied to our lives and livelihoods, is that at the theoretical level it is full of implausible idealizations. Economic agents are regarded as perfectly rational (look at the fragility of 'sentiment' in any stock market, and allow yourself a horse-laugh: it is not alas too cynical to remark that there the dominating appetite is greed, and the dominating emotion that succeeds greed's over-application is fear), and description of their economic activity at both the micro and the macro level is full of abstractions. For example: the organizing notion used to explain the prices and quantities of goods in a market (a 'perfectly competitive market', the textbooks say) is the theory of supply and demand. Simply put – as expressible in the graph we drew as students to illustrate the inverse relationships between the quantity of goods available and their price, and their price and the demand for them – if prices go up demand falls, and if quantity of supply goes up prices fall, and if prices fall demand rises, which increases prices: and so on and on, up and down, seasick fashion. No doubt this happens frequently enough even in imperfect markets to justify its apotheosis into the 'law' of supply and demand. But there are so many exceptions, contingent on other interests and needs on the demand side, and so many factors on the supply side, that the relation between price and demand is vastly more complex than this. Take just the one example of diesel and petrol prices: as the British experience of taxes on motor fuels shows, demand for them is remarkably price-insensitive. Motorists will buy fuel for their cars even if they have to sell their grandmothers to do it, not out of manic love (see elsewhere in these pages for an account of this phenomenon) for their cars, but because of the imperatives of mobility in the contemporary Western economy. From heavily taxed tobacco products to rising food prices the same relative invariance of demand is found, with no elegant curve of diminishing demand crossing the elegantly rising price curve, but a jagged one of enforced and reluctant reductions in demand when critical choices have to be made between competing needs, dropping to zero at the ultimate crisis point when the motorist can genuinely no longer afford to drive, or – vastly worse – when the starving man dies.

There are many special fields of enquiry in economics relating to labour, law, trade, management, agriculture, developing economies, public finance, welfare, the environment, and more. Modern economics aspires to the condition of a science more than a social science, in making central use of mathematical techniques and game theory.

Despite Adam Smith's pre-eminence in economic history, he was preceded by those who thought about interest and value in medieval times, and by the 'Physiocrats' of the French Enlightenment who thought seriously about the relation between production and income. Smith's *Wealth of Nations* inaugurated classical economics, from which Marxist economics descends by dissent, influenced by Ricardo's views. Macroeconomics owes its independent existence to the seminal work of John Maynard Keynes's *General Theory of Employment, Interest and Money* (1936), which governed thinking on employment for many years afterwards, his view being that market forces by themselves will not ensure full employment, because high unemployment levels would damp effective demand in the economy by creating a barrier to growth. Although this theory was important, his instrumental role, as a lover of opera and ballet (he was married to a Russian ballerina), was in bringing the Arts Council of Great Britain into existence.

The founding assumption of standard or 'neoclassical' economics, mentioned above, is that economic man is a rational agent who dispassionately seeks to maximize his self-interest. And as suggested by the accompanying remarks, this assumption is empirically challengeable. One of the counter-theories to neoclassical economics is 'behavioural economics', which seeks to offer a more realistic account of how and why people make the economic decisions they do.

Behavioural economics turns on a set of observations about the actual practice of *homo economicus* – economic man – as an ordinary individual with an ordinary psychology. First, he is a herd animal, influenced by what others do; perhaps because he is not quite sure what to do himself he copies others, or he acts in ways that he thinks will gain their approval or avoid their disapproval. As a corollary of this, he will try to do what he thinks is right, especially if his actions are transparent to others. He is a creature of habit, and he has an individual character which typically determines how he will behave in line with the values, traits and habits that constitute it. Most people are not especially good at working out complex problems, and therefore rely on their 'instincts' or past experience or hopes; they tend to place too much weight on recent or close-at-hand factors, and too little on objective data or remote facts. The great majority of people are 'loss-averse' and inclined to hang on to what they have got rather than risk losing it; but a few are wild risk takers, and sometimes unpredictably so. Entrepreneurs number a higher proportion of such individuals among their ranks – and it is the entrepreneur who invites ordinary folk to invest in his schemes.

Neoclassical economics, in its endeavour to be as much as possible a quantitative science, ignores these psychological considerations. For example, it does not ask how people's preferences are formed, nor does it take into account the non-rational motivations for their choices and actions. It assumes that each agent can be considered independently as a calculating machine with a single interest, which is maximization of its advantages. It assumes that the agent knows what is required for the realization of his aim.

Across a certain field of economic explanation, this assumption, it must be granted, works well enough. If I want a small economical car for town use my choice will be made from a suitable range of models in a way exactly conformable to the neoclassical scheme. But most of life, and certainly most economic decisions, are neither so straightforward nor so simple in the fit between required knowledge and aim. Behavioural economics seeks to approach economic behaviour from the much richer, more nuanced and various direction of actual human psychology. It is an important new departure in economics, not least because of its public policy implications, where it suggests that changing people's habits, norms and expectations is a more potent way of influencing economic activity than assuming that each individual is a separate calculating unit fully equipped to act, and fully intent on acting, in its own interests even at others' cost.

See: ADVERTISING, CAPITALISM, CONSUMERISM, EGOISM, WEALTH

EDUCATION

The aim of a contemporary education is mainly to equip the young with sufficient levels of literacy, numeracy and basic knowledge for participation in the complexities of modern work and society when they attain adulthood. This is a response to the conditions of modern life, where the skills that a training in literacy and numeracy impart are in some ways more important than the content of such subjects of study as history and literature, though not of course than the content of science subjects. The exigencies of society accordingly impose constraints on public education so that it can produce young adults capable of taking an active and successful part in economic and social arenas.

This, though, makes contemporary education a rather partial matter. To see why, note the sharp contrast between the idea of education prevalent in the contemporary world and the ideal of education in classical antiquity. It is a contrast that some educational institutions do their best to minimize – some private schools and great universities cherish the classical ideal enough to try to incorporate aspects of it in the modern curriculum. The difference can be explained by the ancient Greeks' own distinction between a training in the trades and crafts of commercial life, which they described as *banausic*, and education proper, which they saw as the process by which the young were encouraged and enabled to strive for refinement of character and the development of moral virtues, and to be equipped to make 'a noble use of leisure' as Aristotle put it.

True, the elitist implications of this view resulted in some people thinking that participation in trade and industry is beneath the dignity of an educated man – a silly attitude, and an unfortunate one, but alas too prevalent even in recent times. Obviously enough, the right thought is that both aspects of education are necessary, and mutually fructifying. The trouble as some see it is that in present attitudes to education the emphasis has gone too far in the banausic direction.

The belief that education is something that happens between the ages roughly of five and twenty, and that what happens in the workplace thereafter is a short-lived affair of 'training' and later 'retraining', puts a barrier in the way of thinking that learning should be one of the main features of the whole of a human life. But so it should. The reasons are numerous; the chief is the ethical thought that we have a responsibility to ourselves to be informed, knowledgeable and reflective, aware of what is happening in the world and able to be a good participant in debates and decisions concerning our lives and societies.

Everyone is familiar with the processes of school education, and many with those of university education. Mainly for these reasons, talk of education tends to prompt the thought of schools, playgrounds, teachers, classrooms, exams, and the like: a repertoire of concepts that fills the horizon of thought about what the word 'education' can encompass. Accordingly few think, or think often, about the education provided by literature, film, television and theatre, by museums and art galleries, by travel, by encounters with other people in work and social life, and by the totality of experience itself. For the same reason they therefore do not think of these other sources of instruction as providing education of the emotions, sensibilities and attitudes.

Once one begins to think in these much wider terms, one sees the world and everything in it as a university, and as providing many opportunities to the receptive mind. The best schools and universities make use of these other and broader opportunities for instruction; queues of school children at the city museum, at a theatre matinée, in a party travelling abroad, exemplify this accessing of the wider domain. Yet that domain lies in wait every day for people of every age: it is a fruit that has only to be reached to be plucked.

In the world at large nearly a third of all children of primary school age are not enrolled in school. The proportion of those deprived of a chance of education rises steeply through the age groups for secondary and tertiary education. The result is that considerably less than half the world's population, located almost exclusively in underdeveloped parts of the world – the connection is obvious and two-way – has the educational attainment of a high school graduate of the American system. Apart from the waste of talent and opportunity this entails (how many village Hampdens, how many mute inglorious Miltons?), it forms part of the explanation of the persistence of superstition and religion, very often in forms that are retrogressive and occasionally dangerous. This illustrates the truth that lies behind the half-joke, 'If you think education is expensive, look at the cost of ignorance.'

Theories of education, efforts to design appropriate curricula, experimentation with techniques aimed at making mathematics and reading easier, the aims and methods of training teachers, the funding of school systems and expensive research-based institutions of higher education, are among the perennial topics of discussion in the educational sphere. But there is no community or society which any longer rejects the idea that education is both a good and a necessity, not even the remote tribes of the Amazon and Papua New Guinea whose traditional ways of life deal with their own educational needs quite differently.

In advanced economies education has to meet an increasing diversity of specialized needs. One result has been to obscure the importance of broadly liberal aspects of education, aimed at the person rather than the future employee. The study of mathematics and science is essential in the modern world; but so too is the study of literature and history. The former equip individuals to address the world of work, the latter to address the personal, social and political demands of life. Neither is sufficient alone, though the latter might be so on a richly provisioned tropical island. What gives concern is the diminishing of the latter in the standard round of education, for they are about the elements of civilized human existence.

See: CIVILIZATION, ENLIGHTENMENT, EPISTEMOLOGY, FREEDOM OF SPEECH, VIRTUE ETHICS

EGOISM

Egoism is the view that self-interest is the correct basis for morality. A distinction is often drawn between the idea that as a matter of fact people always act in their own perceived self-interest (psychological egoism), and the idea that self-interest *should* be the basis for morality (ethical egoism).

Ethical egoism recognizes that it is often in an agent's self-interest to benefit others, because at some point it will be of benefit to himself that he has done so – or in general it will be an insurance that others, if there is an established practice to this end in which he takes a part, will act to his benefit at times when he needs them to do so. But he will not act to others' benefit out of motives of altruism, which involves benefiting others purely for their own sake, irrespective of his own good.

Proponents of ethical egoism argue that it is rational to act in ways calculated to produce one's own good. It was offered as a defence against those, not least among them Joseph Butler (1692–1752), who attacked the psychological egoism which had been taken as a datum by some, for example Thomas Hobbes and Bernard Mandeville. Butler argued that among the things people desire is the welfare of others, but also things that harm themselves (for example, revenge); and he held, as others subsequently have done, that in any case self-love and benevolence are not necessarily at odds, because it can make us happier to produce happiness for others.

Nuances of usage between 'egoism' and 'egotism' suggest that the former labels the view, aired above, that self-interest is the basis of morals, whereas 'egotism' is the excessive self-reference of the individual who cannot resist speaking and thinking about himself before all others – who can be said, in short, to suffer from 'I-strain' in both conversation and the transactions of daily life. Obviously the two are related, but differences of nuance or emphasis are always worth preserving.

See: ALTRUISM

ENLIGHTENMENT

The Enlightenment is the movement of thought in eighteenth-century Europe and North America that placed reliance on reason, championed the autonomy and rights of the individual, advocated scientific approaches to social and political problems, promoted science itself, and opposed absolute monarchy, organized religion, superstition and priestcraft as barriers to human progress. Its watchwords were rights, tolerance, freedom of thought, science, and the 'social contract' as the basis of political society.

It might be more historically accurate to say that the Enlightenment covers the whole period from the Reformation in the sixteenth century until our own day, despite reversals and setbacks and the various vigorous would-be 'counter-Enlightenments' responsible for them, because the scientific revolution and the retreat both of absolutism in government and the hegemony of religion over people's minds are important factors in providing the conditions that have transformed life and society in what have, as a result, become the advanced liberal democracies of the Western world.

But the core event of the Enlightenment is the impact on French thinking of the work of two Englishmen, Isaac Newton and John Locke. It was under their influence that the *philosophes* of France, among them Denis Diderot, Jean le Rond d'Alembert and François-Marie Arouet, better known as Voltaire, undertook their respective great projects of reforming the world by the light of reason.

The classic definition of the concept of 'enlightenment' in this historical context is to be found in an essay ('What is Enlightenment?', 1784) by one of the movement's greatest sons, Immanuel Kant, who wrote, 'Enlightenment is man's emergence from his self-imposed immaturity. Immaturity is the inability to use one's understanding without guidance from another. This immaturity is self-imposed when its cause lies not in lack of understanding, but in lack of resolve and courage to use it without guidance from another. *Sapere Aude!* [Dare to know] – "Have courage to use your own understanding!" – that is the motto of enlightenment.'

Neither Kant nor any of his contemporaries believed that they had actually attained enlightenment. They meant rather that they were making progress towards it; Kant remarked, 'If it is now asked, "Do we presently live in an enlightened age?" the answer is, "No, but we do live in an age of enlightenment."'

In describing the immaturity of the intellect as consisting in a state of need for guidance by another, Kant expressly attacked the authorities who sought to keep the human mind thus subordinate. The intellect needs liberty in order to mature, but in every aspect of life, he wrote, liberty was lacking. 'Nothing is required for enlightenment except freedom; and the freedom in question is the least harmful of all, namely, the freedom to use reason publicly in all matters. But on all sides I hear: "Do not argue!" The officer says, "Do not argue, drill!" The tax man says, "Do not argue, pay!" The pastor says, "Do not argue, believe!"'

The iconic work of the Enlightenment is unquestionably the *Encyclopédie* edited by Diderot and d'Alembert. One of their principal targets in attempting to free the mind of man was religion. 'In vain, oh slave of superstition,' says Nature to Mankind in Diderot's *Supplement to Bougainville's Voyage*, 'have you sought your happiness beyond the limits of the world I gave you. Have courage to free yourself from the yoke of religion ... Examine the history of all peoples in all times and you will see that that we humans have always been subject to one of three codes: that of nature, that of society, and that of religion – and that we have been obliged to transgress all three in succession, because they could never be in harmony.' The result is, said Diderot, that there has therefore never been 'a real man, a real citizen, a real believer'.

Although the repudiation of religion's hegemony over thought was important it was not the sole concern, but rather the starting point for the project of encouraging each individual to think, to rely on reason, and to apply the lessons of science as a guide to building good lives and a good society. The Enlightenment project was accordingly a creative and reforming endeavour, based on the idea of freedom.

The Enlightenment has of course always had admirers and detractors, either too enthusiastic or too vehement respectively, not least among the latter those detractors who blame it for everything from Robespierre's Terror to Nazism and Stalinism. In fact the horrors of human history since the French Revolution have largely been the result of counter-Enlightenment outlooks. Where Enlightenment thinkers argued for the autonomy of the individual and the rights of man – jointly implying a pluralistic society – and accorded authority to reason and science, very different things were extolled by the welter of opposed movements: Romanticism with its offspring of nationalism, racism, and the praise of war, the totalitarianisms which attempted to revive the kind of absolutism once exercised by Church and monarchy. We tragically know the results all too well.

As this shows, the various forms of counter-Enlightenment have been just as significant for recent history as the Enlightenment itself. Contemporary opposition came from those who disliked the implications of Enlightenment thought for the religious and political status quo; yet fiercer opposition came later from those who experienced those implications actually bearing fruit in the nineteenth and twentieth centuries. Thus it is that the Enlightenment is seen as indictable for the excesses of the French Revolution, as meriting the Romantic reaction to its rationalism and formalism, and as the ultimate source for both Fascism and Stalinism. There are even those who, this time rightly, recognize that it is responsible for 'liberal' values, but who think this is a bad thing (they paradigmatically include conservative Americans for whom 'liberal' is a pejorative term denoting someone who poses a threat to 'family values', the freedom of the market, and the right to own guns). And of course it remains a *bête noire* for all those who see it as challenging what they think matters most to the human spirit in its need for encounters with the mystical, the ineffable, the numinous, and the divine.

The Enlightenment's first opponents were of two broad kinds: those we would now describe as politically right-wing – ranging from clergymen to thinkers like Edmund Burke and Joseph de Maistre – and those we now call Romantics, for whom imagination, nature and emotion are more important than what they regarded as the Enlightenment's reductive and mechanical rationalism.

Burke argued that the Enlightenment's attack on tradition and religion – for him the respective sources of legitimacy in matters political and moral – was the direct cause of everything bad about the French Revolution. He vigorously opposed the Enlightenment's claim that the ultimate source of political authority is the people. For the *philosophes* of the Enlightenment this idea was simply obvious, and it has proved to be (despite Burke and later conservatives and reactionaries) the underpinning of Western liberal democracy since. But in the eighteenth century the word 'democracy' was a term of horror, and 'the people' were regarded as anarchic and dangerous.

Romantics treated the Enlightenment's espousal of science as implying the claim that scientific progress is the only kind of progress there is, and that history and human experience can only be understood in mechanistic, even deterministic terms. Recoiling from this supposed view, the Romantics placed emotion above reason, and celebrated the subjective, the visionary, the personal, and the non-rational. They saw moods and passions as sources of insight and truth, and gave first place in their praises to such experiences as the individual's passionate reaction to natural beauty. This is in a way odd, for Enlightenment attitudes are natural successors of the classical admiration for order, balance and harmony in music, architecture, art and poetry. That is a valid aesthetic, even if it is not the whole story. Romanticism deliberately contrasted this aesthetic with another applauding the spontaneous and various, trusting emotions to discover better principles of beauty and excellence than reason can.

Of course one would not wish to be without the best of either the Enlightenment or the Romantic legacy. But it is worth insisting that the uncritical embrace of Romanticism aided the survival of many shibboleths that the Enlightenment sought to extirpate – for a chief example, superstition.

The big question at the heart of debates about Enlightenment values concerns the place of reason in the good life. The Enlightenment view is, in sum, a reprise and application of Socrates's famous dictum, that 'the unconsidered life is not worth living'. One main opponent of the idea that reason is the key is religion, which claims that revelation, whether in the form of mystical experience or scripture, conveys otherwise undiscoverable truths from outside ordinary human experience. Relativism is another opponent, arguing that different truths, views and ways of thinking, even those that contradict each other, are all equally valid.

In arguing by contrast that reason, despite its fallibilities, is the only legitimate standard for enquiry, Enlightenment thinkers well understood that reason itself has imperfections and limits, and demands responsibility and care therefore in its use; think of Voltaire's satire on the excessive rationalist optimism of Dr Pangloss in *Candide*, and of the critiques of reason by those arch-Enlightenment figures, David Hume and Immanuel Kant.

A famous later critical reaction to the Enlightenment illustrates how its optimistic and progressive outlook came to be seen by critics in an opposite light. In *The Dialectic of Enlightenment*, whose authors Max Horkheimer and Theodor Adorno began it as a conversation between them in a New York kitchen during the worst days of the Second World War, the argument is that the ideas and principles of the Enlightenment had metamorphosed into their opposites. The Enlightenment extolled individual freedom, but it had become a form of enslavement by economic forces. Science was urged as the rational alternative to religion, but 'scientism', itself assuming the guise of a salvation myth promising scientific explanations and solutions for everything, simply replaced religion and came to exert the same maleficent influence.

Horkheimer and Adorno regarded their attack on scientific rationality as their key argument, because they thought they were witnessing, in the horrors of the Second World War, the realization of its malign threat. The *philosophes* of the eighteenth century believed that the objective character and pragmatic success of science would promote the interests of freedom and tolerance. But Horkheimer and Adorno argued that scientific rationality has its own dynamic, which gradually makes it turn against the values which facilitated its own rise. It therefore changes from being a weapon against repression into a weapon of repression. Believing its dreams of progress, drunk on its successes, triumphantly increasing its mastery over nature, Enlightenment's chief ornament – scientific rationality – becomes a nightmare, and everything it had set out to destroy re-emerges in new and worse forms – chief among them, so Horkheimer and Adorno argued, Fascism.

The analysis offered by Horkheimer and Adorno was greatly influential in the Frankfurt School, whose debates were widely followed in the years after the Second World War. It does not however survive scrutiny. They saw the idea of scientific mastery over nature as leading to the idea of totalitarian mastery over people, a mastery exercised by those into whose hands the levers of power, both economic and political, had been put by the material progress that the Enlightenment made possible. As they put it, 'instrumental rationality' had become 'bureaucratic politics', and the worst form of the latter was Nazism.

But the implausibility of this is obvious. Nazism drew its strength from the peasantry and petit-bourgeoisie, the people who felt most threatened by capital's advance to power. Horkheimer and Adorno misidentified the true source of the new oppression: the descendants, so to speak, of the people who originally had most to lose from Enlightenment and therefore reacted with hostility to it – namely, and literally, the reactionaries. If Nazis had lived in the eighteenth century, they would have defended absolute government against the 'instrumental rationality' which then expressed itself as aspirations to secular democracy. And so, indeed, would Stalinism have done, of which Horkheimer and Adorno were not so critical – though by their own argument they should have been.

Just as Horkheimer and Adorno were not the first to attack the Enlightenment, they were not the last. Postmodernism denies the basic premises of the Enlightenment's 'grand narratives', and the institutionalized opposition to Enlightenment embodied in the very nature of most religious and some major political outlooks remains. The project of championing the Enlightenment cause, therefore, remains likewise.

What people mean today by 'Enlightenment values' is an updated and somewhat idealized – but no less valid and admirable – version of the values that the eighteenth-century Enlightenment embodied. They can be listed as a set of commitments: to pluralism, individual autonomy, democracy, the rule of law, tolerance, science, reason, secularism, equality, humanistic ethics, education, and the promotion and protection of human rights and civil liberties. None of these are mere abstractions, and the difference they make to the lives of individuals is vast. Only compare the life of the ordinary man and woman in a Western country today with the lives of their forebears three or four centuries ago, or with many of their fellows today in developing countries, especially those where religion remains a dominating influence over people's lives. The transforming effect of Enlightenment ideas in history is plain to see: and as admirable as it is plain.

See: EDUCATION, EQUALITY, HUMAN RIGHTS, HUMANISM, LAW, LIBERTY, ROMANTICISM, SECULARISM

EPISTEMOLOGY

Epistemology is the branch of philosophy concerned with the nature of knowledge and how we acquire it – this latter not in the sense of education, but rather the question of how enquiry can be so conducted that it will lead towards truth rather than error, or at least so that it will yield responsible belief. *Episteme* is the Greek word for 'knowledge'.

Plato took the view, shared by everyone since, that one cannot know what is not true – that is, that anything which is an object of knowledge properly so called must be true. He further thought that what is true must be perfect and eternal. But since (he said) everything in the world revealed to us by our senses is temporary and imperfect, so that the most we can aspire to in our investigation of it is opinion or mere belief, nothing in the empirical world can be an object of knowledge. He accordingly proposed that there must be a realm of perfect, unchanging and eternal entities which he called 'Ideas' (or 'Forms'), of which the multiple, imperfect and ever-changing copies in our world (which he called 'the Realm of Becoming' because everything in it is always becoming something else – the acorn turns into an oak, the oak becomes a pile of planks, the planks become a ship) are poor reminders.

They are indeed literally reminders, Plato said, because we could not possibly deduce the existence, still less the nature, of the Ideas from these impoverished instances of them in our experience; so he concluded that we have immortal souls which in their disembodied state were in direct contact with them. At conception or birth we forgot all this knowledge; the processes of education and experience are partial reminders of what we once knew. (I explain Plato's views more fully in METAPHYSICS below.)

Few have been prepared to construct so heroic a theory in order to formulate an epistemology, but all have agreed that the minimum that knowledge can be is *justified true belief*. The requirement for appropriate justification is obvious; one cannot claim to know something merely on the basis of (say) dreaming it or choosing on a whim to believe it. The requirement that what is known be true is likewise obvious; as Plato said, one cannot know a falsehood (although of course one can know *that* a belief, proposition or theory is false, which is a different thing). And of course one must at least believe what one hopes to know, for that is how the mind must entertain the thought 'that p' where 'p' is a proposition expressing the putative item of knowledge.

A short way of explaining why this discussion matters so much, if it is not already obvious, is that it concerns the distinction between fact and opinion. How, if at all, can we distinguish them? What are the techniques and methods of enquiry that will lead us to the former and correct the latter?

The justified-true-belief model of knowledge has, as one would expect, had many holes picked in it by philosophical debate, mainly with a view to exploring what kind and degree of justification are required for the model to stand up. A simple argument shows where the biggest hole is. One can believe a true proposition and have a justification for doing so, but the justification can be the wrong one for holding that belief. For example: suppose you believe that Fred is in the next room because you heard Fred's favourite tune being strummed on Fred's peculiar-sounding guitar. Fred is indeed in the next room, so your belief is true; but he has taught a friend to strum his favourite tune on his peculiar guitar, and it is the friend strumming. Your justification for holding this true belief is therefore not the right justification in the circumstances. So if you claim to know that Fred is in the next room on the basis of the evidence you employ to justify that claim, you cannot be said to *know* that Fred is there; you only or merely believe that he is. And very often, indeed, our beliefs are merely beliefs because the justification for them is insufficient to make that belief amount to knowledge.

This example shows that the justification condition in the justified-true-belief model needs shoring up. A number of suggestions are in play. One is that the methods we employ in seeking knowledge should be reliable under some suitable definition of 'reliable'. Another is that they should 'track the truth' at each stage of enquiry. Some theories, far more modestly – or pessimistically – ask us to accept that efforts to acquire knowledge are fallible, and that knowledge claims must therefore always be regarded as likewise fallible.

The fallibility point reminds us that the central motivation for constructing a theory of knowledge is the need to meet sceptical challenges to the possibility of knowledge, either globally or in one or another particular domain – for example, in ethics, history, or the sciences. In consequence a considerable portion of epistemological debate has focused on scepticism, chiefly with the aim of refuting it or at least showing how it fails to subvert our normal certainties about what we claim to know.

Sceptical challenges take the form of reminding us about the normal human propensity for error, and the fallibility of our powers of perception, reasoning and memory. How can we ever exclude the possibility – however remote and implausible it might seem to suggest that this possibility exists – that we are dreaming, deceived, in error, or subject to hallucination or plain perceptual misjudgement, at the moment when we claim knowledge of something? Even so obvious-seeming a claim as that I know there is a desk in front of me as I write these words is vulnerable to sceptical challenge: how can I be one hundred per cent certain that I am not dreaming at this very moment, given that we often do not know we are dreaming when we dream, but believe that events unfolding in the dream are actual and true?

From Descartes in the seventeenth century to Bertrand Russell and A.J. Ayer in the twentieth century, the effort to meet sceptical challenge has been the central motivation in developing epistemological theories in modern philosophy. In this period, in fact, the history of epistemology is mainly the history of responses to scepticism. At times sceptical challenge has been seen as a serious threat to the project of attaining knowledge, at times it has been seen as a merely heuristic device aimed at clarifying the task of constructing a decent theory of knowledge. In either case scepticism sharply illuminates what needs to be done to explain the nature of knowledge and to identify the optimal means of getting it; so that even in enquiries about the assumptions and methods of enquiry in natural science, social science and history, epistemology's fundamental dilemma lies in the background.

In the tradition of philosophy there have been two major schools of epistemology, the Rationalist and the Empiricist. Rationalists hold that knowledge as such can only be attained by reason, for example by rational excogitation from first principles, self-evident truths, or 'the given'. For some Rationalists we innately possess at least knowledge of logical and moral truths, and perhaps also (though not as extensively as Plato thought) some fundamental principles of reality in general. For Empiricists, as their name tells us, it is sense-experience and observation – that is, enquiry into the way the world actually is – that form the basis of all knowledge. Stated in terms of this crude opposition, it would appear that Empiricists have no use for reason or Rationalists for the data of experience; but of course they respectively do; it is the question of the ultimate source and authority of knowledge on which they differ.

See: ETHICS, METAPHYSICS, PHILOSOPHY, SCEPTICISM

EQUALITY

Equality is an ethical and by extension political ideal with a long history. It is central to the philosophy of Mo Zi in ancient China, is discernible in early Christianity, was the desire and demand of the Peasants' Revolt of 1381 and of the English Civil War's Levellers in the seventeenth century, and it has its most famous expression in modern history in the French Revolution, with its noble aspiration to 'equality, liberty and fraternity'. One might cite the socialist and communist movements of the nineteenth and twentieth centuries as further embodiments of the ideal of equality, but in practice the societies in which were tried the experiments of these two -isms were so imperfect that they tended to experience the equality of suffering, deprivation and oppression rather more than any other kind.

The idea of equality is a complex one. A general formulation of the ground for asserting equality as an ideal is this: there is no intrinsic feature of any individual or group which entitles them to preferential treatment in any respect over any other individual or group, or a greater share of any good than the share of any other individual or group. This way of putting equality's ground registers opposition to such views as that some are entitled to more or better than others because they are 'nobly born' or racially superior, or some such.

Attempts to give a definition of equality quickly prove problematic. 'Equality' unqualified does not make much sense; we need to specify the respect in which people are to be regarded as equal, or are to be treated equally. There is equality of opportunity, equality before the law, equality of rights, equality of income, political equality, and even the strict distributive equality in which each individual receives the same benefits and resources as every other. Does talk of equality comprise all of these, and if not, surely we do need to particularize? Should we not ask if all these equalities are equally desirable or equally necessary? Does the basis of equality as a value lie in the fact that it promotes justice in society? If so, does that imply that justice is different from equality? Might it possibly be that justice is what really matters even more than equality as such? What of the thought that people are not, after all, equal in endowments, historical advantages and disadvantages, and the accidents of history?

The question just asked is important because contingent facts of history, geography and biology mean that individuals in different parts of the world and different tracts of time have very unequal starting points in the race for life's prizes. If absolute or unqualified equality is a practical impossibility, what can the ideal of equality apply to?

Obviously enough, despite this last point, there is a stubborn thought at the heart of thinking about equality. It is that racism, sexism, ageism and other forms of discrimination are flatly unacceptable. This in turn means that we need a workable concept of equality in properly qualified respects to achieve their eradication.

One way to begin is to see what is implied in requiring that two people be equal or equally treated in some respect. An old woman and a fit young sportsman are very unequal in their athletic ability and dietary needs, but they should be equal before the law, equal in receiving medical care when they need it, and equally entitled to vote in elections. So they have equality as citizens, though they are unequal in age, sex, athletic prowess, and dietary requirements. If we tried to make them equal in these latter respects – or even just in one: say in their food intake – we would do them as much harm and injustice as if we tried to make them unequal in the former respects.

For some, the difference between the two sorts of equality in play in these remarks shows that what actually matters in this debate is an underlying idea not of equality but of *equity* – that is, fairness.

'From each according to his ability, to each according to his needs' is a famous call for equity; it is not a call for equality. It implies that one should interpret equality in the political and legal senses as resting on principles of justice, just as one would appeal to justice to explain inequalities of treatment in respect of the diet needed by an old woman and a sportsman respectively.

Appeal to the concept of justice helps with the other problem mentioned – that individuals can be very unequal in matters of natural endowment, historical and geographical accident, and more, and yet should be treated equally in fundamental respects that are independent of these variations. This fact can be accepted and the overriding importance of justice asserted here too, this time in allowing a distinction between people having unequal needs but equal rights to their needs being addressed – which would result in differences of treatment justly motivated.

This captures the idea stemming from ancient philosophy that justice consists in 'giving each his due', but adds to it the idea that an individual's due is itself a matter of just apportionment. In ancient times, if you were a woman, a barbarian or a slave, your due was less than that of a male Greek adult. Having a lower status than an adult Greek man did not mean that you had no entitlement to just treatment, it just meant that your treatment would be just according to your station. What the Enlightenment added was the view that everyone merits the same dignity and respect as everyone else. This was the result of discussion about natural rights and the social contract, which started from the idea that in the 'state of nature' before social distinctions and political structures change things, everyone is equal in rights (though not in endowments: hence the need for the protection that society offers), and that when people come together in social groups they never completely forfeit their right to autonomy and liberty. For Rousseau social inequality is caused by the institution of property; property is unnecessary in the state of nature, and once it begins to exist it proves harmful, most especially when the ownership has become unequal as a result of property being institutionalized and inherited from generation to generation, some people gaining more than others.

Enlightenment conceptions of equality premise the idea of shared humanity: we each have equal rights because we are equally human – the French Revolution's *fraternité*. Some religious writers argue that this idea was not only present in Christianity, but responsible for these applications of it in Enlightenment thinking. This is a puzzling claim given that, at best, commitment to Christian beliefs carries promise of posthumous equality only, whereas Enlightenment thought saw it as applying to the here and now, and as the desideratum for political action; and moreover Christian doctrine separates the sheep from the goats depending upon the success of Christian obedience in the vale of tears, and indeed some versions of the doctrine (notably the Calvinist) say that the Elect are nominated from all time, and are few: which is a variation on a familiar aristocratic theme.

But the important point is that the political and legal equality of all individuals is a notion far different from one asserting differences between people on grounds of race, sex, 'nobility', and the like, putatively justifying discrimination between them as a result. Once it is accepted that each person counts as one, the rest follows.

If the ideas of equality and equity ultimately turn on that of justice –

as noted, a debated point – then evidently the idea of justice is one that requires closer analysis. It is addressed elsewhere in these pages.

See: ENLIGHTENMENT, FEMINISM, HUMAN RIGHTS, JUSTICE, LIBERTY, SLAVERY

ETHICS

The term 'ethics' has two main related meanings. In its ordinary general use it denotes the principles and attitudes which regulate the behaviour of individuals, groups or corporate bodies, the aim being to identify what they ought to do, in the sense of identifying what is the right or good thing for them to do. As a branch of philosophy, it is the study of concepts such as *good, right, evil, wrong, moral obligation, duty,* and of the kinds of reasoning (often called 'practical reasoning') used in working out what one should do in given circumstances, and more generally how one should live.

The key question in ethics concerns this last matter – how one should live, or what kind of life is best – but for a time in more recent academic philosophy (in particular in twentieth-century university philosophy in the English-speaking world, and still in many of its university courses of study) the analysis of ethical concepts and styles of reasoning came to occupy centre stage exclusively, with practitioners of that kind of philosophy disclaiming any special authority to prescribe the best kinds of life. In this respect they abdicated a responsibility not just that past philosophers felt themselves to be under, but that every one of us should feel himself or herself to be under; which doubly removes contemporary philosophical ethics from its parent trunk.

In still more recent years the study of ethics has been galvanized in some quarters by neuroscience and psychology, with contributions from anthropology, economics, sociobiology and primatology. Proponents of this approach to the study of ethical questions regard it as a new synthesis capable of revealing the biologically evolved culture-forming brain functions that underlie moral responses, decisions and sentiments. Real-time experimental work using functional MRI scans in which sub-jects are presented with scenarios, choices and dilemmas shows which structures in the brain are involved, and among other things conclusively establishes the relation of moral cognition to emotion, which – although it is scarcely news – places what had been based on insight and intuition on a firm empirical basis

It has to be said, though, that although a great deal of value can be expected from this empirical and interdisciplinary work, it prompts at least the following two considerations: first, such work is entirely descriptive, and the major aim of ethical reflection is not descriptive only but normative – that is, is aimed at helping us decide what to do. Secondly, the circumstances of ethical life are mainly social, that is, ethical decision and action lie in the interpersonal domain, in the formal and informal institutions of social living, in the complexities of relationships. Looking at what happens inside an individual skull can tell us much, but not everything.

Think for example of 'mirror neurons', neurons which activate in one monkey's brain when it watches another monkey perform a certain task. The neurons in the watching monkey's brain are the same as those actually being employed in the performing monkey's brain, so the watcher's brain is mirroring the performer's brain, suggesting that this is how we – as primates too – understand what others are doing, and by extension how we empathize with them – a crucial consideration for ethics. But if the watcher sees a performer do something wrong, no doubt the same neuronal mirroring is occurring; but the mere fact that it is, is not enough to explain the difference between empathizing, approving, being indifferent, being opposed or hostile, condemning, or feeling horror. Again, other parts of the brain will of course be involved in producing one or other of these complex states in the watcher – but why one state rather than another? We can imagine two watchers, their mirror neurons similarly activated, but one approving and one disapproving: why? Will brain function alone provide a full account of why moral codes are as they are?

Neuroethics, to coin the appropriate term, is clearly going to tell us much. It will undoubtedly help to tell us how things should or ought to be too: the question is, how much will it help in this applied and normative task? For it is equally clear that there is a large gap between descriptive facts about brain functioning and the principles on which I resolve an acute moral dilemma, a gap which the addition of whole tracts of historical, sociological and circumstantial considerations still does not quite fill, though they are essential too.

The distinction between ethics as doctrine which offers to guide life and to identify goods worth pursuing, and ethics as analytic reflection on concepts and methods of reasoning, is standardly marked by calling the former 'normative ethics' and the latter 'meta-ethics'. Much of the academic ethical debate mentioned above as focusing only on concepts is thus meta-ethical. It is of course impossible to formulate a normative ethics without meta-ethical reflection; the point is whether the latter is to absorb all the oxygen of thought about ethics in the arena where there is most competence for reflection, leaving society's conversation with itself about the good and the bad, the right and the wrong, to newspaper sound-bites, prejudice, and special-interest pleadings.

There is an interesting distinction to be noted between 'morals' and 'ethics'. The former word, derived from Latin, is related to 'mores' (customs) and has the sense of 'correct or proper behaviour'. The term 'ethics' derives from Greek and has the sense of 'way of life, character'. From these etymologies one can immediately derive the suggestion that ethics is a broader concept than morals. Ethics is about what sort of person one is, and therefore comprehends but is more inclusive than one's morals. An example shows how to understand this: what colour one paints the front door of one's house is an ethical matter, but (unless it is an especially offensive colour that badly upsets the neighbours) it is not a moral matter. Thus one's aesthetics, one's manner of living, one's choices about things that are not focally or even at all moral matters, are part of one's ethics (one's *ethos*, one's general way of being). Morality is more narrowly concerned with what is right or wrong in one's behaviour especially as it impinges on others.

One of the great questions in meta-ethics is whether ethical value is an objective matter, that is, whether good and bad, right and wrong, are properties of states of affairs, persons or actions, independently of human beings and the choices and preferences that their human nature and their experience lead them to, or whether ethical value is the product of human sentiment and emotion entirely. Another way of putting the latter point is to ask whether our moral values are subjective.

In this connection the labels 'objectivism', 'cognitivism', 'realism' and their opposites are frequently applied in meta-ethical debates. Objectivism can best be characterized as the view that ethical assertions are true or false independently of our interests, preferences or desires. When objectivism takes the form of ethical realism it consists in the claim that objective moral facts exist independently of us, and it is this fact that gives our assertions about them their truth-value. Objectivism sometimes takes a form called 'cognitivism' to imply not the existence of ethical facts and properties but the knowability of ethical truths.

The view directly opposed to objectivism is subjectivism, the view directly opposed to cognitivism is 'non-cognitivism', the view directly opposed to ethical realism is 'ethical anti-realism'. Reflection on these three pairs of labels reveals that there are significant differences between the ideas in play, as follows.

Ethical anti-realism is the view that there are no objectively existing moral properties or facts, and that therefore ethical assertions are not true or false, but have uses – to persuade or dissuade, to express attitudes or feelings (thus 'emotivism' is a form of ethical anti-realism), or to lay down norms, or to express acceptance of them or conformity to them.

But there can be widespread agreement about norms or moral sentiments in a community, so anti-realism is not necessarily subjectivism, the view that moral judgements are premised on personal attitudes, feelings or responses. On the subjectivist view, to judge that something is wrong is to say 'I think it is wrong' without anything following as to whether it would be judged wrong by others, or is in fact – independently of what anyone thinks – wrong. This latter view would be objectivism, and would take either a cognitivist or realist form.

Subjectivism is a form of relativism, but it is not the only form, because a relativist view could be one that says whole communities agree about moral values, but differ from other communities that internally agree on exactly the reverse values. This latter kind of relativism is not subjectivism, but subjectivism is relativistic, and if any two or more people happen to coincide in their judgements, it will be an accident that they do so.

It is an especially interesting question whether an objectivist view should take the form of realism about ethical facts and properties, or whether instead it should take the form of cognitivism, which is an effort to dodge the ontological question about the existence of ethical facts and properties, focusing instead on the truth and falsity of ethical judgements.

A principal objection to realism is that such putative ethical objects as 'the good' or properties such as 'being good' or 'being right' are what the philosopher John Mackie described as 'queer'. They are not like sticks and stones and other obviously existing things, yet there is nothing else for them to be like. G.E. Moore and other ethical realists thought that ethical objects and properties are simply *sui generis*, and cannot be defined other than by being displayed, as in the case of primary colours: one cannot define yellowness other than by displaying a sample of the colour yellow. A corollary of their view is that just as eyes and nerve-endings and ears are required for detecting the presence of physical objects in the world, a special faculty called 'ethical intuition' is required for detecting ethical facts and properties in the world. It is this that Mackie roundly rejected.

But even though one might agree that there are no ethical things or properties in the way that there are physical things and properties, there is – says the cognitivist – no need to take the next step that someone like Mackie is forced to take, given that our moral discourse mimics our factual discourse by making claims about things, by describing them, and generally by regarding them as if they were therefore capable of being judged true or false. 'That car is painted green' and 'that action is morally wrong' both look like factual claims; on a Mackie-type view the belief that the latter is a factual statement is an error. Indeed on a Mackie-type view the fact-stating appearance of moral discourse in general has to be accounted for by saying that we are systematically in error in interpreting it as fact-stating. But the cognitivist says that even without a realist commitment to ethical facts and properties, ethical statements can be true or false: the interest in this position lies in the question of what *makes* ethical propositions true when true and false when false, given that there are no putative moral states of affairs acting as truth-value makers, as there are in statements about the physical world. One suggestion is that moral discourse is like a game defined by its rules – chess, say – so that a moral statement can be true in a sense analogous to a chess move being correct within the rules, or even more pertinently: can be true in the way that it can be true that the king is checkmated (as defined by being threatened with capture and unable to move out of that threat). This suggestion does not satisfy all critics: for whereas a correct move in a game is contingent on the rules of the game, which one can accept or reject – one need not play the game – the cognitivist's ambition for ethical claims seems to be that they are categorically true and therefore binding. So the problem about what makes ethical claims true or false remains.

See: BIOETHICS; BUSINESS ETHICS; EPISTEMOLOGY; ETHICS, HISTORY OF; METAPHYSICS; PHILOSOPHY

ETHICS, HISTORY OF

Philosophical reflection on ethical matters is probably as old as human consciousness itself, but in the Western tradition its systematic inception is generally attributed to Socrates, who sought to encourage his contemporaries to pay attention to the question of how they should live. As a young man he had attended philosophical lectures and debates on the origin and nature of the universe, which in the nature of the then state of science were inconclusive and apt to go in circles, and it exercised him that people were devoting attention to such matters when they were seemingly indifferent to their own moral health. Plato has Socrates urge self-understanding and the achievement of harmony in the soul as the basis of the well-lived life, and his theory of knowledge and metaphysics both served the idea that an eternal Form of the Good, as the highest of all perfections, existed as that to which all sublunary good action and intention aspire.

Aristotle was of a more practical turn of mind, and indeed identified 'practical wisdom' as the means by which people could identify the middle path between extremes of vice as the proper route through life. Thus courage is the mean between cowardice and rashness, generosity is the mean between tight-fistedness and profligacy, and so forth. If an individual cannot work out the middle path for himself, he should imitate those who can; and by practice might eventually attain to practical wisdom himself, for Aristotle saw ethical living as something one could practise and make into a habit.

Aristotle's reason for identifying the exercise of practical wisdom as the path of virtue was that possession of reason is the highest distinguishing mark of humankind, and living according to it is what constitutes goodness.

Critics say that Aristotle's doctrine of the middle path is middle-aged, middle-class and middlebrow, and to some extent this is reinforced by Aristotle's own description of the successfully virtuous individual as a self-satisfied individual with a stately walk. He described this individual as *megalopsychos*, which means 'great-souled'. In Latin 'great soul' is *magna anima* from which we get our 'magnanimous', and as this suggests Aristotle's conception of the good man was in effect what came to be called in English a 'gentleman', not in the class sense but in the sense of one who is considerate of others, honest and decent, possessed of integrity and sound principle. Thus understood, the charge of 'middle-aged and middlebrow' can be seen as not very constructive.

The great work in which Aristotle set out his ethical views is the *Nicomachean Ethics*, so called because it was edited from his lecture notes by his son Nicomachus. It has a chapter in it on friendship, which is very striking; Aristotle thought friendship to be the highest and best of all human relationships, and he is eloquent in his discussion of it. A friend, he said, is another self, so that his interests will be as one's own interests, and his fortunes as one's own. Although there is beauty in this idea, it is not wholly persuasive: for surely a true friend recognizes his friend's difference from himself as well as their community of interest, and allows his friend the margin to be himself. For this the requirement is generosity, tolerance and understanding – which when exercised are marks of the surest kind of friendship.

After Aristotle the uncertain and often unsettled nature of life in the Hellenic period gave rise to ethical doctrines that stressed inner strength and security – *ataraxia* or peace of mind – as the desired goal of life. By far the chiefest of the ethical schools was Stoicism, which formed the outlook of educated people for more than half a millennium before Christianity officially became the outlook of the Roman world. Stoicism's main doctrine was that one should cultivate indifference (in the strict sense of this term) to what one cannot alter or influence in the vicissitudes of life, and self-command in respect of all those things over which one has control – such as one's fears and appetites, desires and hopes. By this means one will live courageously and serenely, exercising self-mastery and otherwise accepting the inevitable.

The two greatest exponents of the late ethical outlook of Stoicism were a slave, Epictetus, and an emperor, Marcus Aurelius, whose *Meditations* remain a classic. As a philosophical school Stoicism also embraced distinctive and subtle metaphysical and epistemological theories, from which its ethics derived. The Stoic outlook has remained influential in Western culture, both because it continued to be the basis of educated sentiment, and because its main tenets were adapted into Christianity once a richer ethics was required for this latter than the New Testament alone provided.

Another ancient school that taught the way to *ataraxia* was Epicureanism. Its founder Epicurus thought the hedonism of the Cyrenaic school too extreme, and although he preached what looked like the same doctrine – 'pursue pleasure and avoid pain' – he had a much more disciplined conception of what pleasure and pain are. He argued that the conventional pleasures of eating, drinking and sensuality carry within them the seeds of pain, and are accordingly to be avoided, and true pleasures – the intellectual pleasures of enquiry, gaining knowledge, discussing with friends in the shade of a tree, sipping water and eating bread when hungry – are to be preferred. This is an Epicureanism quite opposite to what the term has since come to mean.

The Epicureans, and to an even greater extent the Stoics, saw engagement and involvement in the world of affairs as desirable and even a duty for the citizen. One movement among their contemporaries wholly disagreed; these were the Cynics, followers of Diogenes, who was in effect a hippy who preached dropping out of society altogether, and living an individual self-contained life as close to nature as possible. Diogenes

accordingly went about naked, masturbated in public, and scorned everything conventional.

From the time that Christianity became the dominant outlook of
Europe until the seventeenth century, there was very little discussion of
either the foundations or the principles of ethics, because it was assumed
that answers about what to do, how to live and what is good were settled
by the Church, whose authority was complete and which could invoke
God's commands as the basis of value. In the eighteenth century, following the liberation of thought made possible by the Reformation and the
scientific revolutions of the previous two centuries, debate resumed on
foundational matters, not least because philosophers had again allowed
themselves to acknowledge that 'God is good' is not a tautology, and that
therefore the question of the nature and basis of goodness is a matter that
both can and must be discussed independently of theology.

In the eighteenth century such thinkers as David Hume, the Earl of
Shaftesbury, Francis Hutcheson, Bishop Butler, Bernard Mandeville and
Immanuel Kant between them shaped the outlines of the debate that has
since continued. The two major trends that emerged from it were consequentialism and deontology, the first in essence consisting in the claim
that the primary target of moral evaluation is the outcomes of actions,
the second consisting in the claim that the target of moral evaluation is
the intrinsic moral character of acts, actors and situations, independently
of consequences. In the nineteenth century the consequentialist theory
known as 'utilitarianism' became dominant in Anglophone ethical discussion, taking a variety of forms as it was more and more intensively
debated, and as the debate continued into the twentieth century. At
the outset utilitarianism recommended itself as a practical theory that
could be applied by rule of thumb, for its motivating idea was that an
act is good if it promotes a balance of good (or happiness, or 'utility')
over bad (or unhappiness or 'disutility'). Young men sent out to govern
jungle districts in the British Empire were equipped by it to conduct
their administrative affairs, no doubt much helped by having a relatively
straightforward, practical notion of right and wrong to apply.

With the professionalization of philosophy in the academy in more
recent times, the meta-ethical debate has focused on theories, concepts
and methods of 'practical reasoning'. Driven by needs outside the academy
there has risen a swathe of new areas of discussion under the label 'applied
ethics', such as medical ethics, business ethics and environmental ethics,
together with such offshoots as 'just-war theory'. The irony is that ethics
always used to be applied, and the drift of academic philosophy into

purely abstract domains has meant that in order to recover the function of trying actually to determine what should be done in difficult cases, a new pursuit with a new name has had to (seem to) come into existence. Ever in search of justification for their existence, academics then poach the new debates and drag them into the desiccating atmosphere of their studies, there to render them impotent and irrelevant again by means of polysyllabic refinements, distinctions, trifling objections, counter-theories, improbable counter-examples, pedantic minutiae and a drowning flood of neologisms. In the midst of this, of course, there is a nugget or two of genuinely useful insight; most of the rest is spoil, in the circumstances a multiply useful term.

One of the more valuable contributions of recent ethical debate is Bernard Williams's observation that ethics is not a subject that can be left to the ministrations of philosophers alone. It also needs historians, psychologists, anthropologists and novelists, dramatists and artists of all kinds. Since the true subject matter of ethics is debate about the best kind of human life, we need all the resources we can get to enrich and inform it. And as this implies – so reflection will show – one of the goods of the ethical life is the quest for it itself.

See: EDUCATION, ETHICS, PHILOSOPHY, VIRTUE ETHICS

ETHNOCENTRISM

Ethnocentrism consists in judging other cultures according to the norms and standards of one's own culture. Because that invariably means treating the standards of one's own culture as right or best, ethnocentrism tends further to consist in feelings of superiority, and can lead too naturally to racism (discriminatory attitudes against other races on the supposed grounds of their inferiority) and xenophobia (dislike and lack of acceptance of foreigners).

The term was coined by the American anthropologist W.G. Sumner in *Folkways* (1907), but almost all nineteenth-century social science, most notably ethnography, anthropology, and history, was strongly ethnocentric in its assumptions, and markedly so in respect of colonized peoples. Many of the latter were regarded as 'primitive' by measures relating to the degree of complexity of their institutions, their literacy (or lack of it), their scientific and technological knowledge, and what Europeans and North Americans regarded as their moral development (or, usually, lack of it – as supposedly displayed by lack of decency in dress. In Central Africa, diseases introduced by white missionaries were aided in their potency by the clothing that the latter obliged native people to wear – and which they did, whether wet or not, day and night, thus decimating local populations.)

The remedy for ethnocentrism is to attempt to understand the beliefs, value systems, institutions and practices of cultures not one's own in the light of their own context. A step beyond this is to say that these beliefs, values and the rest have equal validity with those in any other culture; this, which is one main form of political reaction to ethnocentrism, constitutes cultural relativism, and it is controversial because whereas one could understand the place of (say) female circumcision in certain cultures, one might otherwise and emphatically regard it as unacceptable.

In a book called *The Authoritarian Personality*, written in reaction to the Nazi atrocities of the 1930s and 1940s and subtitled 'Studies in Prejudice', Theodor Adorno, Else Frenkel-Brunswik and Daniel Levinson argued that ethnocentrism fundamentally consists in hostility to 'out-groups' and is a common trait of psychological types also attracted to reactionary authoritarian ideologies. Their diagnosis of ethnocentrism's attractions for such is that they help 'ingroup' bonding. This phenomenon is naturally enough also exploited in the allied ideology of nationalism.

See: ACCOMMODATION THEORY, MULTICULTURALISM, NATIONALISM, RACISM

EUTHANASIA

Literally understood, 'euthanasia' means 'a good death'. That is what everyone hopes for in the end, usually in the form of a naturally occur-ring, easy, pain-free death in sleep at an otherwise healthy old age. Death by illness, accident, murder, war injuries, a badly carried out suicide, and any other death-inducing process that involves physical or psychological suffering, or both, do not count as euthanasia in this literal sense.

Euthanasia has come mainly to mean the deliberate ending of life by acts or omissions – acts such as turning off a life-support system, omissions such as withholding treatment from an elderly patient with pneumonia. Euthanasia of these kinds is called 'passive euthanasia' and is regarded as both lawful and morally acceptable.

Active euthanasia takes place when someone is given death-inducing treatment of some kind: an injection of potassium chloride, suffocation, an overdose of barbiturates with alcohol.

Despite appearances, there is no moral difference between these sup-posedly different kinds of euthanasia. Deliberately not doing something is an act just as much as doing something is an act. The concept of sin in theological ethics recognizes that it can take the form both of commis-sion and omission; sins of omission do not carry less responsibility than sins of commission. Choosing not to do something, withholding a good on purpose to bring about a foreseen end, is as culpable (sometimes as praiseworthy) as acting to bring about a foreseen end. The law makes it a crime not to stop at an accident to offer help; that too counts omission as commission. It follows that passive and active euthanasia are the same thing in being deliberate choices whose outcome is the same.

It is a only a matter of sentiment that passive euthanasia appears more acceptable than active euthanasia. What drives this point home is the realization that, because of compassion and sympathy, active euthanasia is performed far more often than most people realize or would even like to consider. Not trying to address the agonies, whether physical or mental, of someone in the terminal phases of an illness is so cruel that not many medical practitioners can allow themselves to take steps that actively prolong those agonies. And this often means taking steps not just to palliate but to abbreviate them. Not to do this would be to treat people with less kindness than most pet owners accord to their animals, for it is considered merciful to animals to end their lives swiftly and easily when they suffer without hope of recovery. Happily for humans suffering in the same way, in hospitals, nursing homes, hospices and sickrooms everywhere, doses of analgesics are, when need arises, raised to levels that effect euthanasia, and the legitimacy of the proceeding is protected by the 'doctrine of double effect', which states that because the practitioner's primary aim was to alleviate suffering, the anticipated but unintended life-shortening side effect is inescapable and therefore justified.

But here too, just as with the alleged distinction between passive and active euthanasia, appeal to the doctrine of double effect is merely a conceptual convenience. Given the empirical certainty that death will result from increasing doses of morphine, claiming that one's intention was only to relieve pain and not to expedite death is a conceptual sleight of hand. In any case, expediting death is the ultimate palliation, the last available form of pain relief, a fact that is as well understood as acted upon in efforts to relieve suffering.

When the idea of physician-assisted death is discussed, whether refer-ence is to its direct enactment in passive and active euthanasia, or under the cloak of 'double effect', the point is standardly made that it is flatly wrong, because practitioners are bound by their medical code of ethics to save, protect, and enhance life, or at least to minimize the suffering caused by injury or disease. In the United States, the Hippocratic oath clause that says 'To please no one will I prescribe a deadly drug, or give advice which may cause my patient's death' is still often cited. The main meaning of this clause, of course, is that a doctor will not give in to pressures from family or the CIA or anyone else to end the life of a person who does not wish to die. But often a stronger interpretation is given, to make the clause entail that a practitioner must also not accede to a request from a patient for help to die. This is the interpretation given by opponents of medically assisted suicide. Yet it would seem obvious that a practitioner who refuses to help a badly suffering, terminally ill patient to die is in fact failing in his Hippocratic duty to care for the patient appropriately; which suggests that the stronger reading of that clause is not the correct one.

This said, the question of active involvement in helping a patient to die remains a real and justifiable concern for medical practitioners, for after all their primary responsibility is wherever possible to save life, repair injuries, cure disease, or at least palliate suffering. Accordingly the following practical suggestion might be made: that a medical speciality of thanatology (a term from Greek *thanatos*, death) be introduced, most appropriately as a sub-speciality of anaesthetics. Thanatologists should practise within a framework of law, supervised by a hospital ethics committee, so that all thanatological treatment is properly approved, monitored, and recorded. Because only thanatologists will be engaged in helping those to die who have chosen death and demonstrated that their choice is a stable and intelligent one, everyone else working in medicine will continue to operate under the assumption that their concerns are solely to save life, cure disease, and ease suffering. This would have the added benefit of clarifying the murkily grey area in which many medical practitioners at present work, given the fact alluded to above that deliberate life-shortening treatment, for compassionate reasons, is a commonplace on the wards and in the sickrooms of every land.

The complaint will assuredly be made that if life-ending treatment becomes available in this organized way, it will be abused by someone somewhere. This is probably true, though it is within the competence of mankind to administer itself in ways that reduce the potential for abuse, and in any case it is not acceptable to allow great suffering to continue for fear that here and there someone might commit a wrong. In the

Netherlands, Switzerland and the state of Oregon in the United States, euthanasia under specified conditions is permitted, and the experience of those jurisdictions does nothing to give comfort to people who think that once the door is opened to such treatment, hospitals will hasten patients' deaths to free up beds, greedy relatives will persuade their elders to die once the will has been signed in their favour, and so on. These canards are produced mainly by religious lobbies whose members think prolonged suffering in illness and age is acceptable because a supposedly merciful deity is in charge and has the sole prerogative over suffering and death – as if the 'sanctity of life' embraced the sanctity of pain, suffocation, the indignities of soiling oneself incontinently, and a lingering drug-hazed incompetence at the last. What would count as relief and release for such people is described as murder by the anti-euthanasia lobby, consisting of healthy people whose certainty that their theological and moral beliefs are true is unshakeable.

One of the central arguments in favour of euthanasia is that individuals should have the right to decide when and how they die, and should not be left to bear the sufferings and indignities of terminal illness or extreme old age if they do not wish it. Individual autonomy and freedom of choice are at stake here, and it has to be remembered that all of a person's rights are fully engaged even as he lies ill or dying, for dying is an act of living, and does not reduce a person's entitlement to assert his rights if he remains competent to do so.

See: BIOETHICS

EVOLUTION

Biological evolution is the process by which living things descend with modification, both in the sense of changes in gene frequency in a given population as one generation succeeds another, and in species as they diverge from a common ancestor. All life has a common ancestor; through descent with modification the amazing diversity of species arises over time, small changes in inherited traits being passed on if they confer reproductive advantage, thus reflecting the adaptedness of a species to its habitat.

Evolutionary changes are driven by one or both of two main mechanisms. One is natural selection; the other is 'genetic drift'. In the first, heritable traits that prove helpful in adapting a reproducing population to a given environment are 'selected for' accordingly, and therefore become more frequent in the population, whereas traits which prove disadvantageous in the relevant respects die out. Different (and somewhat more controversial) is the idea of 'genetic drift', hypothesized as a process in which random changes occur in the frequency with which traits appear in a population, influencing the reproductive chances of the affected individuals. In the theory of natural selection, changes that are advantageous to reproductive success tend to be passed on, and by small incremental steps contribute to the modification of the species itself. In the case of genetic drift change happens regardless of whether it is advantageous to reproductive success.

Any group of organisms whose members can successfully breed with one another to produce fertile offspring constitutes a species. It frequently happens that subgroups of a species become geographically separated, and over time genetic changes accumulate within each that make them no longer able to interbreed. When this happens 'speciation' has occurred; in effect two or more new species have separated out from one. It is the origin and change over time of species which is the principal focus of evolutionary theory, but the powerful insights thus afforded provide a basis for theorizing in biology and other disciplines that has proved immensely fruitful.

By the mid-nineteenth century comparative anatomy and the fossil record had together taught biologists that species evolve, but there was as yet no understanding of the means by which this happened. The answer – natural selection – was discovered by Charles Darwin. The 'modern synthesis' (an expression coined by Julian Huxley in the title of a book setting out these new ideas: his book was called *Evolution: the Modern Synthesis*) was effected when Darwin's discovery was combined with the genetic discoveries of the Slovenian monk Gregor Mendel. Darwin had identified the mechanism, Mendel (although he did not realize it at the time) the units, of evolution; the resulting theory is extremely powerful and overwhelmingly attested by experiment and observation.

The 'modern synthesis' was required because although Darwin had correctly identified the mechanism of natural selection, there was no consensus about how it worked in detail. Darwin himself came to favour a form of Lamarckism (the thesis that acquired characteristics are heritable), and when experiment in the 1880s undermined this view (lots of mice had their tails cut off, but their offspring were still born with long tails) other theories were advanced. Then the full possibilities of Mendel's work with pea plants became important; his ideas were rediscovered in 1901 but not fully appreciated until the end of the First World War in the work of Sir Ronald Fisher, who was both a statistician and a biologist. Fisher showed how Darwinian natural selection and Mendelian genetics were consistent, and from that starting point the modern synthesis of evolutionary biology was worked out in increasing detail.

A key moment for evolutionary biology was the 1953 discovery by Crick and Watson of the double-helical structure of deoxyribonucleic acid (DNA). DNA can 'unzip' to replicate itself, thus constituting the mechanism by which heritable material can be transmitted from one generation to another. Biologists knew that the unit of heritability was the gene; they now knew the molecular structure of that unit and therefore how it works.

One result of Darwin's own reservations about whether natural selection could be the sole mechanism of evolution was his development of the idea of sexual selection, in which the heritability of some traits is explained in terms of reproductive competition between members of a species – mainly between males competing for breeding partners. For Darwin the peacock's tail could not be explained otherwise, given that it does not appear to have anything other than disadvantages for peacocks in the battle for survival. Darwin's great contemporary Alfred Russel Wallace did not agree with him about sexual selection, on the grounds that it imputed to peahens and other non-human females too great a capacity for aesthetic judgement. This question continues to be debated; one theory denies that we have to impute aesthetic sensibility to females (and sometimes males) of avian and other non-human species – nor even to humanity itself – but instead merely an evolved capacity to respond to cues of health and reproductive fitness. Another reputable theory suggests that something a lot more like aesthetic sensibility is indeed at work in sexual selection; Fisher proposed that if the nervous system of the female of a given avian species was such as to make it prefer, say, blue plumage on males, the result would be that blue plumage would increase in the population, the preference and the incidence of blue plumage mutually reinforcing each other.

In 1972 Stephen Jay Gould and Niles Eldredge proposed the idea of 'punctuated equilibrium' as a modification of evolutionary theory. Their idea is that species are generally stable, and do not change for long periods, but then change and diversification occur in sudden rapid bursts, usually at the margins of a species where groups might have become isolated, or moved into an especially propitious environment away from the rest of the species, there to reproduce successfully. The relatively small gene pools ensure that the descendants of the original group cease to be able to interbreed with descendants of the original species or members of the other new descendent species – thus in a relatively short time bringing a new species into being, which would itself in turn enjoy relatively long periods of stability.

Rapid speciation events are known as 'cladogenesis'. This term is not tied to punctuated equilibrium; it is a general term for branching evolution, whether punctuated or not, as opposed to 'anagenesis' which means evolution without branching. 'Anagenesis' and 'cladogenesis' are terms coined by the palaeontologist George Gaylord Simpson, one of the contributors to the formation of the Modern Synthesis; they refer to different parts of the evolutionary process, one denoting the branching part and the other the 'change within a non-branching lineage' part.

One advantage of the Gould–Eldredge idea is that it predicts what is in fact observed, namely, that evidence of speciation is not typically found at fossil sites, for the good reason that the evolutionary process is occurring somewhere other than where a given species' remains are located. That is, the expectation that intermediate steps between an ancestral and an evolutionarily descendent population will occur at the same site is always likely to be disappointed precisely because evolutionary change requires that the intermediate stages should occur somewhere other than in the parent population's habitat.

Some further empirical evidence for the view is provided by the coral-like bryozoans, which display very long periods of stability interrupted by short periods of rapid diversification. But actually the Gould–Eldredge proposal does not diverge very much from Darwin's own view, as Richard Dawkins showed in his book *The Blind Watchmaker*. Darwin did not assume that the rate of evolutionary change was uniform or constant, for although he thought that evolutionary processes are slow and gradual, 'gradual' does not have to mean 'smooth'. But there is a difference between Darwin's ideas and the Gould–Eldredge version, which Dawkins characterized in terms of 'speedism', describing the latters' view as 'discrete variable speedism' and Darwin's view as 'continuously variable speedism'. (Other differences between Gould's and Dawkins's views are explored fully in Chapter 9 of Dawkins's *The Blind Watchmaker*.)

A related concept is 'adaptive radiation', understood as the process in which species evolve rapidly to occupy an empty niche in an environment. For example, on the Galapagos Islands where Darwin collected the data that gave him the basis for his theory, there are more than a dozen species of finches, all descended from a single species, which have evolved differently from one another in order to exploit different parts of the islands' food supplies. Thus some have powerful husk-cracking beaks, others fine beaks for probing into small spaces. Some have adapted to feed on leaves, some on insects, others on seeds, some even on the blood of sea-birds; some have adapted to live on the ground, others in trees. The ancestral species was a ground-dwelling seed-eating finch; its descendants are mainly differentiated by the shape and size of their beaks. Between them they beautifully illustrate the operation of natural selection.

One merit of mentioning debates and differences of view within evolutionary theory is that its critics and opponents, among them so-called 'intelligent design' advocates, take the appearance of disagreement among evolutionary biologists as evidence of weakness in the case for evolution. Nothing could be further from the truth: it indicates the vigorous nature of research and debate in the field, and the controlling place of observation, experiment, evidence and reason within it. For example, creationists sought to exploit Gould's remarks about the fossil record and its relation to gradualistic theories of evolution; Gould responded by denouncing the misuse of his views by 'the scourge of creationism', as he put it.

Evolutionary theory is powerfully combined with palaeontology to explore the history of life on Earth, and not least the story of human origins. Detailed research continues into many aspects of evolution and its mechanisms, but as the organizing theory of modern biology it is overwhelmingly well established and attested, and stands as one of the great achievements of science.

See: BIOLOGY, BIODIVERSITY, CREATIONISM

EXISTENTIALISM

Existentialism was a much discussed philosophical view in the decades following the Second World War, the horrors and destruction of which were, for existentialism's major contributors and those interested in their work, a prime motive for it. Commentators on existentialism find its roots in the writings of Kierkegaard, Nietzsche and Edmund Husserl, and they nominate its principal exponents as Jean-Paul Sartre, Albert Camus, Karl Jaspers, Gabriel Marcel and Martin Heidegger. Among these thinkers it is the first two who were most influential in the 1950s and 1960s, not least because they expressed their respective versions of an existentialist outlook in literary forms as novels, plays and essays.

Existentialism would be interesting only as an historical phenomenon, symptomatic of a difficult period in Western history and not a substantive contribution to the age-old ethical debate, if there were not enough intrinsic interest in its ideas to invite further attention. But indeed there is.

It is a concomitant of an atheist view that whatever meaning attaches to human existence is found in it or imposed on it by human beings themselves, for one premise of atheism is that no purpose is established for mankind from 'outside'. In their respective ways Sartre and Camus made the gratuitous character of human existence central, emphasizing the fact that individuals simply find themselves 'thrown' into the world without external purpose or guide, as a blind outcome of natural events. They gave the name 'absurdity' to this accidental and purposeless brute fact of existence. Camus dramatized the philosophical conundrum which absurdity represents by saying, at the outset of his essay 'The Myth of Sisyphus' (1942), that the great philosophical question is: Shall I commit suicide? For if one answers in the negative, it is because one has a reason to live; there are things one regards as valuable to have, to do or to be. But since these things are not given from without, they have been chosen by the individual himself, and in choosing them he confers meaning on his existence.

This puts matters schematically. Even more schematically one might describe the net result of the views put forward by Camus and Sartre in terms of their nomination of four values which individuals, in 'creating themselves' in the face of absurdity, can impose on the antecedent meaninglessness of existence to give it value: namely love, freedom, human dignity, and creativity. Freedom is not only a value but a condition of being able to choose these values; Sartre describes the possession of a free will as an 'agony' because it forces us to make choices in the face of existence's emptiness. Indeed Sartre thought that choosing and deciding are stressful enterprises, and ultimately solitary ones, and further that the business of living one's choices is an effort, a painful endeavour; so his is not an especially reassuring view. But he saw the endeavour as inescapable if life is to have a meaning, for without it one would have no choice even of approximating its goal, namely 'authenticity' – which means living according to one's beliefs, taking responsibility for the consequence of one's actions, and accepting the agonies of one's freedom.

It is right that critical reaction has demanded that the central values of this version of existentialism – love, dignity, freedom, creativity – should be further explained, for as they stand they are near-vacuous concepts to many, and with many contested possible interpretations. But this in turn merely says that the sketch given just indicates the starting point for a conversation; the premise – that it is the business of individuals to inject value into their lives by choices that they are vertiginously free to make – is a potent one, and marks out a fruitful place for a debate about those concepts to begin.

'Absurdity' is the key notion applied by existentialists to the human condition, meaning by it that there is no extrinsic meaning, purpose or value to human existence: it is 'absurd' in being wholly accidental and in itself pointless. As Camus put it in that influential essay 'The Myth of Sisyphus', 'Man stands face to face with the irrational. He feels within him his longing for happiness and for reason. The absurd is born of this confrontation between the human need and unreasonable silence of the world.'

But this characterization is not intended to be, as it at first appears when so baldly stated, pessimistic or nihilistic. Rather, it is the starting point for the claim that individuals must, in response, create meaning in their lives by asserting the value of freedom, creativity, and love, and attributing dignity to human beings thus condemned to be self-creating and self-valorizing. This is the basis of existentialism.

A certain form of fideism in Christianity states that it is a proof of the truth of Christian doctrine that it is so absurd. 'Credo quia absurdum est' wrote Tertullian: 'I believe because it is so ridiculous' (that is, to claim that the deity was born as mortal man, etc.). The trouble with this invocation of absurdity is that the response to it is arbitrary; one could believe anything whatever if the fact of absurdity licensed grabbing at any old idea. For the existentialists, by contrast, the claim is that the values chosen justify themselves when life is lived according to them, without any additional apparatus (a story, a myth, a scaffolding of beliefs) being required to bolster and interpret them.

'The theatre of the absurd' has its roots in the climate of thought of which Camus's doctrine of the absurd is a characteristic feature. The idea that humankind stands at odds with a universe not properly adapted to it is a theme in the background of much of the work of Samuel Beckett, Eugene Ionesco, Jean Genet and Harold Pinter (among others). The characters in these works are troubled and displaced, unable to attach sense to the world they find themselves lost in, and which seems obscurely to menace them.

The bitter experience of the Second World War, the collapse of religious certainties, and the fragmentation and vertiginous experimentation of much of the earlier twentieth century's avant-garde, conspired to produce the bewilderment, arbitrariness and insecurity explored in these plays. To grapple with these themes, innovative dramatic styles and uses of language and silence became a distinctive feature of the genre.

In the existentialist philosophy of Jean-Paul Sartre (1905–80) the concept of bad faith (*mauvaise foi*) plays a crucial role. Sartre employs the term to denote the state into which individuals get themselves if they refuse to accept that they are 'condemned to freedom' in their lives, where their fundamental existential task is to create an essence or meaning for themselves, since they have neither when they enter the world. People display bad faith, or indeed live in bad faith, when they deny their freedom – which they do because of the anguish it threatens to cause them – by avoiding their duty to take responsibility for themselves, thereby allowing themselves to be treated as objects. Yet freedom, for all that it causes anguish, is what is distinctively human, and its exercise is what creates value in an otherwise absurd and abandoned existence.

The theme of bad faith is a constant in Sartre's novels as well as his main philosophical work *Being and Nothingness*.

See: ATHEISM, ETHICS, METAPHYSICS, PHILOSOPHY

EXPERIMENTAL PHILOSOPHY

Since classical antiquity the dominant conception of philosophy has been that it is an a priori activity of thought, aimed at understanding the world and mankind, by analysing concepts and constructing explanatory overviews of the nature of reality and the good. In more recent philosophy, mainly in the English-speaking world since the beginning of the twentieth century, the constructive or synthetic ambition has been abandoned or much downplayed, and philosophy has been mostly devoted to the analysis of concepts.

To say that both synthetic and analytic philosophy are a priori is to say that they proceed by armchair speculation, that is, their method is enquiry into our ideas by means of thinking about them carefully and rigorously rather than conducting empirical investigations such as occur, for example, in psychology and sociology in the form of surveys of attitudes, opinions, beliefs and traits.

Some philosophers have become dissatisfied with the a priori nature of their pursuit, not least because it relies on a procedure they call into question, namely, consulting 'intuitions' about moral questions, knowledge, rationality, and other central topics of philosophical enquiry. These philosophers accordingly seek to introduce an experimental element into their theorizing, typically by conducting surveys or polls to ascertain the attitudes, beliefs or intuitions of samples of people, thus avoiding reliance on an armchair-only view of what is 'intuitively' the case with respect to some concept.

The 'experimental philosophy' movement which has thus arisen, calling itself 'X-Phi' and using a burning armchair as its symbol, has invited immediate criticism on the grounds that it seeks to do what the empirical social sciences do, only less well – bearing the same relation to empirical psychology that 'performance art' does to professional acting and theatre: a clumsy and etiolated mimicry of the real thing. At times this criticism seems all too well justified. Some of the work done by experimental philosophers consists in surveys of the students in their classes – scarcely a representative sample and usually a very small one, and usually also based on a questionnaire amateurishly devised by the philosophy professor himself or herself. For example: one such was a survey of sixteen philosophy students, seven men and nine women, who were asked whether they believed their male or female sex to be an essential fact about them, rather than an accidental one. Five men said No and two Yes, while seven women said Yes and two No. This result certainly looks interesting, and a large-scale survey of attitudes might well confirm the difference, and lead the way to further insights into male and female self-perceptions based on sex, gender, social and working-life differences, and more. But as it stands it is at best informal and potentially very misleading, and illustrates the risk of experimental philosophy being a poor cousin of empirical social science, or if not, of ceasing to be philosophy.

This latter eventuality, however, might be no bad thing – certainly the experimental philosophers themselves must have an inclination to think so. For if they did they would be doing no more than acknowledging an important fact about the history of philosophy, which is that it is always in the business of trying to bring itself to an end by finding better and more accurate ways of answering the questions it asks. This is what happened with the rise of the natural sciences in the sixteenth and seventeenth centuries: philosophers found ways of investigating the natural world that at last began to yield substantive answers, in contrast to the armchair speculations and brain-spun theories of the preceding, mainly Aristotelian, tradition. The experimental philosophy movement might be doing nothing less than recapitulating that happy turn of events in those seminal centuries.

As it happens, though, it would be wrong to think that experimental philosophy would, if well done, simply turn into empirical social science. This can be seen by noting that empirical work can only be, and in any case only aims at being, descriptive. Once a survey has found a trend, the task of analysing and understanding the trend remains; and there might be policy decisions or recommendations to be made on the basis of that understanding – which is to say, there is often a significant prescriptive element at stake too. In experimental philosophy the targets of enquiry include moral beliefs and the nature of knowledge. It could never be enough merely to poll opinions as to what counted as right and wrong or as instances of knowledge as opposed to mere belief; quite likely the polling results would invite analytic investigation rather than settle the questions that prompted the surveys in the first place.

A pivotal point in the debate over experimental philosophy concerns, as noted, its practitioners' objections to the appeal to 'intuitions' in conceptual analysis. Philosophers construct 'thought experiments', hypothetical situations in which the application of concepts can be tested to see where they apply and where their application begins to seem suspect or strained, thus showing what they can properly be taken to mean. Thought experiments involve investigating what is possible, what could or could not be the case, given certain counterfactual situations ('counterfactual' – as the name implies – means 'contrary to how things in fact or actually are'). Imagining scenarios and thinking what it would be plausible to say or think about them using the concepts under examination is an illuminating exercise – so philosophers have always standardly thought – because it turns on what is involved in competent use of concepts and the language in which they are expressed. Obviously, if someone pointed at a table and said 'that's a blackbird', and meant it seriously, we would surmise that his concepts of tables and blackbirds were non-standard at least, for we can specify the conditions that have to be satisfied for the concepts of tables and blackbirds to be applied in standardly correct ways. This is a very simple example of a scenario used to illustrate a point about concept possession and application, and about language use; it would be unnecessary to conduct a survey of one's students (by presenting them with a table and a questionnaire asking 'is this a table or a blackbird?') to make the same point.

On the other hand, experimental philosophers are surely right to point out that saying 'it seems reasonable or natural to say ...' as the sole test of a concept's application – this being a typical way in which intuitions are invoked – is not sensitive to the fact that how an American and a native of Papua New Guinea might respectively conceptualize something is likely to be very different, so that what seems natural to think for one would be very unnatural for the other. Such facts have to be taken into account, and cannot be identified in the first place by means of conceptual analysis itself. Thus, large differences in moral outlook and practice, or attitudes to what counts as knowledge and the means of acquiring it, or how the world itself is carved up into objects, events and their attributes, call into question the security of relying on intuitions about what it is right to think or say (in one's own culture? in one's own language?) on any of these matters.

And it is not just the spectre of relativism which raises questions about the a priori reliance on intuitions in conceptual analysis. If you ask the same question of two groups of people, one in delightful and relaxing surroundings and the other in a dirty, smelly, cramped room, you tend to get significantly different answers conditioned by those circumstances. Thus, experimental surveys of people's attitudes to crime and punishment have been found to be markedly influenced by the environment in which they are questioned: the less pleasing the environment, the harsher the attitudes reported.

No doubt controversy about experimental philosophy will continue, at least for a time; but it is now firmly on the scene, as shown by the publication in 2008 of a volume entitled *Experimental Philosophy* by Oxford University Press, by the increasing number of conferences on the subject, and by the fact that some leading university philosophy departments have begun to advertise for tenure track positions in experimental philosophy.

See: PHILOSOPHY

FALSIFIABILITY

Falsifiability is a key notion in the philosophy of science of the Austrian-British thinker Karl Popper (1902–94), serving as the criterion of demarcation between science and non-science.

Almost anything can be counted as evidence in favour of a theory, Popper said, so unless what so counts is the outcome of an especially crucial or 'risky' prediction, citing corroborating evidence is nigh worthless. (The paradigm of a risky prediction was the one stating that light would be seen to bend round the sun under the influence of gravity in the 1919 solar eclipse. It did bend; and this was a crucial test of Einstein's theory of relativity.) Instead, a genuine scientific hypothesis is one which itself specifies the conditions under which it is false.

Popper argued that science proceeds by 'conjecture and refutation'. Ideas, however generated, are submitted to rigorous testing in the form of efforts to prove them false. If they survive, they are not thereby guaranteed to be true, but they can be employed so long as they remain unrefuted. If they are falsified by the test then they must be set aside, and a better hypothesis devised.

A major criticism of Popper's falsificationist theory is embodied in the Quine–Duhem thesis (owed to W.V.O. Quine and Pierre Duhem), which states that hypotheses cannot be refuted on a one-by-one basis, because they come in a package with an entire setting of other hypotheses and theories that give them their meaning. Popper replied that this criticism applies only to a crude view of falsificationism, which in fact admits that a form of natural selection applies, eliminating those hypotheses that do less well in explaining phenomena and fitting with other hypotheses and promoting those that do the opposite.

Another criticism is that complete falsification of an hypothesis is as difficult to achieve as complete confirmation. What if what appeared to be a falsifying counter-instance to an hypothesis were an experimental error, or an instrumental aberration, or a freak result? Granting that it is exceedingly difficult to see how any hypothesis could be conclusively verified by what, in the nature of the case, must be a finite range of experimental results, is it not the case that falsifying an hypothesis is tantamount to verifying the negation of the hypothesis?

Although there are problems with Popper's 'falsificationist' model, its ideal of rigorous empirical challenge is a healthy one, for it characterizes science as a rational and critical enquiry capable of progress. So too is Popper's belief that non-scientists can legitimately criticize science for failing to abide by its own avowed standards.

See: SCIENCE

FASCISM

There is a technical definition of Fascism as a political philosophy, and an extended characterization of political systems that are widely described as Fascist because they share a number of the disagreeable features of a more strictly Fascist system, and both merit mention – not least because too many of the world's regimes are, or have uncomfortably reminiscent features of, Fascist systems in the extended sense.

The classic statement of Fascist philosophy has to be the entry written by Benito Mussolini, with the help of Giovanni Gentile, in the *Italian Encyclopaedia* (*Enciclopedia Italiana*) published in 1932. By then he had been in power for ten years, and therefore as the coiner of the term *fascismo* and the leader of a Fascist state, he had an excellent grasp of the concept from both the theoretical and practical points of view. It proceeds as follows – and though I paraphrase, these are nevertheless the unvarnished sentiments of Mussolini himself.

Fascists, wrote Mussolini, do not believe that perpetual peace is either possible or useful. On the contrary, they renounce pacifism and the cowardly renunciation of struggle, and accept that only war brings out the most noble qualities of human beings. Fascists love life and despise suicide, but nevertheless see life as a duty to engage in noble struggle and conquest, above all for the sake of others now and in the future.

Fascism, wrote Mussolini, is the opposite of Marxian Socialism, which explains history simply as the conflict of interests between social groups. The Fascist denies the economic conception of history and the idea of the class war. Instead, he believes in holiness and heroism, which is to say, in actions wholly uninfluenced by economic motives.

Fascism, wrote Mussolini, also repudiates and combats the whole ideology of democratic politics. It denies that the majority, merely because it is the majority, can direct human society. It affirms the immutable, beneficial and fruitful inequality of mankind, and denies the myths of happiness and progress.

The twentieth century, wrote Mussolini, will be a century of authority, of Fascism, the century of the state; the nineteenth century attempted to be the century of the individual, but the twentieth century will be the century of the collective.

The Fascist state organizes the nation, wrote Mussolini, but leaves a sufficient margin of liberty to the individual, except for the useless and possibly harmful freedoms which are not essential. On the question of which freedoms these are, the state alone decides.

For Fascism, wrote Mussolini, the growth of empire, by which is meant the expansion of the nation, is an essential manifestation of vitality. Empire demands discipline, duty and sacrifice, which explains many features of the Fascist regime, including its severe measures against those who would oppose it with outworn doctrines of the nineteenth century.

'If every age has its own characteristic doctrine,' wrote Mussolini, and here I am no longer paraphrasing, 'there are a thousand signs which point to Fascism as the characteristic doctrine of our time. For if a doctrine must be a living thing, this is proved by the fact that Fascism has created a living faith; and that this faith is very powerful in the minds of men is demonstrated by those who have suffered and died for it.'

The foregoing might be regarded as more braggadocio than statement of political creed, given the marked failure of Mussolini's Italy to follow him into the glories thus envisaged, and the undignified end of the dictator himself – all the more undignified for the swaggering and strutting that preceded it.

Yet from this bloviating account it is easy to derive the central tenets of the view. Fascism is a political philosophy that is nationalistic, avowedly authoritarian, and seeks the supremacy of the race or nation over others through the sacralization of power. It seeks national unity by invoking racial, cultural or religious bonds, and by identifying internal and external enemies and threats. It takes its name from the *fasces*, the bundle of rods tied round an axe which in ancient Rome was the symbol of authority. The Roman fasces were carried by lictors who assisted magistrates in their duties; a single rod is more easily broken than when a number of them are tied together, hence the bundle's symbolization of strength; and the rods themselves were individually used by the lictors to punish offenders at the magistrates' direction.

The regimes of Mussolini, Hitler and Franco are cited as classic examples of Fascism. In the first two cases the leaders of the states in question sought to recover former greatness – Mussolini no doubt had Roman imperial dreams, whereas Hitler viewed defeat in the First World War and the collapse of the German economy as sources of humiliation of a *Volk* which only recently – under Bismarck – had begun to realize its world-historical destiny as the master race.

Purists argue that Nazism – National Socialism – should not be described as Fascism, because its focus is race and everything that goes with it – racial purity, racial destiny, anxieties about pollution and subversion by inferior races (the Jews, the Slavs, negro peoples) – whereas in Mussolini's original brand of Fascism it is the State which is the primary focus. This somewhat splits hairs, as shown by the wider pejorative use of 'Fascist' to describe any anti-democratic nationalistic authoritarian regime; for if the epithet can apply informatively to Franco's Spain and Suharto's Indonesia, to the Greece, Argentina and Burma ruled by juntas of generals, and to theocratic regimes such as those run by Taliban groups in Afghanistan, then it certainly applies to Hitler's Germany.

In the extended use of 'Fascist' as a pejorative, the term can apply to individuals and sub-state groups as well as states, and to some aspects or actions of governments which are not otherwise correctly describable as Fascist. What is meant in these usages is the connotation of some or all of the jack-boot features of Fascist states in the classical sense just described.

A Fascist or proto-Fascist state in the extended sense is characterized by its ultra-nationalism, including the over-use of flags, symbols, songs and slogans glorifying the nation and its leaders – or quite often: leader, singular; the leader principle is a feature of classical Fascism as the dictatorships of Mussolini and Hitler amply show.

In such regimes there is not much use for, or presence of, democracy, civil liberties, or due legal process. Human rights are arbitrarily and extensively violated; summary arrest, detention without trial, and capital punishment for offences which include political opposition and dissent, are typical. The military are greatly in evidence in all this, and have high status and a lion's share of resources. The judiciary is invariably in the pockets of the leaders, and if there are elections they will be a sham, rigged, jerrymandered, or influenced by various forms of coercion.

There is in such regimes close control of the media and extensive censorship. 'Security' considerations are claimed to be paramount, both against enemies within (political opponents, human rights activists) and real and supposed enemies without. Both are appealed to by Fascist regimes as a reason for military spending and authoritarian laws.

Typically such regimes are conservative economically and morally, favouring business and industry over working people, outlawing trades unions, and entertaining perennial suspicion of intellectuals – writers, artists and academics, from among whom the leadership of dissent often arises.

While characteristically harsh on crime, with the police and secret services having wide powers to snoop, arrest and detain, the regimes themselves tend to be corrupt, riddled with hidden scandals, nepotism, and straightforward crime – all under the protection of impunity.

These features are dismayingly ubiquitous in the world today; traces of them are uncomfortably discernible even in Western liberal democracies, especially as fears over security and terrorism prompt governments to restrict traditional civil liberties in the mistaken belief that doing so will provide a measure of protection.

It is needless to offer criticism of Fascism as an ideology and as both an historical and a contemporary fact. It condemns itself out of its own mouth and record.

See: ABSOLUTISM, DEMOCRACY, POLITICS, TOTALITARIANISM

FEMINISM

Feminism is a complex set of overlapping movements in the political, social and cultural spheres aimed at promoting and defending the interests of women in society. One way of expressing the aim of this set of movements would be to say that feminists seek to achieve equal rights with men, not least equal pay for equal work; but some more radical feminists wish to bring about a dispensation in which male status and pay cease to be what define women's aspirations.

So diverse are the perspectives and concerns of feminism that it cannot be accounted a single ideology. Nevertheless there is a core of questions on which much feminist activism and theory focuses, including questions about the nature of sex and gender and their social construction, women's experience, violence against women, the historical and institutional basis of patriarchy (male domination) and the correlative subjection of women, stereotyping and sexual objectification, the right methods required for combating the forces and factors that militate against the achievement of feminist aims, and much besides.

The very first feminism on record might be found in Aristophanes's play *Lysistrata*, in which the women of Athens and its allies decide to force their menfolk to stop the Peloponnesian War by refusing them sexual favours until they do so. They succeed. If organized activity by women had continued and diversified into areas of social injustice affecting women, the episode dramatized by Aristophanes would have become feminism proper.

One has to look to the eighteenth century to see the first proper intimations of organized feminist consciousness, in the views of the Marquis de Condorcet and later in the writings of the remarkable Mary Wollstonecraft. The term 'feminism' was coined in French (*féminisme*) by the socialist Charles Fourier, and John Stuart Mill's *The Subjection of Women* (1869) gives it one of its best early statements; the book begins with the words, 'The object of this Essay is to explain as clearly as I am able ... that the principle which regulates the existing social relations between the two sexes – the legal subordination of one sex to the other – is wrong itself, and now one of the chief hindrances to human improvement; and that it ought to be replaced by a principle of perfect equality, admitting no power or privilege on the one side, nor disability on the other.'

The first great victories for feminism are arguably those of suffragism – the campaign for the vote – and access to universities and medical schools. Both campaigns began in the nineteenth century and by the 1920s were more or less assured of victory if not already victorious. But these gains served only to highlight many remaining barriers to fairness; for example, women with university degrees were still denied access to jobs carrying influence, power and high remuneration, either being refused access outright or meeting the 'glass ceiling' that prevented them from rising above a certain level of seniority.

The gainers of the qualified victories just mentioned are often called 'first-wave feminists'. The second wave was given its impetus by two influential books, Simone de Beauvoir's *The Second Sex* and Betty Friedan's *The Feminine Mystique*. In the turbulent 1960s, with many interconnected social and political upheavals occurring – not least the civil liberties movement in the United States over the rights of African Americans – together with a sexual revolution spurred by the contraceptive pill and liberalized attitudes, feminists found many opportunities to advance their case.

In the early 1970s in the United States two events favouring the situation of women occurred: the Equal Rights Amendment to the US Constitution was passed by Congress (though not ratified), and the Roe versus Wade abortion case accorded women 'the right to choose'.

Since these major battles, feminism (now as 'third-wave feminism') has taken many forms ranging from the liberal to the radical – from the quest for social and economic equality with men to separatist rejection of men, from theoretical interests to activism, from assertion of equal rights to arguments for special protections for women that (for example) include limiting male free speech (centrally focused on pornography), and much besides – and there are also movements that deny the male–female dichotomy altogether ('Queer Theory'). On some classifications there are at least two and perhaps three dozen identifiable types of feminist movement. Whereas most people of either sex in the advanced world agree that equal pay and opportunity should be available to all equally qualified people irrespective of sex, race, or any other putative ground of difference, few agree with the extreme feminism exemplified by Andrea Dworkin's claim that all penetrative sexual intercourse is rape.

Feminism of all stripes has benefited from the work of eloquent and powerful advocates for various of its aspects and movements, among them Susan Brownmiller, Judith Butler, Mary Daly, Carol Gilligan, Germaine Greer, Catherine MacKinnon, Juliet Mitchell and Sheila Rowbotham.

In view of the fact that the future health and safety of the world depend on the economic, educational and political advance of women, not least in Third World and developing countries, and among these not least again in the Middle East and parts of south Asia, it seems that the most vigorous and assertive feminist action should be targeted at a dramatic improvement of the lot of women in these places. Among Arab women in the Middle East the literacy rate is only 47 per cent; in parts of central and east Africa girls are subjected to the horrors and dangers of female circumcision; in many parts of Africa it is found that if women receive just a few years of elementary schooling, they have fewer and healthier children, and gain access to rights and benefits that ignorance seals from them.

If 'First World' women who have the means and the knowledge to help their sisters in these disadvantaged circumstances would strain every sinew to do so, the prospects not just for the women themselves but for the world as a whole would be transformed. The feminist challenge should surely place this struggle at its centre.

See: ACTIVISM, EQUALITY

FREEDOM OF SPEECH

There are two bedrock civil liberties without which the very idea of civil liberty is empty. They are freedom of speech and due process of law. Free speech is fundamental because without it one cannot have any other liberties. One cannot claim or exercise liberties, or defend them when attacked; one cannot defend oneself when accused, or accuse those who do one wrong; one cannot have democracy in which information, views and policies are expressed, debated and challenged; one cannot have education worth the name, if there are things that cannot be said; one cannot express one's attitudes, needs, feelings, responses, anger, criticism, support, approval or beliefs; one cannot ask all the questions one needs to or would like to; and for all these reasons, without free speech one would be in a prison made of enforced silence and averted thought on important matters.

So fundamental is free speech that in the United States the First Amendment to the Constitution, in the document that constitutes the Bill of Rights for American citizens, is an express protection of the rights to freedom of speech and the press, to assemble, to petition the legislature, and to think and believe freely in matters of religion and non-religion. Indeed every human rights instrument, from the United Nations' Universal Declaration of Human Rights (article 19) to the European Convention on

Human Rights (article 10), and most written constitutions (even those that window-dress tyrannies) have clauses protecting free speech. Note that many of these instruments quite rightly prefer the term 'freedom of expression' in cognizance of the fact that 'expression' is broader than 'speech', for it includes artworks, theatre performances, novels, dance and much besides that is not specifically or only speech as such. However, 'free speech' and 'freedom of expression' are functionally synonymous in the civil liberties sense, and are widely understood as such.

The fundamental justifications for freedom of expression are as follows. First, it is an intrinsic right of every individual not to be forced to think, speak and believe at the dictate of others, but to do these things of his or her own free accord. Secondly, it is of the essence to the possession and protection of other liberties that individuals have this right. Thirdly, in the absence of the first two considerations, the full development of the human individual is vastly more difficult and in most cases not even possible. Fourthly, freedom of expression is essential to the interchange of ideas and views, and discussion of them, without which society cannot be healthy or mature. Fifthly, by means of the fourth point it promotes and aids the quest for truth or at the very least sound and responsible knowledge. Sixthly, it is a vital check on government, which can too easily veer into tyranny without it.

As every proponent of freedom of expression must allow, the right to it is not an unqualified one. The standard way of explaining why is to cite the case of someone shouting 'Fire!' in a crowded theatre when there is no fire. Because it can do harm, and because it can be used irresponsibly, there has to be an understanding of when free speech has to be constrained. But given its fundamental importance, the default has to be that free speech is inviolate except ... where the dots are filled in with a specific, strictly limited, case-by-case, powerfully justified, one-off set of utterly compelling reasons why in this particular situation alone there must be a restraint on speech. Note the words *specific, strictly limited, case-by-case, powerfully justified, one-off, utterly compelling, in this particular situation alone*. Give any government, any security service, any policing authority, any special interest group such as a religious organization or a political party, any prude or moralizer, any zealot of any kind, the power to shut someone else up, and they will leap at it. Hence the absolute need for stating that any restraint of free speech can only be *specific, strictly limited, case-by-case, powerfully justified, one-off, utterly compelling, in this particular situation alone*.

For as these remarks suggest, the enemy of all that freedom of expression makes possible – the six points, at least, detailed above – is censorship. It comes as a surprise to most people to learn how universal censorship is, even in contemporary Western liberal democracies. In every sphere and at every level censorship is the norm. Governments censor information before it reaches the public. Newspapers and television news reports do not show pictures of maimed bodies on battlefields, and by their sanitizing censorship inadvertently help keep war going, for the public would be revolted by the truth, and sentiment would swing violently against armed action. Teachers and parents censor what they tell children. Leaving things out, doctoring pictures, maps, reports, news, information, whether for tendentious purposes, political 'spin', or in the supposed interests of the tender-minded recipients, are all forms of censorship. It is ubiquitous and constant. It does vastly more harm than good.

The kinds of circumstances that justify a case for a specific, powerfully justified restraint on free expression are those in which what is at stake are perjury and contempt of court, hate speech, and state or company secrets expressly and justifiably (they are not always the latter) protected by confidentiality requirements. Slander and libel should not be protected by prior restraint of speech, but by remedies after the fact, if a jury decides they have occurred. 'Hate speech' is an important matter, but here one has to be careful to note that hate speech can only justifiably be linked to aspects of people they cannot choose – sex, sexuality, ethnicity, age, and disability if any – whereas their political or religious affiliations, dress sense, voluntary sexual conduct, and the like, are and should be open season for criticism, challenge, and even mockery. Most votaries of religions attempt to smuggle 'religion' into the 'age, sex, disability' camp, and though it might be thought an instance of the last of these, it is not sufficiently so to merit immunity from challenge and satire.

Some of the things people would like to list as appropriate reasons for curtailment of free speech are profanity (swearing), blasphemy, pornography, and insult (other than directed at the sex, ethnicity etc. camp mentioned); and even – *mirabile dictu* – such things as heads of state and 'national identities' are 'protected' from free speech in some places, for example Turkey, where people are legally barred from insulting 'Turkish national identity', for instance by mentioning the hideous atrocity of Turkey's massacre of Armenians during the First World War.

A particular aspect of freedom of expression that has much importance is 'academic freedom'. This is the freedom of those who teach, research and study in academic institutions such as universities and colleges, to pursue enquiry without interference. The pursuit of knowledge and understanding is hampered, if not derailed altogether, by external control of what can be studied; and the silencing of teachers and researchers, especially if they make discoveries unpalatable to one or another source of authority, stands in direct opposition to the quest for truth.

It is a widely and tenaciously held view among all involved with academies of higher education in the world's liberal democracies that freedom to teach, research and study is essential for the communication of ideas, for formulation of the criticism, dissent and innovation required for the health of a society, and for the intellectual quality of its culture. Censorship and political control over enquiry lead to the kind of consequences exemplified by the debacle of biological science in the Soviet Union which followed the attempt to conduct it on dialectical-materialist principles, concomitantly with the expulsion of 'bourgeois' biologists from laboratories and universities.

Although academic freedom seems on the face of it an obvious value, it has been often and widely contested. It does not exist in totalitarian dispensations such as the People's Republic of China, and even in a country with a jealously protected constitutional right of free speech, the United States of America, a variety of formal and informal obstructions to academic freedom exist.

In the '1940 Statement on Academic Freedom and Tenure' in the United States it is conceded that teachers must avoid controversial and irrelevant matter in what they say in the classroom, and although they are free to hold and express whatever opinions they like, they must do so with restraint and make it clear that they speak for themselves alone. This is the opposite of the system that obtained in the German universities from the eighteenth century onwards; there *Lehrfreiheit* meant that professors were free to convert their students to their own way of thinking, and could teach whatever they liked; but were not permitted to express their opinions (especially their political opinions) outside the classroom.

Another component of academic freedom is the autonomy of academic institutions to appoint teachers, specify syllabuses of learning, and choose whom to admit as students.

Since universities ceased to be schools for older adolescents and became research institutions and centres of genuinely advanced scholarship and instruction, with the concomitant professionalization of university teaching so that scientists, historians and such dubious individuals as 'philosophers' and literary theorists came to be paid salaries for their entire lifetimes, they have come to have a dual nature: the sciences have become highly significant motors of change and innovation in society, while the 'humanities' have become, by and large, stagnant and irrelevant pursuits, which do very little for those who study them apart from giving them three or four years' extra maturation time and occasionally an advantage in employment terms because, mainly, of the lucky adjunct that the three or four years in question enabled some of them to read more widely than is usual in the population at large. This single simple fact is a not insignificant one, and is possibly the only reason why a 'higher education' in the humanities has any value. But it could of course be secured far more cheaply and probably effectively if people were just encouraged to read. The intellectual life of Western countries happens almost exclusively outside universities; within their humanities departments jargon-laden nit-picking, the project of speculating polysyllabically more and more about matters of less and less importance, consumes time, energy and resources in a way that sometimes makes even some of its own beneficiaries, in their honest moments, gasp.

Still: it takes a lot of compost to grow a flower. Rather like contemporary art, with regard to which one stoically accepts that many frogs have to be kissed before one of them turns into a prince, the humanities on their life-support machine of salaried tenure occasionally produce something, justifying not just their existence but the freedom – the academic freedom – that allows the miracle to occur.

And having said all that, I shall now retract some of the cynicism (which, *experto crede*, has enough justification to warrant it), and repeat the most significant of the points made above, which is this: it matters that there should be places where ideas are generated and debated, criticized, analysed and generally tossed about, some of them absurd, some of them interesting, a few of them genuinely significant. For this to happen there has to be freedom to moot radical, controversial, silly, new, unexpected thoughts, and to discuss them without restraint. Universities are one of those places; humanities departments within them make a contribution to this, and as such justify at least some of the cost they represent to society. For this academic freedom, as an instance of freedom of speech more generally, is vital.

See: EDUCATION, ENLIGHTENMENT, HUMAN RIGHTS

FUNDAMENTALISM

Someone who believes in the literal truth of a religious holy text is a fundamentalist of the religion in question. By extension, people with very strong religious commitments which they believe to be close to the founding intentions of their religion are also described as fundamentalists even if they allow some interpretation of their scriptures.

The term originated as a self-ascribed name for the outlook of a group of Protestant Christians in the United States in the early years of the twentieth century, who affirmed a commitment to the 'fundamentals' of Christianity against many forces that seemed to be diminishing or challenging their faith. The group consisted mainly of theologians at Princeton Theological Seminary, but soon spread well beyond. The summation of the outlook appeared as a series of essays published under the title *The Fundamentals: A Testimony to the Truth*, edited by Reuben Archer Torrey, and paid for by a pair of wealthy oilmen brothers, Milton and Lyman Stewart. The targets of fundamentalist thinking included evolutionary theory, Roman Catholicism, liberal theology, 'higher criticism', atheism, philosophy, spiritualism, Mormonism, and Christian Science. As one sees, not all their targets were undeserving.

It appears that religion has experienced a recent resurgence in fundamentalist forms. This has happened not only in Christianity and Islam but also in Hinduism, associated with nationalism in India. Islam is by nature fundamentalist, and its recent history has seen an unleashing of the destructive forces fundamentalism too often contains.

Fundamentalism's manifestations have taken sometimes horrifying forms, from the murder of medical staff working in abortion clinics to the massacre of worshippers in mosques, from small and large acts of terrorism involving mass murder, such as the events of 11 September 2001 in the United States, to open warfare between people of different religious persuasions. In every case fundamentalists, whether or not they use the gun and the bomb in defence or furtherance of their views, are opposed to democracy, liberal pluralism, multiculturalism, religious toleration, secularism, free speech, and equal rights for women. They reject the discoveries of modern science in the fields of physics and biology, and assert the literal and unrevisable truth of their ancient holy writings. All the major fundamentalisms are determined to take control of the states in which they exist, and to impose their view of things onto them.

No doubt the main sources of fundamentalism lie in the increasing secularization of society started by the eighteenth-century Enlightenment, itself fuelled by the advance of science. In the light of both enlightenment and science, religion appeared to be retreating into the domain of private eccentricity, and in most advanced countries had adopted a social and symbolic guise as a way of coping with its loss of literal credibility and public authority. There have of course always been religious enthusiasts who have resisted what they see as attacks on their cherished beliefs; in the earlier centuries of the second millennium they were the critics who attacked the Church for its lack of zeal, its corruption and its loss of true spirituality. In the twentieth century the enthusiasts had a different target: the unbelievers and their liberal, tolerant, secular society whose education and science see religion as at best marginal and quaint, but mainly as an absurdity, a hangover from the infancy of mankind, the withered fig leaf that hid mankind's ignorance and fear in ancient times. Along with secularism came a relaxation of morality – at least, from the enthusiast's viewpoint. All this doubtless felt like an insult, a threat, the work of the devil. To the passionate soldier of God, the sight of an advertisement in which a scantily dressed attractive girl leans negligently on an expensive motor car of phallic design must seem an intolerable incitement and blasphemy. In the case of Islam, the backwardness of Islamic states relative to the advanced West, and the frustration caused by their own Islamic governments, must have seemed an added offence to many, for whom militant forms of Islam provide everything needed in the way of excuse to engage in a violent struggle against the hated enemy.

Some have felt sympathy for those embattled in their beliefs in this way. Others feel sympathy for them for the different reason that they are victims of a false and distorting perception of the world, a view in which they are trapped typically because of their upbringing and circumstances. For the continued existence of religions is largely the product of religious education in early childhood – itself a scandal since it amounts to brainwashing and abuse, for small children are not in a position to evaluate what they are fed as fact by their elders. (The vast majority of religious educational institutions are for young and very young children.)

The main point of interest for present purposes is to ponder for a moment what kind of ethics would be imposed by, say, a fundamentalist Christian government in the United States, if such came to pass. The world has seen Taliban rule in Afghanistan, where music was banned and women had to walk about covered completely from head to foot, two facts quite staggering in their meaning when one contemplates them. And of course the whole of history is an object lesson in this regard. From it one knows that a religious morality imposed by enthusiasts for their faith would controvert almost every tenet of liberal views about tolerance, openness, personal autonomy and choice, and would impose instead a harsh and limiting uniformity on behaviour and opinion, and doubtless even on dress and recreation. It would be done in the name of a God, in the alleged interests of our souls; and it would not reflect or accommodate much in the way of facts about human nature and human occupancy of a natural physical world.

See: CHRISTIANITY, ENLIGHTENMENT, ISLAM, RELIGION, TOLERANCE

FUTURE, THE

In the early years of heavier-than-air manned flight, before the First World War, aeronautical engineers believed that because biplanes flew better than monoplanes of the kind then being tested, aeroplanes of the future would have as many as twelve wings for ultimate stability, manoeuvrabil-ity and lift. As an illustration of how wrong we can be about the future, this is a paradigm. So too is Margaret Thatcher's remark, ten years before she became prime minister of the United Kingdom, that she would not see a woman prime minister in that country in her lifetime. And as an example of the hubris our expectations can involve, the 1988 claim by molecular biologist Peter Duesberg about the human immuno-deficiency virus (HIV) is another classic; he said, 'That virus is a pussy-cat.'

One could cite many others. But the best of them is the assertion by one Charles H. Duell, an officer of the US Patent Office, who said in 1899, 'Everything that can be invented has been invented.' And as an illustration of how wrong we can be about anything at all, there is Charles Darwin's perhaps wishful, perhaps wistful remark in the foreword to his *The Origin of Species* (1859), 'I see no good reasons why the views given in this volume should shock the religious sensibilities of anyone.'

He who would prognosticate, therefore, does so at peril not just of error but of absurdity. Even the simplest and apparently most sure case, a straightforward extrapolation from the present, is very risky. All around us we see developments which, naturally enough, we project linearly into the future, taking too little account of interactions between those developments, changes in moral and political fashion, the unexpected and unforeseen, and the unforeseeable.

Thus, at time of writing, we make all sorts of confident assertions about what the near and medium-term future will bring. But the very speed of change and technological development should make us extra wary. The rapid increase in computing power made possible by super-computers is enabling scientific and technical research to explore many horizons of knowledge hitherto inaccessible. What this will reveal, and what yet further horizons of knowledge it will make accessible, we can scarcely know. We hope to understand the human brain and consciousness; we hope to apply increasing knowledge of the human genome to the prevention and cure of disease, and the repair of injury and ageing; we hope to counteract the effects of human activity on the natural environment and climate by technological means; we hope to explore further regions of space and the hidden corners of our own planet such as the deep oceans, and perhaps not only to understand them better but to learn things of benefit to us there. These remarks relate to things we know we do not know enough about. What about the things we do not yet even know we do not know?

There are nevertheless some likelihoods. Perhaps within a short time of this book being published in ink on paper, as books have been published for over five centuries, electronic technologies will have superseded this traditional form and will deliver text to readers by other means. These words might be read by those means, constituting a self-fulfilling prophecy. Many other activities will likewise assuredly be influenced into new forms by the electronic revolution of the decades preceding the moment that these words were written – new kinds of community interaction, new types of distant and virtual relationships, new forms of education, new ways of delivering medical care, new political realities, new techniques of shopping and trading, even new forms of warfare focused on damaging or interdicting an enemy's communications and electronic landscape where everything from banking to medicine to schooling and voting depends on the touch of a finger to a screen – or on a thought transmitted via a chip adhering to the forehead or a cranial implant, provided shortly after birth in as commonplace a minor surgical procedure as male circumcision once was.

As these last points suggest, the rapid and in many ways vastly enabling current and apparently forthcoming technologies also introduce new vulnerabilities and risks. Among many that could be cited is the way full engagement in the world of electronic connectedness strips away most of one's privacy, and makes one transparent to the world – to the 'authorities', hackers, criminals, and the curious. And by the way, these latter are legion; already no 'celebrity', film star, public figure or politician is quite safe from the gossip-seeking prying of the fast-fingered seeker after data. But even the ordinary electronically wired-up individual is today an almost naked creature in the cyber-reality he inhabits; from credit cards to mobile phones, email to Internet surfing, use of identity cards and bus passes, the individual leaves a bright shining smear of information about himself like a trail in his wake, which anyone interested can follow with the greatest of ease; and in addition there he is on the CCTV monitor as he waits at the bus stop, peers into a shop window, meets friends, sits at the outdoor café, reads the book whose title the camera can pick up and add to the wealth of details about him that a central computer somewhere stores. Fantasy? This is already the reality of a citizen's life in any developed country in the world.

There is an irony to this. Religions once succeeded in making most people believe that they were under perpetual and complete surveillance by an inescapably relentless supernatural eye. The ubiquitous application of electronic surveillance is proof of official religious scepticism – our governments no longer believe in the gods, but trust instead to the eye of the CCTV camera and the electronic communications monitoring device. This is yet another instance of the truth of Theodor Adorno's remark that we humans have over time grown cleverer but not wiser. Perhaps this should be rephrased: our increasing cleverness is making us more stupid.

In his novel *1984* George Orwell contemplated a society in which the authorities could monitor and control individuals in fine-grained ways. One example of how this might work in an already existing nanny-state society like the United Kingdom could be this: 'the authorities' would suddenly speak to you through your television set to tell you that you have been watching too many of the wrong kinds of programme lately, and that you need to vary your viewing diet, and in particular to listen to government advice on diet because monitors in your toilet have picked up an insufficiency of fibre and B vitamins. If you think this is merely a wacky idea that could never happen, I sincerely hope you are right.

At time of writing a distinction is drawn between younger generations of people who are 'technological natives' and older people who are 'technological tourists', that is, rather tentative and not fully competent venturers in the land of computers and powerful mobile phones and the like – they do not know the language well, and miss a great deal of what is happening, what is possible, and what is coming at them with the speed of light in the brave new world of technology. Technological natives, by contrast, consist of those who have grown up acquiring hyper-fast thumbs on their mobile-phone buttons, who read with comfort on tiny screens and take every new development in their stride with relish.

A reasonable near-term prognostication, for some of this is already with us, is that newspapers and magazines will largely if not completely become electronic, film and television will standardly be watched on mobile hand-held devices, houses will become electronic zones in which lighting, heating, cooking, alarm calls, switching on the shower or wall-sized television, and so forth, will be remotely controlled, voice-controlled, timer-controlled, and probably all three – and cleaned by robot. (As to this latter: roll on the day.)

Think of the implications. Will cinemas vanish? Will books and bookshops vanish? The experience of home life will be different – as will the way homes are furnished and arranged, to make robot cleaning and other electronic conveniences more efficient. For some time people have been saying that the electronic revolution will lead to people working from home. This has increasingly happened already, but most people still commute to places where co-workers congregate and perform their tasks in geographical proximity. With climate change considerations and increased technological capability increasing the pressure for new patterns of life, the home-working paradigm could suddenly take off and become the norm, with office working becoming the rarer or only occasional alternative. Workers might go to the central workplace once a week or once a fortnight, the knock-on to commuting infrastructure and townscapes would be considerable, the hours and methods of working would change – as soon as one begins to speculate, one sees a cascade of possible changes following from this one major change.

Not a few of the ideas discussed elsewhere in these pages might seem, in comparison to the crackling novelty of the fast oncoming tide of change connoted here, old-fashioned and outdated. But to think this is again to risk mistaken prognostication. Ideas are resilient things. It is part of both human strength and human tragedy that ideas live so long in human cultures. Consider the protoscientific ideas of antiquity, in which the operations of nature were attributed to the action of invisible but conscious and purposive agencies. You would think that the advance of understanding about our world would have consigned these old ways of thinking to the history books. But no, they survive as today's religions, in contradiction to almost everything we have learned about the world through the advance of science. And they survive not as curiosities or vestiges, but as forces that can still have powerful impacts on the lives, well-being and safety of whole peoples.

We allow ourselves to grow ignorant about ideas, then, at our peril. Given that we can only partially prepare ourselves for the future, the best and most effective way of trying to do so is to understand the past, the present, and the limits on our forward vision: all three will help us be more resilient in meeting the unforeseen, and – even more to the point – in trying to make the future our own by asserting control over present trends.

See: INTERNET, SCIENCE, TECHNOLOGY

GAME THEORY

Game theory is the analysis of strategies involving conflicts of interest, with a view to determining what counts as a rational strategy – and especially to determine when those engaged in making strategic decisions in such circumstances should cooperate and when they should compete for maximum advantage.

Game theory was inspired by the work of the mathematician John von Neumann and the economist Oskar Morgenstern in their book *The Theory of Games and Economic Behaviour* (1944). Apart from the intrinsic interest of the aim sketched above, game theory also promises insight into the difference between strategies appropriate in one-off and in long-term relationships, and into questions about whether game theory models actual human behaviour, and whether ethical rules about cooperation emerge naturally from the strategic relationships between rational agents seeking to maximize outcomes for themselves.

A 'game' in this context is not a cricket or tennis match, but a model of an interactive situation such as a military stand-off, conducting a business, seeking a mate, securing a majority vote, negotiating a choice of technology, and the like. The key idea in the analysis of such situations is rationality, where a rational agent is one who seeks always to maximize outcomes (profits, benefits, income) for himself in any and every situation. This apparently grasping simplification of real human behaviour is in fact a founding assumption in standard economic theory. It helps to do two things that make game-theoretic analysis possible: rational behaviour is predictable, whereas non-rational and irrational behaviour is not; and it dictates what counts as a 'win', namely, an agent getting what he wants, or what is the best outcome for him relative to his aim.

An example of a problem in game theory – and one that happens to have been a major stimulus not just to game theory itself but to debate in many areas of social science and philosophy – is the Prisoner's Dilemma, invented in the course of a lecture at Stanford University in 1950 by the mathematician Albert Tucker. Suppose that two thieves, A and B, have been arrested near the scene of a major crime (which they committed) and are being questioned separately at the police station. The problem they each face is whether or not to confess. If neither confesses they will be indicted on a relatively minor charge of carrying weapons, perhaps getting a year in prison each. If they both confess and at the same time each implicates the other, they will each go to prison for ten years. But if one (say, A) confesses and 'fingers' the other but the other (B) does not confess, then A will go free because he helped the police, and B will go to prison for twenty years. Finally neither of them knows, of course, what the other is going to say, and they cannot collaborate. So, what should each choose to do to ensure the least bad outcome for himself?

In fact, the best outcome for them both is secured if neither of them confesses, because then they will each spend just one year in prison. But each will doubtless reason, 'Either he will confess or he won't. If he does and I do too, we will each get ten years. But if he does and I don't, then he will go free and I will get twenty years. Also, if I confess and he doesn't, I will go free. So my best course all round is to confess.' If each, thus acting rationally, confesses, they both go to prison for ten years, which is not the best outcome available for either.

What has gone wrong here for the thieves is that they have each adopted what is known as a 'dominant player strategy', each separately working out what is best for himself alone. The outcome that results is known as the 'dominant strategy equilibrium'.

The obvious moral of the story is that cooperation is best. Too much of what happens in the world in military, economic and political terms is 'dominant strategy equilibrium' – considerably less than optimal for everyone concerned everywhere.

A cousin to game theory is *decision theory*, which is an application of probability theory to decision-making in economics and other spheres where uncertainty and risk prevail.

The aim of decision theory is to arrive at an assignment of values ('utility functions') to the probable outcomes of alternative courses of action, once all known relevant circumstances have been factored in. One standard tool employed is Bayesian inference, and successful decisions are regarded as those that reach an acceptable compromise between optimal and preferred outcomes (the optimal outcome might not be the preferred one because of risk, time and other factors). Such outcomes are known as 'satisficing' outcomes, this technical neologism denoting the trade-off between satisfying, sacrificing and sufficing.

Bayesian theory is the philosophically influential view that a measurement of probability is a measurement of a given statement's plausibility. It is specifically opposed to probability theories that turn upon the relative frequencies with which random events occur. There are a number of other decision-theoretic techniques besides Bayesian inference, but they all have in common the aim of providing a relatively simple way of showing what choices exist once a set of objectives, a set of alternative routes to their realization, and a set of consequences for each, have been specified. Decision theory does not itself pretend to help in the choice of any of these factors.

It is more correct to talk of 'Bayesian theories' than a single such theory. They have in common the fact that they derive from a theorem proved by the Reverend Thomas Bayes (1702–61), a Presbyterian minister and amateur mathematician. His proof of a special case of what is now called Bayes's Theorem was published only after his death, in a work called 'An Essay Towards Solving a Problem in the Doctrine of Chances'. It was prepared for its publication in the *Transactions of the Royal Society* in 1763 by Bayes's friend, the celebrated Dissenting divine and polymath Richard Price. The term 'Bayesian theory' has only come into general use in the course of the last century as philosophers working in the theory of knowledge have become increasingly interested in applying concepts of probability to problems of knowledge, belief and rational acceptability.

In essence, a Bayesian view of probability has it that probability is a measure of the degree of belief that a rational individual would accord to a given statement.

Of tangential interest to all the above is Benford's Law, a statistical law predicting that in any randomly sampled number sequence, 1 appears as the first digit in 30 per cent of cases, and 9 appears as the first digit in 5 per cent of cases, with the numbers between appearing with decreasing frequency, thus: 2 appears as first number in about 17 per cent of cases, 3 appears as first number in about 13 per cent of cases, and so on down.

Dr Frank Benford was a physicist in the employ of the General Electric Company in the United States. He made his discovery about the decreasing frequency of occurrence of first digits from 1 to 9 in 1938, and the theorem he derived has since proved a powerful tool for detecting fraud, tax evasion, embezzlement, and computer problems.

The theorem is as follows: if 1 is certainty and 0 is impossibility, then the probability of any number 'd' from 1 to 9 appearing as the first digit in any number is log to the base 10 of $(1 + 1/d)$.

This law applies to numbers drawn from any source and scale, whether they are the numbers quoted on the stock market in any currency, or the numbers that randomly appear on a page of a newspaper, or the populations of towns in a given state. The larger the sample of numbers, the more closely the distribution of their first digits fits Benford's Law.

Auditors know that if the numbers that appear in (say) a tax return or company balance sheet do not conform to Benford's Law, there is a good chance they are less than honest.

GLOBALIZATION

Globalization is the process by which the world has become increasingly interrelated and interdependent in economic terms, and in terms of international political and legal relations. It is a process which has been continuing, with gradually increasing rapidity, since the transoceanic voyages of Portuguese, Spanish and English explorers in Renaissance times, and the consequent trading and then imperial activities for which these voyages laid the basis. As this suggests, globalization in effect therefore means the spreading of European (and in more recent times American) influence, culture and ideas along with the often enforced opening of relationships with the places and peoples thus reached.

The term itself was coined in the 1960s, but became a household word only in the 1980s and 1990s with the first organized campaigns of disquiet about the way international companies were exploiting workers and markets in developing countries. Dictionary definitions of 'globalization' captured what protesters disliked: 'globalization n. the process which enables financial and investment markets to operate internationally, largely as a result of deregulation and improved communications' (Collins). The visible manifestations of the kind of wholesale imposition of Euro-American economic imperialism were the Coca-Cola and McDonald's logos on main streets everywhere in the world, and they were seen as marks of everything corrupting, crass, insensitive, and destructive of local values and practices that the West was exporting willy-nilly in its hectic pursuit of profit.

It is no surprise that the globalization of the last half-century should be so powerfully driven by economic activity. This is what motivated the Portuguese explorers of the fifteenth century, and in the post-SecondWorld

War world the establishment of international agreements and institutions to revive the world economy had globalization as an express aim. The famous Bretton Woods conference of the Allied nations in 1944 set up the International Bank for Reconstruction and Development and the International Monetary Fund (IMF), and signed the General Agreement on Tariffs and Trade (GATT) which paved the way to the founding of the World Trade Organization (WTO). Another product of Bretton Woods, set up a year afterwards, was the World Bank. The conference also agreed a system of exchange rate management which remained effective until the early 1970s. All these initiatives were aimed at free trade between countries and an expanding global economy. The US Secretary of the Treasury, Henry Morgenthau, described the Bretton Woods agreements as heralding 'the end of economic nationalism'. That is precisely what globalization represents.

A more neutral account of globalization describes it as the process of making things known, done, available or possessed worldwide – such as Internet access, telecommunications, medical knowledge and benefits such as vaccines, transport technologies, political ideas, art and music, books, and much besides. The distribution of these more positive things is very unequal across the world, and is always determined by money, but without doubt if some sections of the world's population were denied access to these positive things, there would be even more vociferous protests at the injustice involved.

From the beginnings of the modern globalizing process in the fifteenth century the key has been communications. Transoceanic voyaging needed ships and sailors equal to the task; the successive advent of steamships, railways, the telegraph, telephones, aircraft, and now the Internet has increased communicative power and with it contact, trade, migration, and the increasingly intimate relations between economies which have now reached a point of genuine interdependence, such that serious problems in any of the world's larger economies threaten disruption in them all.

The negative effects of globalization to which protesters draw attention include the fact that despite all the international arrangements and agreements that have promoted globalization, there is still not fair trade in the world, and the chief victims are producers in poor countries. This is partly because business in rich countries is far better equipped to work the international system, and also because richer countries protect their agricultural and other sectors so that producers in poor countries cannot hope to compete with them.

The protesters also point to the destruction or at least deleterious alteration of traditional ways of life and cultures, and – somewhat differently – the generation of tensions when cultures feel threatened by the boorish-seeming insensitivity of cultural and economic colonization. For example, some of the film and television images that pour out of the United States and Europe are regarded with dismay by traditionalists in Muslim-majority countries, making them anxious for their daughters' morals and the fabric of their societies. This can generate hostility and deepen divisions even as the world itself grows closer, forcing different peoples and traditions to jostle cheek by jowl in arrangements that chiefly benefit the stronger and richer among them.

Anti-globalizers are a coalition of groups of environmentalists, trades unionists, left-wing activists of various degrees, fair-trade campaigners, and the inevitable few who like tearing down fences and throwing bottles. With the exception of the last, these groups have a number of valid points to make about the negative aspects of globalization, the strongest being the unfairness of globalizing arrangements to the weaker participants in them. They also express legitimate concerns about the fact that some international corporations are more powerful than any single government, and are laws unto themselves as a result. Without question such corporations have at times acted in very exploitative and harmful ways, and despite the recent climate of demands for more ethical business behaviour there is no guarantee that harmful activity has stopped.

One of the sharpest voices in the debate about globalization is that of Noam Chomsky. He points out that the term has two quite different senses. One, associated with the internationalist hopes of left-wing movements, denotes international integration, cooperation and mutuality among peoples. The other is the financial and commercial sense in which the world is opened to the search for profit by corporations and investors 'and other sectors of power', as Chomsky puts it, who do not care about individual people very much.

Globalization does however have positive aspects too. It promotes the flow of goods, labour, capital, technology and knowledge around the world, and thereby can increase wealth in poor countries, provide opportunities for education and health care for their populations, promote cooperation and the exchange of knowledge and skills, and hold out hope that an economically more interdependent world, which concomitantly will be a mutually more knowledgeable world, might therefore prove to be a more peaceful one too.

See: ACTIVISM, ECONOMICS, INTERNET, WEALTH, WESTERNIZATION

HINDUISM AND BRAHMANISM

Brahmanism is the ancient religion of India, existing more recently under the name of Hinduism. More accurately, it is a complex and diverse set of beliefs and practices which ultimately can be traced to a basis in four collections of ancient scriptures: the Vedas, Brahmanas, Upanishads and Sutras.

The term 'Hinduism' now applied to the religion or family of religions of India, Nepal and the Sri Lankan Tamils is a coining first made by eighteenth-century Westerners interested in India's religious traditions. The word 'Hindoo' was indeed once the general ethnic term for inhabitants of the Indian subcontinent. 'Hindu' has long since been accepted by Indians themselves as descriptive of the collection of more or less loosely related religious beliefs and practices to be found in their country. At time of writing there are about a billion subscribers to one or another form of that religion, making it the third-largest world religion after Christianity and Islam (in that order). It has far more ancient roots than either of them, and almost certainly than Judaism too.

The dates given for the composition of the ancient books on which Brahmanism/Hinduism ultimately rests vary widely. The Vedas are given an earliest date by some of 1500 BCE, while others claim that they were written as early as 3000 BCE. On the more usual conservative estimate, the dates are: Vedas 1500–800 BCE, Brahmanas 1000–600 BCE, Upanishads 800–500 BCE, and the Sutras 600–400 BCE.

The Vedas are a collection of hymns and incantations praising the gods and accompanying rituals of sacrifice and exorcism. The Brahmanas are a miscellany of commentaries and glosses on the Vedas for use by Brahmins (priests). The Upanishads contain speculations on the nature of the universe and the destiny of mankind, while the Sutras are compendiums of guidance on rites and customs.

In its earliest form, which might informatively be called 'Vedism', Brahmanism was a relatively straightforward polytheism in which the principal deities were Indra, god of war, and first among the gods; Varuna, upholder of the law; Vishnu the sun god (also known by many other names and accordingly possessed of many attributes); Siva the dancer and destroyer; Agni, the god of fire and benefactor of man, early known as 'the first priest'; and Soma, god of the eponymous plant which when eaten gives wonderful visions and promises immortality. The Vedas display belief in a heaven for the good and a hell for the bad, and prescribe animal sacrifice to secure the gods' blessing and forgiveness. The spirits of ancestors were also tenderly worshipped, and provided with soma and rice in feast-offerings (*sraddhas*) to secure their protection and help.

After this early period Vedism developed in two different directions, one of them a religion for the masses, the other more esoteric. The first kind, popular Brahmanism, was a priest-dominated, ritualistic religion of strict observance and ceremonies, in which the powerful and aristocratic priestly (Brahmin) class came to prominence. It was during this development that society became fixed into a rigid caste system.

Asceticism flourished especially in the Brahmin caste, encouraging many men to leave their families once their children had grown to adulthood, and to live extremely austere lives, surviving by begging. Known as *Sannyasis* or *Yogis* they practised meditation, seeking union with the divine in the trances thus induced.

From the later Vedic hymns a theology was developed in which the concept of a supreme creator and omnipotent lord figured, first known as Prabjapati and later Brahman. The Upanishads and Brahmanas are the scriptures of this development, and the system of thought they express is called Vedanta. This name literally means 'end of Veda', which betokens the view that the Upanishads reveal the real meaning of what the Vedas say, in teaching ultimate emancipation from the cycle of death and rebirth. The various Brahmanas constituted efforts to organize and systematize the teachings of the Upanishads, but all that their differences of interpretation succeeded in doing was to give rise to a plurality of schools of Vedanta. There are ten major such schools – Advaita and the rest – and between them they constitute the chief philosophy of Hindu religion to the present day.

A key concept in Vedanta is that of *atman*, which means 'self'. The Upanishads teach that our ordinary view of the self is mistaken, resting as it does on sense experience and the activities which involve us in using our bodies (eating, walking, talking and so forth). Therefore we need to learn a technique of self-discovery, resulting in the realization that the self is pure objectless consciousness. This in turn is identified (in Advaita Vedanta) with the ultimate ground of all being, Brahman, union with which or absorption into which is the goal of existence, and is infinite bliss. (Advaita literally means 'not two', which means that it is a denial of dualism – specifically, the dualism of the individual self and Brahman, the universal soul.)

Vedanta was and is too arcane for the majority, however, so the popular form of Hinduism which has persisted since it grew out of the original Vedic religion takes the form of one of two cults: either the cult of Vishnu the Preserver (whose avatars are Krishna and Rama), or the cult of Siva the Destroyer. Worshippers of Vishnu are known as Vaishnavas, worshippers of Siva are known as Shaivites. Their respective traditions date from about the fifth century BCE. In order to retain an at least nominal association with the original Brahmanist tradition, Advaita Vedanta theology incorporates these two deities with Brahman in a *trimurti* or trinity.

Hinduism, like all polytheistic religions (or more accurately, for most versions of Hinduism, 'henotheistic' religions, meaning those in which there is one deity which takes many forms), is traditionally tolerant. But political Hinduism has become a force in recent decades, partly in response to politicized Islam in the subcontinent of India, and it has a tendency to be nationalistic, right-wing and intolerant. One result has been violence against Muslims and Christians. This development has stemmed from the movement for *Hindu jagaran* ('Hindu awakening') started in the nineteenth century, from the *Hindu Mahasabha* ('Great Hindu Assembly'), a political party started by Pandit Mohan Malaviya in 1909 advocating *Hindu rastra* (rule according to traditional Hindu law – analogous to calls by Islamists for rule by Sharia law), and from the idea of *Hindutva* ('Hindu-ness) put forward by Vir Savarkar in the 1930s, to distinguish Hindu culture from Hindu religion (*Hindu dharma*). Nationalistic Hindu parties controversially call for *Hindutva* to be a criterion for citizenship of India, and their attitude in this respect is characterized by an emotional patriotism, all the more interesting for the fact that prior to British imperial dominion in the Indian subcontinent, the region consisted of many independent states encompassing many different forms of Hinduism and Islam. Such is the virtue of that dangerous set of fictions that goes under the name 'nationalism'.

See: BUDDHISM, CLASS, RELIGION

HISTORY

An interesting ambiguity infects the word 'history'. It can either denote past events, or it can denote the study of past events.

In the first sense 'history' comprehensively refers to everything that has happened in the period of time into which, by all means of research including archaeology – that is: by means of 'history' in the second sense – we can cast light over human affairs. This in practice takes us back about 10,000 years; before then the history of humankind and its evolutionary antecedents are the province of palaeoanthropology.

History is one of the indispensable studies. No person can be educated or civilized who does not make a study of history, and a habit of reading history. This is because it stands alongside literature and the arts as one of the richest and best sources of understanding human experience and the human condition, and it equips us to understand ourselves, to organize our lives and societies, and to meet the future as best we may. As the saying derived from Thucydides has it, history is philosophy teaching by examples.

The key question in reflection on the nature of history is this: is history in the first sense – as past human time – the creation of history in the second sense – the process of historical enquiry – or can we be sure that we are capable of discovering objective truths about what happened in the past? The reason for raising this question is that, obviously, the past no longer exists and is not accessible to investigation other than by way of what remains of it in the present – documents, monuments, ruins in the ground. In the present we find these remains and we construct interpretations of them. Both the remains and our interpretations are contemporary with ourselves. Because history in the second sense – enquiry into the past – familiarly consists in narratives forged in the present, it is no wonder that historians often disagree among themselves about their interpretations.

Although the idea that history – the realm of past events – is like a place spread out 'behind' us, which we could visit and explore if only we had an H.G. Wells time-travel machine, is only a simile, it tends to dominate our imaginations because it is naturally associated with our belief in its objectivity: there are facts of the matter about what happened in the past, and history (as enquiry) has the job of discovering what they are. Our sense of realism is offended by the thought that the past is an artefact of the present, particularly when we meet with 'revisionism' about history, for example as when it is denied that the Nazi Holocaust of Europe's Jewish peoples happened. As this example shows, the question whether history is an art that creates or a science that discovers is not an idle one. It comes down to asking whether there is such a thing as historical truth, and if there is, to what extent we can know it.

The intriguing and problematic ambiguity in the word 'history' is a very ancient one. The word derives from ancient Greek *istoria*, which means enquiry. But by the fourth century BCE the word *historikos*, meaning reciter of stories, was in use alongside *historeon*, meaning 'enquirer'. This raises the question of which category to place the first great historians into, these being Herodotus, Thucydides, Polybius, Livy, Sallust and

Tacitus; and indeed it remains a question still, though today there is an acknowledged division between popular narrative historians (the likes of Arthur Bryant, say) and coal-face archival research historians (most academic historians) who certainly merit the label *historeon*.

As it happens, the historians of antiquity understood the problem very well. Thucydides (surely an *historeon*) roundly criticized Herodotus (on this view an *historikos*) for his anecdotal history, which jumbles together tales, facts, legends and speculations about the great struggle between Persia and Greece. Thucydides says at the beginning of his account of the Peloponnesian War that historical enquiry should restrict itself to contemporary events which can be verified by direct observation. He practised what he preached; he served in the Athenian army, and wrote about what he had experienced or could check with those who had experienced what he wrote about.

Until the Renaissance, history was the province far more of the *historikos* than of the *historeon*. But from the seventeenth century, inspired by developments in science and philosophy and the intellectual spirit that lay behind both, the idea of a more scientific form of historical enquiry emerged. It was motivated largely by work on documentary sources, not least because principles had been established for authenticating manuscripts. By the first half of the nineteenth century, in a period of flowering scholarship in Germany, it was possible to believe that a completely objective knowledge of the past was attainable – the past 'as it actually happened' in the words of Leopold von Ranke, the doyen of nineteenth-century historians.

Von Ranke is described as a 'positivist' about history not only because he believed in its objectivity, but because he thought that it is governed by inductively discernible laws. John Stuart Mill agreed with this view, adding the thought that psychological laws figure among them too. This kind of view makes history a true science, its laws being comparable to natural laws and its truths being discoverable by the same kind of empirical research.

This positivist view of history was vigorously opposed by a group who came to be known as the Idealists, notable among them Wilhelm Dilthey. These thinkers were influenced by the philosophers Kant and Hegel, whose views led the Idealists to argue that history is not like natural science in studying phenomena from an external perspective, but rather is a social science which studies its phenomena from the internal perspective of human thought, desire, intention and experience. The positivists thought that historical enquiry is an empirical study of objective facts; the Idealists viewed it as an exercise in 'intellectual empathy' designed to achieve an understanding of what earlier people felt and thought so that we can understand why they did what they did.

This did not mean that all the Idealists regarded history as merely subjective; Dilthey argued that it remains an objective matter because the books, letters, art, buildings, and other products of human experience exist in the public domain and serve as the materials making 'intellectual sympathy' possible. However, some of the most notable of his fellow Idealists disagreed; Benedetto Croce argued that history is always subjective because there is no way for the historian himself to be absent from its construction.

The theories just sketched constitute 'philosophy of history'. It is allied to historiography, which is discussion of historical techniques and methods. But it must be distinguished from 'philosophical history', a label for grand theories of history's metaphysical significance as advanced by Hegel, Marx, Spengler and Toynbee. Like von Ranke these thinkers regard history as manifesting laws, but they add the very different claim that it is moving towards a climax or goal, that it unfolds teleologically or purposively, or at any rate with some form of final state waiting at the end of the process. This view is part neither of history nor of the philosophy of history, but of metaphysics, or wishful thinking.

See: EDUCATION

HUMANISM

In its current main sense, 'humanism' denotes a family of views premised on a commitment to the idea that ethics and social policy must be based on our best understanding of human nature and the human condition. It is a concern to draw the best from, and make the best of, human life in the frame of human lifetimes, in the real world, and in sympathetic accord with the facts of humanity in the world. By immediate implication, therefore, it rejects transcendentalist claims about the source of value and morality, in particular those associated with religion. It is not the same thing as either secularism or atheism, but it has a natural affinity with both and especially the former.

A humanistic view is a starting point, not a finished body of doctrine. There can be and indeed is much debate about what the human good is and how it can be attained, and that debate ranges from matters of ethical theory to the practicalities of politics, with humanists voicing different positions across the range. What they have in common is the starting point that such debate is about humanity in the real world, not the supposed intentions and commands of supernatural agencies to which human nature must be twisted to conform.

The word 'humanism' has had a variety of different senses and uses since its first coining in the Renaissance. But although the word has a relatively short and complex history, the main current meaning just given applies to the great ethical tradition stemming from classical Greek antiquity, older by half a millennium than Christianity, and older by a thousand years than Islam, and much richer and deeper than either of them. This tradition has in fact been the mainstay of Western ethics, for it provides the chief content even of applied Christian ethics, having been borrowed by the Church when, after the Second Coming had apparently been postponed *sine die*, it proved necessary to adopt the substantialities mainly of Stoic ethics. Though if one were to look for a blueprint for the ideal of the 'Christian' it is to be found before the fact in Cicero's distillation of most that is best in the ancient tradition, culminating in his depiction of the Republican *vir* or gentleman.

In the Renaissance the rediscovery of classical letters prompted a spirit of learning that was broader, fresher, more open and humane than the narrow theological obsessions that had dominated the late Middle Ages. This is called Renaissance humanism, and sometimes 'literary humanism', and is chiefly concerned with the study and enjoyment of the humanities.

At this time it was possible for more enlightened people to enjoy the Classics and the wider perspective they afforded, while retaining their religious faith; hence the somewhat hybrid term 'religious humanism' which some with more interest in the first word than the second strive to put into currency. There is an outstanding example of a true 'religious humanist' however: the great Erasmus of Rotterdam, who for a while was highly influential in the culture of Europe, though doubtless his writings had the effect of weaning many away from the narrow confines of religious orthodoxy, a prospect much feared by orthodoxy's guardians. Because the delights of classical literature always threatened to liberate minds in this way, both the Roman and the Reformed Churches in the sixteenth century endeavoured to suppress interest in the Classics, and to substitute something more acceptable. Sebastian Castellio's translation of parts of the Bible into beautiful Ciceronian Latin became a classic in its own right for this reason, because it provided schoolboys with a good Latin model without undermining their morals, as Ovid and Virgil were feared to do.

In the United States some Unitarian and Universalist groups like to call themselves humanists, as to all practical purposes they are; real humanists often remark that such folk take religion out of religion while retaining the name for reasons unfathomable, unless they use 'religion' as a misnomer for 'attitude to life' or as somehow akin to its metaphorical use in 'football is his religion'. Either way the usage merely introduces muddle where there is no need for it, given that the premise of humanism, as described in the opening paragraphs above, is that the most important of all questions, the ethical question of how we should live, is to be answered by appeal to facts about human nature in the real world, and not from supposedly sacred ancient scriptures, transcendental revelations, or religious or supernaturalistic teachings of any kind.

Secular humanism, given its first full expression in the Enlightenment of the eighteenth century, is functionally the basis of the triumph of the West in the succeeding two centuries in science, technology, progress in democratic systems of government, and conceptions of the rights of man. That is quite an achievement.

One of the largest influences on Renaissance humanism, as implied above, is the writings of Cicero, both for the beauty of their language and their rich matter. Erasmus said that whenever he read Cicero's *On Old Age* he felt like kissing the book, and thought the great Roman should be called 'St Cicero'. Cicero was also Petrarch's favourite, and others among his admirers took an oath never to write Latin in any but Cicero's way, and with any but Cicero's vocabulary. One of them was Pietro Bembo (1470–1547), one of the Latin secretaries to Pope Leo X, who with his friend and fellow Latin secretary Jacopo Sadoleto led the movement known as 'Ciceronianism' aimed at standardizing Latin on the Ciceronian example. Bembo had a magnificent library at his home in Padua, wrote beautiful Latin and Italian, and dedicated a dialogue on Platonic love to his friend Lucrezia Borgia, modelled on Cicero's *Tusculan Disputations*.

The Renaissance valued Cicero not merely for his style but for his humanism in the modern sense, expressed as belief in the value of the human individual. He argued that individuals should be autonomous, free to think for themselves and possessed of rights that define their responsibilities; and that all men are brothers: 'There is nothing so like anything else as we are to one another,' he wrote in *On Laws*, adding that 'the whole foundation of the human community' is the bond between individuals, which he said should consist in 'kindness, generosity, goodness and justice'. The endowment of reason confers on people a duty to develop themselves fully, he said, and to treat one another with generosity and respect. This outlook remains the ideal of contemporary humanism today.

See: ETHICS, HISTORY OF; RELIGION; SECULARISM

HUMAN RIGHTS

One of the most significant advances in human affairs in the last four centuries, and especially since the mid-eighteenth century, has been the development of conceptions of rights, as in the phrase 'the rights of man' and 'human rights'. Before the seventeenth century there was little question of anyone having rights who was not able to claim and enforce them through strength, wealth or office, and the majority of people were at the disposal of those with rights, thus constituted, over them.

Monarchs, aristocrats, priests and others with like vested interests had every reason to suppress the desire for rights and freedoms as expressed by participants in the Peasants' Revolt of 1381, or by the Levellers of the seventeenth-century English Civil War, or by workers in early nineteenth-century factories, or by slaves on the sugar and cotton plantations of the New World, or by women almost everywhere and in every period. The struggle to achieve rights and freedoms for the generality of mankind was, therefore, a long, hard and bitter one.

Historians of the concept of rights search the distant past to find intimations of it, for example in the edicts of Cyrus the Great in sixth-century BCE Persia, Ashoka in third-century BCE India, and Muhammad's 'Constitution of Medina' of 622 CE. The sources of the idea of rights now so central to Western Enlightenment-derived ideas of human rights and civil liberties are, however, to be mainly found in the philosophical thought of classical and Hellenic antiquity, and particularly in the thought of Plato, Aristotle and the Stoics.

The idea of rights is a very broad and complex one, much debated in philosophy and jurisprudence, extending across many domains of concern: animal rights, civil rights, gay rights, parental and children's rights, legal rights, natural rights, women's rights, workers' rights, rights at law and in politics; individual rights and peoples' rights; the relation of rights to obligations and duties; and more. A central question concerns the source of rights: are they inherent in humanity, or are they claimed or made? Are they objective, or artificial? If the latter, are they nevertheless valid and binding? Are they universal, or are notions of rights specific to different societies and their members?

The modern idea of human rights – modern in the sense that the first explicit articulation of them dates from the French and American revolutions of the eighteenth century – starts not from philosophical debate about their source, but from a bald and bold assertion: that people have them, and possess them equally. This is exemplified by the first article of the United Nations Declaration of Human Rights (UNDHR), adopted in 1948, which states, 'All human beings are born free and equal in dignity and rights.' The immediate prompt for this reassertion of the Enlightenment aspiration for a universal enfranchisement of human individuals was of course the horrific experience of the Second World War and the atrocities committed during its course, foremost among them the Holocaust of European Jewry. In the light of that experience, few of those involved in drafting and adopting the UNDHR felt much moved to pick nits over its philosophical basis: experience spoke too loudly and clearly for that. And in my view, rightly: sober reflection shows what the minimum requirements are for the possibility of human flourishing, and we know what kinds of human activity and inactivity tend almost invariably to cause other humans to suffer or at least fail to flourish. That is enough to dictate what any human rights document should minimally contain.

Adoption of the UNDHR has been hugely influential, not least as a powerful further step in the development of a rich body of international humanitarian and human rights law which began with the first Geneva Conventions of the nineteenth century but has been given a great impetus by the UNDHR's adoption and the two great Covenants that followed it on civil and political rights and social and economic rights – and moreover in being followed by the beginnings of regimes of enforcement, such as the European Court of Human Rights and the International Criminal Court. This latter endeavours to put to work the much-contested notion of a universal jurisdiction – proponents of the idea of national sovereignty (the United States chief among them) of course dislike this, preferring to see dictators bully and massacre their own people with impunity than to risk having their own officers of state arraigned for crimes against humanity if they have, for example, been involved in initiating or conducting a war.

The UNDHR is the focal contemporary reference point of discourse about human rights. In its preamble it makes an all-important claim and an all-important observation. The claim is that 'recognition of the inherent dignity and of the equal and inalienable rights of all members of the human family is the foundation of freedom, justice and peace in the world'. The observation is that unless human rights are protected by the rule of law, people will continue to be compelled to the last resort of rebellion against tyranny and oppression.

Moreover the UNDHR's drafters recognized the indivisibility of human rights, and therefore the need to bring economic, social and cultural rights into connection with the political and civil rights that were the focus of the French Revolution's Declaration of the Rights of Man and the United States' Bill of Rights. The range of rights was made more specific by the two great UN Covenants which followed adoption of the UNDHR, namely the Covenant on Civil and Political Rights and the Covenant on Economic, Social and Cultural Rights. Whereas the world's most influential Western powers were agreed on the provisions of the first Covenant, there was considerable controversy over the second, the argument being that the most one could do is to state economic and social aspirations and goals, given the contingent nature of what they concern. It seemed to many critics that according people a 'right to work' in economic circumstances where there are no jobs is futile at best.

Other conventions aimed at eliminating racial and sex discrimination, the use of torture, and the protection of children and migrants, function as norms and, upon coming into force after a sufficient number of nations have ratified them, are citable in proceedings of international law. The ideas embodied in all these human rights instruments have a powerful influence on thinking and behaviour, even if violation of them continues: hope has to lie in the future as these ideas become more widespread and more influential still.

At the heart of the concept of human rights are those ideas enshrined in the UNDHR's provisions concerning the individual. They centrally include the right to life, liberty and security of the person; to protection from slavery and cruel or inhumane treatment; to recognition as a person before the law (and therefore to freedom from discrimination, to the availability of effective remedy when appropriate, and to due process); to privacy; to free movement; to marriage and family life; to ownership of property; to peaceful association with others; to participation in politics and government; to education; and to participation in cultural life.

The chief difficulty facing the project of seeing regimes of human rights prevail in the world is that of enforcement. The only body recognized in international law as having the power to enforce human rights instruments is the Security Council of the United Nations. For geopolitical reasons this body is a thing of impotence; China and Russia (as with

Russia's predecessor the USSR) habitually find it useful to stall efforts by the other permanent members, Britain, France and the United States, to see human rights provisions enforced across the world – not that these states are themselves unblemished in human rights respects: but they are considerably better than many others. Among the reasons why this is so is that Russia (think Chechnya) and especially China are major human rights violators themselves, and in any case they like the world to be divided and the United Nations weak (this latter desire they share with the United States). In particular the Chinese actively support regimes where human rights abuses are especially egregious: historically, countries like the Burma of the generals, the Sudan of the Darfur massacres, the Zimbabwe of the dictator Robert Mugabe, and the like; for the twofold reason that it gives China a foothold in those places, and keeps the world distracted.

The effect is that the UN Security Council is an all but ignorable body in world affairs. For a time this was not so; in the 1950s and 1960s hopes for it were higher and its role in difficult situations around the world was much publicized and discussed. The blue-helmeted UN peacekeeping forces were much more evident in news stories, and Secretary-Generals like U Thant and Dag Hammarskjöld were major world figures. The great powers of the United States and the USSR were successfully able to diminish and marginalize the UN's role as interfering with their Cold War spheres of influence. When the Cold War ended, the UN was too far down the ladder of authority to fill the needed gap.

As the UN Security Council is the only body with power in international law to enforce human rights instruments, the United Nations itself is the only body with international jurisdiction for human rights matters. The Human Rights Council (which replaced the ineffective and hamstrung Commission on Human Rights in 2005 – to no greater apparent effect) is mandated to investigate human rights violations and abuses, and reports directly to the General Assembly of the United Nations. It can ask the Security Council to take action by sanctions or direct intervention, and it can refer abuses to the International Criminal Court. The Council consists of representatives of 47 of the UN's 191 member states, chosen by secret ballot in voting by the General Assembly.

There are also a number of UN 'treaty bodies' in the form of committees which monitor particular aspects of human rights, such as compliance with human rights norms, questions of racism and sexism, the status of children and migrants, and the use of torture. There are regional bodies also for Asia, the Americas and Africa (Oceania does not have a regional body but has a good overall record, led by New Zealand

and Australia, despite a number of historically based difficulties with their indigenous peoples).

The chief bone of contention in debate about human rights is the question whether they are universal, or whether religious and cultural traditions qualify or even trump them or some of them. Those who accept this latter view are relativists, and in arguing for an exceptionalist view of their traditions they often claim that the universalist view is in fact merely Eurocentric Enlightenment imperialism, being forced on traditional cultures against their will. In response it has been acidly observed that those who most frequently assert this view are people in power in countries where that power is abused and human rights violations occur. Societies in which the position of women is unacceptable from the universalist human rights standpoint tend to be the most vocal (more accurately: their male populations tend to be most vocal) in denying universalism. Islamic states in particular dislike the rights accorded to women by human rights theory, and have since chosen to announce their own versions of a human rights charter conformable to, or trumpable by, the teachings of the Koran. By such means are the aspirations to a universal code of rights for mankind subverted.

See: ENLIGHTENMENT, EQUALITY, JUSTICE, LAW, LIBERTY

IDENTITY

One of the main things that both unites and divides people is the allegiance they feel to an identity – a national or religious identity in the standard case, or an identity as a member of a particular minority which, for whatever reason, feels itself in some way separate from a surrounding majority. Thus members of an ethnic minority, or of the gay community, might feel that they are distinct from most others around them, and that what identifies and individuates them gives them a deep common bond with those who share that identity.

As the world has grown more global and as societies have become more cosmopolitan, so adherence to a distinguishing identity has become a matter of greater importance for some. A prime example is religious identity: and here a particularly clear example is the desire of some Muslims, not least in non-Muslim-majority countries, to mark allegiance to their religion by wearing traditional dress – in the case of women by covering their heads and sometimes faces, in the case of men by growing beards and wearing a white cap.

The same is true of ultra-orthodox Jews in their eighteenth-century coats, skullcaps and dangling locks of hair, and Christians sporting crosses or crucifixes on chains around their necks. In the public domain these signals in effect announce that the person in question wishes to be regarded primarily under the label of the religion of which they advertise membership.

On occasions of national endeavour, ranging from war to an international sporting event, the idea of community membership – of one's identity as a member of that community – can have emotional resonance. This is a fact that governments and demagogues rely upon when in need of volunteers for armies. In fact they find it relatively easy to whip up nationalistic or patriotic ardour – the two are not quite the same thing, but can have the same effects – and it is interesting to inspect the slogans and symbols which summarize, evoke and provide a focus for the emotional appeal in question. It is well known that the psychology of crowds is very different from the psychology of individuals, and the concepts of national and religious identity relate to the mass mind, the corporate emotion, to which the identities in question belong. For when an individual is operating under the description of one or another national, ethnic or religious identity, he is no longer an individual, but a component of a mass or collective.

The most compelling critique of identity as a divider and over-simplifier, as a falsifier and source of trouble, is to be found in Amartya Sen's book *Identity and Violence* (2007). Describing others or oneself in terms of 'a choiceless singularity of human identity' is the dangerous mistake, Sen says, which not only diminishes individuals but exacerbates differences between them. The aim of his argument is to compel us to remember that a person is not just one thing – only and solely a Muslim, or a Jew, or an Arab, or an American – but many things: a parent, a friend, a teacher, a chess player, a Frenchman, a socialist, a grandson, all at once, a multiple and complex entity whom the politics of singular identity reduces to an empty symbol and stuffs into a pigeonhole.

Sen observes that there is a growing tendency to overlook the many identities people have in place of the single differentiating identity that 'identity politics' seeks to impose. Of course this tendency has always existed; in the past the possession of a singular identity was more a function of practical limitations imposed by illiteracy, geography and poverty, on the one hand, and on the other hand stereotyping by conquering or colonizing powers with regard to those over whom they lorded.

This latter tendency was opposed by the good side of what has since overreached itself as 'political correctness', which urged us to avoid the errors of stereotyping on which racism, sexism and other forms of discrimination rest.

It is, though, right to be reminded that the past was not wholly a slave to the politics of singular identity. There was pluralism and tolerance in past Islamic culture; Akbar, the great Mughal emperor of the sixteenth century, and Saladin, the prince of Islam in the twelfth century, are exemplars who welcomed all faiths and persuasions in their empires. Alas, the unhappy truth about the contemporary world is that those most responsible for insisting on singular identities are Islamist radicals. In contemporary Europe as the twenty-first century gathered pace many young Muslim women chose to wear the niqab – the full veil – as a political statement, asserting their Muslim identity as the most significant fact about themselves – indeed, given the nature of the apparel, the only fact about them – which forces others to treat them accordingly.

Whereas Christian fundamentalists in the United States might consider their faith allegiance to be their main individuating characteristic, they are also Americans, Southerners (perhaps), businessmen or farmers or workers, members of the National Rifle Association, and (in most cases) Republicans. Their identity as Americans of a certain kind is a package deal; just one of these features is not enough to make them Americans of that distinctive kind.

For an Islamist, by contrast, religion and politics are the same thing, and not much else matters by comparison. Overriding singular identities are those that people are willing to die for; in wartime soldiers are encouraged to identify wholly with the cause of their homeland, and to see their potential self-sacrifice for it as glorious – which proves the power and the danger of the idea.

In his book Sen admonishes those in Western countries whose reaction to contemporary Islam is to identify it indiscriminately with Islamism, which of course is simplistic. He is right to warn against this mistake. But he is also right to charge Islamists with playing singular identity politics; to them too his indictment of reductionism and a 'foggy perception of world history' applies, especially when they use it as a *casus belli*.

A problem for debates of this kind is that they reach only those who are already persuaded of the need to dispense with singular identity judgements, and who do so because they already read and think. The arguments are unlikely to reach those whose ignorance and anger make them the ones most in need of persuasion. It is so much easier for people to think both of themselves and of others in terms of singular identities, that getting them to unlearn the habit is daunting work. It is best done by putting people into contact with each other, literally so. Actual contact with individuals of any kind – working with them and socializing with them – makes it hard to think of them in stereotyped terms; and that is the best way to resist the dangers of singular identities. For one thus sees others in all their identities – and finds in them the identities that relate to some among the plurality of one's own.

See: ETHNOCENTRISM, MULTICULTURALISM, RACISM, RELATIVISM, XENOPHOBIA

INTERNET

It is well known that when Communist China's second-in-command, Zhou En Lai, was asked what he thought of the French Revolution, he answered after a thoughtful pause, 'It's too early to say.' This is vastly more true of the world-changing, history-changing phenomenon of the Internet; what it will lead to, prompt, cause, alter, end, begin, distort, pervert, enable and shape is at present almost unimaginable: and it, along with other communication and information technologies, has already transformed the world and human experience within it beyond the rec-ognition of those whose lives have been largely lived before their advent.

I was born in the mid-twentieth century, as jet aircraft were first ap-pearing on the scene. My grandmother was born three-quarters of the way through the nineteenth century, before the motor car was invented. The rate of technological change between those two minor events, and between the second of them and now, if graphically represented, would have the shape of an exponential curve. How might one extrapolate such a curve further?

The origins of the Internet lie in the launch of Russia's 'Sputnik' satel-lite in 1957. Alarmed at the thought of falling behind the USSR in the technological race, President Dwight D. Eisenhower set up the Defense Advanced Research Project Agency (the 'Defense' was later dropped from the title to yield the abbreviation ARPA). Oddly, the first fear generated by Sputnik was that 'the Soviets' would soon be able to bombard the United States with nuclear weapons from space – thus what came in entertainment and Ronald Reagan's mind (the same thing?) to be called 'Star Wars' was the first impulse which, by the typical detours of fate, led to the Internet.

Some of the work undertaken by ARPA focused on an air defence system involving a digital computer network to control a continent-wide aircraft and missile detection capacity. This system was known as the Semi-Automatic Ground Environment (SAGE) and it was run on a network of twenty-seven vast computers each weighing 20 tons and occupying 20,000 square feet – two storeys of a building – and which generated so much heat that no one could stand near them. If their cooling systems failed they would melt in less than a minute. The operators of the SAGE system were located in twenty-four centres of operations and three combat stations, and were linked by long-distance telephone lines. This network gave a hint to the progenitors of what became the Internet, because it inspired Joseph Licklider, who had been appointed head of the Information Processing Techniques Office mandated to research the further applications of the SAGE networking system, to find a way of connecting the computers and not just their operators.

The technology for this (called 'packet switching' technology) was developed by researchers at the RAND Corporation and the United Kingdom's National Physical Laboratory, and applied in the construction of a new device called an 'interface message processor'. When the design was implemented for ARPA in 1969 it was known as ARPANET, and the first communications were passed between the University of California at Los Angeles and the Stanford Research Institute, also in California.

The networking protocol used by ARPANET was soon succeeded by more sophisticated versions, and this in turn resulted in ARPANET being replaced by a network developed independently by the US National Science Foundation (NSF) which saw the potential of linking science departments in universities around the country through its own NSFNET. Part of the impetus for this development was that the US military had separated itself from the ARPANET, thus promoting the idea of an open-access network for researchers unconnected with the military.

The liberal, generous and imaginative conception of the NSFNET's developers – in effect: the idea of the Internet itself, as a global device for all to speak to all and share their knowledge – was the driver behind the NSF's sponsoring of a number of regional supercomputers to enable high-speed computing resources for the American research community. Once connected to the fraternal CSNET (Computing Sciences Network) and then the EUNET which had come into existence to perform the same function in Europe, the Internet was ready to explode across the world. It did so in the early 1990s; by 1995 the US government relinquished control of the Internet to a federation of independent organizations including the Internet Society, the Internet Architecture Board, the Internet Engineering Taskforce, the Internet Research Taskforce, the Internet Corporation for Assigned Names and Numbers, the Internet Assigned Numbers Authority, the Accredited Domain Name Registrars, and Network Solutions Incorporated.

The Internet is quite literally what it says it is: a network or spider's web of many linked computer networks – hence: a net of networks – which are themselves the local networks of universities, businesses, governments and private owners. This network carries messages and information and provides access to the World Wide Web (WWW), a system of hypertext documents carrying text, images and video footage, and accessed through a Web browser facility on a computer linked to the Internet.

The WWW was invented by the British scientist Tim Berners-Lee, a researcher at CERN in Switzerland. He had read a book in his youth called *Enquire Within Upon Everything*, and saw the potential of the Internet as an electronic home for a similar idea. After the required technical development CERN opened the WWW in 1993 as a free resource for everyone.

The main language of the Internet is currently English, though the technical difficulties of handling other scripts are being rapidly overcome, and it is not improbable that the Internet of the future might have Chinese and Hindi characters as its main scripts. In addition to providing access to the WWW as a vast if not always reliable library of resources and information, the Internet's other main use is for electronic mail – email – and for collaboration in research, file sharing and remote access, advertising and marketing, and more. It is also home now to the 'blogosphere', the realm of blogs – the public diaries and opinion sheets of anyone who cares to have one, with the result that a Babel of voices floods the Net, typically anonymous, frequently vituperative and unpleasant, sometimes interesting and worthwhile. It is the biggest lavatory wall in history, on which graffiti multiplies by the nanosecond.

Like any public space, the Internet has rapidly accumulated huge amounts of junk and garbage. But the careful navigator can find a large amount of interesting and useful material there. One of the best things, in my view, apart from instant email communication and access to news, is the availability of out-of-print books and documents.

The disbenefits of the Internet include the worst forms of violent or exploitative pornography – apparently pornography of the ordinary acceptable kind is the most accessed material on the Internet – and hate speech of various kinds, religious nonsense, and terrorist networking. But the benefits of the Internet so far outweigh these that censorship can only be admitted for a very few areas, such as child pornography and terrorism. In China, Iran, Saudi Arabia and certain other places efforts are successfully made to limit citizens' access to general information, news and comment, and to criticism of the regime itself. The authorities there also use the Internet to track down people of dissident views. These are abuses of the Internet, and the risk is that more and more governments will find open access to news, opinion and information an inconvenience, and will begin to follow suit. It might be that the heady heyday of the Internet as a truly gateless field on which we have gambolled at will during the first two decades of its existence will be seen in future as a golden age – or, by the censors, as a primitive age of unbridled and unacceptable access. Time, which has not had to wait long for the Internet to catch it by the tail and then surpass it, will tell.

See: FUTURE, THE; TECHNOLOGY

INTUITIONISM, MATHEMATICAL AND LOGICAL

Intuitionism in mathematics is the view that mathematical entities are constructed by the mental operations of mathematicians. It is opposed to Platonism (that is, realism) about mathematical entities, which holds that numbers, sets, structures – whatever the ultimate mathematical entities are – exist independently of being discovered.

The most accurate way to describe mathematical Intuitionism is to say that it is the thesis that the truth of a mathematical statement consists in its proof. And if to say that a given mathematical statement is true is to say that it is proved, then correlatively to say that a given mathematical entity exists is to say that it can be constructed.

Intuitionism is a radical theory in that it requires extensive reconstruction of significant areas of mathematics. In particular, it does not accept actual infinity, and that demands revisions to set theory and calculus, constructivist versions of each being required.

The most significant figure in the development of Intuitionism in mathematics is the Dutch mathematician L.E.J. Brouwer (1881–1966); the philosopher who has given prominence to intuitionistic ideas in more general application in philosophy is the Oxford logician and philosopher Sir Michael Dummett (born 1925).

Intuitionistic logic differs from classical logic in not giving the classical reading to the truth-values 'true' and 'false'. In standard classical logic truth and falsity exhaust the field of possible truth values, from which it follows that (where 'p' is any proposition) 'p' and 'not-not-p' are equivalent, that is, have the same truth-value. For this logic, the law of excluded middle holds: 'p or not-p' is taken to be always true, whatever the truth-value of 'p' (the law is said to be a 'theorem' of classical logic).

But in intuitionistic logic there are not 'true' and 'false' but instead 'provable' and 'not provable'. One can immediately see that on this reading, 'p' is not equivalent to 'not-not-p', for they respectively say 'p is provable' and 'it is not provable that it is not provable that p'; and this latter does not say 'p is provable'. So it further follows that the law of excluded middle ('p or not-p') does not hold. Rejection of the law of excluded middle is the defining feature of intuitionistic logic.

The significance of the rejection of excluded middle is that in intuitionistic logic 'p or not-p' cannot be asserted unless there is either a proof of p or a proof of not-p. If p is 'undecidable' then there cannot be a proof of 'p or not-p'. Another important consequence of this is that some kinds of proof by contradiction do not work.

A major motive for the work of Brouwer and other pioneers of Intuitionism was that they were troubled by the philosophical implications of the paradoxes of set theory which, at the beginning of the twentieth century, appeared to undermine the foundations of mathematics. It seemed to them philosophically unacceptable that a proof could be given for 'p or q' without either a proof of 'p' or a proof of 'q'. From this problem Intuitionism flowed; and in the way of these things it has ceased to be an abstract problem in mathematics and the philosophy of logic, but has come to have significant uses in computer science, particularly in connection with type systems of functional computer languages.

IRRATIONALISM

In philosophy, this expression can denote either or both of the views that there is no such thing as reason, or that reason is the wrong resource for arriving at any really significant insights about things. Someone can hold the latter, weaker view because he holds the former stronger one, but a subscriber to the latter need not be committed to the former view as well; he might just believe that although there is such a thing as reason, it is not very important.

One who subscribes to the strong view that there is no such thing as reason has to treat its apparent existence in mathematics, science, daily life and elsewhere as an illusion. We think we are reasoning about how to get most expeditiously from one place to another, say, or about how to bring about some desired end most swiftly and economically, but in fact we are not doing so, we merely think we are. This doubtful claim falls foul of a number of objections, not least that it is unclear why the illusion, if it is one, should have arisen in the first place.

The strong view stumbles on the problem that either it is itself supportable by rational argument, in which case it refutes itself, or if it is not so supported, then what is the justification for accepting it?

Those who subscribe to the weaker view, that reason is not what helps us arrive at a grasp of what is important, offer other routes thither: instinct, intuition, imagination, mystical or religious experience, drug-induced altered states of consciousness, meditation, the authority of ancient traditions or scriptures, the teaching of holy men, the demands of blood or race or *Volk* – and so forth.

Such views associate irrationalism with fideism in religion, which is the view that a commitment of faith is the key to wisdom or salvation, meaning by this something like Kierkegaard's belief that to make the leap to what is truly faith one must deliberately fly in the face of reason and evidence.

'Irrationalism' can mean one of two more interesting views also. It can label the view that the definition of man as a rational animal is misleading or even incorrect; human beings might be able to reason but they are, says this view, far better characterized by (say) their aggression or acquisitiveness or sociability or bipedalism or some other attribute than possession of reason. And it can label the view in metaphysics that, contrary to Hegel's dictum that 'the real is the rational' (meaning that reality can be understood), reality is not rational.

ISLAM

The Arabic word 'Islam' means 'submission', 'acceptance' or 'surrender', and as the name of the religion founded in the seventh century CE by the Arab religious, political and military leader Muhammad, it expressly connotes submission to God, referred to as 'Allah' (the God) in Arabic and therefore by all Muslims likewise.

Muhammad is regarded by his followers as a prophet, and, more to the point, the final prophet in the line which began with Adam and includes Abraham, Moses, Noah and Jesus. The message of all the prophets was the same: that there is only one God, who is owed all obedience, service and worship (*tawhid*), and that God requires mankind to do good and avoid evil.

Muhammad as the last messenger came to complete God's instructions to mankind. He is regarded by his followers – Muslims, a name said to have been given by Abraham – as the most perfect man ever to have lived. One of his primary tasks was to institute the five pillars of the faith. The first of these is the *shahadah* or confession of faith: 'There is no God but Allah and Muhammad is his messenger.' The second is *salat*, the performance of the five daily prayers, timed to occur before sunrise, at noon, in the late afternoon, after sunset, and between sunset and dawn. Before praying Muslims must clean their teeth, mouth, nose, face, hands, arms and feet. While praying they must face towards Mecca, where the holy shrine of the Ka'ba is located. Communal prayer is held on Fridays; on the other days of the week Muslims can pray alone or in groups, or in the mosque as on Fridays, as opportunity offers.

The third pillar of faith is *zakat*, which means 'purification' but denotes payment of 2.5 per cent of one's income to the state for disbursement to the needy. The fourth pillar is *sawm* or fasting, which is practised from dawn to sunset every day in the month of Ramadan. Since the fast involves total abstinence from food and drink, there are exemptions for those who are sick, or very young, and travellers. Ramadan ends with the festival of Eid (*Eid al-Fitr*) during which Muslims visit relatives and exchange gifts.

The fifth and final pillar of the faith is *Hadj*, the pilgrimage to Mecca. There pilgrims walk around the Ka'ba, said by Muslims to be God's first house on earth, built by the prophet Abraham. Other authorities say it houses a rock – perhaps a meteorite – that was venerated by pre-Muslim Arabs.

Islam was founded by Muhammad of Mecca, who was born in that city in or about the year 570 CE, and who at about the age of forty, in 610, began to receive revelations from God, conveyed by the angel Gabriel. (Strictly speaking Muhammad's followers do not regard him as the founder of their religion but as the restorer of its true lineaments.) Over the following twenty-three years Muhammad dictated the revelations to those of his followers who, unlike him, could write, and after his death the dictated texts were collected and arranged into the sacred book of Islam, the Qur'an or Koran. This book teaches that in addition to believing in the one God, Allah, the faithful must believe his revelations in the Koran and the messages conveyed by his angels. It also teaches that there will be a Day of Judgement in which the good will be admitted to the joys of Paradise while the bad will be flung into hell-fire.

Because the residents of Mecca were not inclined to accept Muhammad's revelations, preferring their ancestral polytheism, he and his followers left that town and went to Yathrib, later renamed Medina (which means 'city of the prophet'). This happened in the year 622, and is known as the *Hijra* or emigration. It is accounted by Muslims as the founding event of their religion, for it was from this time that the struggles began by which Muhammad conquered most of Arabia, including in 629 his hometown of Mecca. These conquests in turn were the starting point for Islam's subsequent spread over the Middle East, North Africa, Central Asia, and northern parts of the Indian subcontinent, reaching into Spain in the west and eventually as far as Malaya and Indonesia in the east.

After the death of Muhammad in 632 the second phase of Islamic history occurred, a crucial one as it transpired because it saw a fundamental split within Islam itself. There was immediate disagreement about who should succeed Muhammad as leader, and the rival claimants and their backers between them served as the first four caliphs (nevertheless known as the 'rightly guided caliphs') in a tumultuous period for the expansion of Islam and the fate of the faith itself. The first four caliphs were Abu Bakr (632–4), Umar ibn al-Khattab (634–44), Uthman ibn Affan (644–56), and Ali ibn Abi Talib (656–61), who was both cousin and son-in-law to Muhammad. Umar extended the empire of Islam at the expense of the Byzantine and Persian empires to include Syria, Palestine, Persia and Egypt, and Uthman consolidated Umar's conquests.

Internal politics led to the assassinations by rivals of Umar in 644, Uthman in 656 and Ali in 661, and the schism of Islam into Sunni and Shi'a factions. The Sunnis regarded the first three caliphs as legitimate successors to Muhammad, whereas the Shi'as regarded Ali as the only rightful successor. After Ali's murder the caliphate was seized by Mu'awiyah, until then governor of Syria, and he founded the Umayyad dynasty. In the seventy years of its existence the dynasty extended Muslim power to Spain in the west and Sindh in the east. Under its auspices the great mosque of Damascus was built in the location and with some of the materials of the Christian cathedral that had, in its turn, been constructed out of the mighty Temple of Jupiter that the Romans built there on the site of a temple to a yet earlier Arabic deity.

In 750 the Umayyad dynasty was overthrown by the Abbasids, who made Baghdad their capital, and for the next five centuries Islam enjoyed its golden age – even though the Abbasid empire itself soon fragmented into a number of autonomous and eventually independent regions. By 1055 the Seljuk Turks had wrested power from the Abbasid caliph, while still respecting his titular religious position, rather as Japanese emperors continued to rule powerlessly during the shogun eras. The resulting pluralism in the Muslim world allowed poetry, philosophy, art and science to flourish, and debate was free. The thinkers ibn-Sina and al-Farabi sought to import Greek philosophical ideas into Islam; they were successfully opposed by al-Ghazzali. Sufism, which had arisen under the Umayyads as an ascetic devotional sect that disagreed with the worldly avocations of the conquering caliphate, developed (with al-Ghazzali's help) into a mystical movement. Shi'ites split further among themselves owing to disagreements about the correct lineage of imams, these being the infallible politico-religious guides who descend from Ali.

From the ninth century onwards Islam's western possessions in Spain and bits of Italy began to be retaken by Christian Europe. Emboldened by these successes, Europe's Christians organized a succession of crusades to drive Islam from the Holy Land. This was an initially triumphant enterprise but in its turn was reversed by later Muslim victories (notably under Saladin, who retook Jerusalem during the Second Crusade).

Islam's golden age was brought to an end by the Mongol invasions which eventuated in the capture of Baghdad in 1268. In the following centuries the Mongol khanates in the overrun former Muslim lands themselves converted to Islam, opening the way for the religion's spread into Central Asia and, under the Mughals eastward and the Ottomans westward, into the development of major empires.

The two main branches of Islam to emerge from the faith's early history are, as noted, the Sunni and the Shi'a sects. The former constitute the great majority of Muslims. They follow the path laid down by Muhammad as recorded in the Koran and the *hadith*, sayings reported in addition to what is written in the Koran. There is a variety of legal schools and theological traditions within Sunni Islam, all acceptable and accepted by most Sunnis, although as with most religious movements there are those who disapprove of too much latitude and seek to restore the purity of doctrine. The Salafi sect is an example. The Wahhabis are an especially austere sect, who would deserve the name of fundamentalists if the religion as a whole was not one in which fundamentals play such a significant role.

While according greatest authority to the Koran itself, Sunnis say that its suras (chapters) should be understood in the light of sound *hadiths*, and interpreted in the context of the Koran as a whole. Believing that faith and works are equally important, and that Allah has a plan for the world and the individuals in it, Sunnis emphasize the controlling influence of Islam for matters of government and public policy. This includes regarding Shari'a (law) and the collective interest and opinion of the Muslim community as sovereign.

The Shi'ites constitute Islam's second-largest branch, though they are far less numerous than the Sunnis. Their name 'Shi'a' means 'faction' or 'party' and 'Shi'at Ali' means 'the party of Ali'. They believe in the Imamate, that is, the divinely ordained succession of leaders after Muhammad, the first of which in their view was Ali. The imams have absolute authority in matters of doctrine and tradition. In addition to believing in the succession of imams Shi'ites have their own preferences as to which *hadith* are genuine or significant, and they have their own tradition of jurisprudence.

Shi'ism is subdivided into a number of sects, the main one being the Twelvers, who believe that twelve imams succeeded Muhammad, the last being Hujjat ibn Hasan ibn Ali, the Mahdi or saviour, born in 868 and since then hidden by God until the time comes for his appearance to save the world. His hidden state is known as 'The Occultation'. Other Shi'ite sects include the Alawi and the Ismaili groups, the latter with its own subdivisions – one headed by the Aga Khan, whose followers include some of the most modern and secularized of all Muslims.

There are other Islamic sects: Qadianis, Yazidis, Abadites, Kemalists, Druze, Zaydis, Dawoodi Bohra, Sufis (among whom there are a number of orders), Al-Ahbash, Mahdavi, and more – it is hard for an outsider to count them accurately, since many are subdivisions, offshoots, or regional or ethnic variants of others. There can be bitter differences among them, though; some do not regard others as Muslim at all, which is a harder line even than recognizing them as Muslim but heretical.

An Islamic concept that has come much to the notice of non-Muslims in recent times, not least because of the atrocities committed by a band of terrorists in the name of Islam in New York and Washington on 11 September 2001 – events which accelerated some dismally unhappy changes in the world – is *jihad*, a word that means 'struggle' or 'striving', and is glossed by some Muslim authorities as 'struggling to the utmost of one's power and effort to contend with disapproved objects'. Suitably qualified it refers to matters of morality and faith, as an internal matter; left unqualified it is interpreted as struggle against opponents of the faith and the unbeliever (the *kufr*). Among Shi'as and Sufis a distinction is drawn between the 'greater jihad' and the 'lesser jihad', meaning by the former a spiritual struggle, and by the latter, warfare against enemies. This latter sense has the weight of Islamic jurisprudence behind it, relating not just to struggle against apostates and criminals, but to those who refuse to submit to Islam.

No mention of jihad can pass without raising the question of Islam in the contemporary world. It should properly seem odd to ask the question at all, for Islam is a major world religion, comprising 20 per cent of the world's population, and it is as much a 'Western' religion as a religion specific to any other region such as the Middle East, Pakistan or Indonesia, because there are millions of Muslims in Europe and North America, the majority of them natives of the countries in those areas.

At the same time, though, it has to be accepted that many of the values, beliefs and practices in Islam, and certainly in some versions of Islam, do not sit comfortably with the dominant Enlightenment-paradigm values of the Western world, and it is a fact that some of the tensions that exist in the world arise precisely from that fact. Consequently a number of legitimate and pressing questions arise about how Islam relates to such movements and the ideas that inspire Western polities, such as globalization, secularism, pluralism, democracy, tolerance, human rights and especially women's rights, environmentalism, business and finance, and in general Western 'liberalism'.

There is no automatic suggestion here that Islam is incompatible with all or even any of these things, but neither is it clear that how they work in Western liberal democracies is always consistent with some versions of Islam or some Muslim groups. Among the most urgent projects in today's world is clarifying exactly how these questions are to be answered, and if the answers are dusty ('Ah, what a dusty answer gets the soul/ When hot for certainties in this our life!' wrote George Meredith), what should then be done.

It will be gathered from the tenor of remarks about Christianity elsewhere in these pages that this writer does not hold any brief for religion in general, and this applies here too. Much might be said, not least about the associated texts and traditions, which come as quite a surprise and profound disappointment to a first-time examiner. But this simple, if not simplistic and infantilizing, faith is not at all good at taking criticism or satire, usually a symptom either of lack of self-confidence or of unquestioning and unquestionable iron conviction, or – which is worse – both; and it is the faith which at present anyway has an extremely violent fringe from which murder has come, continues to come, and can all too readily come in response to perceived insult or threat. This is a disgraceful fact: but fact it is, and one therefore does well·to remember the story of the philosopher and the ghost, in which the former chose to assert his claim over the latter by treating it as circumstances required.

See: CHRISTIANITY, JUDAISM, RELIGION

JUDAISM

Judaism is one of the oldest surviving religious traditions in the world – it might vie with Hinduism over questions of antiquity – and in almost every account it is described as 'the oldest monotheistic religion in the world'. That it was not monotheistic until about the middle of the first millennium before our common era is not often mentioned, but the evidence for belief in a multiplicity of gods (these being the gods of other tribes whom the Jews were strictly forbidden to follow) abounds in what Christians call 'the Old Testament'.

The tribal deity of the Jews would seem to have started as a volcano god, appearing as a burning bush on a mountaintop and a pillar of smoke in the distance. The Jews' own traditions suggest that as a people they emerged from the area between the great civilizations of the Nile on one side and the Tigris and Euphrates on the other, but spent time as an underclass in Egypt, doubtless having been impressed into service under one of the powerful pharaonic dynasties.

Jewish history, apart from the legends of the earliest patriarchs Abraham, Isaac and Jacob, starts with the exodus from Egypt under Moses – perhaps himself an Egyptian, but accorded a Hebrew ancestry by means of the basket-in-the-Nile story. After forty years of wandering in the wilderness under Moses they conquered the land called Canaan – by remarkably bloody means, replete with massacres and much enslavement of women and children – and settled there in twelve tribal zones. Canaan approximates to an area covering today's Israel, Sinai, south-western parts of Syria and western Jordan.

The development of the Jewish religion is intimately connected to the history of the Jewish people, which they regarded as being the same thing as the story of their relationship with their deity. Regarding themselves as especially elected by their deity – who eventually became the one and only God; all the others were demoted to devils and finally to non-existence – it was impossible for them to see their history, battles, vicissitudes and triumphs as anything other than the fraught relationship with a being who, to outside eyes anyway, appears remarkably fickle, intemperate, vindictive, not very intelligent, partial, and unreliable. This unappealing deity is of course a projection from the quarrelsomeness of the Jewish people themselves, as portrayed by their own documents, which testify to much bickering and disagreement about most things, not least their religion, which for them – for the reasons just mentioned – was a matter of politics.

Jewish observance – the feasts and holidays of the religion, and its rituals – are closely tied to their history. One of the great feasts is the Passover, commemorating the occasion on which God sent a plague of death on the firstborn children of Egypt to punish the Egyptians for their treatment of his chosen people. The Jews placed a sign on their houses so that the angel of death would pass over them in his murderous work. (This kind of detail – the inability of a supernatural being to tell the houses of Jews and Egyptians apart unless there was a notice attached to the front door – seems to do nothing to set off a gullibility alert among the faithful.) Because of this connection between doctrine and history, and because of the internal divisions of Judaism into more and less conservative and orthodox sects, the following outline of the religion's doctrines is summary.

Today Judaism is describable as a monotheistic religion whose principal teachings are contained in the Tanakh as interpreted in the Talmud and associated texts. The Tanakh is the Jewish Bible, roughly speaking what Christians call the Old Testament; the first five or Mosaic books of the Tanakh, called the Torah, are regarded as divinely revealed – denying this is regarded by many as heretical.

The founding act of the religion was a covenant between Abraham and God, recorded in Genesis 12–17, in which the latter promised the former to 'make him a great nation' which would occupy the land from the Nile to the Euphrates. The mark of this covenant was to be circumcision of all male children. Somewhat confusingly, Abraham was also promised to be the father of many nations, but nothing is said about where they will live. This desire for many progeny is the wish-fulfilment dream of any herding people, longing for the increase of their flocks, for that is their wealth.

There are in fact a number of covenants between the deity and various patriarchs and prophets, revealing the patchwork-quilt character of the Tanakh. In Genesis 8–9, a passage embodying memories of floods that the peoples of the great Middle Eastern rivers assuredly passed down with embellishments over many centuries, God makes a covenant with Noah, somewhat shamefaced at having massacred humanity by drowning almost all of it. He then promises not to do this again, and fixes a rainbow in the sky as a mark of that covenant; he puts all plants and animals under mankind's control, commands capital punishment for murder, and outlaws eating meat with the blood still in it.

Other covenants were made with Jacob, Moses and David, and nearly a dozen with the whole people of Israel. Although the various covenants contain injunctions and rules, and embody a contract to the effect that if Israel will observe them faithfully then God will prosper them, the greater part of Jewish belief and practice is embodied elsewhere: in the rabbinical literature (notably the Mishnah and the two Talmuds) and the legal tradition based on the Torah, said to contain over six hundred commandments, although many of them are restricted in application – some to men only, some to the priestly castes only, some only to those living in the traditional lands of historical Israel.

It is needless to say that the combination of theology, tradition, and the love of argument and contention rather characteristic of the Jewish mind, has made a massive tangle out of these sources, so that almost everything and nothing can be said to be a component of Jewish doctrine. The twelfth-century Spanish-Jewish philosopher and rabbi Moses Maimonides endeavoured to formulate the principles of Jewish faith, though his 'Thirteen Principles' took a long time to emerge from controversy and neglect and to become in part more generally accepted. Since they are practically the only authoritative summary of articles of faith a non-Jew would find if looking for one, they bear statement, and are as follows.

I am – so Maimonides requires a true Jew to say – completely certain that the Creator made all things and is, was and will always be the creator of all things. I know with complete certainty that he is One alone, and ever was and will be. I know with complete certainty that he is immaterial; and that he is the first and last of all things. I know with complete certainty that he is the only being to whom it is right to pray. I know with complete certainty that the prophecies of Moses, our teacher, are true. I know with complete certainty that the Torah is what was given to Moses; and that it will never be changed or that any other law will come from the Creator. I know with complete certainty that the Creator knows all the thoughts and deeds of mankind. I know with complete certainty that the Creator will reward those who keep his commandments and will punish those who do not keep his commandments. I know with complete certainty that the Messiah will come; I wait every day for his coming even though he tarries. I know with complete certainty that the dead will return to life whenever it pleases the Creator to bring them back.

This statement of faith cannot be regarded as on a par with the Christian's Nicene Creed, say, and earlier Jewish critics of it were quick to point out that, traditionally, Judaism had always been more a matter of practice than belief: to be a Jew was to adhere to the customs and to perform the rituals, rather than to subscribe to a set of dogmas. However, as time has passed Maimonides's principles have acquired something of the status of a creed, not least among Orthodox groups.

Mention of Orthodox Jewry prompts a remark about the variety of Jewish denominations which, like their Christian and Muslim counterparts, differ in doctrine and practice from one another. This variety is great, ranging from Humanist Judaism which is cultural and non-theistic, to extreme forms of orthodoxy as represented by Haredi Judaism and its subset of Hasidic Judaism. Haredi Judaism is absorbed by painstaking and minute observance of ritual, dress and taboo. Votaries are recognizable by their odd tradition of wearing eighteenth-century garb, as if something happened then that froze their then customary wear into articles not of clothing but of faith.

Despite its name, Conservative Judaism is somewhat more open to the need for adjustment to changing circumstances in the interpretation of law, while Reform (sometimes called Progressive or Liberal) Judaism is the most open and relaxed form of all, though perhaps that accolade is even better merited by 'Reconstructionist' Judaism. Both forms allow men and women to sit together in synagogue, and do not fetishize ritual and observance as their Orthodox brethren do.

Given the importance both of history and of observance to the character of Judaism, one cannot neglect to mention the large number of important feasts and holidays. The first in order of frequency is the Sabbath (Shabbat), the weekly rest day that occupies the twenty-four hours between sundown on Fridays and sundown on Saturdays. A ritual meal is eaten on the Friday evening, and more observant Jews avoid 'work', which includes switching on lights, driving a car, pressing the buttons in an elevator, or purchasing anything.

The three major holy days of the Jewish calendar are Sukkot or Tabernacles, commemorating the forty years of wandering in the wilderness under Moses's leadership, Shavuot or Pentecost, commemorating the deity's gift of the Torah on Mount Sinai, and Pesach or Passover, commemorating the Exodus. This is the feast at which unleavened bread is eaten; on the morning of the Seder – the feast, held in the Jewish family home rather than the synagogue, at which the Haggadah is read, celebrating the liberation of the Jews from Pharaoh's slavery – all leavened bread is burned and the home meticulously cleaned to expunge all traces of it.

The holy days of the Jewish calendar are Rosh Hashanah, or Day of Remembrance, and Yom Kippur, the Day of Atonement, for which Rosh Hashanah is a preparation. Rosh Hashanah is the Jewish New Year, and the ten-day interval to Yom Kippur is a time of reflection and repentance; Yom Kippur itself is the Jews' most solemn holy day on which they are meant to fast and seek forgiveness for sins. Rather as Christmas attracts non-religious Christians, Yom Kippur is an observance that attracts non-religious Jews, who may participate in the meal on the eve of the fast day, say the Kol Nidre prayer at the beginning of the service at the synagogue, and even wear white clothing as the Orthodox do. Blowing a ram's horn is a feature of this period, but the blast of the horn that ends observances on the day following Yom Kippur is especially significant.

Hanukkah or the Festival of Lights was a minor holiday until fairly recently; because it is close in date to Christmas it has come into fashion as a Jewish alternative or analogue to Christmas activities in the United States and elsewhere. It commemorates the rededication of the Temple in Jerusalem after its desecration in 168 BCE by the Seleucid ruler Antiochus IV Epiphanes, whose soldiers had slaughtered a pig (a very unclean animal in Jewish lore) in the Temple precincts. This happened in the conflict between the Seleucids and the Maccabees; the latter triumphed over the former, allowing rededication of the Temple to occur.

If Hanukkah is a happy holiday season – it lasts eight days, reprising the eight days on which the Temple lamp miraculously burned though only having enough oil in it for one day – Purim is even more so. Celebrating the survival of the Jews of Persia despite a plot to massacre them (an event recorded in the Book of Esther), it involves eating, drinking, dressing up, and having a party. More religious observances should be like this; perhaps if all were, the world would be the better for it.

Most traditions take notice of important transitions in life, such as birth, coming of age, marriage, and death; in Judaism these transitions are observed with particular ceremony. As with other traditions, boys and men tend to have more importance in community eyes than girls and women, so the Brit Milah (circumcision rite on the eighth day of life) and the Bar Mitzvah (at age thirteen; for girls there is a Bat Mitzvah at age twelve) loom large in early life. At the end of the wedding ceremony in a synagogue the groom smashes a glass underfoot to remind everyone of the Temple's destruction and the dispersion of the Jews. Mourning for the dead likewise has its formula, notably the Shiva (the seven evenings of wake in the home of the deceased).

Until the destruction of the Temple in 70 CE two inherited priestly castes, the Cohens and the Levites, officiated at ceremonies; the Cohens performed the sacrifices and the Levites sang the psalms. Today descendants of these lines are called respectively first and second to read the Torah in synagogue. They no longer exercise priestly functions, though some believe that when a third Temple arises they will again be required to do so. For almost all the last two thousand years every Jew has been his own priest, though for the more important religious observances the presence of at least ten adult men (or for more liberal Jews, ten adults) is required. Although a rabbi is not necessary for a congregation, the latter is most likely to have one; he is a scholar who can answer questions about Jewish law and custom so that the congregation can manage its affairs properly. Some congregations also have cantors to sing the traditional music.

Among the outstanding facts about people of Jewish faith is that their contribution to mankind's arts, sciences and humanities is out of all proportion to their numbers, and through the last two thousand years they have been the victims of repeated persecution and oppression, often of the most horrendous kind. Neither fact appears to have much to do with their beliefs, though each fact may have something to do with the other. The disgraceful fact of anti-Semitism is discussed in the article thus headed elsewhere in these pages.

See: ANTI-SEMITISM, RELIGION

JUSTICE

The concept of justice is as much discussed as it is important, because it plays a key role in ethics, law and politics. The idea of 'distributive justice' is central, because it puts to work the intuitions and experiences we all have about fairness and its absence in our lives and societies. Which social benefits and burdens are to be distributed to whom, and why to some and not others? Are there any grounds for sometimes making unequal distributions, or exempting some members of society from a share of the duties and burdens expected of most? One way of framing these questions is to ask, 'In what ways and circumstances should people be treated equally, and in what ways and circumstances should they be treated differently? What justifies the treatment in each case?'

Fundamentally, justice is about the arrangement of relationships in a society. One of the great modern theoreticians of justice, John Rawls, said, 'Justice is the first virtue of social institutions, as truth is of systems of thought.' It is argued by empirical psychologists and animal ethologists that instincts of justice are hard-wired, as experiment and observation repeatedly show; the example of the innate sense of justice in children is well known. The ancient Greeks were, as with so many things, the first to rate the possession of a sense of justice, and moreover one on which one acts, as a virtue.

Views about the nature of justice have been various: Plato defined it as harmony or balance in the state, thinkers of a religious stamp have attributed it to the ordinances of a deity, and in modern European thought (that is, from the sixteenth century onwards) one influential idea has it that justice arises from natural law, in which each individual has a claim to his or her due by nature, a claim that no subsequent arrangement of society can trump; while another, very different and even more influential idea is that justice is the product of a social contract.

This last idea has considerable influence on contemporary philosophical debates about justice, not least because of the use made of it by John Rawls in his seminal *A Theory of Justice*. He speculates on what we would choose by way of arrangements in a society if – before entering it, and without knowing what position we would occupy in it or what natural endowments or other advantages we would have or lack – we were invited to think about how we would like that society to be organized. Rational reflection would, he argued, prompt us to desire that each person should have an equal right to the most extensive basic liberties compatible with the liberties of all, fair access to opportunities for each, and the greatest benefit to the least advantaged consistent with the benefit of all. These would in his view constitute the principles of justice for the society, and in essence they equate justice with fairness.

Rawls's theory is describable as liberal or left-leaning, and was opposed by a conservative or right-leaning argument by Robert Nozick, who claimed in his *Anarchy, State and Utopia* that justice is served when a person possesses some good (especially property) because it was justly acquired in the first place, perhaps by the work of one's hands in clearing wilderness for agriculture, and justly transferred by sale or inheritance. Governments which dispossess people, without their consent, in order to redistribute their goods to others – in the interests of greater equality, say

– are guilty of theft. He regards taxation for the purpose of redistribution of wealth as theft.

Questions of justice also arise in connection with punishment. Is justice served only by retribution, as in the 'eye for an eye' tenet of the Old Testament, and the correlative justification given for capital punishment of murderers ('a life for a life')? If punishment of those who break the law is intended to rehabilitate them, or protect society from them, or deter others from doing the same, in what sense is justice served by their implementation?

As important, if not more so, the idea of justice in law is closely allied to the idea of due process, and of the transparency, consistency and good order of legal proceedings. If legal institutions are not designed to ensure that the administration of justice is scrupulous and proper, then they risk failing to deliver justice. 'Justice must be seen to be done in order to be done' is a component of this. The independence of the judiciary, the fair examination of evidence and argument by both sides, rules of evidence and disclosure, and expert attention to the requirements of legislation and the pronouncements of precedent, figure in the institutional arrangements aimed at ensuring that justice is done. Even the best efforts in these directions sometimes fail, as with all things made by humankind: which, incidentally, is one main argument against capital punishment.

Common sense applied at any point in the history of a society should always be able to reach a consensus about what distributions of benefits and burdens count as fair. Reflection should also always confirm the inalienability of such fundamental political and legal rights as the right to vote and the right to equal treatment before the law. This entails that certain rights are universal, namely those that regimes of human rights are designed to protect. Accordingly a society that recognizes justice as the foundation of equal treatment in certain respects, and equitable treatment in all other respects, has the makings of a good society. 'Equality, and where equality is unjust, equity' would be its entirely appropriate slogan.

See: ENLIGHTENMENT, EQUALITY, HUMAN RIGHTS, LAW

LAW

Odd as it may seem at first to say so, one of the most distinctive things about humanity, one of the things most conducive to civilization, and one of the things potentially most important for the safety, liberty and flourishing of human individuals, is law. I mean law in the sense of 'law of the land', law as framed by legislatures and applied by judges, law as what organizes and regulates interpersonal and institutional relationships. Without it what we have is merely a state of nature, where might is right and we get what we can and suffer if we cannot. Law came into existence because natural power is not equally distributed among people, and the protection of the weak against the depredations of the strong is a necessity if the weak are to have any chance. Given this, it is of the first moment to understand the nature of law, and what has been said and thought about it in the counsels of the learned.

The laws governing the activities of people in societies, and attributed to the authorship of gods, kings or parliaments, are in essence stipulative or imperative: someone, or some organization, decides that things shall henceforth be done in thus-and-such a way; and if the decision is properly taken – or backed by the validity, and perhaps the power, of the legislating authority – it becomes law for those to whom it applies.

This sketch of course begs many questions, and prompts others. Philosophical debate about the nature of law is called 'jurisprudence', and modern discussions of it begin with John Austin (1790–1859) and his *The Province of Jurisprudence Determined* (1825). He defined law as a command given by a sovereign and enforced by a sanction, where a 'sovereign' is an identified common superior (whether an individual or a body) which the majority of a given society's members habitually obey, and which is itself supreme. This 'command' theory of law seems obvious, and Austin was not its first exponent; Jean Bodin in *Six Books of the Republic* (1576), Thomas Hobbes in *Leviathan* (1651) and Jeremy Bentham in *A Fragment on Government* (composed 1776) took similar views. Austin is, however, its first systematic proponent.

A crucial feature of Austin's view is rejection of the concept of 'natural law' (not the same thing, note, as 'law of nature' in the scientist's sense, which is simply a statement of observed regularities). It had long been argued that man-made laws are valid only if they do not conflict with a higher law, such as the law of God; the validity of law, in other words, is related to its moral content. Austin rejected this, saying that if a law is commanded by a sovereign, it is ipso facto valid, irrespective of its morality. This is called 'positivism' and turns on holding that the question whether a law is a law is one thing, and the question whether it is morally acceptable is quite another thing.

Austin's plausible-seeming theory was eventually challenged in an important work by H.L.A. Hart, *The Concept of Law* (1961, new edition

2005). Hart showed that laws as they in fact exist in societies are not like orders backed by threats, as the command theory states. Nor is Austin's theory of unlimited sovereignty satisfactory, because legislative bodies or individuals are typically constrained in their powers – say, by a constitution; and can in certain circumstances be checked by external agencies – say, a court; and might ultimately owe their authority to something else – say, an electorate. Hart's view of the nature of a legal system turns instead on the idea of 'rules of recognition', which enable us to recognize laws by identifying their sources – whether some or all of parliament, courts, and constitution.

But Hart accepted Austin's positivism, which led to a celebrated debate with L.H. Fuller about the relation of law and morality. What was at issue between Hart and Fuller can be vividly illustrated by an example of law in action that had taken place during the dozen years before they debated each other in the pages of the *Harvard Law Review* of 1958, those events being the anti-Nazi trials in Germany.

Something like the ancient idea of 'natural law', whose first traces are evident in Plato and Aristotle, but which flowered in Stoicism and such works as Cicero's *On Duties* and Marcus Aurelius's *Meditations*, and which later assumed a central place in Roman Catholic legal thinking under the influence of Aquinas's *Summa Theologica*, was invoked by German prosecutors after 1945 when they tried people whose defence was that they had acted in obedience to Nazi laws. The courts held that those laws were 'contrary to the sound conscience and sense of justice of all decent human beings'. Fuller applauded the German courts' decision, arguing that a legal system must have an 'inner morality' to justify it, where this phrase denotes possession of such features as generality, consistency, and clarity. Hart responded that it confused matters to say that a law is not a law if it is evil, rather than recognizing it as a law but an evil one which needs to be opposed or changed. This is not a rejection of the idea that a relationship exists between law and morality; rather, it is a rejection of the idea that a law is a law only if it is moral. Hart's central point was that we need to hold apart the concept of 'law as it is and law as it ought to be'.

Austin's reason for rejecting natural law theory, as with David Hume before him in *An Enquiry Concerning the Principles of Morals* (1751), was that it attempts to deduce an 'ought' – a statement of what should be done – from an 'is' – a description of natural facts about the nature of human beings, their proper goals, and what helps them flourish. Others pointed to the opposing claims made by appeal to the concept;

for example, John Locke held that democracy is enjoined by natural law, whereas Robert Filmer argued the exact contrary on the ground that God, the author of such law, 'did always govern his own people by monarchy'.

If Fuller revived the idea of natural law in modified form, J.M. Finnis revived it much more directly. In his *Natural Law and Natural Rights* he argued that there are 'human goods' – such as acquiring knowledge, enjoying oneself, having friends – which are attained by exercising 'practical reasonableness', the methods of which guide behaviour and therefore constitute the content of natural law. 'Sound laws,' he states, derive from 'unchanging principles that have their force from reasonableness'. The morality and law debate remains vitally important.

As with all philosophical debates, discussion of the nature of law immediately spills into discussion of closely related concepts. In this case the most important are *rights* and *justice*. Some of the greatest contributions of twentieth-century jurisprudence have been made in discussion of these fundamental concepts: the classics are, on the first, Ronald Dworkin's *Taking Rights Seriously* (revised edition 1978), and on the second, C.H. Perelman's *The Idea of Justice and the Problem of Argument* (1963), John Rawls's *A Theory of Justice* (1971), and Robert Nozick's *Anarchy, State and Utopia* (1974). (See the respective entries for HUMAN RIGHTS and JUSTICE for separate comment on them.)

There are important differences between the types of law known respectively as 'common law' and 'civil law'. The essence of common law is precedent, whereas that of civil law, whose roots lie in the law of Roman imperial times, is statute. Common law first evolved in England, and followed its empire across the world. Its former colonies, including the United States (except for Louisiana), are largely common law jurisdictions therefore.

Common law is judge-made law, and its guiding motivation lies in the idea that the commonly agreed good sense of experienced people will discern what natural justice requires on a case-by-case basis. This is worked out in the adversarial setting in which a case is tried, the 'trying' consisting in the weighing of the merits of the arguments and evidence adduced by both sides in opposition to one another. The decisions reached provide the precedent for how later like cases are to be resolved, so that a body of judgements builds up, guiding and regularizing. The principle at work is expressed in the Latin tag *stare decesis*, 'to stand by decisions [made]'. This is to be done until the decisions in question have become, by the workings of time and change, outdated and unjust. This qualification is vital, because without it the system of accreted laws would have no flexibility, and would not be able to evolve in response to new needs and circumstances.

Custom and tradition are involved too, influencing the manner in which trials are conducted, dictating what is proper in the way of argument and evidence, appropriately regulating the role of witnesses, and governing the powers of presiding judges. Since the nineteenth century statute has come to play an increasingly large role in common law jurisdictions, especially in the criminal law, though in many instances the supervening statutes simply encode and tidy common law precedent. In the civil law arena, for a notable example in tort, common law and case-based argument remain.

Perhaps the most significant date in the history of common law is 1154 CE, when Henry II ascended the English throne. To him goes the credit for generalizing common law to his entire kingdom, displacing the variety of local legal customs and traditions that had prevailed until then. Moreover he abolished a plethora of arbitrary punishments, and introduced the jury system. It was his regularization of the administration of justice that brought him into conflict with the Church, which was jealous of the privileges and independence of its canonical courts, and from this flowed the 'martyrdom' of Thomas à Becket.

The common law framework of the United States is supplemented by a Constitution which, in addition to setting out the main lineaments of the instruments of governance and the balances that obtain among them, accords to citizens a set of inalienable rights. It also gives individual States in the federation scope to enact their own laws provided that they do not conflict with federal law, although latterly codes of uniform procedure have resolved various inconsistencies that arose as a result of too great a divergence in States' rights.

Most legal regimes in the world, though, are civil law regimes. Civil law rests historically on Roman law, and in particular on the *corpus juris civilis* of the Emperor Justinian (535 CE). It was developed in the Middle Ages by scholars and jurists into a system that was common throughout much of Europe until the Westphalian settlement of the seventeenth century gave an impetus to increasing national diversity in institutions and legal codes.

These, however, retained much fidelity to their roots while incorporating new thinking and practices, especially during the eighteenth-century Enlightenment. The prime example of such developments is the Code Napoléon. In the Far East, and especially Japan, nineteenth-century modernization drew much from the German civil law model, because

Germany's then rise to world power status was much admired by Oriental modernizers.

The essence of civil law is legislation. It aims at consistent and comprehensive codification of law, the ideal having originally been that the law would therefore only require application. In practice the inescapable nuances of individual cases mean that judges in civil law jurisdictions have to interpret, reason, and seek guidance from precedent, so that the actual practice of a judge in a civil law court has a good deal in common with a judge in a common law court.

There is, though, a very significant difference between judges in the two traditions. It is that whereas in common law jurisdictions judges are drawn from among the ranks of practising attorneys, barristers (and, increasingly, solicitors), in civil law jurisdictions they are trained and appointed separately from the practising lawyer cadres. This difference extends yet further into the investigatory and inquisitorial role played by civil law judges in criminal cases.

If there is one thing that draws a line between civilization and barbarism, it is the rule of law. It is a bulwark against arbitrary power, it provides remedies for the injured, its due processes are a safeguard – imperfectly so, but far better than none at all – against injustice and miscarriage. As human attempts go it is imperfect and occasionally corruptible also, and requires constant attention and renewal; it can be barbarously used and abused – history is full of examples of consciously discriminatory laws, for notable examples, against Jews, black people and women. But taken in the round it exemplifies the human attempt, when at its best and most thoughtful, to order things in the direction of what is right, fair and good, impartially considered. Not one of us would choose to live outside a regime of law; all of us would surely wish to live under just, impartially administered, sensibly revisable laws.

In modern Western liberal democracies one of the main problems with law is the difficulty of changing it when it has become obsolete. Some cite this as a virtue, saying that it is better that laws should change ponderously and slowly. Others say that needless injustice is inflicted while an outdated law continues to operate, too often surviving past the demise of its point or usefulness. In early nineteenth-century England when people could be hanged for stealing bread, juries simply stopped convicting because of the unjust harshness of the penalty; when laws become unenforceable, or lose their moral authority, reform beckons – and it would be desirable to have somewhat more nimble reform than is standardly the case.

But law matters, and although it is a source of immense profit to those who engage in it and a source of immense frustration and heartache to those who fall at the wrong angle into its vastly grinding wheels (think Jarndyce versus Jarndyce) – and although yet further it is better to have as little to do with it as possible – it is nevertheless a very good thing that it exists.

See: CIVILIZATION, HUMAN RIGHTS, JUSTICE, PUNISHMENT

LIBERALISM

Liberalism is a political outlook premised on the realization, by moderate constitutional means, of socially progressive ideals, the establishment and protection of civil liberties, the rule of law, and government by consent.

This definition is most likely to be recognized by those sympathetic to it in the country of liberalism's birth, namely England, and countries influenced by English traditions. It found its first formulation in the treatises on government and toleration by the seventeenth-century philosopher John Locke (1632–1704). In France definitions of liberalism tend to place greater emphasis on secularism and egalitarianism. In America the word has pejorative connotations for those on the right wing of politics, betokening secularism, left-wing political and economic views (in fact and in practice extremely mild ones, given the American setting), and a defence of civil liberties of a kind to inflame right-wing opposition, as relating (for example) to homosexuality, abortion, sexually explicit cinema films, and irreverent and even blasphemous art.

The central concept in liberalism is *liberty*. In the view of liberalism's first major prophets, John Locke and John Stuart Mill, individual freedom is a basic given, and anyone who would limit individual freedom in any way is under an obligation to make an ironclad case for doing so. That in effect means that the very idea of government has to be justified. An example of how that is to be done is provided by the 'social contract' theorists, chief among them Thomas Hobbes, John Locke (again) and Jean-Jacques Rousseau, who argued that in a state of complete and universal individual freedom – in short: anarchy – the strong prey upon the weak, and the quality of life for all is low. By yielding some of their personal sovereignty, individuals benefit from the protection and aid given by membership of society (for Thomas Hobbes, the protection in question is afforded by an absolute ruler), and these benefits are what justify government.

See: DEMOCRACY, HUMAN RIGHTS, LIBERTY, TOLERANCE

LIBERTY

Individual freedom in political and religious outlook, in speech, in a variety of choices affecting personal life and work, and in movement within, from and to one's own country, constitutes liberty in the chief political sense of this word. It has to be contrasted immediately with licence, which is wholly unbridled freedom to do and be even those things that interfere with the liberties of others, and might cause them harm. As this suggests, liberty cannot be absolute; it must be consistent with the interests of others. But this suggests a need for watchfulness against spurious minimizations of liberty on the specious grounds that they interfere with the interests of others.

Liberty has been very hard won in the Western tradition. It involved struggles against the hegemony of religion that put to death those who refused to conform to its orthodoxy, absolute monarchy based on the notion of 'divine right', slavery, ignorance, the subjection and disenfranchisement of women, criminalization of association for political and trades union purposes, and much besides.

Libertarianism is an extreme form of advocacy in favour of liberty. It preaches absence of legal and institutional restraints, even those devised to protect the weak against the strong, and its logical limit is anarchy, which literally means 'no rule', that is, no ruler. Conservatives and reactionaries, fearful of what they think would be the disorder and rapine that would ensue on an anarchic or libertarian dispensation, seek always to regulate, even to the extent of legislating on private moral matters such as what is to count as acceptable in sexual activity between consenting adults. This shows where the balance must be sought between libertarianism – the unfettered right to do as one pleases, even to trample on others – and the unfreedom of a tyranny. Liberty lies between them, closer to the former than the latter certainly, but constrained by the sensible and reasonable need to respect the liberty and rights of others.

Thus between the two extremes of anarchy and strict authoritarianism is the ideal of a well-regulated society in which licence is restricted in the interests of those who might suffer from it, but in which the maximum degree of individual freedom is accorded to all consistent with the good of all. These last six words are the text for much debate in politics and allied fields, for the necessity is clear, as Plato and Thomas Hobbes both argued, that individuals have to forfeit some of their individual freedom in exchange for the benefits of belonging to a community.

Isaiah Berlin introduced a distinction much invoked in discussions of liberty, between 'positive liberty', which is the *freedom to* do and to be much as one desires, and 'negative liberty' which is *freedom from* restraint, limitation or obstruction. The connection between the two is obviously intimate; there can be no positive liberty without negative liberty; the latter is at very least a necessary condition for the former.

Positive freedom is possible only for those who are genuinely autonomous as agents, that is, who are free to choose and act for themselves. It is not just the imposition of constraints by a higher authority or by strict laws that would curb autonomy, but also ignorance or deficits of character such as timidity or weakness of will. For this among other reasons some theorists concentrate instead on negative liberty, which is associated with the idea of rights. If a person has rights that give immunities or opportunities that others cannot interfere with, then it is irrelevant whether he can assert himself as an autonomous agent in choosing and acting as he wishes. Berlin regarded negative liberty as the important kind.

In the contemporary world the degree of liberty enjoyed by citizens of a state has become one of the chief measures of the degree to which that state counts as developed, stable and civilized. The closest that history has come, in general, to this ideal is the contemporary Western world, although it is an illusion to think that its constituent members have actually achieved the full realization of democracy, individual liberty, and the rest of the desiderata which supposedly define a modern Western 'liberal democracy'. Economic freedom and its consequences (including the relationship between wealth and political power) are far more characteristic of these dispensations than the actuality of those aspirations by which they define themselves.

See: DEMOCRACY, FREEDOM OF SPEECH, HUMAN RIGHTS

LOGIC

Logic is the study of reasoning and argument. That innocuous definition, with which a course of study might begin, masks a deal of scepticism about logic as applied to human affairs; many have pointed out that logic is the means by which we arrive at silly conclusions with great confidence, and that logic might lead with inexorability in one direction while our hearts and hopes tug relentlessly in another. Much that matters most in human affairs appears to be far beyond the reach of logic: and yet without it we would lack almost every advance that humanity has made in the direction of science and civilization.

It is scepticism about logic which keeps nonsense in existence – nonsense dressed in robes, given a seat at government tables, awarded power over the minds not just of the ignorant and illiterate but of children who grow up to be adults unable to shake off the unreasoned and illogical fears, hopes and beliefs that had been injected into them in early life. Logic in the general sense of reason can be a remedy for this – for the few brave enough to use it, and to follow its lead.

Logic as a science is not the science of truth, but of reasoning; in addition to reason you need facts; getting the latter, and getting them straight, is a matter of care, common sense, discipline, hard work, and scrupulous enquiry. All these things are beyond the attention span of most, which is why there is so much folly in the world. This is because most reasoning – such as it is – operates not on facts but prejudices and superstitions, and thus it is that people go to war with one another, and spit in each other's eyes.

Logic has three distinct branches. There is formal deductive logic, concerned with the study of valid forms of deductive reasoning. There is inductive logic, concerned with the kind of enquiry and reasoning typical in ordinary life and some of the sciences. And there is informal logic, which is about the many kinds of reasoning employed in debate, in law and politics, indeed in the setting out and defending of theses in any branch of discursive enquiry, and in the fallacies and rhetorical devices typical of such debate. In informal logic both deductive and inductive logical considerations apply, but an important feature is the identification and avoidance of informal fallacies of reasoning, that is, those that do not arise because of the form or structure of the argument itself, independently of its content.

In formal deductive logic the concept of *form*, as the very name implies, is central. Formal deductive logic does not study individual arguments, but types of arguments, to see which type is so structured that, if the premises are true, the conclusion is guaranteed to be true also, independently of subject matter. This is what 'valid' means; it is a concept that applies only to the *structure* of arguments, not their content. An argument is *sound* if in addition to having a valid form it also has true premises, that is, if *both* its content and its form stand up. Thus the soundness of arguments is in part a matter of the facts, namely, those asserted in the premises, and partly a matter of how the argument is structured. But to repeat: formal deductive logic is interested only in this latter matter – the form or structure – and its aim is to identify which types of argument are valid in virtue of their form so that *if* true premises are supplied, that form will guarantee a true conclusion.

Inductive arguments, by contrast, if they are good ones, only make their conclusions probable to some degree. That the degree of probability can be very low despite the argument appearing plausible can be shown by an example of the simplest form of induction, 'induction by simple enumeration', in which a wholly general conclusion is inferred from a limited number of particular premises: 'This swan is white, that swan is white, the next swan is white ... so all swans are white.' Some swans, in fact, are black; some are even black and white.

Inductive inference always goes beyond what the premises say, whereas deductive inferences contain no new information in the conclusion, which is simply a rearrangement of the information in the premises. Consider: 'All men are mortal; Socrates is a man; therefore Socrates is mortal.' All that has happened is that the terms occurring in the argument have been redistributed to yield the conclusion.

But although there might be no new information in the conclusion of a deductive argument, it can nevertheless be psychologically informative. This is shown by the story of the duke and the bishop. A famous bishop was the guest of honour at a country party hosted by a duke. At one point the duke left his guests to order something from his servants, and the bishop entertained the company by telling them that when, long ago, he was a newly ordained priest, the first person whose confession he heard was a multiple murderer of an especially vile kind. The duke thereupon returned, clapped the bishop on the shoulder, and said, 'The bishop and I are very old acquaintances. In fact, I was the first person whose confession he heard.' The rest of the guests, evidently logicians to a man, hastily left.

The first systematic study of logic was made by Aristotle. With additions and extensions, especially by logicians of the medieval schools, his logic remained an apparently completed science until the nineteenth century. But then, in the hands of the mathematicians Augustus De Morgan, George Boole and especially Gottlob Frege, it was transformed into mathematical or 'symbolic' logic, an instrument of far greater range and power than Aristotelian logic. One of the innovations that made this possible was the development of a notation for expressing more and more complex notions. (The notation now standard is derived from one first devised by Bertrand Russell and Alfred North Whitehead in their *Principia Mathematica*.)

Aristotelian logic rests on three so-called 'laws of thought', the *principle of identity* which states 'A is A', the *principle of non-contradiction* which states 'not both A and not-A', and the *principle of excluded middle* which states 'either A or not-A'. (Augustus De Morgan showed that the latter two are merely different ways of saying the same thing.)

An example of the way inferences were explored in the framework of Aristotelian logic is afforded by the 'Square of Opposition'. Taking the letters S and P to stand respectively for Subject and Predicate (in the sentence 'the table is brown' the subject is 'the table' and the predicate is 'brown'), one can describe the four standard forms of the proposition as follows:

A: universal affirmative 'All S is P'

E: universal negative 'No S is P'

I: Particular affirmative 'Some S is P'

O: Particular negative 'Some S is not-P'

Arranging them thus:

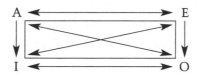

allows one to read off the 'immediate' inferences: A *entails* I, E entails O, A and O are *contradictories*, as are E and I; A and E are *contraries* (they can both be false together, but they cannot both be true together) and I and O are *sub-contraries* (they can both be true together, but cannot both be false together). Making up appropriate versions of an English declarative sentence to put in the place of A, E and the others quickly demonstrates what all this means; take the example A: All men are tall, E: No men are tall, I: Some men are tall, O: Some men are not tall.

The main object of study by Aristotle and his tradition of logic was the syllogism, an argument form in which a conclusion is derived from two premises. In his *Prior Analytics* Aristotle defined syllogistic reasoning as a discourse in which 'Certain things having been supposed, something else necessarily follows from them because they are so.' A standard example is, 'All men are mortal; Socrates is a man; therefore Socrates is mortal.' This is an example of a categorical syllogism, and it consists of two premises – a major premise 'All men are mortal', a minor premise 'Socrates is a man', and the conclusion that can be inferred from them, 'Socrates is mortal.' It will be noted that in this syllogism the major premise is a generalization, whereas the minor premise and conclusion are particular. The Aristotelian tradition classified all the forms of the syllogism according to the quantity (all, some), quality (affirmative, negative) and distribution of the terms in the premises and conclusion, devising mnemonics for the 256 thus identified: Barbara (AAA), Celarent (EAE), Darapti (AAI) and so on, the letters AEIO being explained in connection with the square of opposition above. Of these 256 forms only 19 are valid (and even some of these 19 are controversial).

The new 'symbolic logic' is a far more powerful and extensive instrument than the traditional syllogistic. Its use of symbols alarms people who do not like the look of anything that smacks of mathematics, but a little attention at the outset shows that far from being alarming, they are extremely useful and clarifying.

In the standard way of notating this logic, lower-case letters from later in the alphabet are used to stand for propositions: p, q, r ... and a small set of symbols is coined to show the relationships between them: & for 'and', v for 'or', → for 'if ... then ...', and -- for 'not', thus:

> p&q (pronounced 'p and q')
>
> pvq (pronounced 'p or q')
>
> –p (pronounced 'not p')

The operators '&' and the rest can be very simply and informatively defined by 'truth tables', thus (where 'T' stands for 'true' and 'F' for 'false'):

p	q	p&q
T	T	T
T	F	F
F	T	F
F	F	F

This shows that the only time 'p&q' is true is when 'p' and 'q' are individually true. If either or both of them are false, 'p&q' is false. This defines the meaning of '&' in the logic calculus. For 'v' ('or') matters are thus:

p	q	pvq
T	T	T
T	F	T
F	T	T
F	F	F

This shows that 'pvq' is true if at least one of p or q is individually true, and is only false if both are false. This defines the meaning of 'v' in the logical calculus.

With these simple elements, and intuitive use of brackets to keep all clear, forms of arguments can be explored for validity or otherwise. For example: from the premises 'p → q' and 'p' one can always deduce 'q', no matter what truth-values are assigned to p and q individually. Write this argument as:

$$[(p \rightarrow q) \& p] \rightarrow q$$

and one can show that this is a logical truth by making a 'truth table' thus:

p	q	p → q	(p→q)&p	[(p→q)&p] → q
T	T	T	T	T
T	F	F	F	T
F	T	T	F	T
F	F	T	F	T

The fact that 'T' appears in all four rows under the arrow in the last column shows that the whole string [(p → q) &p] → q is T no matter what the individual Ts and Fs are of the components. This is a 'logical truth' or tautology; it follows that any argument of the form:

Premise 1: p→q

Premise 2: p

Conclusion: q

is valid.

This form of argument happens to be called *modus ponens*. One can use truth tables to test for the validity of the following:

Premise 1: p→q

Premise 2: q

Conclusion: p

and

Premise 1: p→q

Premise 2: --q

Conclusion: --p

One will find that the first is a *fallacy*, called 'the fallacy of affirming the consequent' (in p→q 'p' is the 'antecedent' and 'q' the 'consequent', here being 'affirmed' by being used as the second premise), because there is an 'F' in one of the rows under the arrow in [(p→q)&q] → p, thus:

p	q	p → q	(p→q)&q	[(p→q)&q] → p
T	T	T	T	T
T	F	F	F	T
F	T	T	T	F
F	F	T	F	T

In cases where an 'F' appears in *every* row under the final operator, one has not merely a fallacy but a *logical fallacy*.

The second example is, however, a logically valid form of inference, as its truth-table will show; it is known as *modus tollens*.

These are the rudiments of the 'propositional calculus', which deals with arguments involving whole propositions. But the real work begins when one adds a few powerful devices to this calculus, transforming it into the 'predicate calculus' by getting inside propositions. This is important, given that propositions assert that all or many or a few or some or at least one of a certain thing has a certain property; and we wish to understand validity in terms of this finer degree of structure using quantifier ('how many') expressions.

To this end lower-case letters from the end of the alphabet x, y, z are used to stand for individual things, and the quantifier symbols (x) and (Ex) are used to denote respectively 'all things x' and 'at least one thing x' (this latter doing logical duty for all other quantifier expressions short of 'all', for example 'some', 'many', 'the majority', 'a few', 'three', 'four', 'a million', and so forth). Upper-case letters from earlier in the alphabet F, G, H stand for predicate expressions such as ' ... is brown' and ' ... belongs to the Queen'. So the sentence 'the table is brown' would be symbolized as (Ex)(Fx&Gx), pronounced 'there is an x such that x is F and x is G', here standing for 'there is an x such that x is a table and x is brown'.

Equipped with supplementary rules allowing *general* expressions of the form (x)Fx to be 'instantiated' to give individual expressions of the form Fa (using lower-case letters from the beginning of the alphabet to stand for particular individuals), arguments can be tested for validity as before. Thus *modus ponens*, represented above by [(p → q) &p] → q, might look like this in quantified guise:

$$(x)\{[(Fx \rightarrow Gx) \& Fx] \rightarrow Gx\}$$

The instantiation rules allow us to rewrite this as:

$$[(Fa \rightarrow Ga) \& Fa] \rightarrow Ga$$

which one can plainly see is an instance of *modus ponens*.

Discussion of inductive logic often occurs in connection with discussions of scientific methodology, for the obvious reason that scientific enquiry concerns contingent matters of fact, and the process of formulating a hypothesis or prediction and then testing it empirically can never have the conclusiveness expected in deductive logic, except perhaps when an hypothesis has been shown definitely to be mistaken.

The interesting thing about inductive reasoning is that it is always invalid from the point of view of deductive logic. Its conclusions, as mentioned above, always go beyond what is licensed by the premises. Accordingly much of the debate about induction concerns the sense in which it can be regarded as justified. A sticking point seems to be that the only available justification for induction is itself inductive, namely, that it has worked well in the past. If this is not to be merely circular, then the underlying assumption that the world is a consistent realm in which laws and patterns of occurrence remain stable and reliably repeat themselves, has to be accepted as a general premise. Attempts to justify this premise can only themselves be inductive; so if they are made they simply reintroduce the circularity that the assumption is intended to make virtuous rather than vicious.

Inductive inference can take a number of forms. Induction by simple enumeration has been noted; there are also – and more generally better – inductions taking the form of causal inferences, statistical and probabilistic inferences, and arguments by analogy, all of which, when responsibly controlled and their defeasibility accounted for, are of use in practical concerns and scientific investigation. Opinion polls infer from representative samples of the population to overall views, generally with a good deal of reliability; that is one compelling example of how effective controlled induction can be. An argument in support of induction might proceed by appealing to the concept of rationality: one who does not take seriously the conclusion of an inference such as is involved in thinking 'I'd better take an umbrella because rain looks likely' is behaving irrationally. If it is rational to take the conclusions of inductive inferences seriously, that fact justifies induction.

A celebrated twist to the debate about induction was given by the American philosopher Nelson Goodman. He argued that the problem could be recast as one about how we justify thinking that our description of things in future depends on our description of them now. For example, we think we will be entitled to describe emeralds we encounter in future as green, because all emeralds so far encountered in history have been green. But consider this: suppose one makes up a new word, 'grue', to mean 'green until now, and blue after a future date X'. Then the word 'grue' applies to emeralds just as legitimately as the word green, because emeralds have been green until now, and the definition of 'grue' only requires that they turn blue in the future. Now, obviously we think that we are better justified in taking 'green' to be the right description for future emeralds than 'grue'. But on what grounds do we think this? After all, the evidential basis for both descriptions is exactly the same – namely, that all past and present emeralds are green.

In addition to inductive logic and formal deductive logic there are other domains of this science, in which logical principles and notions are put to work in exploration of allied ideas. So there is 'fuzzy logic', concerned with domains containing vague terms and imprecise concepts; 'intensional logic', concerned with domains where context violates the ordinary workings of logic (for example, by interfering with the reference of certain terms); 'deontic logic' concerned with reasoning, chiefly in ethics, involving ideas of obligation (expressed by such words as 'must' and 'ought'); 'many-valued logic' in which there are more than just the two truth-values 'true' and 'false'; 'paraconsistent logic', which contains, accepts and manages contradictions; 'epistemic logic' in which the operators 'believes that' and 'knows that' occur; and others.

LOGIC, FALLACIES OF INFORMAL

For everyday use, the identification of fallacies in informal logic is of great value. There are many of these, and many of these many are standard rhetorical devices that politicians, advertisers, even friends and lovers, use to try to persuade other people in order to get their way.

First it is useful to be reminded that an argument can be valid in form but unsound, either because one or more premises are false or because a fallacy has been committed. Consider this syllogism, for example: 'Nothing is brighter than the sun; a candle is brighter than nothing; therefore a candle is brighter than the sun.' This is valid but unsound, because a fallacy – the Fallacy of Equivocation – is committed by it. This fallacy involves using a word in two different senses, as happens with 'nothing' in the first and second premises, thus unsoundly allowing the nonsense conclusion to be drawn.

Some of the commonest fallacies, not a few of them employed on purpose to mislead, are as follows.

The Fallacy of False Dilemma works by offering an alternative – 'either we have nuclear weapons or the country will be in danger of attack' – which pretends to be exclusive in the sense that no other options are possible, whereas in fact several other options exist. The Slippery Slope Fallacy involves saying that if X happens or is allowed, Y and Z and so on will inevitably follow. 'If you give your son a mobile phone he will next want a television in his bedroom and then a car.' The Straw Man Fallacy occurs when someone attacks an opponent or a point of view by representing him or it in its weakest, worst or most negative version so that he or it is easy to knock down.

The Fallacy of Begging the Question, more illuminatingly known as Circular Reasoning, involves assuming in the premises what the argument claims to prove as a conclusion, for example, 'God exists because it says so in the Bible, which was inspired by God.' People nowadays typically misuse the expression 'begging the question' to mean, 'prompts or invites or urges us to ask the question'. These latter formulations should be used if that is what one means to say; 'begging the question' should be reserved to its proper meaning of 'arguing circularly'.

A number of fallacies turn on the illegitimate use of emotion to get someone to accept a conclusion which does not follow from the offered premises. One is the 'appeal to force': 'believe what I say (do what I tell you) or I will beat you up' (*argumentum ad baculum*; this, though it puts the matter more bluntly than usual, is the essence of divine-command moralities).

A second is the 'appeal to pity': 'I will be upset, hurt, troubled, miserable if you do not believe or do what I say'; 'I'm poor'; 'I'm offended'; 'I'm from a minority'; 'I've been discriminated against' (*argumentum ad misericordiam*. The joke example given for this fallacy is the man who has been convicted of murdering his parents and who asks for the court's leniency on the grounds that he is an orphan.) Associated with this is the idea that people who have been victimized or who have suffered are therefore good, or right, or can be excused for bad things they do.

A third is 'prejudicial use of language', which means using emotive or laden terms to 'spin' the view taken of something. Racist and sexist language provide one kind of example, another is the use of euphemism to hide the real purpose of something; so Idi Amin's death squads were called 'public safety units' and the CIA calls assassination of unfriendly foreign leaders 'extreme prejudice'.

There are also the fallacies of appealing to 'what everyone thinks' (*argumentum ad populum*), to what people in an authoritative position think (*argumentum ad verecundiam*), or the claim that no one knows the answer so you can believe more or less what you like (the argument from ignorance or *argumentum ad ignorantiam*). None of these are good grounds for accepting a view or believing anything.

A very common form of fallacy is the *ad hominem* argument, which is an attack on a person rather than his or her argument. It takes different forms; there can be direct abuse of an individual, insinuations and hints that associate the individual with bad people or happenings, ridicule of the individual, and redounding a charge on the individual ('you too', *tu quoque*).

Equally common is the use of biased statistics, introducing red herrings to distract people from the true thrust of an argument, reasoning that if y happened after x then it happened because of x (*post hoc ergo propter hoc*), and generalizing from just one or a very small example of something. These are all fallacies.

And so finally is attributing a property of part of a whole to the whole itself – which we know to be wrong because we know that a school of whales is not itself a whale. This fallacy, called the Fallacy of Composition, is one applied to groups and nations all the time: 'I met a Frenchman who was impolite, so the French are an impolite nation.'

Although fallacies of informal reasoning are often deliberately employed to win arguments by trickery, thus persuading and coercing people into a way of thinking or a belief, it is also very frequently the case that we each reason badly because we commit one or more such fallacies without realizing it. A course in 'straight and crooked thinking' (to borrow the title of a celebrated book on informal reasoning by Robert Thouless) would be to everyone's benefit – and it does not commit the fallacy of composition to say: to the world's benefit as a whole therefore.

LOVE

Love is a various and, to quote a well-known song, many-splendoured thing. There is love of parents for their children and children for their parents, the love of friends, the love of workmates and comrades who have been through testing times together, the love of people for their pets, and the erotic and romantic love of which so many poems, novels and films speak, relating often to youthful or young adult experience of finding and bonding with an all-important other, though such love is not monopolized by any one age group.

English has just one inadequate word to denote all these different emotions – these bonding, affectionate, caring, needy, desiring, dependent, nurturing, passionate, painful, ecstatic, erotic, romantic emotions – and the kinds of relationships that involve them. The Greeks, with more nuance, had several names: *agape, storge, philia, ludus, eros, pragma,* enabling them to discriminate more finely among them.

Agape means disinterested love for one's fellow human beings. In Latin it is *caritas*, whence our 'charity' (and less coldly, 'cherish'). It has come to be the form of love that Christian moral practice extols, following the injunction of Jesus to his followers to 'love one another' (John 13.34–5) and 'love your neighbour as yourself' (Matthew 22.37), and St Paul's saying in I Corinthians 13:13 that love is greater than its companion virtues of faith and hope.

Agape once denoted 'love-feasts', common meals or communion services among early Christians, commemorating the Last Supper. In time the communion service or Mass was separated from the common meal, the idea of confounding the mystical events of the Mass with a social event coming to appear sacrilegious to a later age.

In the sense of 'brotherly love' which it is a moral duty to feel for one's fellow human beings – as opposed to the sense of brotherly love felt by actual siblings, or that arises spontaneously among comrades-in-arms or people who have shared similar vivid experiences such as tragedies: this is *storge* (sometimes *philia*) – *agape* is enjoined by other moral traditions, not least by Mohism in ancient China, whose founder Mo Zi (470–390 BCE, making him an almost exact contemporary of Socrates) taught the doctrine of *bo-ai*, whose meaning embraces both 'impartial concern' and 'universal love' as the attitude to be cultivated towards all others.

Erotic love is sexual, sensual, physical and emotional passion. It is characterized by intensity, physical longing, exclusivity, intimacy and profound sexual desire. It can transform the world for the mutual participants in it, and it can also give rise to unrealistic and over-optimistic views, or in adverse circumstances apocalyptic passion, a sense of cosmic tragedy and despair, even (as in the immortal tale of Romeo and Juliet) suicide. In the guise of obsession, incontinence and volatility it is better described, as it was by the Greeks, as *mania*. Manic love, if indeed it is love, was thought by the Greeks to be an infliction, more a punishment than anything else, from the gods; and not a few of them thought the same of erotic love too.

Ludus is playful love, the love of light-hearted friends, or the affection of people who are not deeply in love but jest and spar and enjoy each other's company more as a recreation than as something more serious.

Storge denotes the love of deep and genuine friendship (again, *philia* might be the more accurate word for such friendship), the love that members of a well-functioning family share, the love that evolves between married couples after many years together. It is a calmer bond, supportive, premised on good mutual understanding and acceptance.

Pragma is pragmatic love, not always distinguishable from the form of storgic love just mentioned; it is a love of the mind as much as and sometimes more than the heart, often felt or engaged in for practical reasons such as the advantages conferred by marriage or long-term partnership.

Sociological research into the respective proclivities of men and women as classifiable in terms of these concepts suggests that men are more prone to ludic and erotic forms of love, women to pragmatic and storgic forms, especially when it comes to settling down and raising a family. Physiological research into aspects of love has identified the role of the hormone oxytocin in bonding between individuals; it is secreted in response to close physical intimacy such as cuddling or sex. Other physiological factors are obviously implicated in the blushing and palpitations experienced by a besotted individual when thinking about or encountering the beloved. Smell and other cues have been hypothesized as playing a major part in attraction and bonding, and erotic and manic love (as the latter name implies) have quite a lot in common with psychosis.

Some researchers apportion love in the romance-leading-to-marriage sense into three phases, each with its own chemical basis. The first stage, infatuation and lust, is driven by the hormones testosterone and oestrogen (testosterone is active in women also; it is what might be called the horniness hormone). The actual falling-in-love stage seems to have a great deal to do with a set of neurotransmitters know as monoamines, in particular dopamine and adrenalin. The former is activated by cigarette smoking and cocaine as well as the presence of the beloved; the latter is responsible for the flushing, blushing and racing heart characteristic of high passion. Serotonin is also very much involved; it is the chemical of madness, and is responsible for the temporary lunacy associated with the honeymoon phase of infatuation.

Finally, and if all goes well, there is bonding, which is what makes the relationship last if it is going to last, and this is where oxytocin comes in, and with it (if the results of scientific study of the erotically energetic prairie vole are generalizable to humans) vasopressin also.

Functional MRI scanning of the brain (fMRI) reveals definite patterns of brain activity associated with thinking of the beloved or seeing images of him or her. A notable feature of the scans is that they show suppression of activity in the prefrontal cortex, an area of the brain that is excessively active in people suffering from depression.

Before and as part of prompting the chemical processes just described, the 'body language' of individuals plays a major part in attracting or repelling others. Sexual signals sent by hair, cleavages, curves, the female and male body shapes in general, eyes, gestures and body position, subliminally perceived likenesses to oneself or to parents (experiment reveals that women like smells that remind them of their fathers), all play definitive parts. This suggests, not surprisingly, that love is a deeply biological matter. It is known that most mental computation is carried out by the brain non-consciously. The reasons why any two people fall for each other and pair off, whether for the short or the long term, tend therefore to be for reasons that – whatever rationalizations they give to others – they do not themselves really understand, for they lie too deep for reason.

Loving someone else, and in the case of erotic and romantic love of being loved in return, is among the highest and best of all human experiences. People do not always love well, in the sense that being in love can make them obsessive and jealous, desirous of entrapping those they love, engrossing their attention to themselves alone and seeking to own them body and mind. In the infatuation phase, when the heat of passion fuses two into one, both parties typically desire this exclusivity; but it is easy to see how destructive it can be in longer-term relationships, and also in parent–child relationships where neither smothering by the former nor too great a dependency on the latter's part is healthy.

But loving well – which takes thought and generosity, forbearance and sometimes pain – is a marvellous thing to give another and thereby the world, and it can summon everything that is truest and best in the person who so loves. Love like that would indeed be kind, long-suffering, not easily provoked, neither envious nor contemplative of evil, selfless, full of hope for good things and of endurance when bad things come, rejoicing in the truth, and in the other's good. When love is like this, it is the best of all the states and experiences of which humanity is capable.

MARXISM

Marxism's founders, Karl Marx and Friedrich Engels, regarded themselves as having articulated a general theory of the world and human society which amounts to a comprehensive political philosophy and a blueprint for action. Their approach to examining the nature of society and the way it changes over time, and to discerning the way it will change in future, was intended to be scientific; they took it that the dynamics of history are, like the things that happen in the natural realm, subject to laws which can be identified and described. The chief recommendation of their approach was its promise of a scientific theory of society, which would replace the suppositious notions of religion, hero-worship and utopianism.

The revolutions that brought communist states into existence in the early and mid-twentieth century, most notably Russia and China, were ostensibly based on Marxist principles, though in each case these were extended or modified by the theories respectively of Vladimir Lenin and Mao Zedong – and in each case in circumstances far from the developed industrial capitalism that Marx regarded as the essential precursor to a proletarian revolution.

The basis of Marxism is a theory of economic relationships. In working out his economic theories Marx insisted that they cannot be separated from historical and social considerations. The technical study of wages and profits might seem to belong wholly to economic theory, but they cannot be fully understood until they are placed into the fuller picture of relations between employers and workers, which in turn requires an examination of the historical context of those relations.

The key social relations underlying economic factors are those, said Marx, that obtain between classes in society. The simplest definition of a 'class' is: a group of people who get their living in the same way and therefore share certain interests in common – or more accurately: who share certain self-interests in common. A favourite example for Marxists is the contrast between feudal landowners and serfs. Members of each class wished to get the most for himself from the other: the barons from the labour of the serfs, the serfs from their own labour for themselves and their families. Hence arose class conflict, almost constantly at an individual level, often (as with the rising of Wat Tyler and the peasants in 1381) as a class struggle expressed in revolutionary terms.

Feudalism was succeeded by capitalism as, first, specialized production enabled the rise of a merchant class, acting as middlemen who bought surplus produce and exchanged it for the goods and services of other producers in other places, and as, secondly, some producers began to employ their fellows, paying them wages for their journeyman labour. From this latter development arose the two essentially interrelated classes, the industrial capitalist class and the industrial working class.

The struggles that brought about these shifts of power and economic relations are described by Marxism as revolutions; Marx's own examples are the English Civil War and the French Revolution. Neither movement interpreted itself at the time in terms of a violent change of economic relationships, instead seeing themselves as the application of certain ideas and ideals; but as Marx remarked, 'Just as we cannot judge an individual on the basis of his own opinion of himself, so such a revolutionary period cannot be judged from its own consciousness.'

Although the struggle between classes is regarded by Marxist theory as the principal driving force in history, two accompaniments of the process have to be borne in mind. One is the growth of mankind's power over nature by means of science and technology, and the other is the change of moral outlook occasioned by the change in social relations between classes. A given morality simply reflects the organization of society at a particular phase in its development; recognizing this immunizes one against seeking 'principles of morality' that hold good universally and permanently. Most ideas are class ideas, in particular the ideas of the dominant class prevailing at the given historical moment.

Ideas, thus, are secondary to the material facts of the forms of production in a society; they embody what the then dominant class requires to keep itself in control. But when contradictions arise between prevailing conditions and new forces of production, new ideas arise too. For another favourite Marxist example: when the first merchant middlemen encountered feudal restrictions on trade, they began to desire a change in the rules leading to greater freedom of action and a greater say in such matters as fixing taxes. Thus although ideas arise from material conditions, they can influence and direct them too when conflicts within the material conditions occur – as occur they must, given the class conflicts they embody.

These ideas about social evolution constitute 'historical materialism', Marx's philosophy of history. Historical materialism describes the dynamic between material conditions and the struggles of rising classes against the vested interests which wish to preserve those conditions for their own benefit. But the point is not merely to describe this process, but to help those oppressed by it to change it permanently for the good; once people understand how history works, they can take charge of it and direct it to ends that are good for all. As Engels wrote, 'The objective, external forces which have hitherto dominated history will then pass under the control of men themselves. It is only from this point that men, with full consciousness, will fashion their own history.'

From this account of Marxism one can see its chief lineaments and elicit its chief assumptions. It is not so obvious to an observer today that the 'industrial working class' is an object of callous and conscious exploitation by lazy and Machiavellian capitalists as it was to Marx, who lived in a London where grinding poverty and its immiseration of slum-dwelling proletarians contrasted in razor sharpness with the wealth and ease of the rich bourgeoisie in Mayfair. It seemed impossible to Marx that this state of affairs could or indeed should be remedied by incremental reform; revolution appeared to be the only escape for the oppressed majority, alienated from themselves by the conditions imposed by the capitalist form of production.

The theory just described is now sometimes called 'classical Marxism' to register the fact that any number of theorists and activists have added, subtracted and modified it to suit changing conditions or special circumstances – as did Lenin and Mao for the backward agricultural economies in which they instituted their revolutions.

Despite the exclusive implication of its name, Marxism is the joint brainchild of Karl Marx and Friedrich Engels. The two men first met in 1844, and began a lifelong collaboration which produced a number of seminal works, one of the earliest being the famous *Communist Manifesto* of 1848. Engels was the son of a wealthy industrialist and was therefore able to support Marx while the latter spent his long years in the British Library in Bloomsbury researching and writing his monumental *Das Kapital*, still unfinished when he died in 1883. Engels edited Marx's literary remains and wrote a number of important works himself. He survived Marx by twelve years.

Marxism was the inspiration and the invocation of the communist revolutions of the twentieth century, but since the collapse of the USSR and the repudiation of Marxist economics by the Communist Party of China, and indeed since the empirical failure of socialism in general, which shared a number of Marxist or Marxist-influenced views about public ownership of the means of production in a centralized economy, Marxism has ceased to be a platform for concrete political action. (Some, with justice, will say that neither Marxism nor socialism has ever been properly tried anywhere; the regimes appropriating these labels have never proved worthy of them.)

But Marxist ideas have remained highly influential as a cultural and philosophical force, not least in the analysis and criticism of trends in the arts and media, in certain schools of sociological thought, in feminist thinking, and as a stance for independent critics of almost everything. In the pick-and-mix world of the comfortably salaried, leather-jacketed polytechnic lecturer, Marxist rhetoric can be combined with (say) Lacanian ideas – or indeed any ideas – to provide dissidence à la carte. Some of these rhetoricians would be horrified if the arrangements they attack actually ceased to function, and still more horrified if they were required to roll up their sleeves and manage the alternative, perhaps with starving human individuals to feed and angry violent mobs to placate. But so it goes: the vocation of critic is one of the most comfortable and enjoyable of all vocations, providing one is never challenged to administer the opposite of what one impugns.

See: CAPITALISM, COMMUNISM, POLITICS, SOCIALISM, TOTALITARIANISM

MEANING, THEORY OF

A central concern of analytic philosophy since the early twentieth century has been the question of how meaning attaches to the uttered sounds and written marks that constitute language. Philosophical interest in language is motivated by the conviction that understanding how language works takes us a long way towards understanding both thought and the world. This is because the world shapes and is shaped by our thought about it, while thought, in its turn, is expressed, communicated and accessed through language. So investigating language – and more precisely: the phenomenon of linguistic meaning – turns out to be an important though indirect way of investigating how the mind relates to the world itself.

It is important to be clear about the nature of *philosophical* interest in language, by discriminating between it and linguistics, which is the empirical study of language structure and functioning.

One simple and at first plausible view of meaning rests on the paradigm of proper names such as 'Jack' and 'Jill', which function simply as labels. This suggests that the meaning of a word is the object it denotes; thus 'table' means (because it denotes) a certain sort of furniture. Of course not all words mean by denoting; such syncategorematic words as 'if', 'but', 'and' and the like get meaning 'in context', for obviously there are no ifs and ands in the world for the words 'if' and 'and' to name. But otherwise, says this view, a word's meaning is what it labels.

This idea is, however, shown to be false by two considerations. How could even a simple labelling relation between a sound (or mark) and a thing in the world be established without recourse to pre-existing conventions of naming? There is first the ambiguity of ostension (how does the learner of English know that I mean a nearby piece of furniture rather than, say, its uses, colour, or texture when I point in a certain direction and say 'table'?). Then there is this problem: 'table' is used, in conjunction with a demonstrative ('that table') or an article ('the table', individuated by context), to pick out some particular table on some particular occasion; but the word itself does not denote this or that particular table, but can be applied indifferently to any member of the class of tables, for it is a general term. But what does it mean to say that a general term functions like a proper name? Is there something – a class of things, or a concept, or an 'abstract idea' – it denotes?

The second consideration is decisive. Two words or phrases can refer to the same thing but have different senses, as 'the morning star' and 'the evening star' exemplify; they both denote the planet Venus, yet they differ widely in connotation. Accordingly it is out of the question to make a simple identification of the meaning of a word with its referent.

The denotative theory invites a charge of absurdity too. If the meaning of a term is the object it denotes, it would be possible to pull the meaning of the word 'handkerchief' from one's pocket. But this is nonsense, and so too is the idea that the meaning of 'handkerchief' is all the handkerchiefs there are, were, and will be.

Denotation, therefore, cannot constitute meaning. Nevertheless, the original intuition regarding the way proper names function, and the fact that reference is central to our use of language, raise important questions. Manifestly, there are classes of expressions that do, or can be used to, refer to items in the world. How does reference work? What do we have to know, if anything, to use a referring term successfully? These are the very first steps in the complex and far-ranging enquiry that tries to understand the nature of meaning in language.

It seems obvious from the grammatical and lexical differences between languages that the sounds and marks which carry or contribute to meaning are conventional items, that is, are the product of an implicit agreement between members of the linguistic community in question to attach a given significance to them. But this is something that applies only at the surface level of language, according to Noam Chomsky and those he has influenced; for them language has a deep structure, innate to the brains of human beings, which permits any infant to learn any language if exposed to it. Chomsky points out that small children acquire a knowledge of the grammar of their community's language despite only ever being offered a fragmentary and degenerate example of it, in the form of the scanty half-finished sentences they hear in the linguistic environment of their early years. This suggests that there is a 'deep grammar' hard-wired into human brains that supports the particular surface grammar of the language spoken by the community into which an individual is born.

By itself this does not achieve the philosophical goal of explaining linguistic meaning. For this a wide range of phenomena have to be understood, some of which have been claimed to be the key factor in meaning. One is the way that the *use* of words and sentences enters into giving them meaning. Another is the work done by the intentions of speakers in seeking to communicate with others. A third is the way that expressions can be used to pick out things or events, describe them, convey facts about the manner in which they exist or happen, and much more. A fourth is the nature of the relationship between mental states and language, and between both of these and the world (or more generally the domains) over which thought and talk range.

One suggested entry into the complex of questions raised by the concept of meaning is to say that the key lies in employing the notion of a 'truth-condition', thus: the meaning of a sentence is given by stating the conditions under which it is true, and the meaning of the sentence's constituent words is the contribution they make to the sentence's meaning. On the face of it this looks trivial, for in effect it asks us to take the statement ' "snow is white" is true in English if and only if snow is white' as giving the meaning of 'snow is white'. But note that the first occurrence of the words 'snow is white' is enclosed in quotation marks to show that the words are being quoted rather than used, and that the rest of the sentence is about it – as in this case: ' "la neige est blanche" is true in French if and only if snow is white'. Here English is the *metalanguage* and French the *object language*, and the meaning of the object-language sentence is being given by stating, in the metalanguage, the condition under which it is true.

This truth-conditional theory of meaning has been highly influential in recent philosophy, but it has been opposed by those who think that the concept of *use* is a more satisfactory key to an account of meaning. One reason is that the truth-conditional approach requires that declarative sentences all be determinately true or false whether or not we know which, thus appearing to put what is required for grasp of meaning beyond our epistemic powers. This entails what critics see as an over-strong 'realist' thesis to the effect that there are facts of the matter about everything, even if we do not know or can never know what they are; and that it is in virtue of them that all sentences are determinately true or false, again whether or not we know which. But if we cannot know these things, how can we grasp the meanings of what we say in terms of them?

Another reason is that in any case it is a fact about language that expressions change their meanings with change in the way they are used, so the conventional nature of meaning is respected by the use theory, which at the same time places meaning and grasp of meaning squarely within the competence of ordinary speakers. The use theory is most associated with the later work of Ludwig Wittgenstein (see his *Philosophical Investigations*), but a version of it is implied by the influential work of Michael Dummett, a leading critic of the 'realist' truth-conditional approach.

One must distinguish between philosophy of language, as just sketched, and both 'linguistic philosophy' and 'ordinary language philosophy', in which latter version this approach to philosophy flourished mainly at Oxford University in the 1950s. In essence both labels denote the view that philosophical problems are the spurious result of misunderstandings about the way language works, and if only we would pay very careful attention to how we speak, and if we resist the temptation to assimilate one way of speaking to other ways, we will avoid generating the pseudo-problems in which – so proponents claim – philosophy mainly consists.

Wittgenstein was a leading influence in this respect. In his *Philosophical Investigations* he advanced the view that expressions in language acquire their meanings from the way they are used in given areas of discourse that he called 'language games', rather as the nature and significance of the chess piece called a 'bishop' are determined by its role in the game of chess. If one took the bishop and tried to use it in draughts as it is used in chess, the result would be muddle and nonsense. In just this way, said

Wittgenstein, if an expression is used out of its proper linguistic habitat it will give rise to muddle, and such muddles are what philosophy consists in. Proper attention to language will thus 'dissolve' philosophy.

In Oxford in the 1950s the leading figures of Gilbert Ryle and especially J.L. Austin applied the technique of careful and precise examination of the way words are ordinarily used to make a similar case. Neither their approach nor that of Wittgenstein survived the compelling individual charisma of their proponents. It is easy to see why: one might know all the different ways in which the words 'true' and 'truth' are used, and yet be all the more rather than less puzzled, as a result, about what truth is; so far from solving the problem or quietening the desire to understand what truth is, the variety of uses and senses will stimulate the desire for a deeper understanding.

See: METAPHYSICS, PHILOSOPHY, POSITIVISM AND LOGICAL POSITIVISM

METAPHYSICS

Metaphysics is the branch of philosophy that enquires into the ultimate nature of reality. It seeks to determine what genuinely and fundamentally exists, and what existence itself is. It asks whether, in addition to physical reality, such things as deity, abstract objects such as numbers, and values such as goodness and beauty, exist in the universe, and if so, in what way.

This enquiry acquired its name by accident. When the editors of Aristotle's works had completed their task of organizing his lectures on physics, which with exemplary straightforwardness they named *The Physics*, they turned their attention to his lectures on (as Aristotle himself put it) 'being qua being', that is, the nature of ultimate existence. At a loss for a name, they ended by calling it 'the book that comes after *The Physics*' (*meta ta physika*) – thus: *metaphysics*. Somewhat confusingly, this label came to serve as a general term for what we now call 'philosophy' until a mere century or two ago, because 'philosophy' was once the generic name for what we now call 'science' or more generally still, 'enquiry'.

Aristotle's metaphysics concerned the nature of primary substance (that which exists in its own right) and causation, including the 'first cause' of all things. Descartes gave metaphysics a renewed impetus by saying that the universe consists of two essentially different substances (that is, different in their essences), namely, matter and mind, the former being defined as 'that which occupies space' (*res extensa*, 'extended stuff') and the latter 'that which thinks' (*res cogitans*, 'thinking stuff'). The immediate problem with this dualistic view is that it is mysterious how two such utterly different substances can interact, as they must do given that thoughts prompt movement of arms and legs, and that physical impingements on the body give rise to such mental phenomena as pain and pleasure. In response many have argued that there are not two different fundamental kinds of thing in the universe, but just one: this monistic view can take either the form of mental monism (there is only mind in the universe; a view held by Bishop Berkeley) or material monism (there is only matter in the universe; a view held by most philosophers and scientists).

Kant held that the three great topics of metaphysics are God, the freedom of the will, and the immortality of the soul, and he wrote his *Critique of Pure Reason* to explain why it was that, in the century and a half before his own day, philosophical enquiry had failed to make progress with regard to these three subjects, whereas in the same period the natural sciences had taken immense strides. His answer was that when reason tries to apply concepts beyond their proper role in organizing empirical experience, the result is illusion and error; and that is what happens when efforts are made to prove the existence of a deity, or to show that the soul is immortal and free.

A useful distinction between 'descriptive metaphysics' and 'revisionary metaphysics' was introduced by the British philosopher P.F. Strawson. The former consists in an examination of the way we in fact think about the world; it identifies the concepts we use, and traces the connections between them, including the order of dependence between the more and less fundamental among them. Revisionary metaphysics, by contrast, seeks to correct our beliefs about reality, typically by eliminating talk about certain types of thing in favour of talk about more basic types – for example, eliminating talk about minds and mental phenomena in favour of talk about the functionings of brains, thus giving a putatively more accurate account of what the universe contains (this is known as 'reductionism'). Historically the two most influential and debated theses in metaphysics are *Idealism* and *Materialism*.

Idealism is the thesis, or more accurately the family of theses, whose fundamental claim is that the universe is mental, that is, that mind is the basic reality, or that reality is an expression of mind or thought.

There are considerable differences between varieties of idealism. For

George Berkeley the universe, including all finite minds such as our own, exist because they are conceived by an infinite mind, which he identifies with the traditional Christian God. Absolute idealism, first developed in the writings of Fichte and Schelling and brought to its fruition by Hegel, regards the ultimate reality as 'Spirit', which is progressing dialectically to a full realization of itself, becoming increasingly actual through the growth of human consciousness in history.

Most discussion of idealism includes Kant's 'transcendental idealism' under the label, but this is an error. Kant did not think that ultimate reality is mental, which is the defining feature of an idealist theory. Rather he put forward a thesis in epistemology to the effect that the reason why scepticism about the possibility of knowledge is incorrect is that our minds contribute a priori features to the way the world appears to us. A simple illustration of what he means is that the colours objects appear to have are the result of an interaction between light reflecting from the surface of objects and the way our eyes and brains are constructed. If the latter were different, objects would seem to have different colours, or none; so we have contributed something to the way the world seems. This summarizes the essence of Kant's claim. From it he deduced the reason why investigation of great questions about the freedom of the will, the immortality of the soul and the existence of God has made no progress, unlike the great progress in the natural sciences. That reason is that we mistakenly try to apply to those questions the concepts which properly only apply to empirical experience. In consequence we get into a muddle and find that we can prove contradictory conclusions about them.

Under the influence of Hegel's views, British philosophers of the later nineteenth century embraced versions of absolute idealism, motivated by a desire to find a view of the universe less at risk from the implications for religion of Darwinism. Chief among them were T.H. Green and F.H. Bradley. The most significant idealist of the later twentieth century is the British philosopher T.L.S. Sprigge, who with the American Nicholas Rescher has formulated a version of idealism influenced by elements of pragmatism.

Materialism is the thesis that reality ultimately consists of material – in the sense of physical – things and processes. Materialism also entails rejection of dualism, which is the claim that the universe consists of both matter and mind; and it views abstract entities (things that exist outside space and time, such as numbers) as merely artefacts of language and not as independently existing things; this is known as 'nominalism'.

In denying mind–body dualism, materialists are committed to the view that mental phenomena such as intentions, beliefs and desires are in fact identical to neurological phenomena occurring in the brain or central nervous system. This is a powerful example of a reductive thesis; it claims that a completed science of the brain will show how reference to mental items can be replaced by reference to activities in brain structures alone.

The earliest materialists are the Atomists of classical antiquity, Leucippus (fifth century BCE) and Democritus (fourth century BCE). Their theory is that the universe is composed of tiny atoms ('atom' means 'cannot be cut') that move in the void, clumping together as a result of differences in their shapes and sizes and thus forming all things with their various properties. A beautiful expression of this view, together with its consequences for moral questions, is given in the outstanding poem by Lucretius, *De Rerum Natura* ('On the Nature of Things'), written in the first century BCE.

Revival of atomist ideas in the seventeenth century gave impetus to the adoption of materialism in the thought of Thomas Hobbes, and more significantly in the development of scientific thinking in that period, at this juncture in physics and chemistry but not biology. The latter became a conquest of materialism with Darwinism in the nineteenth century – although by this point a better term would be naturalism, to denote the idea that science rests on the premise that its objects of study are natural entities and processes, defeasibly describable in terms of natural laws.

By the twentieth century the association of the term 'materialism' with the metaphysics of the early modern period (the seventeenth and eighteenth centuries) persuaded many to employ the term 'physicalism' instead, denoting the view that everything that exists consists in or is a product or property of physical things and processes. This is the majority educated view today in metaphysics and science alike.

One of the deeper questions in metaphysics is whether there are any 'brute facts', by which is meant facts that have to be accepted, no alternative or argument possible. An example of a brute fact might be: 'something exists'. On that, at least, not even the most trenchant sceptic, idealist, solipsist, Buddhist or nihilist could disagree.

In philosophy the expression has a more particular meaning, first conferred on it by Elizabeth Anscombe in contrasting facts that depend for their existence on there being institutions or practices that define them, and facts that do not depend on such things. These latter are brute facts. An example is a piece of gold used as money. The fact that the piece of gold is money that can be exchanged for other things at an agreed rate depends upon the existence of social institutions of the appropriate kind. The fact that the piece of gold is a piece of gold is by contrast a brute fact, requiring no institutions or social practices for it to be so.

Not only the contrast but the connection between brute facts and social and institutional facts is central to John Searle's argument in his book *The Social Construction of Reality*. For Searle, social facts are intentional mental facts, and the existence of mental facts ultimately depends on the physical – and in particular biological – facts that give rise to consciousness and experience. Hence social facts are rooted in physical facts. Nevertheless, though all physical facts are brute facts in being objective and not dependent on our attitudes or preferences, some social facts can be either subjective or objective. The fact that a given piece of printed paper is a dollar bill, and thus has a certain exchange value, is a function of the attitude we take to it, and therefore is a social fact. But it does not follow that this social fact cannot be objective; for if there is enough, and stable enough, intersubjective agreement about it, it becomes an objective fact.

Consistently with his naturalistic and materialist viewpoint, however, Searle's point is that ultimately social facts rest on brute physical facts in the way described, and for that reason it is the connection rather than the contrast that matters.

A view that suggests greater complexity in these issues might be extracted from the debate among the founders of logical positivism concerning whether there are indeed any brute, theory-independent facts, or whether the data upon which science turns are themselves in some way constituted or determined by theory. The idea here is that we never approach the world, or the making of observations of the world, naked of the presuppositions and concepts that themselves make our experience possible (this indeed was Kant's central point). So we can never claim that some among our observations are observations of brute facts about how things are independent of us. In science, our hypotheses tell us what counts as evidence for and against them. In ordinary experience, our faculties are always in play, somewhat as a veil between us and the world we encounter through it – indeed, by its means. Searle and others might reply that we have ways of discounting for subjectivity and the contribution of our faculties; this is what science itself always strives to do. If this is right – but as we see it is a controversial point – then we do have access to brute facts.

Philosophy was memorably described by Alfred North Whitehead as 'footnotes to Plato', suggesting that many of the main themes and ideas of philosophy spring from the fertile genius of the great Greek thinker, pupil of Socrates and teacher of Aristotle, from both of whom he doubtless took inspiration for his explorations of the central problems of philosophy. Because of his importance to the tradition of Western thought it is worth saying a little about his outlook.

Plato held that knowledge can only have as its objects things that are perfect, eternal and immutable, for knowledge must be of what is true, and truth must have these three characteristics. But here in the world of ordinary experience things are imperfect and changeable, so we cannot have knowledge of them but only opinions about them.

But this raises a problem: how do we know anything about what is perfect, eternal and immutable? The imperfection and transience of things in the ordinary world would never be enough to suggest the perfect and eternal paradigms (the 'Ideas' or 'Forms' as Plato calls them) of these ordinary things, existing in a realm somewhere beyond the ordinary world. Nor can we infer the existence of such things from the character of ordinary things, firstly because these imperfect ordinary things lack the power to suggest the Forms of which they are such poor copies, and secondly because the human intellect lacks the power to draw the required inference from these poor copies to their perfect originals.

Plato therefore concluded that the Forms in what he called the Realm of Being (as the place in which true and full existence is alone to be found) must have been known by us when we were in a prior state, existing as disembodied minds before we came to occupy a human body with all its limitations. He offered arguments to prove that we have immortal souls that can exist independently of body, and suggested that minds are frequently reincarnated after periods spent in direct intellectual contact with the Forms. The reason that minds do not have knowledge of the Forms when implanted in a body is that the process of embodiment causes minds to forget what they know; so what we think of as learning is not in fact the acquisition of new knowledge, but the remembering of what was forgotten. This is known as the 'doctrine of anamnesis', where 'anamnesis' literally means 'unforgetting' (amnesia is forgetfulness; an-amnesia is un-forgetfulness or memoriousness). So to teach someone something is in reality (according to Plato) to remind that person of what was known but has been forgotten. The word 'education', derived from the Latin *ex* meaning 'out of' and *ducere* meaning 'to lead', suggests a discernible impress of the Platonic view of what is really happening in education – namely, a bringing out of what is already there.

The highest of the Forms in the Realm of Being is the Form of the

Good. (Other high Forms include Beauty and Justice; Plato was not so sure that there are Forms of Mud and Hair.) He offered a striking allegory to explain the difference between ordinary belief and opinion, on the one hand, and knowledge on the other hand, with knowledge of the Good as the apogee. This is the Allegory of the Cave. Imagine that all your life to date you have been a captive in a cave, sitting with your face towards the cave's backmost wall. Behind you is a fire around which your captors sit and walk. On the back wall of the cave you see shadows pass and repass, thrown by your captors as they move about the fire. Then imagine that you are freed from your bonds, and allowed to walk around the cave; you see the fire and your captors properly, and understand how the shadows were caused, and recognize the difference between real people and shadow people.

But finally you are allowed out of the cave into the daylight, and at last you see the fullness of reality itself, not lit by a mere fire, and certainly not just a matter of shadows, but the fullness of real existence, lit by the brightest object in the heavens: the sun itself.

The sun is the Form of the Good; seeing the real world in daylight is knowing the truth; walking in the cave by firelight is having the sort of belief that the best empirical experience and mortal reasoning can give; imprisonment among shadows is opinion and even illusion.

The dialogues by Plato in which these views are put include the *Phaedo*, the *Meno*, and the *Republic*.

From this sketch it can readily be seen why the label 'Platonism' is applied to the view that abstract entities exist independently of thought or talk of them. Platonism in mathematics is, one might actually say, the source of Plato's Platonism about everything else – which is to suggest that Plato held the views he did because the mathematics of his day was fully Platonistic already. It had already arrived at stable conceptions of numbers, points, straight lines, and other such entities, in abstraction from things in the ordinary world that exemplify them (spots, stripes, straight-edged tables). In geometry lines have no width, and points have no dimensions at all; they are idealizations. Without idealization of these things Euclidean geometry would not be possible. Similarly, the natural numbers (the counting numbers 1, 2, 3 ...) probably developed long beforehand from the need to differentiate between the sizes of collections of actual objects, such as cattle or bundles of corn. But the Greeks reasoned abstractly about number, and already knew not only about prime numbers (those that are divisible without remainder only by themselves and 1) but that there are infinitely many of them – a fact discovered by pure reasoning, not by empirical enquiry. Thus the world of numbers had become a realm of its own, unrelated to collections of actual objects in the empirical world.

Moreover – and this was assuredly the epiphanic point for Plato – the truths of geometry and arithmetic are eternal and unchanging, and they are graspable only by reason. This point was what encouraged so many in the philosophical tradition at large to be rationalists in epistemology, for to them mathematics is the paradigm for what knowledge must be, and for the infinite superiority of reason over sense experience as the royal road to its acquisition.

In short, treating the ideal or abstract objects of mathematical thought as constituting an independent realm about which discoveries can be made is not merely a natural way of thinking, but in fact describes the actual assumption of most mathematicians, even if they would (when presented with a philosophical challenge as to whether they mean that numbers 'really exist' in the way that sticks and stones 'really exist') not be happy to answer in the affirmative. But they would doubtless still hold that mathematical research results in *discoveries* – that is, that pre-existing but unknown mathematical truths can be uncovered. This is a claim challenged by espousers of Intuitionism, who argue that all mathematical entities are 'constructed' by the process of doing mathematics, in which the concept of truth should be replaced by the concept of proof.

'Platonism' is, as the word itself suggests, the name given to Plato's philosophy. But it is also, and now more generally, the name given to any theory (but mainly in mathematics) that says that abstract objects exist. An abstract object is one that exists neither in space nor time. Concrete objects – the ordinary physical objects in the world such as sticks and stones – exist in both space and time; thoughts and feelings exist in time (and in the form of neurological events in the brain, in space); but mathematical objects such as numbers and functions, and 'universals' such as redness and roundness, exist neither in space nor in time (for whereas there are individual red things and round things, it is not clear whether redness itself and roundness itself exist above and beyond them). Such things are therefore described as 'abstract objects'. And Platonism is the view that such things really exist.

Perhaps the greatest dispute in medieval philosophy was the quarrel between the 'Realists' (Platonists) and 'Nominalists' over the existence of universals, the former holding that universals really exist independently of particular things, the latter saying that they are just names (hence 'Nominalists') that we use as a convenience for marking the similarities between things (thus, 'redness' is a word that helps us think and talk conveniently about the similarities between particular red things).

See: EPISTEMOLOGY, PHILOSOPHY

MIND, PHILOSOPHY OF

Among the most important and puzzling questions yet to be resolved by human enquiry are those that relate to the nature of mind and its place in the physical world. There are in fact many questions linked together here, chief among them these: what is mind, and what is its relation to body? How should we best understand our ordinary common-sense concepts of such mental phenomena as belief, desire, intention, emotion, reason and memory?

These concepts, together with others relating to our ways of having sensory experience, constitute a 'folk psychology' giving us a picture of ourselves as perceiving the world around us, acting in it on the basis of reasons, and successfully interpreting the thoughts and experiences of other minds like our own. Is this a satisfactory picture, or should it be replaced by one more accurately based on concepts drawn from neuro-science and the study of information-processing and computation?

Central to the history of attempts to answer these questions are problems about the mind–body relation, and the nature of consciousness.

It is customary to begin discussion of the mind–body problem by noting how the views of René Descartes gave it an especially sharp form. He argued that everything that exists falls under the heading either of material substance (matter) or mental substance (mind), where 'substance' is a technical term denoting the most basic kind of existing thing. Using ideas suggested by his Aristotle-influenced predecessors, not least in employing the notion of 'essence' which means 'a fundamentally differentiating characteristic', Descartes defined the essence of matter as occupancy of space, and the essence of mind as thought. But by thus making 'extended stuff' and 'thinking stuff' so different he seemed to render insuperable the problem of explaining how they can interact. How does a bodily event like pricking oneself result in the mental event of feeling pain? How does the mental event of thinking 'It's time to get up' cause the bodily event of rising from bed? Descartes himself did not have an answer – although for a short time he thought that mind and matter interact through the pineal body in the brain; but then he realized that this does not solve but merely hides the problem.

Descartes's successors had to resort to heroic solutions to the problem that his theory, known as Substance Dualism, had bequeathed to them. Malebranche suggested that mind and body in fact do not interact, but only seem to; for on each occasion that a conjunction of thought and bodily action is required, God causes the appropriately corresponding occurrences in each realm. For example, God sees that I feel hungry, so he makes my body go to the kitchen and cut a slice of bread; then, following my consumption of it, he causes a feeling of satiety in my mental realm. This doctrine is known as 'occasionalism' since on each occasion that a correlate is required in one realm for what is happening in the other, God provides it.

Leibniz did not require the deity to be so remorselessly busy. He agreed with Malebranche that the essential differences of mind and matter mean that they cannot interact, but proposed an alternative explanation of how nevertheless they appear to. This is that God had set going the mental and material realms in exact unison at the universe's beginning, so that they thereafter act in parallel with each other. The two realms are like a pair of clocks, one with a face and hands but no chime, the other with a chime only, which seem to be connected because whenever one shows the hour, the other strikes it. But their concordance is the result not of a connection, but of the fact that the clockmaker set them both going at precisely the same moment, so that ever thereafter their respective activities parallel each other. This theory is therefore known as 'parallelism'.

But it is evident that these brave efforts to explain away the dilemma of Cartesian dualism are very unsatisfactory, even if – as many do not – one supposes that there is a deity, and that this deity designed the universe in such a way as to have it operate in these improbable ways. Critics say that if an omnipotent deity exists, we might reasonably expect it to find a way of making mind and matter interact causally, as they seem to, without resort to such ad hoc means as those proposed. Moreover, Leibniz's view carries a heavy extra cost: it requires that the history of the universe be immutably fixed in advance, which means that there is no such thing as free will, and that therefore all our beliefs about ourselves as moral agents – making choices for which we can be praised or blamed – are false.

The theories of Malebranche and Leibniz are efforts to accept the substance dualism of Descartes and to find ways round it. The obvious alternative to dualism is monism, the view that there is only one substance underlying all things. Three monistic possibilities suggest themselves.

One is that the only substance is matter. The second is that the only substance is mind. The third is that the only substance is something other than mind or matter, a neutral substance which gives rise to them or of which they are different expressions. Each of these three possibilities has been adopted as a solution to the problem of mind. Mentalistic monism is better known as idealism, the thesis that mind and its ideas constitute the basic reality. The third option described was adopted by William James and Bertrand Russell under the label 'neutral monism'. But it is of course the first option – the reduction or annexation of all mental phenomena to arrangements, properties or functions of matter – which has been most discussed: the varieties of materialism.

Under the influence of developments in empirical psychology, one response to dualistic views of mind was behaviourism. This can best be described as the theory that the right way to deal with such mental concepts as pain, emotion and desire is to talk instead of people's observable behaviour in given circumstances. Proponents of this view lay much stress on the fact that how people behave is publicly accessible and describable, which means that interpreting mental phenomena in terms of what people actually do removes the difficulty experienced by earlier enquirers, who had to rely on subjective introspective reports as the basis of their enquiries. A sharp way to characterize the behaviourist view is accordingly to say that it offers translations of our talk about mental phenomena into talk about how people act, as in this example: 'X is in pain' is replaced by 'X is wincing, bleeding and groaning' – and this, says the behaviourist, gives us an objective and perspicuous account of the meaning of 'pain'.

Among the leading psychologists to promote this view were B.F. Skinner and J.B. Watson, and versions of their views were developed by the philosophers Gilbert Ryle and W.V.O. Quine. Between the earlier work of the psychologists and the more nuanced views of the philosophers there are a number of differences, but all forms of the theory face the same crucial difficulty. This is that behaviourism does not in the end succeed in eliminating reference to the fundamental mental phenomena of belief and desire which figure in almost all our explanations of behaviour. A mere description of a man's body moving into a shop and reappearing with a packet of biscuits attached to one hand would not amount to an explanation of what he was doing. His beliefs about the availability of biscuits in the shop, his desire for biscuits, and so on, would be indispensable to such an account. Generalizing, something vital is left out if we try to analyse 'X desires a biscuit' into 'if such-and-such circumstances obtain, X goes into shops and reappears with packets of biscuits' – unless the reference to beliefs and desires has been covertly smuggled into the 'such-and-such circumstances' clause.

A far more influential materialist monism is the 'identity theory', which asserts that mental states are literally identical with states or processes in the brain. In its earliest form it asserted that types of mental phenomena are nothing other than types of brain occurrences, but this was quickly seen to be too strong, for a particular mental event (a mental image of the Eiffel Tower, for example) might in my brain consist of the activation of one set of cells while in your brain it might consist of the activation of a quite different set of cells, the difference arising from our different developmental histories. On this more plausible view, in which a mental phenomenon is nothing other than a particular material occurrence but not a specific type of such occurrence, it is allowable to think that the occurrence in question need not take place in a human or animal brain, but could happen in a computer or some other suitable system.

One interpretation of the idea that a mental phenomenon is 'nothing but' a material one is that as neuroscience advances, we will be able to eliminate the vague, old-fashioned, imprecise mentalistic vocabulary we standardly use. Such a view is known as 'eliminative' because it says that once we have identified the physical processes to which mental entities reduce once we understand them properly, the mental entities will drop out of the picture. Two leading proponents of this view – Patricia and Paul Churchland – say that future neuroscience will be to present 'folk psychology' what modern medicine is to the past belief that illness results from possession by demons.

But the same objection that was urged against behaviourism is urged here, namely, that our mentalistic vocabulary of intentions, beliefs and desires seems indispensable to the explanation and interpretation of human action. The radical revisionist might reply that once we have mastered the new and better conceptual framework in which everything is discussed in terms of neural structures and activity, we will see that the old scheme is thoroughly superseded. But this response, in being not only profoundly revisionary of the way we think about human nature and experience, but in its own right a blank cheque drawn on the future of neuroscience, remains open to scepticism.

Advances in neurology, cognitive science and philosophical under-standing of mental concepts have, however, built an overwhelming case for accepting that the relation of mental to neurological phenomena is very intimate. Given the practical and theoretical difficulties of identifying that relationship precisely, a number of conceptual strategies have been proposed for thinking about it. One is to accept that our ways of talking about mental phenomena and physical phenomena are irreducibly different, even though they are not in fact about different realities. An example explains the idea best. Imagine how a sociologist and a physicist would respectively describe a football match, each focusing upon those features of the events before them which his particular science addresses, and using the concepts particular to each. One speaks of goals, aims, rules, penalties, captaincy, and the like; the other speaks of bodies of measurable mass moving with certain velocities and emitting radiation at certain frequencies. Yet they are both descriptions of the same thing, though different aspects of the same thing. Sometimes such a view is described as 'property dualism', the same thing (brains, or better: persons) being legitimately describable as having two sets of properties which are not reducible to each other, and which answer to different sets of concepts, but which do not therefore entail an underlying ontological duality.

In the absence of a satisfactory way of accounting for the fact that both mental and physical properties can properly be ascribed to the same thing, while not being explicable in terms of one another, philosophers often talk about mental phenomena 'supervening' upon physical phenomena – a somewhat fudging expression which disguises the problem of the exact nature of the relation rather than clarifying it. One implication of the idea of supervenience is that however we finally explain the mental properties of brains, persons, and perhaps (eventually) computers, our concepts of them will still not be reducible without remainder into purely physical concepts. This is suggested by the thought that supervenience is not a symmetrical relation – the physical phenomena on which mental phenomena supervene could exist without subvening the latter, but the converse cannot hold.

Functionalism is the name given to a theory which has been especially influential in accepting materialist monism while leaving aside the question of the exact mind–matter relation. There are a number of versions of the theory, but they are all based on the idea that the way to define any given mental state is by describing its place in a web of causal relations connecting inputs of sensory data, outputs of behaviour, and other mental states. In a sense, functionalism is a descendant of behaviourism, except that instead of simply correlating inputs and outputs, leaving the inner sphere of mental reality a closed 'black box', it offers a series of connected smaller black boxes to put inside the large one, each serving to identify a function that such states as desire, hope, memory, fear, expectation, need, hunger, etc. jointly play in producing given behavioural outputs from given inputs. The functions are abstractly specified; we do not know, or for present purposes need to know, which bits of a brain or computer are responsible for performing them. But we have given ourselves a way of understanding mental states in terms of what they do and how they interact.

But one very large problem with functionalism as just characterized is that it leaves out of account a striking feature of some mental states: the fact that they have a subjective character of which their possessors are aware. Pain, for example, is not merely something which, in combination with other mental states, serves as a way-station in a causal transaction between inputs and outputs. It also hurts; it is felt, experienced, suffered, by its possessor. And it seems sensible to suppose that the felt subjective character of some of our mental states contributes to the functions they perform – obviously, the ability to feel pain has an evolutionary advantage for our species, in alerting us to danger and enabling us to remove ourselves from harmful stimuli, for example.

This brings us to what is by far one of the most important topics in contemporary debate: consciousness.

It might be thought that, in one way, consciousness is very easy to understand, for anyone capable of thinking about it is intimately conscious of being conscious – that is, of the consciousness which attends every moment of our aware experience and thought. Similarly, the consciousness of others is obvious in their faces and behaviour, and we typically have a rich and highly nuanced knowledge of how to read and respond to that evidence – their presence and our understanding of them constitute the commonplaces of social interaction.

At the same time, consciousness is by far the most perplexing mystery facing philosophy and the neurological sciences. It is such a difficult problem that for a long time philosophers avoided thinking about it directly, and scientists ignored it. Some, in the tradition of Descartes, still think that it is too hard for human intelligence; they say that the human brain is not made to understand itself. Others even claim that there is no such thing as consciousness; we are actually zombies, just very complicated ones. In defiance of these views most students of the problem – philosophers, neuroscientists and psychologists, working in concert – have profited from the availability of powerful new investigative tools, especially brain-scanning devices, to watch both healthy and damaged brains actually at work in the processes of learning, sensing, remembering, reasoning, and feeling. One result is a great increase in knowledge of brain function, in the sense of a refined understanding of the correlation between specific brain areas and specific mental capacities.

But as already indicated, all this new knowledge does not amount to an understanding of consciousness, which is far too protean and varied a phenomenon for simple matchings between conscious states and activity in this or that brain structure. In particular, no degree of accuracy in tracing a given mental event to a given brain event can by itself explain how coloured pictures, evocative smells, and harmonious or discordant sounds arise in the head as if it were an inner theatre or cinema show. This is the central problem of consciousness.

There are many suggestions and theories abroad as to how consciousness should be conceptualized. A recent example is offered by António Damásio, who suggests that consciousness begins as self-reflexive awareness constituting a primitive level of selfhood, a powerful but vague awareness of occupying what we later call a first-person perspective. The self and its objects – the things that cause emotional responses in the self – come to constitute a relational model of the world; at this point consciousness is not just a feeling of feeling, but a feeling of knowing. Describing the roots of consciousness in terms of feeling allows us, says Damásio, to explain the central phenomenon of consciousness: the sense that we are each the owner and viewer of a movie-within-the-brain that is our own aware experience, and which represents a world to us of which we are the centre.

Results of research in brain science and clinical neurology fill out this sketch. For example: some patients can still be awake and to some extent aware of their surroundings, and can interact with them, yet in non-conscious ways, showing that consciousness is not the same thing as mere awakeness or awareness. The extra that is consciousness has to have survival advantage, otherwise higher mammals would not have evolved it. Damásio suggests that the appropriate utilization of energy, and the protection of the organism from harm, which are chief goals for any living creature, are much enhanced by an organism being able to place itself in a map of the environment, and to make plans and judgements about the best courses of action in relation to it. Creatures which are merely biological automata, even if highly sensitive to their environment, might do this well enough, but not as well as creatures who are genuinely conscious.

As the foregoing shows, although debate about the mind has come to a widespread consensus that it is part of nature, and amenable to investigation by a variety of scientific and social-scientific disciplines in the way that other natural phenomena are, there are still fundamental mysteries about what it is and how it relates to the rest of nature. When we have weighed, measured, and analysed a lump of rock we have said almost everything relevant to understanding it as a piece of the natural world. But our enquiries with respect to mental phenomena and the brains (so far no other computational systems seem to match brains in this way) which appear to secrete or subvene them have so far left the crucial questions unanswered. The next great leap in understanding the mind and its place in the world will doubtless involve a conceptual and scientific revolution of such magnitude that we at present seem unable to envisage what it will be. The great hope must, though, lie with neuroscience, for despite all the practical and conceptual difficulties that still lie in the way, understanding must start, even if it does not end, with the place where mind takes its rise.

See: NEUROPHILOSOPHY, NEUROSCIENCE, SOCIOBIOLOGY

MULTICULTURALISM

In an increasingly mobile and intermingled world, with greater net flows of immigration from poorer to richer countries and the higher birth-rates of immigrant populations in their new domiciles, the questions of identity, social cohesion, assimilation, and preservation of cultural backgrounds have become jointly more pressing. 'Multiculturalism' is an idea that was supposed to promote overall social cohesion and harmony by allowing people of different ethnic, religious and cultural identities to maintain their differences in what was hoped would be a happy mixed salad of national getting-along-together.

This model is different from the assimilationist one, which requires or at least hopes that immigrants will abandon their culture of origin and adopt the culture into which they have moved. It was thought that the United States' experience of mass immigration in the late nineteenth and early twentieth centuries would provide the model for this, as a great 'melting-pot' that out of the pell-mell diversity of immigration would produce the new American individual. In France the same aim was adopted of according everyone who lives there the single identity of Frenchness, aided by a policy of official blindness to any other distinctions that might have existed before the adoption of the new overriding persona.

The new mobile world also has many migrant labourers moving about it, who do not propose to settle but merely to work for a number of years in a richer country than their own in order to send remittances to their families. In some of the countries that encourage migrant and expatriate labour, for a prime example Saudi Arabia, the strict requirement is that the visitors observe the norms of the host nation, and must do so scrupulously. No display of cultural difference of practice and behaviour is tolerated. This is an interesting fact, because of the contrast it offers with dispensations where cultural differences are accepted with a large margin of tolerance, as in the United Kingdom and the United States.

One of the most welcoming and open-armed of societies until recently was the Netherlands. Following the murder in 2004 of the film-maker Theo van Gogh, who with Ayaan Hirsi Ali had made a film deeply critical of the treatment of women in Islam, Netherlands society was convulsed by anxiety over the large immigrant Muslim community it had welcomed into its midst, but elements of which had turned against it. The Netherlands appears starkly to suggest that when an immigrant community with a markedly different culture from the majority host culture reaches a certain critical mass in numbers, the nature of difficulties thus posed becomes dramatically more acute.

Some countries have significant numbers of immigrants without these sorts of tensions, however – Canada is an example: it has the highest per capita immigration in the world – but a salient difference appears to be that whereas Canada has encouraged immigration by educated, professional people rather than unskilled labourers, European countries such as Britain, the Netherlands, Germany and France have welcomed unskilled immigrants because the kinds of jobs they are prepared to do were no longer being done by native residents. This picture is somewhat muddied by the fact that Australia has selective immigration policies similar to Canada's, but there have been occasional ethnic tensions there – though in these cases it is the next generation or two, the children and grandchildren of immigrants, who have been involved, sometimes reporting that they feel caught between the ancestral and the adopted cultures, the trigger for tensions sometimes being a sense of alienation and continued discrimination.

These last factors have played their part in the periodic and all too frequent eruptions of tension and even violence experienced in Britain and France. In Britain a de facto policy of multiculturalism has had the unfortunate effect of ghettoizing immigrant communities and the generations that succeeded them, so that most people of South Asian origin or descent live in a few cities or areas of cities, overwhelmingly fill the schools in those areas, and experience self-imposed and externally imposed separation from the surrounding majority community. Over 90 per cent of the British population consists of white native Britons, yet in some cities and suburbs the proportion of immigrants and their descendants is over 50 per cent. In the eyes of some critics of multiculturalism, this is stark testimony of its failure.

Is it? Proponents of multiculturalism argue that the values it embodies are too important to give up, and that the ideal of encouraging a benign social diversity should be maintained. They argue this because, first, they point out that efforts to do the opposite will inevitably involve racism and insult to deeply felt religious and cultural sensitivities. They also point out that the effort to eradicate cultural differences will be traumatic for immigrants, because all human beings need cultural affiliations and a sense of identity related to their history and origins.

These views have received support from certain brands of liberalism, not least among them the influential view articulated by Isaiah Berlin. In the absence of universal truths and absolute values, the need to accept and indeed respect differences is, he argued, the best hope of maintaining society in the face of what are in fact not just incommensurabilities in respect of values but the irreconcilabilities that might and almost certainly will arise as a result.

Almost without anyone realizing it, such views have supported, or even been taken to amount to, a claim of right to 'equal recognition' for minority ethnic groups living among a host community – a claim that is emphatically not recognized in Saudi Arabia in respect of its migrant workers, nor for a long time in Germany with respect to its Turkish 'guest workers'. As the philosopher Richard Rorty pointed out, the demand for equal consideration is logically at odds with claims of incommensurability, for one can only accord equal respect if there is some yardstick of comparison that enables one to do so. Of the various solutions proposed for this dilemma, the one that has increasingly come to the fore is that the host community's desiderata of equal respect and status require that immigrants and their descendants accept the norms of the host culture, and seek to integrate with it. What this expresses is the idea that human individuals are equal, but that cultures are not – at very least, not when one is a minority culture at odds with a host culture.

This last idea is a difficult one for liberals to accept. Yet one of the most painful adjustments in the difficult birth of the twenty-first century was the need felt by many who describe themselves as liberals to think again about these matters. They found it hard to say, and yet felt compelled to say, that democracy, civil liberties, science and its methodologies and applications via technology, the rule of law, individual autonomy, fundamentally free choices in personal relationships and other important value-of-life questions, are better or more preferable than monolithic theocratic societies lacking most of these things, for they felt that saying this, though true, smacks of Western cultural imperialism at least and racism – or something approaching it – at worst.

One hope might lie in the significantly different idea of pluralism, itself a cornerstone of liberal thought. A pluralistic dispensation is one in which individuals are free to cherish and pursue values and aims in private, consistently with doing no harm to others, while in the public domain having equal footing with every other individual in respect of the law and access to public social goods and opportunities. In societies still wedded to the multicultural project, the chances of realizing this desideratum are ever more rapidly diminishing. As the claims of minorities in multicultural settings have increased in frequency and volume with the rise of their members' numbers, so the public domain has become an arena of competition, in which there is a Babel of claims for exceptions, exemptions, immunities, privileges, the need for larger equalizing disbursements from the public purse for special interests (thus: all faiths must be given taxpayers' money to run their faith-based schools, perpetuating and indeed deepening ghettoization of communities) – and so on, to the detriment of the common good and social cohesion.

These thoughts suggest that the world has moved beyond the possibility of multiculturalism, and as these words are written a new arrangement waits, with some urgency, to be found.

See: ACCOMMODATION THEORY, ETHNOCENTRISM, IDENTITY, NATIONALISM, RACISM, XENOPHOBIA

NATIONALISM

Nationalism is a political ideology which asserts that the natural political unit is 'the nation'. It has been one of the most powerful political concepts in world history since the nineteenth century, and has a large share of the responsibility for most of the major upheavals and conflicts between then and now.

Nationalism opposes other theories about the legitimate source of political power, for example the appeal to 'divine right' which underpinned absolute monarchies in Europe until the eighteenth century, or class as in Marxist theory. The difference between orthodox Marxism and nationalism is sharp, for whereas nationalism invokes such ideas as culture, ethnicity and language in its effort to define a 'nation', Marxism is internationalist, and premises economic factors in locating moral and political superiority in the global working class.

Despite these oppositions, nationalism is consistent with a variety of other political ideologies, and takes more or less benign forms according to which it is harnessed to, from economic liberalism and democracy to Fascism. After the Second World War some Third World countries adopted a nationalistic form of Marxism, perhaps encouraged by Stalin's earlier pragmatic espousal of 'socialism in one country'.

Although some attribute the rise of nationalism to Enlightenment thought, it is in fact an offspring of the counter-Enlightenment, for whereas Enlightenment political aspirations were towards constitutionalism and democracy as a replacement for absolute monarchy, with no idea of basing political legitimacy in a putative cultural and ethnic unity called 'the nation', counter-Enlightenment thinking, of which Romanticism and belief in non-rational sources of legitimacy such as 'race', 'blood', culture and shared language were potent factors, sought a more emotionally persuasive account of what the natural political unit is.

One reason for the popularization of nationalistic sentiment in the early nineteenth century might be the hostility to French dominance resulting from Napoleon's victories. The pre-war monarchies were restored after 1815, but insecurely; none lasted long, destabilized by the nationalistic movements in the German and Italian states and the Habsburg dominions of the Austro-Hungarian empire. A restless century of revolutions and civil wars eventuated in the enlarging of smaller states into new 'nation-states', such as Germany and Italy, and the fragmentation of the large imperial Habsburg state.

The new nation-states were quick to construct 'national identities' by means of schooling (which involved imposition of a single national language where there had been many local variants before) and the adoption of national symbolism such as flags, insignia and anthems. Many intellectuals and artists enthusiastically supported nationalism; poetry and music were powerful adjuncts to the cause, as in the Czech lands where the Slav population resented the dominance of their German fellow-citizens, and made a conscious and concerted effort to create a national literature and musical culture that deliberately turned its back on Germanism in any form.

In the twentieth century the euphoria and idealism of the first nationalistic impulse, whose main attraction was undoubtedly the prospect of liberation from a disagreeable yoke, had faded, and nationalism had developed into an instrument of far right-wing politics. Fascism in Italy and Nazism in Germany traded on its rhetoric, in the latter case an expanded and expressly ethnic nationalism of the German peoples, or even indeed the Aryan peoples. Just before this happened, however, the appeal of nationalism had reached such an apogee that the idea of 'national self-determination', as enshrined in Woodrow Wilson's Fourteen Points at the end of the First World War, had become a piety, and was universally invoked in the liberation movements of colonized peoples after the Second World War.

Although the ideal unit for a nationalist is a territory-occupying ethnic, cultural and linguistic group (in effect, a tribe, or a tribe writ large), in practice few such units exist except in localized Third World contexts. This suggests a distinction between 'civic nations' and 'ethnic nations', the former consisting of the occupants of a state with a long-enough continuous history as such, of which the citizens – whatever their ethnicity or other differences – regard themselves as proper inhabitants. Historically, the northern and western European states (England, France, the Netherlands) approximate to the civic nation model, whereas the central and southern European states (for example Germany, Italy, Hungary) approximate more to the ethnic model. This latter model is sometimes invoked to explain the greater prevalence of anti-Semitism in countries conforming to it.

Neither model is altogether persuasive; religious differences and linguistic divergences do more to promote nationalist sentiment among different Slavic peoples (for example Poles, Ukrainians, Russians and Serbs) than their ethnic closeness does to promote unity. The truth is that historical, geographical and cultural factors play a far larger role in political history than sits comfortably with theories of ethnic nationalism.

The European Union as a *grand projet* is premised on a rejection of the idea that there is anything inevitable about nation-states competing and sometimes therefore getting into conflict with each other. Indeed it implicitly rejects the idea of the nation-state altogether, with an inclusive form of internationalism or pan-Europeanism as a (very long-term) goal. This is anathema to those who cling to the idea of the nation-state, in the face of the evidence provided by the last two centuries, which strongly suggests, when weighed in the balance, that nationalism is a recipe for disaster.

This last remark might be fleshed out by a critic of nationalism as follows.

Too many of nationalism's roots lie in xenophobia and racism, a fact which has been of service mainly to political demagogues. Disguised as patriotism, nationalism trades on the irrationality of mass consciousness to make intrinsically unacceptable things, notably war, seem otherwise, and indeed even honourable. Appeals to 'Queen and Country', 'The Fatherland', 'My country right or wrong' encourage people to go to war, or to send their sons to war, which means: to kill other human beings – an idea that most would in all other circumstances find merely horrifying.

Nationalists take certain reasonable desires and marry them to unreasonable ones. People wish to run their own affairs; that is reasonable. Most people value the culture which shaped their sense of identity; that also is reasonable. But nationalism goes further, persuading people that they belong to a supposed collective that is superior to, or at least more important to them than, other such collectives, that the existence of other such collectives somehow puts their own at risk, and that the only protection rests in seeing 'us' as distinct from 'them'.

On this basis much cant is talked about nations. Ralph Waldo Emerson (1803–82) spoke of the 'genius' of a nation as something additional to its current citizens; the French playwright Jean Giraudoux described the 'spirit of a nation' as 'the look in its eyes'; other such meaningless assertions abound. The truth is that nations are artificial constructs, their boundaries drawn as a result of (one might more graphically say: in the blood of) wars.

And it is essential to distinguish always between the spurious idea of national identity and the valid idea of cultural heritage. Almost all countries (in the sense of 'states') are home to more than one culture, which is proof enough by itself that nationalism is an artificial construct, of more use to demagogues and separatists than anyone else.

See: COMMUNISM, FASCISM, POLITICS, RACISM, ROMANTICISM, XENOPHOBIA

NEOCONSERVATISM

In the United States of America some of those who had been involved in or sympathetic to the political liberalism and 'counterculture' of the 1960s underwent a reaction to what, as they grew older, they came to regard as the excesses and failures of those movements. These defectors from the left to the right of the political spectrum, carrying with them what they still described (in those early days at least) as 'liberalism', were satirically labelled 'neocons' in the 1980s by the American socialist and writer Michael Harrington, and the label stuck.

Some commentators on the origins of those neocons who became increasingly influential through the Reagan (1980s) and the second Bush presidencies (2001–9) describe their roots as lying in Alcove 1 of the cafeteria at City College in New York where, in the 1940s, a group of Trotskyists met to mourn their prophet and the misdirection of Soviet Socialism. They included Irving Kristol, Melvin Lasky and Seymour Martin Lipset. Under the influence of such teachers as Reinhold Niebuhr and Sidney Hook this group gradually abandoned Trotskyism and gravitated towards the anti-Communist left, where they were joined by Norman Podhoretz. When the Cold War began they took a strong anti-Soviet line, almost outdoing some of the right-wing anti-Soviets of the McCarthy era. Matters were indeed such that the celebrated magazine founded by Irving Kristol, *Encounter*, turned out to be funded by the CIA; there was not much complaint from his fellow ex-Trotskyists when the fact became public.

Two episodes of disillusionment completed the movement rightwards of this early group's inheritors: the first with sixties radicalism, the second with the Democrats after George McGovern's resounding defeat by Richard Nixon in the 1972 presidential election. When Ronald Reagan entered the White House in 1981 almost all of those who came to be called neocons were ready to go the whole way in joining the Republican Party and seeking office under a Republican president.

Neocons have far more interest in foreign policy than domestic policy. As regards the latter the reflex nostrums of right-wing attitudes apply: less tax, less government, libertarianism about matters such as gun control, encouragement of individual responsibility in health care and education, 'faith-based solutions' to social and welfare problems, and so forth. But in foreign policy activism is the aim. This is not so much an al-truistic belief that the US is the world's policeman as a self-serving belief that the world has to be remade to conform to US interests. There have been setbacks to this frank policy: the Iran-Contra scandal (1987) was one such, and oddly the neocons were inconvenienced by the ending of the Cold War as a result of Mikhail Gorbachev's 'perestroika' and 'glasnost', because the clean lines and simplicities of the opposition between two geopolitical blocs, each of which could use the stand-off as an instrument of control in its own sphere, served their interests. It seemed also, for a time, to raise questions about the need for continued high levels of military spending, to which some neocons had profitable links. Happily, terrorism and the need for massive military presence in the Middle East remedied that problem.

By the time of the second Bush presidency the neocons were no longer intellectuals and theoreticians but apparatchiks, still as bold if not bolder in their foreign policy aspirations but no longer thinkers, and apparently therefore no longer very intelligent either, as their handling of matters abundantly suggested. They had become what Jacob Heilbrunn in his book *They Knew They Were Right: The Rise of the Neocons* (2007) calls an 'echo-chamber', producing the sounds of a political and geopolitical discourse that related to a different world, at the latest the Brezhnev world of the 1970s and 1980s, in an entirely inappropriate context – like breaking wind in church.

The misalignment of echo and reality is demonstrated by the fact that whereas the first Bush's Gulf War endeavour (1991) knew when to stop, the second Bush's rematch (2003 onwards) did not, and committed the mistake that the first one had been careful not to: of marching straight into the Mesopotamian quicksands, there to struggle for years at the costs of scores of thousands of violent deaths and billions of dollars overall. On the view being taken here about the trajectory of recent neocon history, the difference is speaking. The neocons argued that the first Bush 'lacked moral clarity', was too influenced by considerations of realism, and was not robust enough in seeking to remodel the world closer to American desires. These were not mistakes they were ready to make when their chance came under the second Bush. Instead, they made a whole raft of worse mistakes.

Some students of neoconservative thinking and its echoes point to the formal parallels it displays to its left-wing origins. Thus, the desire to export democracy across the world is likened to the Trotskyist theory of permanent revolution. This perhaps explains why, at the outset, the second President Bush was not a natural ally of neocon ideas, having little interest in (mainly because he had little knowledge of) foreign parts and their affairs, and disclaiming any intention to engage in 'nation building' abroad (or even at home, as his tax cuts policy immediately showed). The turning point was the atrocious terrorist attack on the United States on 11 September 2001, and is encapsulated in the State of the Union speech given by George W. Bush in January 2002, written for him by neocon David Frum, in which Bush named Iran, Iraq and North Korea as 'the axis of evil' and broached the idea of pre-emptive war. The neocons had at last found their opportunity; what they thought was opportunity they did not alas see was instead a trap invitingly if only part-consciously set for them by Islamist terrorists.

The influence of the neocons in the second Bush presidency seemed to wane in its second term, because not even ideologues can persist with theory in the face of persistently contrary facts. It is a feature of recent Western political history that the more doctrinaire a government is, the greater the eventual train wreck of the political party that formed it. The Conservative Party in Britain had a long decline after the Thatcher era, and the Republican Party in the United States fell into disarray at the end of the second Bush presidency, for much the same kind of reason: going too far, in an age when reasonably competent, reasonably fair managerialism is what electorates seem really to want (in both senses of this word) most.

See: POLITICS, WAR

NEUROPHILOSOPHY

One of the new directions of enquiry made possible by neuroscientific techniques of investigation is neurophilosophy, that is, the influence of neuroscientific insights on philosophical debate about knowledge-acquisition, concepts of the self, attitudes and responses of a moral kind, the making of decisions, and the nature of love, friendship, and sociality generally. For some, and increasingly many, philosophers the value of neuroscience to increased understanding in these and associated areas of enquiry is not only great, but recapitulates the history of mankind's progress in understanding the world: the natural sciences emerged from philosophy once the right way to ask questions, and the right methods of seeking to answer them, had been found. Armchair speculation about the fundamental nature of matter, the relation of mind to matter, the structure of the universe, the secrets of reproduction, and everything else, gave way to empirical and quantitative methods which made vastly more progress with these questions in decades than had been made in millennia beforehand. For neurophilosophers, the aspiration is to see this process repeated in respect of great philosophical questions about the mind, self, free will, morality and rationality, now that real advances are being made in neuroscience.

One example will suffice to show how neuroscience and traditional philosophy can fruitfully interact – and indeed how the former can not merely enrich but correct the 'intuitions' on which much 'conceptual analysis' as the standard methodology of armchair philosophy proceeded. There is an extensive philosophical literature on the related subjects of the self and the will, little of which prepared anyone for the surprising results of commissurotomy procedures. When severely epileptic patients underwent commissurotomy – separation of the two hemispheres of the brain by resection of the commissure or connecting tissue (the corpus callosum) between the cerebral cortices – it was found that the left and right hemispheres could conflict, for example when one hand took an item of clothing out of a cupboard but the other hand put it back, these actions repeating over and over; or when a patient was unable to explain verbally why one of his hands had correctly pointed out an object in an array when he was asked to do so, as if a separate self with its own will existed separately from the self-aware self which had control of language.

The most compelling evidence for the importance of neuroscience to philosophy comes from studies of the differences in brains between more and less social species. Relatively monogamous species such as prairie voles and marmosets have a high density of receptors in their brains for neuropeptides that conduce to bonding, the chief of these being vasopressin and oxytocin. In non-monogamous species such as montane voles and rhesus monkeys the relative density of these receptors is markedly less. Oxytocin is released during peaceable social activities, damping the flight-or-fight reaction prompted in threatening situations, and increasing the degree of bonding between the participants.

Such findings impinge upon our understanding of what is involved in human societies and individuals as regards marriage, parenthood, friendship, loyalty, patriotism, indeed social structure generally – most of these things accorded high value and all hitherto believed to be features of evolved moral and social rationality (and for many, the demands of a deity). If these features of human community are determined by, or even just to some extent influenced by, the relative density of oxytocin receptors in certain areas of our brains, our understanding of them becomes significantly different.

And indeed the experimental work carried out in neuropsychology powerfully supports the thesis that oxytocin is a crucial factor in human interrelationships. For example: in one experiment oxytocin was administered by nasal spray to a group of people before they engaged in an economics game called Investor. They were found to exhibit greater levels of trust and cooperation than the control group who had not been given the oxytocin spray.

More compelling still is what has been learned about 'mirror neurons', which enable even small babies to mimic the facial expressions of others. When one monkey watches another performing a task, the same neurons in his brain are activated as are activated in the brain of the performing monkey; his brain is passively modelling what the other monkey is up to. Given that empathy and mutual understanding are key components of the very possibility of morality, this neurophysiological evidence is highly suggestive.

There must of course, and rightly, be careful scrutiny of the way in which, and the degree to which, neuroscientific enquiry can give us insights into the deep questions of human morality and society. What goes on inside individual heads has to be put into informative relationship with what arises from the interactions – the debates, conflicts and cooperations – between people in groups and communities, and these latter obviously involve larger and in many respects different phenomena. But the evidence already to hand shows that there can no longer be speculation about morality and society, about human relationships, needs, desires and interests, which ignores the increasing flood of evidence about the brain's involvement in them all.

See: NEUROSCIENCE; MIND, PHILOSOPHY OF

NEUROSCIENCE

Neuroscience is the study of how the brain works. Given the exquisite complexity of the brain and its functioning – the brain has been described as one of the most complicated things in the universe – this is a challenging and profoundly interesting field of enquiry, and obviously a very important one. If the most ambitious prognostications for neuroscience are borne out, study of the brain will eventually explain nothing less than human nature itself, and with it morality, art, love, and everything else of value or moment in experience.

Neuroscience is conducted at several levels of structure, starting at the molecular level and proceeding to the cellular level, the systems level, the behavioural level, and finally – most complex of all – the cognitive level.

The stuff of which the brain is made consists of an amazing variety of molecules, a large number of which are found only in the nervous system. Molecular neuroscience studies the way neurons intercommunicate, grow, control what flows into and out of them, store information, and more. Cellular neuroscience studies the nature and functioning of connected groups of molecules, to find out how they link up, how different groups become dedicated to different functions, how they influence each other, and how they perform their computational tasks. When cellular structures group into systems, such as the visual cortex occupying a large area of the back of the brain, they constitute an identifiable mass of circuitry working in a highly coordinated way. Systems neuroscience studies brain structure and activity at this level.

Behaviour is the outcome of integrated functioning of systems in the brain and nervous system, so behavioural neuroscience seeks to discover the basis in brain function of (for example) memory, dreaming, and gender-specific characteristics. Even more complicatedly, cognitive neuroscience attempts to understand how the brain gives rise to the highest features of mental activity such as language use, reasoning, moral judgement, imagination – in general: to mind.

There are broadly two arenas in which neuroscientific enquiry is conducted: clinical neuroscience and experimental neuroscience. They are by no means exclusive of each other but obviously have distinguishable goals. Thus, clinical neuroscience is motivated by efforts to understand the brain and its operations for the purposes of effective endeavour in neurology, psychiatry, neurosurgery and neuropathology. Much has been learned about the brain from the deficits experienced by sufferers from one or another kind of brain injury or disease; and advances have been made in helping people who have suffered brain injury or disease as a result.

The disorders of brain and nervous system that clinical neuroscience aims to understand better include Alzheimer's and Parkinson's diseases, cerebral palsy, multiple sclerosis and other degenerative diseases of the nerves, schizophrenia, depression, epilepsy, stroke and head injury. The desire to make progress in dealing with these devastating conditions speaks for itself. The complexity here is obvious: abnormal thought and mood, as respectively present in schizophrenia and depression, are plausibly thought to be caused by brain malfunction, and identifying where and how these malfunctions occur in the brain is the challenging task. It is also a task of great urgency: in the United States more than 2 million people suffer from schizophrenia, and all forms of clinical disorders of thought and mood jointly cost the country over 1.5 billion dollars annually at time of writing. On all scales this is a problem of epidemic proportions, and clinical neuroscience and the associated field of psychopharmacology are the leading hopes for addressing it.

Experimental neuroscience ranges even more widely still. The specialists who engage in it include the psychobiologist, interested in the biological underpinnings of behaviour, and his colleague the neuroethologist who studies species-specific behaviour in relation to the brain of a given species; the neuropharmacologist, interested in the effects of various drugs on the nervous system; the neuroanatomist and neurochemist, respectively interested in the layout of the brain and the chemistry of the central nervous system; the developmental neurobiologist, interested in how brains grow and mature; and the computational neuroscientist, who employs mathematics and computing techniques to model the way brains work.

A lot of neuroscientific study proceeds by way of experimentation on animals, which raises ethical concerns over animal rights. It is distressing to see pictures of cats and monkeys with wire-trailing electrodes sticking out of their skulls, and even more distressing to think of some of what they are subjected to in the course of experiments. But not all neuroscientific experimentation exploits animals; the development of functional magnetic resonance imaging (fMRI) has enabled investigators to look inside human heads during real-time experiments, including cognitive and behavioural experiments, to see what the brain is doing; and this resource has been rich in results already.

Before the study of the brain had begun to reach its present levels of sophistication, researchers relied largely on observation of behaviour to infer what might be happening in the brain, given that much brain activity is expressed in outward activity. Head injury and intracranial vascular disease and tumours which led to specific deficits such as loss of speech or motor ability provided major clues to brain function. But the advent of scanners able to give high-resolution images of brain structures, and moreover able to reveal brain structures in the very process of activating in response to stimuli and tasks designed to evoke them, has taken observation right down to fine levels of structure. This is tantamount to opening the head, burrowing down into successive layers of the brain, and observing it actually at work.

See: NEUROPHILOSOPHY, SOCIOBIOLOGY

ORTHODOX CHRISTIANITY

The form of Christianity practised in 'the East' – that is, in what used to be the Byzantine world and adjacent areas into which Christianity of that form spread – is known as 'Orthodox Christianity'. There are fourteen or fifteen 'autocephalous' ('with their own heads') Orthodox Churches in mutual communion; the most senior of them is the Patriarchate of Constantinople, and they include the Greek, Russian, Ukrainian, Moldovan, Serbian, Latvian, Finnish, etc. etc., Orthodox Churches. There are also a score more which are not in communion with these, called such things as 'the Russian True Orthodox Church', 'the Russian Old Orthodox Church (Novozybkovsaya Hierarchy)', 'the Russian Orthodox Old-Rite Church (Belokrinitskaya Hierarchy)', 'the Church of the Genuine Orthodox Christians of Greece', 'the Orthodox Church of Greece (Holy Synod in Resistance)' – and so on and endlessly on for the usual split-off, quarrelling, disagreeing, mutually loathing sects which exemplify the great brotherhood of Christianity. The Orthodox divide further into 'Old Believers' (most believers tend to be such) and 'Old Calendarists' (why there should be quarrels over the calendar when the point is eternity and 'eternity' means 'outside time' is anyone's guess: but then the feasts of the faithful have to be observed at the right dates, or would be, if anyone knew definitively what they are).

Orthodox Churches give their functionaries extraordinary titles. So, for example, a 'protosyncellus' is the chief deputy of the bishop of an eparchy. This helpful definition is not much clarified by the interesting fact that the name derives from the Greek *sygkelloi*, one who shares a cell; the syncelli were the lads who shared a cell with their bishops 'to witness to the purity of their lives' and (or perhaps 'or') to perform the daily spiritual exercises with them.

As the foregoing suggests, the definition of Orthodox Christianity might as well be something like 'Christianity of a more than usually comical kind'. Alas, this description applies too generally to be of much help in differentiating the Orthodox from anyone else. The best one might be able to do is to point out that Rome and Constantinople fell out so seriously in the eleventh century of our common era (more precisely, 1054 CE) that they went their separate ways. This was the Great Schism, although in fact there had been many earlier differences, and they had many causes: the linguistic difference (Greek versus Latin), the differently evolved theologies, reluctance felt by the Orthodox patriarchs, especially of Constantinople, to accept the authority of the Pope in Rome, and the usual minutiae on which murder and war are so often premised, such as the word *filioque* ('and [from] the Son') – a tremendous sticking point for people with nothing better to do than argue over whether the Holy Spirit 'proceeds' from the Father alone, or from the Father AND the Son. Rome was for Yes on this point, Constantinople for No. The dispute is truly academic, given the doctrine of the unity of the Trinity (sic), namely, that the Father and the Son are One, so whatever 'proceeds' from one by the law of identity 'proceeds' from the other. But this is theology; and therefore a massive split ensued, right down the middle of the Christian world.

It was, by the way, the rather inaptly named Patriarch Photias I of Constantinople who decreed that AND was heretical, thus laying the slow foundations for his city to become the capital of the Islamic world a few centuries later. On the Orthodox Church website there is a photo of the Hagia Sophia in Constantinople with its Muslim towers digitally removed to show what it was like in its heyday.

Despite the internal variety of Orthodox Christianity, something of its nature might be captured by comparing it with its chief rival, Catholic Christianity. The Orthodox adhere to the Nicene Creed without 'and the Son', as noted. According to the cognoscenti, the difference between adding and not adding these words is vast; it is the Catholic Church which added them, stirring up trouble. After all, as one helpful but therefore misnamed Orthodox professor, Dr Alexander Roman, has written (note the capital letters), 'The Orthodox Church ... accepts, on faith, Christ's words in the Gospel, that the Father is the Unoriginate Source of the Life of the Trinity, with the Only-Begotten Son and Holy Spirit Proceeding from the Father Alone. We cannot know how the Begetting of the Son and the Proceeding of the Spirit from the same Father is different, only that it is and this distinguishes the two Persons.' (The claim that we do not know how the Begetting and the Proceeding differ seems theologically doubtful, at least for the reason that Mary was involved in the former *by means of* the Holy Spirit, whose Proceeding therefore had to Precede the Begetting, and Was Involved In It – various analogies for this springing readily to mind.)

Another difference is that the Romans use the 'Words of Institution' as the consecrating formula in the Mass (that is, for consecrating the Eucharist; the words are 'This is my Body ...') whereas the Orthodox employ for this purpose the entire Canon, the anamnesis, the Words of Institution and the Epiclesis (that is, the invoking or calling down) of the Holy Spirit – thus at vastly greater length with greater expenditure of incense and ritual.

The two Churches differ on original sin. The Catholics, following Augustine, think we inherit Adam's sin. The Orthodox think we inherit the consequences of his sin, namely death. Since this distinction is too fine to make a difference to the fact that we are all therefore condemned to death and a tendency to sin like Adam – to say nothing of the other recorded marks of the kindly deity's annoyance, namely having forever to eat our bread in the sweat of our brows and suffering agonies in childbirth – it seems hardly sufficient to cause a Schism. But (this is religion after all) it did.

The Orthodox do not have purgatory, do not recognize the sovereignty of the Pope, and claim that they are older than the Roman Catholic Church because Peter and Paul preached first in the East – and in many places – before doing so in the West in just one place (Rome); and moreover that the supposed primacy of the Pope among patriarchs owes itself to the accident of Rome being the earlier of the two capitals of the empire (the other of course being Constantinople).

The two Churches also differ on the Virgin Mary. To remove Mary from the descent of Adam's sin upon her, Rome (late in the day: 1854 to be exact, in Pope Pius IX's bull 'Ineffabilis Deus') decreed that she had 'immaculately' conceived; but the concept of her perfection and sinlessness of course far antedated this. Since the Orthodox do not think that humanity inherits the sin of Adam, it follows that neither did she; therefore this doctrine is from their point of view otiose. They worship her, as the Catholics do, as the 'Mother of God', laden with all perfections.

The Orthodox pride themselves in having two-dimensional icons so that we are reminded that we cannot penetrate the mysteries of heaven by means of the senses, whereas Rome permits statues. This is of a piece with Rome's efforts to define and defend its faith by means of reason and philosophy (for example, claiming that God's existence can be proved), whereas the Orthodox rejoice in basing everything on faith and not trying to reconcile faith and reason where they clash (which is everywhere). 'The Orthodox Church' (says one explainer) 'makes no effort to prove by logic or science what Christ gave his followers to believe.' This saves a deal of trouble.

A very large difference between the two Churches is that the Orthodox appear to believe that by Christ paying himself as ransom to the devil, who holds the power of death, he has made it possible for all to escape death and become like God – that is, to be deified. Rome does not think that the creatures of God will become gods, and they think the death and resurrection of Christ constituted the paying of the debt incurred by Adam.

The Orthodox, it seems, do not kneel on Sundays. Unlike the Catholics', their Eucharistic bread is leavened, and they take communion in 'both kinds' (wine and bread, not just bread as with Catholics). Orthodox clergy can marry, and they wear beards; Catholic clergy are the other way round in both respects. The Orthodox worship facing the east; Catholics can worship in any direction. Catholic deceased go to Purgatory to purge their sins; Orthodox deceased wait in 'the abode of the dead' (Hades) until the last trump, at which time their souls rejoin their bodies to be judged; the good go to heaven and the bad and unbelievers go to hell where they are tortured for all eternity in fire. (So Hell is evidently a physical place with a very big furnace; it has not so far been detected by astronomers or geologists, but perhaps it will be especially created by the all-loving deity when the time for setting fire to sinners arrives.)

There is much more; but this perhaps suffices to outline some of the tenets of Orthodoxy, though doubtless the fissions within the Orthodox realm make for many further differences not just among themselves but with Rome.

The Orthodox Churches are more conservative even than the Roman Catholic Church, and its votaries deprecate the reforms that recent Popes have introduced, as placing a yet larger gulf between them and Rome. A notable feature of Orthodoxy is its ritual, which is elaborate, long-winded, darkling, smoky, with rather splendid deep chanting and lots of robes. Orthodox Church buildings often have sharp spires and onion-shaped domes in close profusion, brightly painted and looking like a stage set for the *Nutcracker* ballet.

See: CATHOLICISM, CHRISTIANITY, PROTESTANTISM, RELIGION

PHILOSOPHY

'Philosophy' is derived from a Greek word literally meaning 'love of wisdom', but it is better and more accurately defined as 'enquiry' or 'enquiry and reflection', giving these expressions their widest scope to denote efforts to understand the world and human experience in it. This is how the word 'philosophy' was understood right into the nineteenth century of our common era; in the most general and comprehensive sense it meant what we now call science as well as what we now call philosophy, and today's distinction between science and philosophy gradually came to be marked by calling the former 'natural philosophy' and the latter 'moral philosophy'. This latter expression now more narrowly denotes ethics, but in its original acceptation it embraced ethics, aesthetics, theory of knowledge, metaphysics and logic – that is, philosophy in the now current sense.

The aim of philosophical enquiry is to gain insight into knowledge, truth, reality, reason, meaning and value. Other human endeavours, not least art and literature, explore these same matters from a variety of directions and in their own way, but philosophy mounts a direct investigation of them in the hope of bringing at least more clarity to them and the concepts deployed in them – and perhaps and at best, answers to the questions they prompt.

In earlier times, before distinctions were drawn between the subject matter and methods of the natural sciences, social sciences and humanities, philosophy was a large part of the vocation of almost all educated minds. The Greeks of classical antiquity are credited with originating Western philosophy in this broad sense, because they enquired freely into all things, not starting from religious or traditional assumptions but premising their thinking on the belief that human reason and observation are competent to the task of asking the right questions about what matters to humanity, and seeking answers to them.

The Greeks speculated about the origin and nature of the physical universe. They debated the ethical and political circumstances of mankind, and proposed views about their best arrangements. They investigated reason itself, and attempted to define truth and knowledge. In doing so they touched upon almost every major philosophical question, and founded the great tradition of philosophical enquiry which has continued, and continued to grow, to our own day.

For a long period, from about the fourth century to the seventeenth century CE, thought in the Western world (which for most of that time meant Europe) was dominated by Christianity. This does not mean that there was no philosophy, but most of it served theology or was constrained by the perceived inconvenience or danger of potential conflicts with theology. But by the seventeenth century, as a result of the several centuries of developments labelled, for historical convenience, the 'Renaissance' and 'Reformation', there had occurred a liberation of philosophical thinking from theological government, with therefore a concomitant rise of natural science and renewed independent thought about the principles of politics and morals.

Philosophy is a highly productive and consequential enterprise. An eye cast over the intellectual history of the modern world (from, say, 1600 CE onwards) would see that in effect philosophy gave birth to natural science in the seventeenth century, to psychology in the eighteenth century, to sociology and linguistics in the nineteenth century, while in the twentieth century it played a significant part in the development of cognitive science. No doubt this somewhat simplifies matters, but not by too much, because philosophy is enquiry into important and central concerns that are not yet well understood, certainly not well enough understood to constitute self-standing branches of study. When the right questions and the right methods of answering them become apparent, the area of enquiry in question can become an independent pursuit. For a major example: as soon as philosophical speculation about the nature and properties of the material universe had identified appropriate methods of asking and answering its questions – in this case by empirical and mathematical means – the enquiry ceased to be philosophy and became natural science.

One might almost say that philosophy's aim is to bring itself to an end, by finding the right way to deal with its questions so that independent trains of enquiry can take over and produce concrete results – as with science – where once there was doubt and disagreement, unclarity and difficulty. A great deal of disagreement, unclarity and difficulty remain in some of the areas of most vital concern to us: in ethics especially, where questions about the right and the good continually press in almost all areas of human experience, but also in relation to questions about consciousness, scientific truth (witness the debate over evolutionary theory in biology and the conflict with religion), and more.

But to say that philosophy seeks to bring itself to an end by finding the right questions and right methods of enquiry for a subject matter – as with the natural sciences – is really just a manner of speaking; for the individual enquiries that philosophy has given birth to find themselves confronting philosophical questions all over again at the limits of their advance – think of fundamental physics and cosmology, and the speculations that arise because the frontiers of ignorance have once again been reached.

As a pursuit and as a discipline studied in universities, philosophy's three main divisions are metaphysics, epistemology and ethics (see the separate entries for each in these pages). In universities students are also expected or at least encouraged to study the history of both ancient and modern philosophy, because doing so advances understanding of major philosophical problems and discourages reinvention of the wheel as a square or triangle. As an extension of its central enquiries philosophy also examines the assumptions, methods and claims of other areas of intellectual endeavour, as in the 'philosophy of science', 'philosophy of history', 'philosophy of psychology', and more. Along with the vital questions of ethics, further questions about value arise in two different directions: one is about the best arrangements for the communities in which people, as social animals, are bound to live – this is political philosophy; the other is about other kinds of value in experience, particularly aesthetic value, found or postulated for the domains of art, beauty, and the encounter with both.

Each of the three main branches of philosophy has a separate entry in this dictionary, but a brief word about each is appropriate here.

'Epistemology' or 'theory of knowledge' concerns the nature and sources of knowledge. The questions asked by epistemologists are: What is knowledge? What are the best means of acquiring it? In addition to defining the nature of knowledge, epistemology attempts to meet challenges to our hopes or pretensions to have knowledge, in the form of sceptical doubts about whether knowledge is possible.

'Metaphysics' is the enquiry into the ultimate or fundamental nature of reality. Its questions are: What exists? What exists ultimately or basically? What is existence itself? Under this label lie questions about the difference, if there is one – and if there is one, the relation – between body and mind, and whether or not there is a God. So major are these questions that they are sometimes said to constitute separate sub-branches of metaphysics, labelled 'philosophy of mind' and 'philosophical theology' respectively.

'Ethics' is the most immediately familiar branch of philosophy to non-students of philosophy. It consists in the examination of questions about the values by which we live our lives. It enquires into the nature of the right and the good, and discusses theories about the basis on which we should choose, act and judge in the moral sphere.

It is finally relevant to note that there are several major traditions of philosophy in the world, separated by geography and history, but unsurprisingly sharing a very large number of similar concerns.

In the Western world philosophy is much as described in the preceding paragraphs, although in the last century or so there has been a divergence between 'analytic philosophy', practised mainly in the Anglophone world, which is piecemeal, highly technical, and deeply sensitive to and informed by logic and science, and 'continental philosophy' (a misnomer, for though it alludes to continental Europe it is practised in Britain and North America too), which deals in metaphysics, sociology, and social and historical criticism in sometimes larger terms. Leading figures in the analytic tradition are Bertrand Russell, Ludwig Wittgenstein, A.J. Ayer, Karl Popper, W.V.O. Quine, P.F. Strawson, Donald Davidson, Saul Kripke, Hilary Putnam, and others – this list names a mixture of British and

American thinkers, but analytic philosophy is a collegial endeavour and contributions to its debates come from every quarter of the Anglophone and European worlds, with Australia as a net contributor. Leading figures in continental philosophy include Edmund Husserl, Martin Heidegger, Jean-Paul Sartre, Michel Foucault and Jacques Derrida.

India has a powerful philosophical tradition, and the questions debated by its major schools of thought are close in character to the questions of the Western tradition. Some hold that the earliest development of philosophy in Greek antiquity owes debts of influence to the earliest Indian schools. Surveys of this rich tradition distinguish between the orthodox (*astika*) philosophies and the heterodox (*nastika*) philosophies, the former including the Samkhya, Vaisesika and Nyaya schools, the latter including Buddhism and Jainism. In Samkhya one finds discussion of questions about metaphysics, causation and conscious; in Vaisesika one finds discussion of categories, the whole–part relation, and atoms; in Nyaya, causation, epistemology and truth. In each case the debates and concerns have close parallels to their cognates in the Western tradition. Practical ethics and strong traditions of atheism and humanism have a significant place in Indian thinking too, a fact less appreciated in the West, whose perceptions of Indian thought and practice are dominated by yoga and strains of mysticism and Indian religion.

China also has rich and long-standing philosophical traditions. The most famous is Confucianism, a set of doctrines in ethics and political philosophy primarily about the duties of rulers and the best ordering of the state. Legalism and neo-Confucianism had more actual influence on the practice of political life in Chinese history, but in individual ethics original Confucian precepts have always been held in esteem, and reputed to govern the outlook of nobles and scholars. Daoism likewise is a personal ethic premised on a complex metaphysical view of the nature of reality; because of its relative lack of concern for matters public and political its influence in Chinese culture is far less pervasive than Confucianism.

Less known than any of the other Chinese schools, but of great intrinsic interest in itself, is Mohism, whose logical and ethical doctrines are fascinating and instructive. Its founder Mo Zi taught brotherly love and the equality of man, which did not please rulers and their aristocracies. A striking fact about China is the absence of organized religion, for which widespread eclectic superstition of a capacious and laissez-faire nature substitutes; thus, a Chinese family will employ a Buddhist priest, a Daoist priest, a Confucian priest and a Christian priest at a funeral, to cover all bases, as it were – but the dominating practice was traditionally ancestor-worship, and in many places to this day family graves are swept, and cakes and paper money laid upon them, to keep the spirits of ancestors supplied, happy and helpful.

Reflection on the philosophical traditions of the world prompts one to wonder at the curious mixture that is humankind. Human beings can be intelligent, curious and inventive, prone to question and enquire, to speculate and discover. They can also be credulous, superstitious, lazy-minded and fanciful. It was once remarked that the persistence of religious belief is not the result of lack of imagination, as some have said, but of too much imagination filling the place of ignorance. There is something in this; the stories of religion can be quickly and entertainingly told and readily understood, whereas a mastery of physics or biology takes time, patience and above-average mental powers. These same virtues are required in philosophy.

See: AESTHETICS, EPISTEMOLOGY, ETHICS, METAPHYSICS

POLITICS

When people define politics as the 'art of the possible' they are being sanguine; it might better be described as the 'art of the near-impossible', because it is the process by which groups, communities, nations, or citizens of a state try among themselves to decide what to do, how things should be run, how social goods should be apportioned, how relations of authority and power should be managed – including who is to have power, for what purposes, for how long, and to what extent. Because there are inevitably differing interests and opinions in any group, the processes of politics involve efforts variously to reach compromises, or to gain control of decision-making and decision-executing processes by securing the reins of authority; this is the typical political process in any society, whether democratic or dictatorial. The means may differ (elections, revolutions, military coups) but the underlying aims and goals are very similar. Questions arise concerning the legitimacy of how authority is gained and held; much of the theoretical discussion in politics concerns this central point.

Political science is the study of political processes; political philosophy is the study of political ideas, theories and concepts. Debate about these matters is very ancient. Its first developed roots lie, as so much else in the Western tradition, with the Greeks of classical antiquity. The first full treatise of that tradition is Plato's *Republic*; Confucius predates him as a political thinker, but did not leave a treatise of the extent and cogency of Plato's famous book, his views instead being transmitted by a tradition of disciples, recorded in the *Analects*.

Speaking generally, it can be said that power takes a variety of forms: the power to reward and to punish; the power conferred by knowledge, expertise or talent, and by success or accomplishment; the power gained by legitimate processes which communities agree upon; the power gained by force or strength.

The key question about legitimacy of power is not the same as the reason why people obey those who hold it, for obvious enough reasons. If power is held by force, prudence may well lead people to acknowledge it. If someone assumes power through sheer charisma, the widespread psychological propensity people have to desire to be led will come into play. Tradition and constitutional arrangements are the main sources of legitimacy for power in almost all societies.

Confucius addressed himself to the question of what makes a good ruler, and his view was that a good ruler is in essence a highly ethical individual, whose example and loving concern for his people will ensure that the state functions well. In addition, if each member of society assiduously performs the duties of his station (more accurately, his various stations) in life – if 'the minister is a minister, a father is a father, a son is a son' – there will be harmony and smooth functioning. This utopian vision is not especially consistent with reality; it is not hard to imagine, or indeed to find, examples of good rulers without good subjects.

Plato, an aristocrat who objected profoundly to the democracy under which he lived in Athens because he saw it as rule by the ignorant mob, argued that the best political arrangement would be rule by an educated elite ('philosopher kings'), who would be selected early for their intellectual gifts and specially trained for their task; who would own no property and therefore would be immune to corruption; who would not marry but would live collegially with one another. Children would be produced by couples selected for their intelligence and beauty, taken from their mothers to be educated together in public schools, and then apportioned according to their aptitudes to one of the three orders of society: the rulers, the soldier class, and the ordinary people.

It was Aristotle who defined man as the 'political animal', and like Plato and Confucius held that ethics and politics are continuous: the good life for individuals requires a good society as its setting in order to make it possible. He conducted an empirical examination of different political arrangements, studying the constitutions of various city states, and one of his conclusions was that each acceptable form of government had inherent in it the danger of degrading into an unacceptable form: thus, kingship could decay into tyranny, aristocracy into oligarchy, and what he called 'polity' – citizens ruling collectively by agreement – could degenerate into ochlocracy (mob rule) – though the word Aristotle used to denote this unacceptable arrangement was 'democracy'.

Two thinkers proved influential in political thought at the beginning of the modern era in Europe: the seventeenth-century thinkers Thomas Hobbes and John Locke. In his *Leviathan* Hobbes argued that people join together in political communities in order to escape the harsh condition of the state of nature, the free-for-all war of all on all in which life is nasty, brutish and short. The mutual contract into which people enter to escape this condition involves giving up part of their original liberty to secure the goods of mutual protection and order, made possible by their submitting to the authority of a sovereign power. This power Hobbes defined as 'nothing more than the personal embodiment of orderly government', the word 'personal' suggesting a single individual – a king – but which could be interpreted as a body of men.

Locke, in adopting the fiction of a social contract also, and coupling it with an argument against the doctrine of 'divine right of kings', came to a view different from Hobbes. He did not see the state of nature as an anarchy of mutual hostility, but as a domain in which individuals possess 'natural rights' which are not abrogated when they combine together into civil society. The doctrine of natural rights states (as Locke puts it in his *Second Treatise of Government*) that everyone is equal and independent, and that 'no one ought to harm another in his life, liberty, health or possessions'.

Jean-Jacques Rousseau's *The Social Contract* advances the idea of the natural freedom and equality of man (it famously begins 'man is born free but is everywhere in chains'), and argues that the source of political legitimacy is 'the general will' of the people. For Rousseau the exercise of sovereignty always aims at the public good, which can conflict at times with the interests of individuals; and more to the point the 'general will' can sometimes be mistaken about what is genuinely for the best. To adjust such conflicts society needs a lawgiver to frame a constitution.

The contradiction implicit in Rousseau's view between the general will and individual interests was one motive for John Stuart Mill's insistence on the need for protection of minorities and individuals in a democracy. In his view the highest political good is liberty, and the only legitimate reason for limiting anyone's liberty is to protect the interests of others. Liberty includes freedom of speech, and one important good served by liberty is that the widest range of experiments towards good individual lives is made possible by it – always subject to the 'harm principle' stating that no one has a right to harm others in the enjoyment and exercise of their liberty.

Karl Marx was Mill's contemporary, and these two thinkers have arguably had the most influence on political thought and practice since their time. Marx saw history as a succession of class struggles, of which the phase through which he himself lived consisted of the struggle between the capitalist bourgeoisie and the industrial proletariat. Indeed the Industrial Revolution was bringing the conflict between workers and owners of capital into crucial conflict, Marx argued, with the inevitable outcome of the historical process being the triumph of the proletariat and the eventual emergence of a classless society in which the means of production will be owned by the people. In the transitional stage leading to a genuinely communist society, namely the 'socialist' stage, the state would own the means of production. Marx's utopian ideal of a free, classless, sharing society was also internationalist; he believed borders to be a feature of the imprisoned state of man, which would wither away with the state itself as true communism was attained. None of the practical would-be implementations of Marxist theory have worked out in anything like the way he predicted or desired, so far.

Each of the main ideas involved in systems of political organization – democracy, liberalism, socialism, communism, totalitarianism, Fascism – is to be found sketched under its own heading elsewhere in these pages.

See: COMMUNISM, DEMOCRACY, FASCISM, LIBERALISM, LIBERTY, MARXISM, SOCIALISM, TOTALITARIANISM

POSITIVISM AND LOGICAL POSITIVISM

Positivism is the view that theological and metaphysical enquiry can lead only to nonsense, and that all genuine knowledge must be rooted in and testable by sense experience. It thus has close affinities with empiricism and naturalism.

The first great exponent of positivist thinking in modern times, although he did not use the label, is David Hume. He gives a classic statement of the fundamental positivist outlook at the end of his *Enquiry Concerning Human Understanding*: 'If we take in our hand any volume:

of divinity or school metaphysics, for instance; let us ask, Does it contain any abstract reasoning concerning quantity or number? No. Does it contain any experimental reasoning concerning matters of fact and existence? No. Commit it then to the flames, for it can contain nothing but sophistry and illusion.'

The term 'positivism' itself was coined by the French thinker Auguste Comte (1798–1857) and employed in the title of one of his chief works, the *Cours de Philosophie Positive* (6 volumes 1830–42). Comte derived his views from a number of sources, starting with John Locke and including the Enlightenment thinkers, chief among them Hume and Kant, and incorporating also the philanthropy of Saint-Simon.

In Comte's view, history shows that all sciences pass through three stages: the theological, the metaphysical, and finally the positive, which – in rejecting the superstition of theology and the speculative illusions of metaphysics – bases itself firmly on empirical enquiry. In ascending order of complexity, he said, the six fundamental sciences are mathematics, astronomy, physics, chemistry, biology, and sociology.

But Comte also thought that human beings need something like a religious practice and commitment to satisfy their spiritual needs and provide a basis for their morality. As a substitute for the false superstitions of traditional religion he invented instead the Religion of Humanity, complete with a catechism, services, a hierarchical priesthood and calendar of feast days, all on the model of Catholicism. The object of worship was the 'Great Being' (humanity itself) in the Great Medium (world-space), and the 'fetish' is the earth – thus the Trinity of Positivist religion. It is an illuminating comment on Comte's ethics that he is the coiner of the word 'altruism', which he used to describe the attitude that positivist religion was to inculcate in its practitioners.

After Comte's death his movement split into two. The orthodox or mainstream succession was led by Pierre Lafitte, who maintained both the scientific and religious aspects, the latter complete with priesthood and ritual. It achieved a following in Sweden, England, and parts of South America. A breakaway group led by Emile Littré rejected the religious aspect and emphasized the scientific aspect alone. For Littré, positivism was in essence a method, the empirical method applied in the natural and social sciences. He rejected religion and argued that the true ethical aim of positivism is the progress of humanity, achieved by understanding humanity through science and education, caring about it through practical policies, beautifying it by means of the arts, and enriching it through industry.

In its philosophical aspects Comte's positivism had great influence among thinkers as diverse as John Stuart Mill, Herbert Spencer, T.H. Huxley and others. One of Comte's greatest admirers in England was G.H. Lewes, consort of George Eliot and author of the *Biographical History of Philosophy* which ends with Comte as the final word.

The methodological aspect of the positivist outlook was also congenial to Ernst Mach (1838–1916), the Austrian physicist, physiologist and philosopher who did significant work on Doppler effects in optics and acoustics (his is the name in 'Mach number' denoting the ratio of the speed of an object to the speed of sound), studied sensory perception, and made valuable contributions to the philosophy of science. Albert Einstein said that Mach was a forerunner of his own theory of relativity because of what has become known as Mach's principle, namely, that everything in the universe ultimately affects everything else in the universe.

Mach's philosophy of science is a classic form of instrumentalism, that is, the view that scientific statements and theories are not true or false, only more or less useful. On this view scientific terms such as 'electron' do not refer to really existing things, but to useful fictions which permit successful prediction and application; the terms are 'instruments' or 'tools', hence the label for the theory. Instrumentalism accordingly has affinities to pragmatism, and stands in opposition to scientific realism, which as the name suggests holds that the terms of scientific theory really do refer to actually existing objects, and that accordingly scientific theories are genuinely true or false.

Mach's views in their turn influenced the scientists and philosophers who constituted the Vienna Circle in the city of that name after the First World War. The Circle included Moritz Schlick, in whose rooms it met at the University of Vienna, Otto Neurath, Herbert Feigl, Rudolf Carnap, Gustav Bergmann and Friedrich Waismann. Karl Popper and Kurt Gödel had some association with it, and two of its members (Schlick and Waismann) had meetings with Ludwig Wittgenstein, though his *Tractatus Logico-Philosophicus* was far from persuading everyone in the Circle (as Carnap later revealed).

The best way to present the logical positivist's outlook is as a theory about what constitutes meaningfulness – just as asserted by Hume in his famous remark about 'sophistry and illusion', which positivism effectively adopted as its slogan. The logical positivists argued that statements are genuinely meaningful only if they are either logical or mathematical statements, in which case their truth-value is settled by the meaning of the terms occurring in them, or they are empirical statements which can be verified or falsified by empirical investigation. (See the fuller discussion of VERIFICATIONISM below.) Everything else is strictly 'nonsense' in the literal and neutral meaning of this term, 'non-sense'. Ethical, religious and aesthetic remarks fall into this category, and at most have emotional or persuasive content for those who utter and hear them.

Factual and analytic statements constitute science. Moritz Schlick believed that at base science rests on direct observational reports (called 'protocol sentences'), and that the observational terms occurring in them are ostensively defined (that is, defined by literally pointing at the things being spoken about). He wrote, 'there is no way of understanding any meaning without ultimate reference to ostensive definition, and this means, in an obvious sense, reference to "experience" or possibility of "verification"'. The equation of 'experience' with 'possibility of verification' is interesting; having the experience which protocol sentences report is just to realize the possibility of verification – that is, to make verification actual.

In an influential paper Carnap argued that scientific knowledge ultimately rests on protocol sentences, which report the observations that verify or falsify hypotheses. The protocol sentences themselves, consisting in incorrigible reports of observations, require no further verification. Schlick agreed, writing that protocol sentences are 'the unshakeable point of contact between knowledge and reality ... we come to know these absolutely fixed points of contact, the confirmations, in their individuality; they are the only synthetic statements that are not hypotheses.'

Otto Neurath pointed out a serious problem with this account. It assumes that protocol sentences are incorrigible because they directly and neutrally correspond to experience-independent facts. But protocol sentences cannot be incorrigible, Neurath said, because at best it can only be a conventional matter which propositions count as 'basic', and no statement, not even a putative protocol sentence, is immune to revision or rejection. 'There is no way of taking conclusively established pure protocol sentences as the starting point of the sciences. No tabula rasa exists. We are like sailors who must rebuild their ship on the open sea.' We begin our enquiries already bearing a rich apparatus of assumptions and theories, and the result of our enquiries is sometimes to make us change or replace some of these – like planks of wood being replaced in a ship at sea – and this further means that the test for truth is not whether a given statement corresponds with reality, but whether it coheres with already accepted and tested statements.

Neurath's view paves the way for theories such as the one advanced by the American philosopher W.V.O. Quine, who argued that observation is not neutral but 'theory-laden', that is, that our observations are conducted in terms of our antecedent theories, which therefore determine what we observe. As actual scientific practice shows, this means that if an observation does not fit with what is expected it is as likely to be ignored, dismissed as aberrant, or attributed to error, as to make us change our theories to accommodate it. But if theory is carried to observation, then the 'meaning' of observation terms, and the notion of observational confirmation of theory itself, is established in advance – logically speaking – of observation; and observation therefore cannot play the part desired for it by Schlick and Carnap.

Whatever the merits of particular forms of positivist views, the importance of the general thrust of positivism is great, for it is the deep background of almost all serious work in science and social science and the trends in analytic philosophy most closely identified with them. A statement of that background might look like this: that knowledge properly so called is positive knowledge, that is, empirically based, evidentially constrained, subject to revision in the light of new evidence or better reasoning, disciplined by rational evaluation, constrained by common sense, and always sceptical, challenging, hard-nosed, informed, and rigorous. Among other things therefore it is a scythe to the fancies and fairy tales in which humanity has cocooned itself in its eagerness for explanatory narratives that are easy to understand and comforting, derived from the deepest wells of our past ignorances. It is the intellectual attitude of humanity's emerging maturity, or at least the promise of its emergence one day – we hope – soon.

See: EXPERIMENTAL PHILOSOPHY, METAPHYSICS, PHILOSOPHY, VERIFICATIONISM

POSTMODERNISM

If you are a relativist about values, if you are sceptical about Enlightenment ideals of liberal humanism, if you are a pessimist about progress, if you lack confidence in the idea of a 'grand narrative' premised on the belief that liberty and knowledge can be made to increase by the endeavour of mankind while human suffering and tribulation concomitantly diminish, then you are a paid-up 'postmodernist'.

Like all such, given the defining characteristics of the outlook, you do not have much that is positive to say. Your chief reason for asserting these relativist, sceptical, pessimistic views is to oppose those who hope for progress, who try to make a case for the universality of ethics, and who think that contemporary constitutional democracy is both an improvement on feudalism and absolute monarchy, and preferable to dictatorship.

You are a beneficiary of all that Enlightenment optimism has achieved, but you repudiate it now. You are not an external opponent of the liberal democracies in which civil liberties and the rule of law permit you to say these things – that is, you are not a subscriber to one of the monolithic ideologies of e.g. religion or Stalinism which know their one big truth about how things are and the right way things should be done, and therefore force everyone to conform even on pain of death. No, you are not an external opponent but an internal opponent, with criticisms but no solutions other than (for example) to believe that all answers to questions about the human good, from all traditions and viewpoints, are of equal validity.

Well: one advantage of such a view is that it provides a happy release from the demand to do much thinking and acting; the task of trying to discern what is true, or what is best, or what is most convincing, among the welter of opinions, views, wishful thinkings and dogmatisms that abound in the world, is after all hard labour. From this postmodernism frees us, for it tells us that they are all equally valid in their own terms, and it is not merely fruitless but wrong to suggest otherwise. (Wrong? But postmodernism gives us no standard even to say this. A certain self-defeating invitation to silence is close in the offing here.)

Proponents of postmodernism, or at least those who set out to explain it sympathetically, ascribe to Jean-François Lyotard's *The Post-Modern Condition: A Report on Knowledge*, published in 1979, the source of the twin claims that the 'grand narratives' of modernism (about progress, science, rationality) have lost their credibility, and that therefore authority in all its forms, including cultural and epistemological authority, should be disdained. Some commentators link this stance to the tradition of scepticism stemming from ancient philosophy, and to similar-sounding views in Friedrich Nietzsche, with his announcement of the death of God and the illusory nature of knowledge and morality.

But the term 'post-modern' predated Lyotard – it occurs in the title of Charles Jencks's influential treatise *The Language of Post-Modern Architecture* in 1975, and was being bandied about in the 1960s in connection with contemporary dance and literature. In all cases the same general outlook was connoted. Jencks described postmodern architecture as a rejection of the functionalism and formalism of modernist architecture, and the substitution in its place of pluralism, ambiguity and pastiche in styles. This is the architectural analogue of the philosophical rejection of foundations and absolute truth.

There is an immediate implication for politics. If anything goes, and if (to quote Jean Baudrillard) 'reality is not what it used to be', what are we to say about social and economic justice, human rights, democracy, legal reform, good government, the whole arena of pressing political and social concern? If there is any aspect of human endeavour which, by reason of sheer practicality and urgency, resists the footling-about and intellectual posturing of academics with too much time on their hands and too much egoism in their souls, politics is surely it.

And as it happens there is a case to be made for saying that this is where the postmodernist attitude gets its hardest test. Consider Lyotard's claims about the failure of confidence in the grand narratives of Enlightenment progress in science and rights, and the march towards liberation of hitherto disenfranchised peoples who had historically been subjugated by priestcraft and absolute monarchy. Lyotard described his view of this failure as an 'extreme simplification' for the sake of his argument. To see just how extreme his simplification is, consider the claim he accepted from the Adorno–Horkheimer thesis that the Enlightenment was ultimately responsible for Nazism and Stalinism, on the grounds that its privileging of rationality led to bureaucratic managerialism and eventually the tyranny of these two -isms. His own failure, as was theirs, is to see the flaw in this argument, namely, that the -isms are paradigmatically counter-Enlightenment phenomena, aimed at repressing the drives towards pluralism, personal autonomy, democracy and protective regimes of rights that limit central power over individuals, which the Enlightenment had proclaimed and enabled.

Given that the main concerns of progressive political thought lie precisely in the arena of social justice, civil liberties and empowerment of the people, and given that these very ideas are pillars of the Enlightenment 'grand narrative', a rejection of the latter destabilizes efforts to achieve anything concrete in respect of them. If postmodern attitudes and fealties are to withstand scrutiny, their advocates have to have an answer to the political challenge implicit here.

Some of the most energetic debate about postmodernism has taken place in critical and cultural theory, and it is there that its chief agonists are to be found, among them Frederick Jameson and Terry Eagleton. One focus of criticism is well summed up by Jürgen Habermas's remark that 'issues of truth and right reason are inescapably raised by any discourse that presents itself for serious appraisal in the mode of diagnostic commentary', which of course postmodernist theorizing does.

By undermining its own claims to be part of 'diagnostic commentary' and to merit 'serious appraisal' by rejecting the notion of standards by which such appraisal can be conducted, postmodernism has had little real impact in philosophy, but far more in a simulacrum of philosophy, a sort of ersatz, easy, do-it-yourself philosophy that calls itself 'literary theory', where various playful because inconsequential forms of jargon-rich lucubration take the place of substantive commentary. Postmodern thought thus appears as a kind of *reductio ad absurdum* of the professionalization of the humanities in higher education when real content has been exhausted and salaries have still to be earned.

Because of the key place occupied in postmodern thought by the 'extreme simplification' of Lyotard's animadversions against 'grand narrative', it is important to note that this latter does not entail the idea of a coherent historical plan unfolding to a predetermined and/or perfected end. Francis Fukuyama made the same mistake from the other end of the telescope, thinking that a final Hegelian synthesis had been reached by the conquest *über alles* of free market capitalism, signified by the fall of the Berlin Wall in 1989. He should have waited to see whether history would resume in the upsurge of violent Islamism, or the ignominious collapse of the greediest form of capitalism in the global financial crisis of 2008. Fukuyama mistook the meaning of the Enlightenment grand narrative of progress, which is meliorist and fallibilist, and saw it instead as something more like perfectibilism, or millenarianism, or some other fanciful view. By 'meliorist' I mean the view that things can be made better by effort, in piecemeal and incremental fashion, without any assumption that they will one day be made perfect; and by 'fallibilist' I mean the recognition that progress is not inevitable or irreversible; it can fail, or be subject to setbacks, or take a very long time to get not very far.

Yet still: one would be a lunatic to deny that in practical matters of sanitation, child health, dentistry, street lighting, housing, education, and a million such besides, things have got better since the eighteenth century for many in the world; and likewise in respect of liberty, democracy, secularism, science, technology, the rule of law, and a thousand other respects. Those who see no progress from medieval feudalism to modern liberal democracy have a serious problem; yet that is the implication of postmodern views, thus demonstrated to be after all an unintelligent extrapolation from discussion of architecture, where it would have done better to remain.

See: ENLIGHTENMENT, RELATIVISM

PRIVACY

All human rights conventions include a provision defending privacy. The reason is a good one: privacy is an essential for human beings, who need it just as much as they need food, water and affection. It is a right that protects a vital margin of individuality: thoughts, ideas, memories, desires, intimacies with others, projects and plans, the complex experience of selfhood, are matters that mainly and sometimes exclusively concern only individuals themselves, and which no one else has a right to trespass upon. Individuals must be able to control access to these aspects of their own lives, and admit others to it or parts of it only by invitation when they can trust the invitees.

A person needs to be able to rest from the scrutiny and interventions of others and the world at large. He needs to be able to relax, let down his guard, be wholly himself, breathe freely, shut out the demands and prying of others so that he can refresh and restore himself in the private space of his personal, intimate life and his own thoughts. One form of torture, and a highly damaging one psychologically, is to keep a person under constant scrutiny and exposure: the psychological friabilities of some who court celebrity are exposed by the relentless invasion of privacy by tabloid newspapers and the public hunger for gossip that they feed.

A large part of the importance of privacy as a human need and right is that it helps people keep at least some control over how they appear to the world. Most people seek to be acceptable to society, for obvious psychological and practical reasons. It could be awkward and even disabling to have certain of one's sentiments and personal habits publicly known, especially any that are conventionally unacceptable. Again, at their first outset one's endeavours and projects are generally too immature to bear outside scrutiny; they need to be nourished in private before they are ready.

But the primary reason is that a degree of privacy is fundamental for autonomy and psychological health. Even lovers need to retain a degree of privacy from each other; to be unable to have a reserve of selfhood is to be bereft of a self altogether.

Yet at the same time, most people are intensely curious about other people's lives and doings, which explains the relish people have for gossip, newspaper revelations about 'celebrities', soap operas where viewers can be flies on the wall witnessing fictionalized versions of other lives, and for the traditional staples of film, drama, biographies and novels. All these sources of data about other people answer an important need: our voyeuristic impulse to research human experience continually, as a way of informing our sense of selfhood and our own possibilities for living.

It might be asked whether there is not a contradiction between our voyeuristic interest in others and our need for privacy for ourselves. Are people being dishonest in desiring to know about others what they themselves seek to conceal? The answer is No. Except in the grey margin between the mainly anonymous lives of the majority and the exhibitionists who clamour to expose themselves publicly, there is a genuine consistency between our curiosity and our reticence. They are connected; it is precisely because there are things we wish to keep veiled that we wish to peep behind others' veils – to find out whether we are normal, and safe, and whether we are coping or falling short. A kind of negotiation results, a transaction essential to us as social animals, in which we simultaneously try to discover as much, and to reveal as little (except to intimates), as we can.

On the larger question of governmental and legal invasions of privacy, matters are clear enough. Properly warranted scrutiny of email messages, telephone calls and mail is an unpalatable but necessary weapon in the fight against crime and terrorism. It is a price to pay for security. Your cyber flirtation with an emailer in Oregon will merely amuse an official eavesdropper, but your plan to blow up Congress deserves to be detected. By contrast, what any consenting adults do in their own homes, even if it involves what others perceive as 'harm' to themselves, is no one else's business. These examples are clear cases on either side of a clear divide. The fact that there will be difficult grey areas in between does nothing to change that. There are always grey areas in everything: they have to be dealt with on their merits, and the only principle that applies in connection with privacy is: when in doubt, let privacy win over curiosity.

So if there are occasions when privacy has to be invaded in the interests of security or investigation of crimes, the invasion has to be licensed as a specific, well-motivated, case-by-case, temporary and limited suspension of what is in general a highly significant civil liberty for the individual or individuals under scrutiny. Any laws that give the security and policing services powers to invade privacy should be limited by sunset clauses, necessitating renewed debate every time their expiry approaches, so that the justification for them can be reinforced – or if the justification itself has expired, for the powers to lapse. This is the right way to proceed on any laws that infringe civil liberties in the real or supposed interests of some greater good than the liberties themselves.

See: AUTONOMY, HUMAN RIGHTS

PROTESTANTISM

When Martin Luther nailed his ninety-five theses to the church door in Wittenberg on 31 October 1517, thereby launching the Reformation – better described as the first one hundred and thirty-one years of murderous intra-Christian strife culminating in the exhaustion of the Treaty of Westphalia in 1648 – he was protesting against the corrupt practices of the Church (which by his act became a smaller entity called the Roman Catholic Church), chief among them the sale of 'indulgences'. This was a money-raising project for the building of St Peter's in Rome, and involved promising people less posthumous suffering in purgatory in exchange for a cash sum.

This act of protest gives Protestantism its name, for all those groups – led by Luther, Zwingli, Calvin and others – that broke with the Vatican subsequently did so because they disagreed with it over doctrine and practice. That they quickly began to disagree with each other too – indeed, that they began to persecute each other (witness the cruelty meted out to the Anabaptists, and Calvin burning Michael Servetus at the stake in Geneva over the Trinity) – is par for the course of things religious, so there are no surprises there. You might say that having begun as Protestants they continued protesting – mainly against everyone not themselves, and for too many of them against everything that added a little fun to life, such as dancing and theatre.

The Church of England, and by extension the Anglican Communion which stems from it, is not a Protestant Church in the same sense as the Lutheran and Calvinist Churches, for it came into official existence by an act of Parliament in 1533–4 to make life easier for Henry VIII's domestic concerns, namely his desire to divorce Catherine of Aragon so that he could marry his mistress Anne Boleyn. The Church in England had anyway had a degree of autonomy and an independent character even before the Synod of Whitby in 664 CE. Legend claims that it was founded by Joseph of Arimathea, who was a trader who bought tin from West Country miners, and who brought the young Jesus to England ('And did those feet in ancient times' etc.) on one of those visits. Later, says the legend, after Jesus's crucifixion, he moved to England and planted a thorn tree at Wearyall Hill near Glastonbury, to which he is also said to have brought some of Christ's blood and sweat in vials, and the Holy Grail, the latter still hidden in a Glastonbury well. His founding of Christ's Church in England thus predates St Peter's mission to Rome.

Among Henry VIII's concerns in his breach with Rome was the desire for a male heir. The Pope did not sympathize with his sense of dynastic urgency, so Henry wisely got rid of the Pope. In addition to founding a new Church Henry thereby also set England on its path of imperial glory, among other things by its independence of the Catholic cause and its freedom from Spanish heirs (luckily not only Catherine of Aragon but her daughter Mary did not succeed in re-routing England through their wombs into becoming an eventual Habsburg province).

Thus the Anglican version of Christianity was founded on a sort of protest after all, and departed the Roman fold in the same period as the other Protestant Churches, and so might be counted among them, if in more dignified and far less doctrinally earnest mode. Doctrinal earnestness came later with Puritans and Methodists and other enthusiasts for the cause.

It is of some interest to peer inside versions of Protestantism, as follows.

Calvinism is the name given to the austere and deterministic version of Christian theology of John Calvin (1509–64), and also by theologians and religious leaders influenced by him, among them Theodore Beza 1519–1605), Franciscus Gomarus (1563–1641), and John Knox (1505–72). In brief, their view is premised on enthusiastic belief in the fallen nature of mankind, and the idea that God has predestined from all eternity those who will be saved and those who will be damned, regardless of what either the saved or the damned do during their lifetimes.

For Calvinism the starting point is original sin, that is, the corrupt and depraved nature of mankind, which nothing that man himself can do – neither works nor faith – will remedy. Only if a man has been elected for salvation from the beginning of time will he be saved. Only God's grace can save man, and he has chosen some to be saved in order to glorify his name.

The fact that neither works nor faith can save anyone who has not been predestined for salvation does not mean that he can do as he wishes; obedience to God's will is a mark of election, and is a gift from God which must be honoured.

Along with the doctrines of the complete depravity of mankind and his enslavement to sin, and the unconditional election of the chosen out of God's mercy, there are three other central pillars of Calvinism: 'limited atonement', which means that Christ's death remits the punishment of sin not for everyone but for the chosen only; 'irresistible grace', which means that no one chosen by God for salvation can resist turning to God and living in obedience to him; and 'preservation of the saints', which means that those set apart by God for salvation will be saved, come what may. Two seconds' thought shows what a ghastly view this is.

As always with ideologies and sects, there are variations and internal differences in Calvinism, but one of the chief early differences arose between the Arminians (followers of Jacob Arminius) and the Gomarists (followers of Gomarus) that led to the Synod of Dort in 1618.

Arminius, a liberal Reformed theologian, held that human beings have free will. He was thus on collision course with Calvinist orthodoxy. Increasingly acrimonious discussion of his views between his followers and loyal Calvinists eventually caused riots to break out in his native Netherlands. The country's effective prime minister, Johan van Oldenbarnevelt, grew concerned, and convened a meeting of leading clergy to discuss a revision of the Reformed Church's Confession of Faith in order to settle matters. The clergymen angrily refused to consider changing the Confession.

This happened in the first decade of the seventeenth century, at the end of which Arminius died. But his followers were determined to continue the fight. They presented a 'Remonstrance' to the assembly of Holland, calling for a revision of the Confession, and demanding that matters of Church and state be kept completely separate. The Gomarists hit back with a 'Counter-Remonstrance', which included a demand that all Arminian preachers should be discharged from their posts. The Arminians asked Oldenbarnevelt for help; the jurist Hugo Grotius, then chief magistrate of Rotterdam, attacked the Gomarists for threatening the safety of the state, the Church's unity, and worst of all the principle of freedom of conscience.

What Gomarists especially disliked was the fact that because Roman Catholics were also believers in free will, this put Arminians into the same (for Gomarists, unspeakably vile) category as Catholics. That explains why Arminian ministers and churches were attacked by mobs.

Prince Maurice of Nassau, the ruler of the Netherlands, began to fear that the dispute over predestination would only be settled by civil war. He and Oldenbarnevelt then also fell out, for Oldenbarnevelt was an

Arminian and Maurice a Gomarist. As a result the Gomarist cause began to get the upper hand.

Prince Maurice convened an assembly of Calvinist divines, with representatives from Germany, Switzerland and England joining their Dutch counterparts in a general synod at Dort. After six months of debates the synod condemned Arminians as heretics. Immediately two hundred Dutch Arminian ministers were dismissed from their posts, nearly half of whom went into exile. Grotius was sentenced to life imprisonment (he escaped two years later), and Oldenbarnevelt was condemned to death. He went to the scaffold the very next day. Thus, in typical fashion, do fraternal and love-thy-neighbour Christians comport themselves.

Puritanism has close associations with Calvinism; Puritans were either Calvinists or shared many Calvinist views on morality. It is the outlook of those Protestant Christians, especially in the sixteenth and seventeenth centuries, who desired to practise a simpler and more austere form of their faith, more in accord with what they believed to be the purity of the primitive Christian Church. By analogy it remains as a term describing anyone who professes or strives for a particularly austere style of life, typically purged of alcohol, swearing, sex or at least forbidden kinds of sex, indulgence, even dancing and going to the cinema because of the dangers to purity they represent. Puritanism in this sense is by no means absent from the world; it flourishes in more devout Protestant corners of the United States (most of whose roots lie in Calvinism itself), in Roman Catholic nunneries, and in the more devout purlieus of Islam.

The term 'Puritan' began as a term of abuse for those in the Church of England influenced by Calvinism during the century following the onset of the Reformation. The conflict between Puritans and the established Church led to their breaking from it and establishing their own sects. Many emigrated, New England in North America being a favoured destination: the establishment of the Massachusetts Bay Colony in the 1620s is the direct result of the hostility directed at Puritans during the reigns of James I and Charles I in England.

The caricature of Puritanism which focuses on its strict moral views and prudery, and its intolerance of such things as dancing, theatre, unseemly dress and violations of Sabbath gloom, is more correct than not. On the positive side can be entered the fact that although Puritans placed great emphasis on faith, divine grace and 'election' (being chosen by God for salvation), they also emphasized individual responsibility before God – 'each man is his own priest' – and this has been seen by some as a spur to the individualism and reliance on reason which characterizes the scientific and philosophical revolutions of the seventeenth and eighteenth centuries. It has also been cited as the source of capitalism and therefore, ultimately, the Industrial Revolution.

Some have also seen the morality of simplicity, thrift, industry, self-reliance, discipline, continence, and loyalty to family and community as founding features of the American spirit. This somewhat utopian view is not wholly implausible: as mentioned, a strong streak of Puritanism remains in the religious Right in America, which has always been an influential force in the country's social and political life. And it is no accident that in his magisterial *Religion and the Rise of Capitalism* R.H. Tawney saw a connection between the Puritan outlook and the economic effects of the thrift, industry, self-reliance and discipline listed above as its characteristics.

These forms of Protestantism make an interesting contrast with the Anglican Church, or more accurately the Anglican Communion, a phrase which denotes all those Churches that are in full communion with the Archbishop of Canterbury, Anglicanism's head, though in a traditional rather than official sense, as a *primus inter pares*. As a matter of historical fact the Communion consists of Churches in former parts of the British Empire, to which the Church of England was exported rather in the same way as cricket and afternoon tea. Because the British Empire was so extensive, the Anglican Communion remains the third-largest Christian grouping in the world (after Roman Catholicism and Eastern Orthodoxy) with about 77 million claimed adherents.

Anglicanism describes itself as 'built on the Bible, Baptism and the Eucharist' (this latter otherwise known as communion or the Lord's Supper or Mass), and all its member Churches therefore share a common ground in scripture, the sacraments and the creeds. They also share a common Episcopalian structure (indeed in the United States the Anglican Church is known as the Episcopalian Church) of bishops, priests and deacons. Note this fact, that it has an ordained priesthood; this is one major difference with the 'Reformed' Churches of true Protestantism.

Anglicanism also prides itself on being an inclusive movement in doctrinal matters, that is, as encompassing a whole range of approaches and tastes from 'low church' – simple services in simple churches, often infected with evangelical zeal and a taste for strummed guitars – to 'high church' – bells and smells, rich vestments and much ceremony. 'High Anglicanism' is also known as 'Anglo-Catholicism' and is now considerably 'higher' in liturgy and ritual than most Catholic services, which, since abandonment of the Latin rituals, have become demotic and pedestrian to a degree. The common bond in Anglican observance is provided by the Book of Common Prayer and its less poetic descendants, and by theology – allowing for the licensed differences in practice, emphasis and interpretation across the Communion – in which it stands on the middle ground between varieties of Protestantism and Western Catholicism. The Nicene Creed is accepted by Anglicans as a sufficient statement of the Christian faith, and they associate themselves with the full tradition of the Gospels, the apostolic tradition of the Christian Church, the teachings of the Church Fathers, and the first four Oecumenical Councils, the first of the four being the Council of Nicaea which denounced Aryanism as a heresy and adopted the Nicene Creed (the following three Councils identified and anathematized several more versions of Christianity as heretical – e.g. Nestorianism, monophytism – and declared the Virgin Mary to be the Mother of God). And so on.

The breadth of Anglican observance is one of the institutional factors that account for its survival. It can be described as 'latitudinarian' although some critics call it Laodicean. Latitudinarianism is the view held by a number of divines in the Church of England in the later seventeenth century, to the effect that the Church should encourage tolerance and mutual comprehension between different viewpoints within it, ranging from high church Tory Anglicanism to radical deism. The sincerity of the individual in holding his or her views was what mattered most to Latitudinarians, rather than doctrinal orthodoxy as one or other wing of the Church sought to impose it.

During the Restoration period (1660–88) the high Tory wing of the Church of England was dominant, and the Latitudinarians, notable among them John Tillotson (1630–94), Edward Stillingfleet (1635–99), and Gilbert Burnet (1643–1715), resisted their influence. After the 'Glorious Revolution' of 1688 which brought William of Orange to the throne of England, the Latitudinarians became the most influential party in the Church, and their tolerant views – very similar to those advanced by John Locke in his *Letters on Toleration* – thereafter held sway.

The evangelical wing of Anglicanism consists of those who have a more earnest, personal, emotional faith, dedicated to the Christian life and often to proselytizing in its cause. Pronouncements by Anglican evangelicals tend to emphasize closeness to holy scripture regarded as 'the immutable word of God' (so, a characteristic tincture of literalism creeps in), and also emphasize such aspects of Christianity as the fallen, sinful, depraved nature of man and by contrast wonder, worship, adoration, obedience, dependence and other attitudes as suitable towards God.

That such views are a calumny on mankind, and that the craven attitude towards the supposed deity is nauseating to a degree, does not need mentioning.

There is something typically English about Anglicanism, or at least the Englishness that once managed to acquire and govern a vast and disparate empire: indifference to doctrinal differences, a muddling-along inclusivity, a genius for masterly inactivity, a mild obduracy, the capacity to endure, the habit of suffering endless defeats only to win in the end, shocking snobbery, racism and callousness disguised as bumbling, and occasional hard-nosed savagery. Though admittedly the Anglican Communion has been light on the last of these categories, it has made up for it with the others.

There are many other Protestant denominations – thousands, in fact, some just one church-hall big – spanning the range from rich, organized and influential, such as the Southern Baptist movement in the United States, to the criminally lunatic. It would be a labour to identify what differentiates them from one another, though one can be sure it is not always matters of doctrine; the individual cupidity, delusion, megalomania, or all three, of (often self-ordained, usually half-baked) pastors and preachers seem to have as much to do with it as niceties of theology.

See: CATHOLICISM, CHRISTIANITY, ORTHODOX CHRISTIANITY, RELIGION

PSYCHOANALYSIS

Psychoanalysis is a psychotherapy – that is, a treatment for mental problems such as anxiety, phobias and the like; but also, for many, a way of gaining self-understanding and freedom from limitations imposed by unconscious concerns or childhood trauma. But whereas the term 'psychotherapy' is the wholly general term for treatments with these aims, 'psychoanalysis' specifically and only denotes the form of psychotherapy based on the theories of Sigmund Freud (1856–1939). It is incorrect to describe any other psychotherapeutic theory or practice by this name.

Freud was an Austrian physician, neurologist and psychiatrist. He began to develop his views in the 1880s while exploring the benefits of hypnosis as a treatment for hysteria in women who displayed no underlying physical disease. He came to the view that their hysteria was prompted by unpleasant memories repressed in their unconscious minds, memories (so he at first thought) of being sexually abused in childhood.

He called this the 'seduction theory'. He later changed his mind and held that the repressed memories were of incestuous desire for the parent of the opposite sex, and this formed the basis of his view that all adult neurosis stems from disturbed or incomplete psychosexual development in childhood.

In his fully mature theory (it was still developing in the last two decades of his life) Freud held that there are three aspects to personality, which he called 'id', 'ego' and 'superego' respectively. The first is the seat of an instinctive primal force which Freud called the 'pleasure principle' and which, as its name implies, seeks gratifications and the avoidance of pain and anxiety. It consists in a pair of conflicting instincts which Freud called 'eros' and 'thanatos', respectively the life force (which includes sex) and the death wish.

The superego is the internalized authority first represented by a father-figure and later by the demands of religion, schooling and society. The superego is the controlling and repressive opposite of the id, whose impulses towards the immediate satisfaction of its desires are resisted by the superego. The superego is the home of conscience, morality, and the sense of taboo, and it comes into existence through the failure of a small boy to compete with his father for his mother's love (thus, in the dissolution of the Oedipus complex) for fear of castration by the father. The Electra complex in the case of girls undergoes an analogous fate in the oppositely gendered sense, with analogous consequences.

The ego plays the often difficult role of mediator between the id and superego, striving to ensure that the demands of each are met. When the conflict proves too great the ego resorts to a variety of defence mechanisms, identified by Freud as denial, fantasy, compensation, projection, displacement, intellectualization, reaction formation, regression, repression, sublimation and compensation. (Anna Freud, his daughter and a major theoretician of psychoanalysis in her own right, rationalized these categories into a shorter list of responses, namely: dissociation, introjection, inversion, somatization, suppression, splitting, undoing, identification and substitution.)

In the final version of his theory Freud had a topology of the human psyche in which the conscious mind is as the tip of an iceberg, with the 'preconscious' as the location of the superego, the unconscious as the location of the id, and the ego moving in all three levels. But the unconscious is the most significant region of mind, for as the home of the deepest instinctual desires and needs it is what drives the individual, and it is the repository of memories and feelings, most significantly painful ones, which have been suppressed from consciousness. It is also the home of unacceptable urges and wishes. The activity of the unconscious expresses itself in symptoms, typically neurotic, and when these are themselves painful or life-disrupting the required treatment is analysis (psychoanalysis). The unconscious cannot be accessed by introspection, but can be investigated by techniques of dream analysis, free association of ideas, and noting 'Freudian slips' of the tongue, and by the analyst's skill at interpreting the patient's avowals and reports during the analytic process.

When Freud first began to develop and publish his views he received a hostile response from many in the medical profession, but partly because of the Zeitgeist of the early twentieth century, and even more because of the remarkable gifts Freud possessed as a writer and creative thinker, his views soon became popularly known and highly fashionable. As happens with anything that captures the public imagination and spreads, it also accumulated heretics and split into opposing groups; Freudian terminology escaped into general parlance there to constitute a half-baked folk-pop psychology; and in more recent decades it has come to be an object of suspicion, especially among some feminists who object to what they perceive as its misogyny and patriarchal attitudes, not least in connection with the idea that women are inferior because they are troubled by their castrated sense of lacking a penis. Freud's defenders describe these feminist objections as products of 'resistance' and 'sublimated penis-envy', both technical Freudian notions.   ·

More severe criticism still has come from scientific and philosophical doubts about Freud's views. Jointly these criticisms have it that Freudian theory is insufficiently empirically based, which calls into question its fundamental concepts and its vastly ambitious aim of giving a complete theory of human nature. Critics argue that the methodology of Freudian theory is very inadequate, because it rests on subjective insights and speculations inferred from them, rather than on objective and repeatably testable phenomena. Its data consist in generalizations from individual cases or at best very small samples – in fact, a handful of well-off bored Viennese women and a couple of exceedingly strange men, if we leave aside Freud's personal introspections and what he learned about his own family, members of which he also analysed. Moreover the reasoning Freud employed relies on analogies, subjective association, memories – some of them false – puns, coincidences, and 'mistakes' (Freud did not believe in mistakes: for him apparent mistakes are in fact unconsciously intentional and revealing). All this presumes that mental life is causally deterministic, which might be right but which raises questions about whether analysis can, in effect, inject a sufficient degree of free will into the process to stop the deterministic process from making the patient unhappy.

Stripped of its apparatus of theory, Freud's fundamental idea looks frankly incredible: that infants sexually desire their parents of the opposite sex, and consequently are jealous and hostile towards their parents of the same sex, and because these feelings are unacceptable they suppress them into the unconscious where they breed conflicts; and that this Oedipus/Electra complex is the key to human nature.

The predecessors from whom Freud inherited the concept of the unconscious as a repository of problem-causing conflicts, among them Jean-Martin Charcot and Joseph Breuer, used hypnosis to access its contents. But Freud, learning from Breuer's experience with a patient called 'Anna O', developed the technique of the 'talking cure' which uses free association and dream-analysis to bring out of the unconscious what is repressed in it. The belief was that once the conflict was made conscious, it would cease to be a source of trouble because there would be a catharsis or discharge of the emotions it generated.

In using his talking cure Freud found (or 'found': we find what we look for) sexual trauma, real or imagined, at the root of his patients' troubles. If patients would not confess to such troubles, and would not talk about their early sexual experiences whether solitary or with others, Freud diagnosed 'resistance'. As mentioned, he at first thought that actual sexual abuse had occurred to his patients as children; later he thought that they were expressing repressed 'infantile wishes'.

The fashionable success of psychoanalysis is not hard to understand. People are tremendously interested in themselves, and are prepared to spend very considerable amounts on talking about themselves on a regular basis for years on end. Moreover, the theory is about sex and relationships – endlessly fascinating to us all – and it holds out the promise of revelations about oneself on a par with what a famous clairvoyant might be expected to say about – so one hopes – one's prospects of marriage, wealth, fame and happiness. The question is whether Freudian analysis is any better than clairvoyance, scientifically speaking; or whether the self-understanding, and benefits of an associated placebo effect arising from the belief that one is 'doing something' about one's fears and inadequacies, would arise as readily from the sympathetic-sounding responses of a computer programmed to repeat one's remarks in the form of a question. 'I didn't get on well with my mother.' 'Why didn't you get on well with your mother?' 'She expected too much of me.' 'What did she expect of you?' and so on until light dawns or weariness supervenes.

See: COGNITIVE THERAPY, PSYCHOLOGY

PSYCHOLOGY

Of all the words denoting areas of human enquiry, 'psychology' must be one of the broadest in scope. It means, of course, the study of the human mind and mental life (though suitably qualified it can be the study of animal minds as well – 'canine psychology' etc.), but the variety of approaches and methods, and the specialist subdivisions of psychological interest, are legion. The work of educational psychologists, developmental psychologists, industrial psychologists, psychoneurologists, psychiatrists, psychotherapists of all stripes from the Jungian and Freudian schools to cognitive behaviour therapy, and more, makes the field a highly diverse and rich one.

As this suggests, the targets of these enquiries are diverse too, from every aspect of the development and normal and abnormal functioning of perception, memory, learning, reasoning, intelligence, emotion, sexuality, and more, to the social expression of and influence upon them by education, work, family life and relationships, and further to their physiological and neurological underpinnings. In the recent development of powerful non-invasive means of studying brain function, for a chief example by means of functional magnetic resonance imaging (fMRI), a great deal has been learned in neuropsychology about the physical basis and correlates of psychological phenomena, though it is accepted on all sides that there are aspects of enquiry in psychology that cannot rely on brain imaging alone.

The mind and its various workings have doubtless been an interest for human beings since the dawn of human experience, and one can see psychological theories presupposed in the myths and legends of antiquity – not least in the highly sophisticated and psychologically insightful mythology of ancient Greece – and in the literature of all ages. But it is in the eighteenth century that theories of mind and mental functioning first began to emerge systematically; the 'associationist' psychology developed by David Hartley and employed by David Hume in his philosophical work is an example of the almost ubiquitous acceptance of the view, dominant at the time, that mentation consists in ideas linking themselves to each other by associations of similarity or habit. In the nineteenth century – specifically: in 1879 – Wilhelm Wundt brought the study of psychology into the laboratory, and this step marks the beginnings of scientific psychology proper. Seminal contributions were made by William James (brother of the more famous Henry) in his *Principles of Psychology* (1890) and Ivan Pavlov (1850–1909) who demonstrated the conditioned response (he trained dogs to salivate at the sound of a bell).

A different impulse was given to psychology by Sigmund Freud (see the entry on PSYCHOANALYSIS) and Carl Jung, younger contemporaries of James and Pavlov, in the direction of clinical psychology, addressing the ambiguous field of human experience between the 'normal' psychological range and the kind of mental pathology that could then be adequately handled only by incarcerating its victims in lunatic asylums.

Whereas the various approaches of James and Freud relied on introspection and subjective data, another powerful school of thought, the behaviourist school, insisted on a different approach to its work. As a term of art in psychology, 'behaviourism' denotes the thesis, first articulated by J.B. Watson in a 1913 article entitled 'Psychology as the Behaviourist Views It', that mental phenomena should be explained wholly in terms of objectively observable behaviour, thus making (or attempting to make) psychology an empirical science. His most notable but more radical successor in the field was B.F. Skinner.

The key idea is that behaviour, in humans as much as in animals, consists in conditioned responses to external stimuli, and that all psychological phenomena can be accounted for in these terms. One consequence is that in the debate about the relative importance of nature (innate mechanisms) and nurture (experience) in learning, behaviourism comes down strongly on the side of nurture. This means that what is learned is the result of conditioning, for which the mammalian central nervous system is in general apt, this being the only mechanism in play – contrast the view otherwise held, that a mind consists of many separate mechanisms adapted to handling different types of problems (see the discussion of modularity in the entry on MIND, PHILOSOPHY OF).

A distinction between 'methodological' and 'scientific' behaviourism is significant here. The former insists that psychology must be an empirical discipline reliant on publicly observable evidence, not on the subjective avowals of the human subjects being studied. 'Scientific behaviourism' is more stringent, in requiring that psychology should concern itself exclusively with the formulation of laws correlating input (stimuli) and output (behaviour), eschewing all mention of 'inner' mechanisms and processes. This means having to do without such concepts as intention and attention, motive and memory.

Today most empirical psychology takes its cue from 'methodological' behaviourism. 'Scientific' behaviourism, which stems from Skinner, is no longer espoused by many. The key advance in empirical psychology lies in cognitive science – drawing on the insights of computing, philosophy and artificial intelligence as well as the various branches of psychology themselves – and the development of brain-scanning techniques which allow real-time investigation of brain function correlated with the performance of mental tasks and the occurrence of emotional and cognitive responses. Coupled with greatly increased knowledge about the physical and psychological effects of brain injury and disease, these advances have pushed psychology and its related fields into an area far in advance of anything that could have been imagined by the eighteenth-century 'associationists' who are the modern originators of psychological study.

It might be mentioned at this point that in philosophy, 'behaviourism' (often called 'analytic' or 'logical' behaviourism) has a meaning related to the family of psychological theories bearing that label. Philosophical behaviourism is sometimes described by saying that statements about mental phenomena are translatable into statements about observable behaviour. In its strongest form the view says that statements about mental phenomena are translatable exhaustively into statements about behaviour; the adverb 'exhaustively' is important, in implying that there is nothing left over – nothing private or hidden in the subjectivity of the person being discussed – when one has described matters wholly in terms of behaviour that can be publicly observed.

See: MIND, PHILOSOPHY OF; PSYCHOANALYSIS

PUNISHMENT

Laws exist to regulate the relationship between people and the states they are citizens of, and between individuals and groups. They also exist to protect property. Without sanctions for breach of law, law is ineffective; and among the sanctions available to the executive arm is, centrally, punishment. In the case of criminal law prohibiting murder, assault, rape, theft and other actions that are deemed to be crimes, punishment can take the form of imprisonment, in some jurisdictions death, or for lesser versions of some of these offences, fines or community service. Such punishments consist in depriving convicted malefactors of things we assume they value: their liberty, their lives, and/or their money.

At the same time, society recognizes limits to the degree of punishment it can impose; a thief can be locked up, but not for ever; a murderer can be locked up, but not just for a month or a year; considerations of proportionality apply to punishment for crime dependent on the seriousness of the crime and society's attitudes to it, and they have to be debated afresh as society develops and changes.

But there are other questions too. Is punishment anyway the right response to crime, or to any infringement of law? Would it not be better to think in terms of rehabilitation, redress, restitution? Do we not lock away murderers to protect the public rather than to punish the offender himself? Are the sanctions available to the law in fact a mixture of these things, or ought they to be?

Theories of punishment fall into two main camps. One is the utilitarian camp, which starts from the view that punishment is only right if it produces good consequences, such as protection of society or rehabilitation of offenders. Since inflicting punishment on an individual is, other considerations apart, a bad thing in itself because it involves the suffering in some form or degree of the person punished, the goodness of the outcome of punishing him has to outweigh the badness of the fact that he suffers, in order for the punishment to be justified.

The other main view is the retributive theory, which comes in a number of versions. In essence it says that if a wrong is committed voluntarily, with the perpetrator knowing that he is committing or has committed a wrong, then he deserves to be punished, and his suffering is just.

It is easy to produce counters to both views. If good outcomes justify whatever we do, then we could inflict suffering on the innocent in order to produce an outcome whose good outweighs the suffering in question. Perhaps we do this when we teach reluctant children how to spell and work out problems in geometry. But would we be happy to extend this principle to, say, whipping people to make them more sympathetic to others' sufferings, or depriving one person of his savings in order to give two other people a useful gift of (his) money?

Or consider the retributivist view: what is the point of exacting retribution if it changes nothing, and in particular does not produce any good beyond the not very admirable satisfaction felt at the fact that someone is suffering who made someone else suffer – that the amount of suffering in history has, say, been doubled?

The very concept of punishment is of course intrinsically a retributive

one – an eye for an eye, says Exodus 21: 23–6; a life for a life – and historically the idea was that anyone who committed a wrong (in some cases
even if unintentionally) had to pay for it – with life, liberty or property
depending on the wrong, though even what would now be considered a
minor crime (stealing a loaf of bread – which the starving sometimes did
in order to survive) might invite the death penalty or transportation to
inhospitable lands across the sea.

In the mid-twentieth century there were optimistic views afoot about
the possibility of using the penal system as – despite the name 'penal'
– an opportunity to rehabilitate offenders and put them back into society
as better and more constructive citizens. This idea is embodied in the
name used in the United States for the prison system; it is there called
the 'correctional' system. By one of those painful ironies that teach better
lessons than most other things, the US imprisons a greater percentage
of its population than anyone else, even though in absolute terms the
Chinese gulag of prisons and forced labour camps is vastly more populous;
so 'correction' would appear to be a mere euphemism for punishment.
Studies carried out by penologists, criminologists and sociologists in the
1970s on levels of recidivism (re-offence) showed that prison not only did
not rehabilitate, but did not deter either – deterrence being the other use
that punishment, or rather the threat of it or of its repetition, is claimed
by some to have.

To these empirical facts was added the voice of philosophers returning
to the idea that punishment is indeed in essence retributive, and properly
so, because it serves the interests of justice that one who causes harm
should pay a cost for doing so, out of the valuables of liberty and property
he has. This does not mean that all the rights of a legally convicted person
are suspended by his being marked as a criminal, only those relevant to
constituting a punishment – an exaction – fitted to the harm he has done
others or society or both.

This view, in the eyes of critics, is implicitly a return to the idea of
punishment as vengeance, and Michel Foucault, in his book *Discipline
and Punish*, added to Nietzsche's insight – that the desire to punish is
a deeply human instinct – the idea that a society's penal system is an
embodiment of its power to control by threats, force, suppression and
even destruction (or at least, to attempt to do so; but in the standard
case successfully), whatever threatens or inconveniences it, or disrupts
its efficiencies.

Against this it can be said that ideas of punishment and rehabilitation derived from the Enlightenment, some of whose leading votaries

opposed the death penalty on humanitarian grounds, urge considerations of justice as tempering or limiting the state power to coerce and destroy. The Enlightenment thinkers also objected to the use of public torture and executions as a macabre spectacle designed to frighten the populace into law-abidingness, for they recognized that the spectacle fed interests in crowd mentality very remote from deterrence.

Foucault challenged the idea that change from corporal punishment to imprisonment was the result of Enlightened and humane changes in attitudes, although he did not deny that such attitudes played a part. Rather, he argued, the rise of imprisonment was of a piece with emergent ideas of discipline, expressed not just in prisons and their regimes but in schools and hospitals as well as the military setting where it more traditionally belonged. He contrasts the last-ever brutal publicly conducted torture and execution in 1757 of a would-be French regicide (Robert-François Damiens), and the order and regimentation of a nineteenth-century prison. The contrast is very striking. Damiens, who tried to kill Louis XV by knifing him, was tortured with red-hot pincers, and molten lead, wax and boiling oil were poured into the wounds thus caused before each of his limbs was attached to a horse, whereupon the four horses were ridden in four directions to tear his body apart. He was thus hideously treated and butchered alive.

The regimented prisoners of the nineteenth-century gaol suggested to Foucault not so much an improvement as a shift of focus to the production of 'docile bodies', fit not just for disciplining criminals but for producing a new order of beings for the industrial age in which the state controls even the minutiae of people's lives. All society becomes a 'carceral system' and whole careers are constructed on the task of disciplining society and its members.

Foucault's arguments suggest something other than their conclusions, implicit and otherwise, by their very existence; namely, that reflective awareness of the structures that bureaucratic societies develop to organize themselves, often placing efficiency above individual rights and interests, can indeed acquire the character that Foucault imputes to them; but that very awareness is a condition of resisting or moderating the 'carcerality' that results; while at the same time, the generally just, proportional, and humane system of dealing with people who commit crimes and do individual and social harm is surely infinitely preferable to the treatment Damiens received. His punishment speaks of anger and revenge, whereas the ideal of a justice system is dispassionate, ordered and fair – even if it is punitive, and even if hopes for rehabilitation (which the penal system must surely keep alive and strive to realize) are not as sanguine as they might be.

See: JUSTICE, LAW

QUANTUM MECHANICS

Quantum mechanics is a fundamental branch of physics concerned with the structure and properties of matter at the microscopic level. It is a mathematical model for predicting the behaviour of matter at the very small scale. It is a powerful and successful model, which underwrites many practical applications, even though it appears to give a radically unintuitive picture of the deep levels of reality. But then, it is a characteristic of human egoism or perhaps timidity to think that every level of reality has to have the same character as it does at the size of refrigerators and armchairs.

Quantum theory arose out of the inadequacy of classical physics, derived and developed jointly from the work of Isaac Newton and eighteenth-century chemistry, to explain a number of increasingly apparent anomalies. When in the mid-nineteenth century James Clerk Maxwell (1831–79) successfully gave a statistical description of the behaviour of gases, he was able to assume that gas consists of tiny featureless atoms interacting as if they were minuscule billiard balls. But then experimental discoveries later on in that century showed that atoms have inner structure, for particles were observed with mass less than the atom of least mass, the hydrogen atom, and moreover atoms were displaying what came to be called radioactivity (the natural disintegration over time of atomic nuclei), accepting and giving electric charge and changing into other atoms. The crucial discovery was made by J.J. Thomson in 1897 when investigating cathode rays; he discovered that the 'rays' were in fact streams of negatively charged particles which he called electrons.

This led to speculation about the distribution of positive charge in the atom. Thomson proposed a 'plum pudding' model in which the negatively charged electrons were 'plums' in a mass of positively charged 'dough'. Thomson's student Ernest Rutherford discovered, by means of his 'scattering' experiments, that the greatest part of an atom's mass and its positive charge are concentrated in a tiny percentage of its volume. He hypothesized that they were focused at the volume's centre, constituting the atom's nucleus. The planetary model that results (this way of describing the model owes itself chiefly to Niels Bohr) posits three kinds of subatomic particles: electrons, protons and neutrons, with the electrons 'orbiting' the protons and neutrons constituting the nucleus. Protons are positively charged particles, neutrons have, as the name suggests, no charge; together they carry most of the atom's mass. Electrons are very 'light' particles, having a tiny fraction of the mass of a proton, and they are negatively charged. The difference in charge between electron and nucleus is what keeps the former in orbit round the latter.

Protons and electrons are always equal in number in a non-ionized atom; when ionized they contain fewer electrons than protons. Atoms differ in the number of protons in the nucleus, and this determines what element it is; thus hydrogen is number one on the table of elements because it has one proton, oxygen is number eight because it has eight protons, and so on.

This classical picture of the atom soon proved inadequate. One simple reason is that, on classical principles, electrons should lose energy as they fly around their nuclei, and consequently spiral into them. But they do not; atoms are relatively stable structures. Moreover it turned out that atoms do indeed absorb and radiate energy, but only at specific wavelengths. Such puzzles as the problem of hot-body radiation and the photoelectric effect showed that a new way of thinking about the elementary structure of matter was required. It came when Max Planck (1858–1947), in the year 1900, showed that he could solve some of these problems by assuming that energy comes in discrete packets, which he called *quanta* (Latin for 'amounts').

Planck himself thought that his idea was merely a mathematical sleight of hand for solving the puzzle of why the colour of radiation from a body which is growing increasingly hot changes from red to orange and then to blue. But in the third of his three famously seminal 1905 papers, Albert Einstein (1859–1955) used Planck's idea to explain the photoelectric effect (that is, why metals produce electricity when light of high enough frequency is shone onto them). The strange thing, as it seemed to Einstein and his contemporaries, is that whereas there was very good experimental evidence that light is a wave – and by the end of the nineteenth century it was assumed in physics that light is indeed such – it behaves as a particle in Planck's solution to the hot-body problem and Einstein's explanation of the photoelectric effect. Which is it: wave or particle? The answer, by now familiarly, came to be that it is both.

At the level of ordinary experience we are familiar with the phenomena of waves and particles, such as waves at sea and individual pebbles on a beach respectively. When a particle moves it carries both mass and energy from one locality to another, whereas waves carry only energy, and are spread out in space. But at the scale of things described by quantum theory this intuitive wave–particle distinction breaks down, and in its place there is a *wave–particle duality* – that is, subatomic particles can behave in a wave-like way in certain situations, and in a particle-like way in others.

Prince Louis de Broglie extended the idea of wave–particle duality from photons to other particles in 1912, in the face of much initial scepticism, but the work of Niels Bohr (1885–1962) confirmed that the interpretation suggested by Planck – that energy comes in packets at discrete intervals on the energy gradient, which is to say: not continuously but with jumps between – is right. Bohr was therefore able to explain how atoms are structurally stable, while being able to absorb and radiate energy; the reason being that the wavelength of an electron always has to have a whole-number value, so that if an electron emits or absorbs energy, it has to do so by jumping to another whole-number wavelength, with no resting place between.

With these developments in place, physicists (chief among them Erwin Schrödinger, 1887–1961, and Werner Heisenberg, 1901–76) were able to work out the mathematics required for the theory. Among the important results is a radically different view of electrons not as particles but in effect as probability smears around nuclei. When electrons absorb or lose energy they vanish from one 'position' in the vicinity of the nucleus and instantaneously reappear at another.

Heisenberg introduced the 'Uncertainty Principle', which states that one cannot simultaneously measure both the position and the momentum of a subatomic particle (where 'momentum' is the mass of a particle multiplied by its velocity). This has profound implications for causality and predictions concerning the future behaviour of particles. On the classical view, if one knows everything about the current state of a physical system together with the laws governing it, one can predict precisely what its future states will be. But Heisenberg remarked, 'In the sharp formulation of the law of causality, "if we know the present exactly, we can calculate the future", it is not the conclusion but the premise which is wrong.'

Quantum theory has equally profound implications for an understanding of reality itself. It states in effect that what happens in the microscopic world is the result of measurement – that is, a quantum state does not have a definite character until it is measured (for example, a particle does not have a definite path until the path is calculated). This is because prior to the measurement being made, the quantum situation consists of a range of possibilities – it is indeterminate – and the measurement settles which of the possibilities counts as actual. This raises a vexing question: must there be a quantum physicist to make a measurement before reality can have a determinate character? How can the actual nature of reality depend upon there being someone to measure it? And in any case, how does reality 'decide', when it is measured, which determinate state it will adopt?

In what has become known as the Copenhagen Interpretation of quantum theory (because it was advanced by Niels Bohr and Werner Heisenberg when working together in that city) the amazing-seeming fact that quantum systems are indeterminate until measured is simply accepted as given; and when it is, all the rest follows happily. But what the interpretation itself asks us to accept is so philosophically and scientifically puzzling that it has remained a major point of debate ever since, with a variety of sometimes exotic theories aimed at resolving matters, such as the *many-worlds* theory (which proposes that all possibilities are actualized by the splitting into different worlds of the world in which the possibilities arose; each of the new worlds is itself continually splitting into new actual worlds from the possibilities in them, with none of the new worlds able to communicate with the others after the split), the *consistent-histories* or 'decoherent-histories' theory (which in essence asserts that the environment of a quantum event acts as the observer and so all such events assume a classical actualized state), *instrumentalism* (which in effect says, 'the theory does not describe reality, but it somehow works, so just get on and use it': or as Paul Dirac more trenchantly expressed matters, 'Shut up and calculate!'), and what is perhaps the least popular alternative, the theory of David Bohm that the universe is an 'implicate order' (there is an underlying 'quantum potential' in the universe which connects all quantum phenomena, whose character is the result of the unfolding of the deterministic structure of the underlying reality).

Einstein himself was never convinced by quantum theory. In what is called the Einstein–Podolsky–Rosen (EPR) thought-experiment, which Einstein took to be a refutation of quantum theory, the following happens: suppose you fire a pair of photons in exactly opposite 'spin' states away from each other in a straight line, then measure the spin state of one, thus (according to the Copenhagen view) fixing which state it is in. It follows that instantaneously the other photon is fixed in the opposite spin state, without anything being done to it. But for this to happen the information about the spin state of the first photon, as fixed by observation, would by hypothesis have to be transmitted to the second photon at a speed greater than the speed of light ('superluminal transference of information'). Yet an important standard assumption of physics says this is impossible: nothing can travel faster than the speed of light. (The photons – light particles – are themselves of course travelling at the speed of light, yet the speed of divergence between them is still only the speed of light, not twice the speed of light.) Therefore there is something wrong with quantum theory. Einstein took this as vindication of his view that the universe is deterministic.

Alas for Einstein, and to the added amazement of all, the EPR effect was experimentally shown to be correct by the work of Alain Aspect in experiments at the University of Paris in 1982. This has proved one of the motivations for continued debate about, and development of, theories such as those mentioned to find other ways of accounting for the apparent anomalies of quantum theory. The debate – which has moved far on, and is fascinating and deep, embracing as it does string theory and much associated speculation – is fascinating.

See: RELATIVITY, STANDARD MODEL, STRING THEORY

RACISM

Discrimination against, hatred for, mistrust of, and bigotry towards others on the ground of their skin colour or other distinguishing features of appearance, such as eye shape, taken to mark them as belonging to a different – and because different therefore inferior, threatening, unpleasing – 'race', is racism.

Racism is not the only form of inter-group prejudice. Nationality, religion, language, speech accent, sex, sexuality, political affiliation, caste or class, disability, indeed almost anything that noticeably separates one group from another or makes an individual stand out as different from some norm, can be invoked as, or merely subconsciously trigger, prejudice and dislike, hostility and discrimination. But skin colour and other physically group-identifying features such as distinctive eye shape, hair type, nose size and form, and more, are the basis of racist prejudice as such.

The most comprehensive definition is provided by the UN Convention on the Elimination of All Forms of Racial Discrimination, which goes beyond considerations of race as such and includes several of the other features that standardly prompt prejudicial attitudes and actions. It reads, 'racial discrimination shall mean any distinction, exclusion, restriction or preference based on race, skin colour, descent, or national or ethnic origin which has the purpose or effect of nullifying or impairing the recognition, enjoyment or exercise, on an equal footing, of human rights and fundamental freedoms in the political, economic, social, cultural or any other field of public life.'

Arguably, the very concept of 'race' is misleading and even empty. Before genetics demonstrated that there are no differences between human beings to support the idea of racial distinctions, anthropologists and others divided humanity into groups on the basis of overt physical traits such as skin colour, physiognomy and hair type. Sometimes such distinctions were aided by self-identification by the groups in question. All groups think of themselves as the norm and everyone else as odd (reflecting the old Quaker saying 'all the world's queer except me and thee, and even thee's a bit odd at times'); thus some tribes of Native Americans called themselves 'human beings' and by implication thereby distinguished others as not quite human beings. That is commonplace, for practically every people has regarded some other people as subhuman or a lower form of life. This in turn has justified slavery and many other cruel and terrible practices.

All this suggests that 'race' is a social construct, and not a genetic fact. Of course there are phenotypic differences among populations of humans, but also within them, and there are gradations or clines in the similarities and differences between populations that cut across phenotypic classifications, for example blood type. Such considerations support the claim that the concept of race has no genetic basis, and still less that the concept of 'subspecies' does. This does not entail that genetic clusters and lineages can be identified in populations which for geographic or cultural reasons have been historically self-contained; but this is just 'family resemblance' writ large – that is, a generalized case of the similarity among members of a family as a result of shared genes. This does not stop the members of two distinct human families from both being humans. And indeed, genetic analyses suggest that there is more genetic variation within 'races' than across 'races' – undermining the concept of race yet further.

Genetics has replaced talk of race among most biologists with such concepts as population, clade or haplogroup, and genetic tracing of human ancestry suggests that all today's humans descend from a single female individual – 'mitochondrial Eve', who lived in East Africa about 140,000 years ago.

There might be no such thing as race, but there is definitely such a thing as racism, and it is an attitude that does not draws fine distinctions between 'race' and 'ethnicity' and 'culture' and other things that make for visible or at least identifying differences between groups. Given this, many systems of law err on the side of inclusiveness as the UN Convention does; thus English law defines a 'racial group' as 'any group of people who are defined by reference to race, colour, nationality (including citizenship) or ethnic or national origin'.

Catch-all definitions of this kind are important in the fight against discrimination, which is a corrosive social evil. Treating people as worth less consideration before the law, or in respect of employment and remuneration, or morally, or in common courtesy and decency, because of their appearance is completely unacceptable. But it is of the first importance to note that there is a difference between protecting people on the grounds of things they cannot choose about themselves, namely, their race, age, sex, sexuality, and disability if any – and things they can choose for themselves, for notable examples their religion and political affiliation. To protect people's religious and political choices from criticism, ridicule and opposition is wrong; not a few countries do this, especially as regards religion – yet another example of the inflated privileges that are accorded religion in most places, despite so often being part of the problem and not part of the solution in many of the world's troubles.

See: ANTI-SEMITISM, BLACK CONSCIOUSNESS, BLACK POWER, EQUALITY, MULTICULTURALISM, XENOPHOBIA

REALISM

In philosophy the term 'realism' denotes a number of different but related theses of great importance.

Realism is the theory that the entities in a given realm (the physical world, the ethical domain, mathematics) exist independently of our knowledge or experience of them – that is, independently of whether or not we know they exist. One immediate implication of this is that the entities in question do not exist because we think about them, something that appears obvious in the case of such physical objects as sticks and stones, but not so obvious in the case of such mathematical entities as numbers or sets, or ethical properties such as goodness and wickedness.

There are various proposals about how a realist view can be expressed in order to make it more explicit. One is to describe it as the claim that truth is a matter of correspondence between (on the one hand) what we say, think or theorize about the entities in a given domain, and (on the other hand) the entities themselves. This might be taken to imply that everything we assert about entities in that domain is determinately either true or false; which appears further to imply that there can only be one complete true description of the domain as a whole. In the case of the world taken as a whole, this would mean that there is only one complete true description of the world as a whole.

If the chief point in a realist thesis is its claim that the truth about any state of affairs is independent of what we do or can know about it, then despite its name 'realism' is not a thesis about reality – that is, about what exists – but rather about the relation of our minds to what exists. The realist says that what exists does so *mind-independently*, that is, *independently of knowledge or experience*; his is a thesis therefore about the extent of our knowledge and its relation to what there is. Philosophers who disagree with this view say that what exists – the same existing things, note – are in some way internally related to knowledge of them. Such philosophers are known as *anti-realists*: for them, see below.

To the unaccustomed eye, the difference between assertions about what exists and assertions about the relation of our minds to what exists might seem small. But the former is a matter of metaphysics (enquiry into what exists in the universe) whereas the latter is a matter of epistemology (enquiry into the possibility and nature of knowledge). Accordingly the difference is very large.

One way of viewing much of the history of philosophy is to see it as a dispute over realism, taking different forms at different times. Plato argued that the only fully existing things are the perfect, unchanging and eternal Ideas in the 'Realm of Being'; the medieval Schoolmen quarrelled over the question whether universals such as whiteness and roundness exist independently of particular white and round things; contemporary philosophy vigorously debates realist and anti-realist theses in the philosophy of language, the philosophy of mathematics, and ethics.

A glimpse into recent philosophical characterizations of realism will illustrate what is at issue. The American philosopher Hilary Putnam describes what he calls 'metaphysical realism' as the thesis that the world consists of mind-independent objects. Indeed he describes the commitment more strongly, as the view that the world consists of a fixed totality of mind-independent objects. And he argues that one who holds this takes it to follow that there is exactly one true and complete description of the world, and that therefore truth consists in a form of correspondence between it and that description. Partially under the influence of the British philosopher Michael Dummett, Putnam puts these points alternatively as the view that metaphysical realism is a set of theses about truth, namely, that truth consists in correspondence between what we say and what we are talking about; that it is independent of what humans do or could find out; that it is 'bivalent' – that is, there are only two 'truth values': true and false; and that as a result of all this, there cannot be more than one true and complete description of reality.

One of Dummett's ways of characterizing realism is to insist upon sharply distinguishing the truth of a proposition from the grounds that anyone has for taking it to be true. Putnam shares this analysis. In his terminology, the claim that truths are independent of knowledge is the claim that 'the world could be such that the theory we are most justified in accepting would not really be true ... rational acceptability is one thing, and truth is another.'

Such a view on the face of it seems intuitive for the world of physical objects, although Putnam and others have argued that in fact matters are otherwise. But as noted, in connection with mathematics and ethics the converse seems to be the case; yet here there are those who argue for the independent existence of mathematical structures and ethical facts and properties.

Anti-realism denotes the family of philosophical theses opposed, as the very name states, to realism. Anti-realism consists in denying that the relations between thought or experience and their objects are external or contingent relations. This is far from the claim that these objects are *causally dependent* upon thought or experience for their existence. Certain forms of idealism (for example, Bishop Berkeley's) put matters this way, and doubtless this is why some confuse idealism with anti-realism. But properly characterized anti-realism is at most the claim (until more is said; as to which, there can be much variety) that no complete description of either thought (or experience) or their objects, can leave out mention of the other half of the equation. That is the essence of anti-realism.

The idiom of relations is especially helpful in this debate. A relation is something that connects two or more things ('the cup is *on* the table', 'the man is *married to* the woman' – these are 'two-place' relations; 'the man is *between* the woman and the boy' is a 'three-place' relation; and so on), although of course things can stand in certain relations to themselves (such as being identical to themselves – a 'one-place' relation).

As the points above imply, one way of describing philosophical realism is as the view that the relation between thought and its objects is contingent or external, in the sense that description of neither relatum essentially involves reference to the other. What anti-realism says in opposition is that relations are internal (essential, necessary), that is, such that to give a full and proper description of either relatum, one has to invoke the other relatum in the process.

The anti-realist's case rests on the following thought: that a moment's reflection shows that the realist claim is a mistake at least for the direction object-to-thought, for any account of the content of thoughts about things, and in particular the individuation of thoughts about things, essentially involves reference to the things thought about. But then it is an easy step for the anti-realist to show that thought about (perception of, theories of) things is always and inescapably present in, and therefore conditions, any full account of the things thought about. And thus the relation between thought (perception, theorizing) and its objects is internal.

This thesis is plausible when one considers thought about mathematics and ethics. It is more controversial in the case of the physical world.

See: EPISTEMOLOGY, METAPHYSICS, POSITIVISM, RELATIVISM

RELATIVISM

If the way we think about the world is essentially conditioned by our history or culture, there is no reason why different people might not arrive at different, even incommensurable, ways of thinking about the world. The possibility that there are different ways of thinking about the world, together with rejection of any claim to the effect that some are better or more accurate (or more moral, etc.) than others, is relativism.

There is a distinction to be drawn between moral or cultural relativism, on the one hand, and cognitive relativism on the other. The former concerns the difference between cultures, or between different historical phases of the same culture, with respect to religious, social, and moral values and practices; that is, with respect to what might be called the 'superstructure' of a culture's conceptual scheme. Cognitive relativism concerns the 'infrastructure', the level of basic beliefs about the world, such as that there are perception-independent, re-identifiable and individually discriminable objects or events, occupying space and time, interacting causally, and bearing properties of various kinds.

On the face of it, cultural relativism is not really relativism, because our being able to recognize that another culture, or historical phase in our own culture, differs from our own in certain respects, presupposes our ability to gain access to the other culture and recognize the differences as differences; which means that enough must be common between our own and the other culture to allow mutual understanding and communication.

It is, however, just this point that is denied by advocates of relativism, who object that the appearance of accessibility is misleading. Far from gaining entry to the alien scheme we have merely reinterpreted it in terms of our own scheme; which is the best we can hope to do, because translation is not possible above an indeterminate level. By 'failure of translation' relativists do not mean the empirically false thesis that no language can be rendered into another, but the philosophical thesis that we can never be really sure which of alternative translations properly captures the sense of the discourse we are seeking to translate.

One arena where relativism proves most challenging or vexing, according to one's outlook, is in matters of morality. A moral relativist is one who holds that what is regarded as good and bad, right and wrong, acceptable and otherwise, legitimately depends on the point of view of the one making the judgement in question. So if two people from different moral standpoints disagree about whether some action or situation, some choice or practice, is good, each is entitled to his view and there is no way of adjudicating between them.

This view essentially premises the claim that moral value is not an objective feature of the world. If it were, then if two or more people disagreed about what is good or bad, only one of them could be right, and relativism would not be acceptable. There are plenty of moral theories which allow relativism; all those of a subjectivist kind, for example those that say our moral judgements arise from our emotional responses or the historical and geographical accident of which culture we happen to be born into, would find it at least as hard to assert that their moral outlook is right and competitors wrong. The characteristically anomalous position of religion is different: though one's religion almost always is an accidental matter of where and when one happens to have been born, one is standardly bound to believe that its morality is correct, and therefore that differing moralities are wrong.

It is important to distinguish between the empirical relativist claim that as a matter of fact different cultures and societies have different moralities, and the philosophical relativist claim that different moralities are of equal value or validity. The former is of course unexceptionable; the latter is where the fur flies. For moral objectivists of any stamp argue that there are moral truths, and any morality that fails to recognize and abide by them is in error.

It should perhaps be regarded as an oddity that the latter position is the harder one to sustain. The defender of moral relativism says that the basis of moral judgements is provided by the traditions, practices, beliefs and experience of a given community or people, so that justifying a moral claim, and recognizing a moral principle as true, can be done – and done conclusively – by appealing to the community's traditions and beliefs.

For some, this view looks compelling. Many examples appear to bear it out; take just one, the example of polygamy. In some societies this is regarded as acceptable and even good, in others quite the reverse, and in each case it is the traditions and beliefs that provide the justification for the view taken.

But then one considers the objectivist's claim that some things – torture of children, murder, unprovoked aggressive war-making, theft, unkindness and cruelty, and so much more – are surely wrong anywhere, for anyone, in any culture or society. This is a claim to the universality of fundamental moral values, and it is a claim that can be made by appeal to facts about human beings and their needs and interests without having to invoke divine command or some other extraneous source of universality.

An irenic suggestion might be that systems of morality are mixed as to their universal and parochial features. On such a view, there are some universal moral truths, and there are some which are more a matter of mores or custom than morality, and can be allowed to differ between groups according to the way that the more fundamental moral principles are applied. For example: it might be a universal moral truth that elderly parents should be honoured by their grown-up offspring. In one society this might be done by buying them a bungalow at the seaside, in another it might be done by killing and eating them when they become infirm. What differs is how the principle is put into practice, though the principle itself is the same in both cases: the principle is a moral matter, its application in practice is a matter of custom.

If this strikes one as an implausible suggestion – and so it does – it is because conflicts between different principles internal to each morality are being ignored, and in ways that do not seem to add up to anything that constitutes agreement in depth. In the offered suggestion, a principle against killing the aged is accepted and observed in one society but not the other, and so here a genuine relativity emerges; only by ignoring it can one say that the differences in mores do not entail differences in moral principle.

Relativism is the natural adjunct, indeed perhaps it is the defining characteristic, of postmodernism. One motivation for it is the desire to respect cultures and outlooks other than one's own, and to retreat from the cultural (and political) imperialism of the past, in which the superiority of European and North American culture was and is arrogantly assumed and then imposed on others. The price paid for this worthy motivation is a loss of purpose and principle in morality itself; what happens is parallel to what is connoted in the remark, 'Don't be so open-minded that your brains fall out.' The hard trick is to find the right way of having principles and at the same time having respect for alternative and even opposing views. But then, no one ever claimed that life is easy.

See: ETHICS, ETHNOCENTRISM, POSTMODERNISM

RELATIVITY

The phrase 'the theory of relativity' denotes two related theories developed by Albert Einstein in the first two decades of the twentieth century. In 1905 he published a paper, 'On the Electrodynamics of Moving Bodies', which set out the basic postulates of the Special Theory of Relativity, where 'special' means 'restricted' because it applies only to objects moving at constant velocities. In 1916 he published his General Theory of Relativity, which takes account of accelerating bodies also ('acceleration' means change of velocity). The General Theory therefore deals with gravity, because it shows that acceleration and gravity have identical effects (the Equivalence Principle).

By the late nineteenth century it was apparent that there was a serious problem in the classical physics that stemmed from Newton's work. This was that the Newtonian account of the relations between moving bodies was not consistent with the equations of electromagnetism discovered by Maxwell. The former is in effect a common-sense theory about how moving bodies behave; for example, if you are in a vehicle moving at 20 miles an hour, and throw a ball ahead of you at 10 miles an hour, the ball's speed will be the sum of these two speeds – 30 miles an hour. In the background of such obvious-seeming facts is the idea that the laws of physics are the same for everyone in uniform motion relative to one another, a notion developed in seventeenth-century physics to provide frames of reference in which to describe and apply the laws. In the ball-throwing case, the vehicle's speed is relative to something stationary outside itself, and the speed of the ball is computed in the same frame of reference by adding the speed of the ball relative to the vehicle to the speed of the vehicle itself. An important assumption in this is that time is absolute – it ticks away regularly no matter what, the same in all frames of reference.

But Maxwell's equations of electromagnetism give the speed of light, c, a constant value of about 186,000 miles an hour (more accurately, 299,792,458 metres per second), independently of whether a light source is stationary or moving, or of the velocity of an observer of the light. If one is sitting in a vehicle moving at a 100,000 miles an hour, and switches on a forward-shining beam of light, its speed will not be c + 100,000 miles an hour, but just c. It seems paradoxical, but whereas two balls thrown towards each other approach at the sum of their individual speeds, two beams of light shone towards each other approach at the speed of light, not (as one would expect) at twice the speed of light.

Einstein's contribution was to show that it is not contradictory to postulate that the laws of physics are indeed the same for all observers in the same frame of reference, yet also to postulate that the speed of light is constant irrespective of frame. Accepting both (with a suitable mathematical adjustment to the former; specifically but crucially, replacing Galilean transformations with Lorentz transformations) involves accepting some astonishing new ways of thinking about nature. For one thing, time no longer appears absolute and invariant, but is slower when measured on a moving vehicle than at a place stationary with respect to that vehicle. Also, objects grow shorter in the direction they are moving, as measured by an observer. And the faster an object moves, the greater its mass becomes. There is no longer any such thing as absolute simultaneity; two events that appear to happen at the same time for one observer can appear to happen at different times to a different observer. And perhaps most famously, Einstein showed that mass and energy are equivalent and interconvertible: this is expressed by the famous formula $E = mc^2$ where 'E' stands for energy, 'm' for mass and 'c' for the speed of light.

Special relativity agrees with Newtonian physics at speeds of motion which are low in comparison to the speed of light, but diverges from it increasingly as speeds become significantly larger fractions of the speed of light. It has been repeatedly tested and confirmed, and found to be vastly more accurate than Newtonian physics. Physicists use the special theory in their work all the time, where it serves as – so to speak – the wallpaper of their thought.

Einstein was helped in developing the General Theory by something that he at first found an annoyance, namely, the demonstration by another physicist called Hermann Minkowski that his Special Theory of Relativity could best be expressed geometrically in terms of a four-dimensional space–time. Einstein had already worked out the equivalence principle, stating that the effects of a gravitational field are exactly the same as the effects of acceleration. Among other things this explains weightlessness as experienced in a manned rocket ship. When its engines are switched off and therefore the rocket is not being accelerated, its occupants will float about inside in 'free fall'.

An immediate consequence of the equivalence principle is that light is bent by gravity. This was not a novel idea, because it was accepted in Newtonian physics that light, thought of as streams of particles called photons, will feel the gravitational force. Einstein's work showed that the effect of gravity on light is twice as strong as Newtonian physics predicts, as a result of the new model of space and time that his theory offered. This was that space–time is itself distorted by the presence of matter in it, just as a stretched-out sheet with a heavy object placed in the middle will be pulled down by the object into a dip. Think of light moving through space–time as behaving like a ball being rolled across a stretched sheet with a weight in the middle; the ball's trajectory will be affected by the slope, and drawn down it towards the weight in the middle. Rolled with sufficient force it will go from one edge of the sheet to the other, swerving round the contour of the slope yet not ending up in the dip with the object – a bit like a golfer's putt that skirts but does not fall into the hole. This is how light travels through space, occasionally being bent by massive objects such as the sun (as demonstrated in a critical observation supporting Einstein's theory in 1919).

In addition to reconceiving space–time as curved and gravitation as the effect of this curvature, the General Theory also predicts the gravitational red-shift of light, gravitational lensing effects, gravitational waves (so far only indirectly verified by experiment), and the existence of black holes. Its power makes it the basis of the standard cosmological model of the universe.

See: BIG BANG COSMOLOGY, QUANTUM MECHANICS, STANDARD MODEL, STRING THEORY

RELIGION

Because it is one of those capacious terms that allow a great variety of definitions, almost all of them devised by proponents or advocates of their own version of what they wish the term to denote, 'religion' has no universally agreed meaning. One major and central sense is that a religion is a set of beliefs about a supernatural agent or agents, and a set of practices entailed by those beliefs, usually articulated as responses to the wishes or demands of the supernatural agent or agents in question. The different versions of Judaism, Christianity and Islam conform to this model, as more diffusely and multiply do the family of beliefs and practices collected under the label Hinduism. So too do the forms of Buddhism which have accumulated deities, demons and other supernatural beings in large numbers – though Buddhism in its original form is not a religion but a philosophy. The distinction between a religion and a philosophy is important and clear, and applies to other philosophies wrongly described as religions, such as Daoism, Confucianism and Mohism in China, Stoicism in the ancient Greek and Roman worlds, and others.

The word 'religion' is standardly used in metaphorical ways – 'football is his religion' – which are interesting for the light they throw on aspects of the nature of what is meant by it. As this example shows, one thing a religion does (and sometimes things are what they do) is to shape, give meaning to, and indeed dominate lives or outlooks, as in the case of devout Muslims for whom the world can never be seen but through the spectacles of Islam.

For a set of beliefs and way of life to constitute a religion there has typically to be an element not just of belief in something supernatural and transcendent, and regarded as sacred, but also a practice associated with this something, taken as a response to it, or obedience to it, or worship of it, or conformity with it. This practice is the expression of the religious commitment, and a chief way of individuating different religious traditions, apart from the doctrines distinctive of each, is by the way their votaries act out their observances.

In the young religions of Christianity and Islam ('young' in the sense of being latecomers on the historical scene) the emotional content is important to some devotees; feelings of awe, reverence, fear, dependence and love are invoked as characteristics of 'true' religious sentiment. The relationship between the deity and the votaries in these religions is modelled on the social structure of an absolute monarchy; kings and tyrants have to be praised, bowed down to, supplicated, feared, fawned upon, obeyed, loved, followed – the negative and positive aspects of the loyalty and submission are packaged together on the premise that the absolute ruler has the right to demand, to punish, and in general to expect absolute submission, while being under no reciprocal obligations whatever, for example to answer prayer or to reward scrupulous practice of faith by giving the faithful what they want. The psychology of 'worshippers' therefore strikes critical observers as interesting; they accept, as the return for their self-abnegating prostration before a deity, a promise without guarantees of posthumous felicity. Here, says the critic, is the analogy: you lend me ten dollars and I say that I might pay you back when you are dead.

As the world has grown more self-conscious and sophisticated, so what was once the world view of goatherds sitting by their tents and pondering the starry sky above them has come to be given far more lavish accoutrements. Thus, religion is the home of spirituality, a sense of the holy and the divine, of transcendent truth, of ultimate things, of all that is deepest, highest, truest, furthest, and generally superlative. There should of course be a clue in this to the human capacity for detecting the poetry of things natural and beautiful, as the human eye, heart and mind thrill to them: but no, this precious possession of mankind has been attributed to gods beyond the horizon of sense.

There might also be a clue in this for the origins of belief in other worlds and other beings, perhaps derived from the experience of our cave-dwelling ancestors in eating mushrooms with psychedelic properties such as the *Amanita muscaria*, or wheat infected with ergot, or foodstuffs or stored liquids which had fermented and made them drunk, or the effects of enforced fasting, fever, exhaustion from long journeys, head injuries from accidents or fights, epilepsy and other brain disorders, madness, whirling dances, even just dreams – and no doubt also, even just plain old make-believe by creative folk who secured a position in the tribe by skill at weaving tales or pretending to be able to communicate with the spirits.

Etymologically 'religion' derives from the Latin (re)*ligere*, to bind or connect, which is a very interesting fact, because it reminds us that Roman religion was a matter of public observance aimed at promoting social cohesion and loyalty to the state by ceremonially reminding everyone, in civic ceremonies of prayer and sacrifice to gods associated with the public weal, of the overarching ties that bound them together. Roman public religion was not a religion of personal relationship with a deity, as in Christianity, and this was true also of the private household religion centred on the *lares et penates*, the gods of the hearth and storehouse – though as with actual and derivative forms of ancestor-worship (*lares* might have originated as ancestor figures) there was a familial tie to the dead, as in China. But honouring the *lares et penates* was still not anything like the Christian idea of worship and prayer; instead it was a good deal closer to the kind of good-luck, bad-luck superstition which still has some folk knocking on wood or not walking under ladders.

It was precisely because of the public bonding aspect of its religion that Rome regarded the early Christians as atheists, because the Christians repudiated Rome's gods and refused to honour them by taking part in the public ceremonies. If the Christians had done so they would otherwise have been left to believe what they liked, for the Roman state was extremely permissive about religion, and let everyone believe what they wished, including all the local gods and goddesses of all the cults around the empire, just so long as, on high days and holidays, they took part in the public ceremonials associated with their allegiance.

It is sometimes said that a typical religion recognizes a dual reality, one sacred – the domain of the gods; heaven – and one profane, consisting of everything in the sublunary world. This is certainly how Christianity and Islam see things, but whether this is a defining characteristic of all religion is not so certain, if only because it is likely that religions earlier than these two (and earlier than the ones from which they syncretistically derive, such as Zoroastrianism) did not divide the universe in this way. For one thing, the gods of the ancient Greeks immanently inhabited regions of the world generally inaccessible to mankind, or at least off limits to mankind, such as mountaintops (Olympus) and underground realms (Hades), to say nothing of groves and forests possessed of that numinous feel that makes the hair stand up on the back of untutored necks.

In line with this it is altogether likely that the earliest 'religions' were in fact rudimentary and anthropomorphic forms of science and technology, in the sense that they were attempted explanations of natural phenomena such as thunder and wind (the former being a big invisible version of a man stamping on the clouds, the latter the same puffing out his cheeks and blowing) – this is the science aspect – and attempts to influence or modify the behaviour of these natural forces, by petition, sacrifice, and taboo – this is the technology aspect.

On this view the anthropomorphized forces of nature were parts of nature, not supernatural entities. Indeed it is easy to think of the ancient Egyptians as feeling their god on their backs every day – he was Ra, the Sun – and to see the process by which the gods gradually had to be pushed out of man's familiar world, first to mountaintops and to caverns underground, and then into the sky, and finally into complete abstractions outside space and time altogether, as greater and greater understanding of nature accumulated among mankind, and came to be organized as knowledge rather than supposition and superstition.

This is part of the explanation of why today the more sophisticated apologists for religion hesitate to give definitions either of deity or of religion itself, in terms that will tie them down to something too specific and therefore refutable by scientific and psychological means. It is a first-rate convenience to be able to say that the deity is a mystery that human minds cannot comprehend, that religion is too complex a thing to define in any straightforward way, and that traditional views of the deity as an old man with a long white beard sitting on a cloud are a mere caricature. Unfortunately for such apologists, the caricature is what most ordinary folk, not just throughout history but even now, have vaguely in their minds if and when they think about such things; so the anthropomorphic and unsophisticated version is the standard.

Doubt, difference and polysyllabic circumlocution define the theologians; among the ordinary punters the doubt is of a different kind. Take Christianity as an example. Stop people exiting a church after a Sunday service and ask them about the details of their faith, and one is sure to find much haziness organized around the tales that form the staple of Sunday School instruction, together with a wide variety of cherry-pickings concerning which bits of the Bible to believe literally and which not to believe literally, which bits to obey, and which to ignore. (Some fundamentalists say: all of the Bible is to be literally believed, but even that view is hard to take literally in its turn, for they would have to kill people who failed to obey some of the Old Testament injunctions, for example.) The only people who attempt to live the literal moral injunctions of the New Testament – namely to give away all your possessions to the poor, and repudiate your family if they do not share your views, and to take no thought for the morrow (no plans, no preparations) – are monks and nuns, or at least some of them. For everyone else this morality, preached by and to people who thought that the end of the world was a matter of weeks or months away only, is an impossibility for the real world. In consequence most of what passes for Christian morality is rather remote from these New Testament teachings, with the exception of the injunction to 'love your neighbour', which in any case a number of other moral systems also enjoin (for example Mohism in China, predating Christianity by several centuries). Instead, when the Church realized that the Second Coming was no longer imminent, a good deal of non-religious humanistic Greek ethics had to be imported, not least from the influential Stoic school of thought, which had furnished the outlook of educated men for half a millennium before Christianity's good luck with Constantine.

Despite the advances of science and education in the Western world over the last few centuries, with a concomitant drop in religious belief especially in Europe, religion still retains a grip on some, and a residual, partial and intermittent hold on others. In the less developed world, and (against the trend of the advanced world) in the United States of America, both the grip on some and the partial hold on others remain significant.

The main reason for this latter fact is that, as institutions, the religions still have a considerable footprint in society, and by this means continue to present themselves as serious versions of the truth of things to children and troubled adults, to which latter they also offer the advantages of fellowship and certainty. Until the terrorist atrocities in New York and Washington on 11 September 2001, non-religious people tended not to be disrespectful to people with a religious commitment, but allowed the latter to continue arrogating a right to speak on moral matters, to teach their dogmas in schools, to be present as significant adjuncts on public occasions, to claim privileges and respect because they had a faith – and so on.

Since the 9/11 atrocities the mask of mutual indifference between the religious and the non-religious has slipped, and there have been very vocal attacks on the credibility, standing and acceptability of religion in the public domain, from such as Richard Dawkins and Christopher Hitchens. Cries of outrage at their hard criticisms and uncompromising tone arise on all hands, from people who seem to have forgotten that when religion was fully ascendant, the likes of Dawkins and Hitchens would not have been offered merely an unfriendly tone and no punches pulled on home truths, but something much more violent: death – death at the stake, with torture as the probable hors d'oeuvre.

Those of irenic mind on both sides of the religious–non-religious divide like to say that there is no conflict between science and religion, which, they say, are indeed compatible – perhaps because they address themselves to different kinds of truths, or to truths about different realms of being or significance. This, however, does not survive scrutiny. Religion and science are direct competitors for the truth about the nature of the universe, its origins, its contents (e.g. as to whether there are gods and perhaps also angels and other supernatural beings in it), and how it works (e.g. whether miracles occur in it, locally and temporarily suspending physical and biological laws). They are also diametrically opposite in character. Science is exploratory, open-textured, testable, and always revisable in the light of new or better evidence or new or better evaluation of current evidence. Faith, by contrast, is said to be at its most admirable – a virtue, no less – when it flies in the face of evidence, as the tale of Doubting Thomas tells us, and as the religious philosophy of Søren Kierkegaard tries to persuade us. No religion tells us what would count as a refutation of its claims and teachings, which reminds us of the principle enunciated by Karl Popper, namely, that a theory that explains everything, and can be falsified by nothing, is empty.

Religious conviction is at very least non-rational. Its sources and justifications lie in emotion and tradition. Some American Christians try to argue that religious faith is rational and indeed scientifically provable; some try to subvert evolutionary theory in biology with a dressed-up form of creationism called 'intelligent design theory'. These endeavours share a destiny with those attempted arguments for the existence of a deity offered by some medieval and later theologians.

It is practically certain that one of the original forms of religion among early humans – and it remains among certain groups of people still – is animism. Animism is defined as the belief that plants and inanimate objects have spirits, so in effect it is an extension of attributions of consciousness to parts of nature beyond the animal kingdom itself. *Anima* is Latin for spirit, and the word 'animal' derives from it to demarcate birds, fish, reptiles and mammals – creatures that can move about, and interact with one another and their environment – both from the vegetable realm and from rocks, water, hills, and the like, for short called 'inanimate nature'. The spirits believed by animists to occupy non-animal things might be ancestors of the currently living, or tutelary genii of given trees, rivers and significant-looking stones.

Animism is par excellence a primitive form of science and technology, science in the sense that it provides explanations of how things behave and why they are as they are, technology in the sense that it offers a means of influencing what happens in the world by means of mimicry (sympathetic magic), prayer, propitiation, sacrifice, observance of taboos, and the like. It thus constitutes an explanatory framework and an attempted solution to the impotence man felt before nature (and in the face of earthquakes, tsunamis, volcanoes and hurricanes, still feels). In short, it is a rudimentary and primitive precursor to science and technology.

The term 'animist' was coined in the nineteenth century by the anthropologist E.B. Taylor to label the belief system of non-literate tribal societies such as those he had studied in Central America. Along with a number of other nineteenth-century anthropological concepts (compare

'Hinduism') it is now regarded as a fabricated classification responsible for helping to promote and sustain racist and colonialist attitudes.

Many traditional religions do however have features that appear animistic by the term's standard definition, not least those (such as ancient Greek religion) in which the powers of nature are personified as gods. But to avoid the racist and colonialist overtones of the name, anthropologists now restrict themselves to the term 'traditional religion' and its cognates when discussing these features. However the term 'animism' is still casually applied by journalists in talking of the religious views of (for example) some African peoples, as when the religions of the Sudan are described as 'Islam, Christianity and animism'.

Popular forms of Christianity in South America and West Africa in particular have assimilated or adapted aspects of animism and other traditional religions into themselves, making a heady brew which explains their ready fascination for the credulous.

Taylor and others thought that animism represented an early version of religious belief, and assumed – as noted above – that as knowledge of nature and natural forces increased, so the spirits became more abstract and fewer in number, departing first to mountaintops and then the sky and finally into non-spatio-temporal abstraction altogether. If history is in some sense the story of the march of knowledge, so the etherealization of supernatural beings, diminishing from concrete realities in the daily lives of humans to theological abstractions of the most abstruse and polysyllabic kind, is very understandable, but hardly commendable.

No account of religion can ignore some of its byways, for example deism, fideism and efforts to square the presence of evil in the world with the existence of a deity.

This last is called 'theodicy', and its main target is the effort to reconcile the existence especially of 'natural evil' such as cancer, earthquake and tsunami with the putative existence of a good and benevolent deity. In Milton's apt phrase, it is the effort to 'justify the ways of God to man'. The term was coined by the philosopher Gottfried Wilhelm Leibniz from the Greek roots *theos* (god) and *dike* (justice), but Immanuel Kant best gives its primary sense in calling it 'the defence of the highest wisdom of the creator against the charge that reason brings against it for whatever is counter-purposive in the world'.

The existence of 'natural evil' as opposed to 'moral evil' (explained by free will) is standardly the greatest challenge to the idea of a benign providence, and has destroyed the faith of many. For such, natural evil is simply inconsistent with the idea of a deity supposed to be benevolent. It implies that either the presence of natural evil in the world is counter-evidence to the existence of a deity, or if there is a deity, then it cannot be a very benign one.

Leibniz famously held that our world is the best of all possible worlds, and he took this to follow from the 'perfections of God's nature'. Indeed he took this to follow with logical necessity, for it would be inconsistent with the deity's combination of benevolence and omnipotence that he should create anything less than the best possible world. But to render the undeniable because all too manifest existence of evil in this best of all possible worlds with the benevolence and omnipotence of the Christian god, Leibniz argued that this world does not have to be, and perhaps indeed ought not to be, a *perfect* world. On the contrary, the *best possible* world might well be one in which earthquakes, plagues, and the rest, serve the interests of the deity's ultimate plan for his creation. A *perfect* world would contain nothing that would test or chasten God's creatures, said Leibniz, so it would not necessarily be the best one for his plan, and therefore not the best for our own ultimate good.

One major thing wrong with this argument is that an omnipotent deity has, by virtue of that omnipotence, the opportunity to create any logically possible world; so, he could have created a world in which his ultimate plan for creation would be realized without the need of innocent suffering, or at least one in which only non-innocents suffer. The alternative is to concede that the deity is either not wholly benevolent, or not omnipotent. Either way he (she or it) ceases to be a deity as traditionally conceived, which leaves open the question of whether taking an interest in such a being would be anything other than prudential.

An interesting sideline in the question of religion is what effective non-believers thought before science, and especially geology and biology, provided insights into the origin and history of the world and life. The answer is 'deism'. Deism is the thesis that a deity created the universe, but is no longer active in it. It is a characteristically English seventeenth-century view, which became widespread in the European Enlightenment in the eighteenth century, in being a fudge: for it had the advantage of serving as an alternative for those who could not take any revealed religion (such as Christianity) seriously, while yet preserving them from the terrible opprobrium of being called atheists, and at the same time providing them with an intellectual fig-leaf over the question of how there comes to be a universe at all. Not until the geology and biology of the nineteenth century were there avenues of thought available for thinking about origins at all sensibly.

Why people should have reached for the fudge of deism is nevertheless a mystery: to answer the question 'why does the universe exist?' or 'why is there anything rather than nothing?' by saying 'because Fred made it' obviously does not constitute an answer, for who or what is Fred? – the arbitrary, ad hoc invocation of something to serve as the first term of a putative explanation is no good, but neither is substituting the word 'God' for 'Fred' – for a substitute is all it is.

Deism was however a sincere option for some, such as Lord Herbert of Cherbury (1583–1648) who is credited with originating it. Herbert outlined certain basic principles for his version of deistic belief: that there is one creator-god, in response to whose creation one should seek to live virtuously, for there will be a posthumous judgement in which good will be rewarded and evil punished. Of these three thoughts only the first remained convincing for, or was avowed by, later deists, who thought that the god who created the universe not only took no further part in it, but had no further interest in it. This was confirmed for many by the existence in the world of natural evil – a view confirmed for them by the terrible earthquake and tsunami that killed tens of thousands in Lisbon in 1755. And that further meant that there would be no posthumous judgement (or even existence).

Although most of the *philosophes* of the Enlightenment were atheists, most called themselves deists, and some actually were indeed deists (such as Voltaire). Both groups joined in opposing organized religion, priestcraft, and above all 'superstition' everywhere, as the most serious of all barriers to human progress. The greatest of the founding fathers of the United States of America were deists: George Washington, Thomas Jefferson, and Benjamin Franklin.

The truth is that 'deism' for most deists was really atheism with a fig-leaf. In an age in which the word 'atheist' automatically suggested 'multiple murderer rapist Satanist embodiment of evil' very few would volunteer the term as a self-description. 'Deist' was thus almost always a euphemism.

In marked contrast to the wellsprings of deism is 'fideism', the belief that reason is irrelevant to the question of religious belief, the special status of which places it above the norms of reasoning and evidence standardly required in other enquiries, such as the validation of empirical hypotheses. The word derives from the Latin *fides*, which means 'faith', and it has its roots in the teaching of St Paul (see I Corinthians, where the faith that moves mountains is extolled as one of the three highest virtues). But as a doctrine it came into its own in the Reformation period, particularly in the views of Luther, for whom faith rather than good works is the route to salvation.

Some religious thinkers in the nineteenth century adopted versions of fideism as a response to the advance of science, thus exempting themselves from having to put their beliefs to the same tests as scientific hypotheses standardly undergo. The most extreme fideist is the Danish writer Søren Kierkegaard (1813–55), who said that faith requires a leap in the face of reason and evidence, and is all the more admirable therefore. What horrors can be justified by appeal to the authority of the non-rational, the traditional, the superstitious, the suppositious, the evidentially unsupported, and so forth, history too often bloodily teaches.

See: AGNOSTICISM, ATHEISM, BUDDHISM, CHRISTIANITY, DAOISM (TAOISM), HINDUISM AND BRAHMANISM, ISLAM, JUDAISM

ROMANTICISM

Romanticism is a movement that flourished in literature, music, art and philosophy from the mid-eighteenth century until the rise of modernism towards the end of the nineteenth century. Its chief characteristics are individualism, expressivity, the paramount importance given to the imagination, the aesthetic and spiritual importance of nature, and the privileged – almost prophetic and legislative – status of individual creative genius.

The relation of Romanticism to the Enlightenment out of which it grew is a complex one. In some respects it is a direct product of the individualism cherished by the Enlightenment, and its humanism; but it is also a reaction to Enlightenment insistence on reason and empiricism. Indeed non-rational sources of inspiration, as for example the emotional response to nature, were taken by Romantics to have higher intrinsic value than the outputs of what they saw as reductive rational enquiry. As Romanticism diffused more broadly into the mindset of the nineteenth century, it sponsored other appeals to the non-rational as a source of political, personal and moral authority, examples being nationalism in politics and the revival of religious sentiment in some quarters (for example, the evangelical movements in the United States and Britain).

Romanticism can be said to have begun in Germany and England

in the 1770s, and by 1830 had become Europe-wide. Its most enduring legacy is to be found in poetry and music; its effect on the latter
especially continues to this day to hold universal appeal. It proved least
successful in painting, and most harmful in politics. It almost killed off
philosophy, and ruined most of what little was done during its period
of first influence; but as Schopenhauer and Nietzsche show it was not
wholly destructive in this quarter, if either of them can be thought of as
Romantic or post-Romantic thinkers. It had a mixed effect on the English
novel though of course a powerful effect on the German one. It almost
wrecked drama, but some of the finest essay writing in English occurred
during the high tide of the Romantic period, though not unequivocally as
a Romantic phenomenon, for there is far too much of the Enlightenment
in the free, individual and rational voice of the best essayists, the prince
among them William Hazlitt.

The arts including literature seem to be the natural place to find
Romanticism at its most flourishing as well as at its most florid. To
capture its mentality and character, there is no better place to look: as
follows.

It might be thought paradoxical to cite drama as one of the casualties
of Romanticism, as just claimed above, and yet to point to the great influence of Shakespeare on the Romantic imagination. Yet what one might
call the 'rediscovery' of Shakespeare is indeed one of the chief sources
of Romanticism. For a time between his death and the late eighteenth
century, Shakespeare had been regarded by educated critics as a violator
of all the canons of dramatic art, and he was therefore written down by
some as rude, ill-educated and a populist, his plays mere crowd-pleasers
which illegitimately and tastelessly mingled comedy and tragedy and
failed to observe the proprieties and aesthetic rules of drama's classical
models. But in the late eighteenth century and afterwards in Britain, and
especially in Germany, Shakespeare came into his own as the type both
of poetic genius and the pattern for dramatic creativity on an enlarged
and freer scale. Schiller and Goethe were directly inspired by his example,
and his exalted (and thoroughly deserved) status attracted painters, com-
posers and other poets to his plays, their themes, their characters, and in
Britain their language.

The same large dramatic spirit partly explains the Gothic aspect of
Romanticism, first appearing in the novels of Horace Walpole, Monk
Lewis and Ann Radcliffe. The Gothic taste diffused itself not just into the
literature of the nineteenth century in the work of such as Mary Shelley,
Charlotte Brontë, Edgar Allan Poe and Eugène Sue, but into architecture

and painting also. In this latter respect it increasingly took the form of a revived Medievalism, so that country houses and civic buildings alike appeared with spires and crenellations, stained glass and heavy wooden panelling. In painting its apogee is the Pre-Raphaelite movement.

In all its avatars Gothicism sought to evoke powerful, non-rational states of mind – the mystical, erotic, hysterical, frightening and black were its base notes. The contrast with Enlightenment rationality and order, and the clarity of the Enlightenment's intellectual and emotional tone, could not be starker. Voltaire and other votaries of Enlightenment sensibility disdained enthusiasm in all its forms, and this is almost certainly why Jean-Jacques Rousseau fell out with them, because his instincts were by contrast Romantic. Feeling, sensitivity, the trembling lip and tearful eye, broken hearts, the torments of disappointed love, were his natural terrain, as they were to become the terrain of Goethe and the poets of Romanticism's finest frenzies. Samuel Richardson had laid something of the groundwork in the panting, bosom-swelling, thinly disguised eroticism of his fiction; Rousseau unleashed the torrents in *The New Héloïse*, his wildly successful best-selling novel that took the eighteenth century by storm and made 'sensibility' the fashion.

The central emerging theme of Romantic literature was love and romance in our modern sense, and it so captured what was expected of poetry, novels and the stage that no story seemed properly constructed that did not end with the marriage of the male and female principals. The narrative arc of much nineteenth-century English literature from Jane Austen through Trollope and Dickens until – near the end – the new and darker realism of Thomas Hardy, George Gissing and their contemporaries followed this model.

Romanticism also celebrated and borrowed from the exotic, as the poetry of Byron and Shelley shows. Spain, North Africa and the nearer reaches of the Ottoman Empire increasingly came to supply painters with subject matter, some of it focused upon a febrile, lazy eroticism languidly basking in foreign heat. This interest, combined with the currents of the Gothic and medieval, the poetic and emotional, the captivation of the mind by fiction and licensed sensation, explains Victorian moralism: this latter was the alarmed, even frightened reaction to the overblown imagination of Romanticism, which reached from hypnotic tales of love sought, lost and regained to excesses of perfumed, hot-limbed sensual art, as much in music as in painting. One might see the Decadent movement of the late Victorian period, variously represented by Swinburne, Walter Pater, Aubrey Beardsley, Oscar Wilde and others, as the over-ripeness implicit in what had become the storm and thunder of Romanticism's first flourishings in the last third of the preceding century.

But without question the single most important element in the Romantic imagination in its first half-century was Nature. This is a topic of vast scope and great importance, for it is one of the pivotal topics of modernity. The Industrial Revolution and the growth of towns divorced many from the countryside and the way of life they understood there, and among the richer members of society the need to return to the country periodically, or at the very least to mimic it in gardens and parks in town, was pressing. Travel and walking in the country had become safer too, not least in places that the eighteenth century was beginning to associate with 'the sublime': mountains, heaths and moors, seaside cliffs, ravines, wild and solitary places where emotions could be stirred and a sense of the world's vastness and indifference to human individuals could be directly experienced. Poets began to celebrate nature – think of Clare and Wordsworth – or to lament its despoliation – Blake – and Rousseau once again led the way in establishing a fashion for immersing oneself in nature to listen to its voices and bathe one's spirit in its beauty and sublimity. His *Reveries of a Solitary Walker* drew people to the lakes and mountains of Switzerland to tread the romantic paths of nostalgia and reverie as he had done. In honour of Rousseau, Hazlitt spent a summer in the Pays de Vaud on the shores of Lake Geneva with its beautiful views across to the Alps behind Evian, and with the romantic Castle of Chillon just a stroll along the vineyard-lined shores.

The passion for nature was genuinely new; there had been nothing like it since the Roman poets had celebrated the virtues of bucolic retreat in the early Empire, though their chief reasons were the self-sufficiency of farm life, and the remoteness from the capital city's dangers and distractions. In the intervening centuries nature was seen as a foe, or at least as intractable; all effort was directed at subduing it, to clear it, fell its timber, plough it up or graze it, build a cottage and a barn on it, render it tame under the hand of man. Wild nature was the reserve of wolves and thieves, journeys through it were long and not infrequently perilous; the idea of delighting in its remoteness, wildness and more dramatic cliffs, ravines, mountains and tumultuous coastlines would have seemed madness to earlier ages.

If Victorian moralism was one reaction to Romanticism, another was the realism in literature of the later nineteenth century and its cognate academicism in painting. Decadence and Impressionism, arguably, are its metamorphosed forms. In music Romanticism lived and flourished long, and both lines of development inspired respectively by Wagner and Brahms – the first of these ascendant – are surely its heirs, so that the moment of contrast between Debussy and Richard Strauss, on the one hand, and the rise of new musical forms including atonal music, on the other hand, makes for an audible end to Romanticism.

Although Romanticism expressed itself most strongly in literature and the arts, bequeathing much that we would not willingly be without, its other greatest expression was something far less happy: nationalism. Nationalism arose from sources as disparate as celebration of vernacular languages, folklore, shared customs and religion, ideas about the racial and/or geographical integrity of peoples and their traditions (an idea propounded in the 1780s by Johann Gottfried von Herder), and the mixed reactions to the French Revolution and the wars that followed – with France first as a model for, then as an enemy of, national aspirations, in the latter case prompting Prussian ideas of *Volkstum* in resistance to Napoleonic imperialism. Johann Gottlieb Fichte was one of the architects of national consciousness, proclaiming in his 1806 invocation 'to the German Nation' that those who share a language and are bound to each other 'by many ties of nature long before human arts bind them' understand each other and constitute an inseparable whole; they are the natural vehicle of progress, and the medium in which 'divinity' expresses itself. As if Fichte's views needed support, there were Hegel's lucubrations on the Zeitgeist as inhabiting a particular people at a particular epoch and driving the dialectic of history towards the ultimate realization of Spirit. Coincidentally, the Zeitgeist then happened to have lighted upon the German people, whose historic destiny was thus assured.

This Fichtean, Hegelian and similar nonsense has made nationalism one of the cancers of modern history, so productive of wars and unrest has it been, and such a hollow god for worship by bloodlust. Some of its apologists see it as a fundamentally democratic movement, opposed to political models in which authority emanates from a king or wealthy and powerful clique at the apex of society; but in fact nationalism so readily lends itself to demagoguery, in which a dictator or power clique serves the same function as a king, that the only difference is in the myth that justifies the arrogation of power: for kings it was historically 'divine right', for demagogues it is 'the nation, blood, race, the ties of language or faith or geography or culture' – or some other handy abstraction on the basis of which enthusiasm for war can be whipped up.

Few clouds are without their silver lining, and of course there is nationalism-inspired literature and art of value (think of Irish poetry and drama, and Czech music), though as with most literature and art hijacked to 'a cause' (think of Socialist Realism) much of it ranges from the questionable to mere dross. The invention of everything from national epics to 'traditional' dress (Scotland's kilt, for example) shows that nationalism and mythopoeia went hand in hand, as one would expect given the artificiality of the idea and the peculiar ferocity of its effects. What an unhappy conjunction in human history has been the rise of ideas of nationalism with the rapid sophistication and destructiveness of weapons of war.

See: ENLIGHTENMENT, LOVE, NATIONALISM

SCEPTICISM

In philosophy, scepticism is a set of considerations which jointly challenge us to justify our claims to knowledge. It reminds us that sense-experience and reason are vulnerable to error or illusion, and asks us how we can exclude the possibility of either when we claim to know.

In more general terms, scepticism is a healthy feature of all enquiry, prompting careful examination of evidence and argument, reminding us not to take too much on trust and to inspect the credentials of the sources and nature of knowledge claims or any other demands on our credence.

The challenge of scepticism defines epistemology. Epistemology's concern is to identify and explicate the conditions for knowledge. Familiarly, one of the most crucial conditions is justification. The problems facing the justification of knowledge claims can best and most powerfully be described as sceptical challenges, meeting which – if possible – will certify that we are sometimes entitled to claim knowledge.

Despite traditional appearances, scepticism is not best described as doubt or denial, nor is it best understood without limitation of subject matter. Scepticism is best not taken as the claim that we are globally ignorant – that is, that we know nothing – for this is trivially self-defeating: if we know nothing, then we do not know that we know nothing. Rather, it is most sharply characterized as a challenge to defend the grounds offered in support of knowledge claims in some domain.

Reminders that our knowledge in given regions of enquiry is incomplete, or provisional, and that a healthy attitude of open-minded scrutiny must greet each new claim in them are perfectly acceptable and appropriate. But they do not amount to scepticism in the sense important in epistemology; in this guise they amount merely to injunctions to proportion assent to grounds – in short, to be rational.

But not only is scepticism not well described as the thesis that we are ignorant, it is not even well described as an attitude of doubt. Such an attitude would premise the view that there is something inherently suspect about our practices of enquiry, a presumption which, when it does not verge on being self-defeating after the manner of global scepticism, loads the dice against enquiry before it has offered what it can claim in its support. There is a colloquial use of 'sceptic' to denote one who is hard to persuade even about the most obvious things – a stance that commits the opposite sin to credulity or too ready assent – which this characterization conveys. But there is as little reason to think in advance that knowledge claims are by their nature doomed as to think that they are all justified. Our interest lies in separating the wheat from the chaff.

It does so when we recognize scepticism in a given domain of enquiry as a challenge to explain the justification for claims made in that domain. The best sceptic does not himself claim anything; he asks for a defence of our justificatory practices in the light of important considerations affecting our ways of getting, testing, employing and reasoning about our beliefs. The considerations in question relate to the nature of perception, the normal human vulnerability to error, and the existence of states of mind – dreaming, hallucinating, being deluded, and the like – which can be subjectively indistinguishable from states that we normally take to be appropriate for reliably forming beliefs. By invoking these considerations the sceptic motivates his demand to be told how, despite them, we can make claims to knowledge.

See: EPISTEMOLOGY, PHILOSOPHY

SCIENCE

The Latin original of the word science, namely *scientia*, means knowledge, but 'science' now denotes not knowledge in general but a particular range both of knowledge and types of enquiry in search of it – namely, knowledge of the physical world, its basis in material reality, and its various contents. It is a general label, comprehending a number of enquiries which share certain methodological and technical commonalities. The main branches of these enquiries include physics, chemistry, astronomy, biology, geology, meteorology, and their numerous subdivisions and interconnections (such as biochemistry and astrophysics).

The commonalities among them are reliance on empirical methodology – observation and experimentation in the gathering and testing of data – and the use of quantitative techniques of measurement and assessment wherever possible. A standard form of scientific procedure is the making of a prediction and the testing of it by experiment. These features of enquiry are distinctive of science; they are what make an enquiry scientific in the modern sense of this word.

Science is to be distinguished from technology, which is the application in practice of some of the findings of science (and of general experience) through the medium of machines or devices constructed to serve identified ends, such as raising water from one level to another, milling corn, moving heavy objects, or enabling communication between people placed at a distance from one another. Before the rise of modern science in the sixteenth and seventeenth centuries CE, what we now think of as science and technology were often pursued indistinguishably from one another and in connection with one another, generally with a technological aim in view. It was the experimental method and the use of mathematical techniques that gave modern science its great impetus in the period mentioned.

That period began – so most agree to date it – with the publication of Nicolaus Copernicus's *De Revolutionibus Orbium Coelestium* in 1543. (This was also the year in which Vesalius published his treatise correcting the anatomical errors of ancient physicians.) This is not such an arbitrary or isolated starting point, despite the fact that there had been several millennia of astronomical observation already, and much proto-science (and some real science) in many of the centuries beforehand. But the world in which Copernicus lived was one which at last had proper standards of measurement employing a number system ultimately derived from India, it had paper and printing, making the communication of ideas more rapid and general, and it had Latin as a common language of research and scholarship. This state of affairs was soon to be further improved by the arrival of valuable instruments – the telescope and microscope not least among them – which had begun as fairground attractions but were soon seized upon by serious enquirers who saw their potential. And perhaps as significant as all these other factors was the defeat at last of religious prohibitions against scientific enquiry.

Ancient times had bequeathed great technological advances, not least the wheel, bridges, aqueducts, other building techniques, and more; but they had also created obstacles to further progress, in the form of authoritative-seeming systems of thought derived from Aristotle, Galen and Ptolemy, which their successors were loath to challenge. In the new mood of the sixteenth and seventeenth centuries these pieties, as with those of orthodox religion, were no longer a barrier: and the minds of Galileo, Newton and others brought a new perspective to bear with astonishing results.

At the same time as the above events were unfolding, the European nations were sending ships across the oceans on voyages of discovery of new lands and wider fields of nature. Naturalists and artists brought home news of vast treasuries of flora and fauna in other climes, and the accumulation of 'cabinets of curiosities' prefigured the first museums. The application of discoveries in chemistry to discoveries in biology had to wait their time; but the microscope was already a vital biological tool, and the classificatory system introduced by Linnaeus was another such in the organization of biological knowledge.

The moment when science started to diverge into different component specialisms was when Alessandro Volta invented the electric battery. This happened in 1800, and the importance of the event was that it made electrolysis possible, enabling the separation of compounds into their elements. Chemistry thus became a self-standing science apart from physics, and began to make enormous strides.

By these means science expanded its empire, rapidly and – because of its methods and conceptual tools – authoritatively. It is a magnificent achievement of the human intellect, indeed it is the greatest of all mankind's achievements, something that can confidently be asserted even though some of what science has done (or rather, has been made to do in the more perverted interests of politics and war) cannot be regarded as good.

It comes as a surprise to many to learn that one of the proximate roots of science in the modern period is alchemy. This is because alchemy has come to be identified in the popular imagination with science's least successful and most notorious aspects, for its chief motivation was not a search for knowledge but an effort to transmute base metals into gold, to find the elixir of immortality or perpetual youth (or at least longevity), to discover magical means to wealth, power, influence, health and love, to poison people undetectably, to foresee the future, and much besides.

Although all this is indeed true of alchemy, it was also – both therefore and besides – an effort to understand nature and control parts of it to good ends (as in its efforts towards medical understanding) as well as more questionable ends. In the absence of scientific method and suitable accompanying mathematical tools, alchemy was haphazard and disorganized, and therefore both serious and quack investigators were able to pretend to be savants.

The two most celebrated aims of alchemy, then, were to change common metals into precious metals, and to find a cure-all for disease and even death. It was believed by many that both aims would be realized by discovery of the 'philosopher's stone', a potent substance that would make this possible.

That the alchemists' assumptions were not entirely arbitrary can be seen from the fact that they premised the theory that all things are made from different mixtures of elements, which they followed the ancients in thinking were four in number – earth, air, fire and water – each with one or more of the four properties hot, cold, wet and dry (thus yielding such compounds as hot dry air, cold wet air, hot wet air, and so forth). If lead and gold differ in the mixture of the elements constituting them, why cannot one rearrange the elements in lead to turn it into gold? They were, as it happens, right in basic principle, though wrong about the constitutive elements.

Work with metals, dyes, herbs, gems and other stuffs in a wide variety of endeavours had been continuous since prehistory, and it is from these that the various aspects of alchemy stemmed. The earliest known alchemical text is the *Physika kai mystika* attributed to the ancient Greek philosopher Democritus, though more probably written by Bolos of Mendes in the third century BCE. Together with a few Egyptian papyri this early record shows that efforts to make gold or increase small quantities of it into greater quantities, and to produce other valuable chemicals, had already been longstanding, as had discussion of utensils, stills and furnaces necessary for the task

Whereas alchemical research as such played its part in the rise of science, a set of beliefs sometimes associated with it played less of such a role: Hermeticism. This was a pre-scientific assault on uncovering nature's secrets and thereby controlling them, which mixed magic, alchemy and esoteric philosophy, and was based on writings supposedly by a legendary figure called Hermes Trismegistos. Some identified this figure with Hermes, winged messenger god of the Olympian pantheon, and also with Thoth, Egyptian god of wisdom; others thought Hermes was a great Egyptian teacher and prophet. 'Trismegistos' means 'thrice-greatest'. In Renaissance and more recent writings the word is spelled, in Latin form, 'Trismegistus'.

An important event in the spread of Hermeticism in the Renaissance is the translation of the Hermetic Corpus by Marsilio Ficino at the court of Cosimo de Medici at the end of the fifteenth century. Cosimo thought that the Hermetic writings were greatly more important than those of

Plato, hence his commission to Ficino for their translation. Ficino had founded an academy, under Medici sponsorship, for the translation and study of Plato, but when a bundle of very old manuscripts containing the Hermetic Corpus was discovered, all attention was turned to it – and with much excitement, because it was found to contain ideas similar in some respects to Neoplatonism, with overtones reminiscent of Neoplatonic Christian thinking. The assumption immediately made was that it represented the most ancient wisdom in the world, and was the source of Greek philosophy and a prefiguring of Christian revelation. But most importantly it was thought to represent lost knowledge of great power and promise.

This view of its antiquity dated to St Augustine and carried his authority, though in his case he placed Moses much earlier than Pythagoras and thought that the Hermetic writings originated sometime between the dates of these two. All these views were however exploded by the careful linguistic analysis of the texts by Isaac Casaubon, published in 1614, showing that the Hermetic writings dated from the third or fourth centuries CE, by one or more people who had had some exposure to early Christian teachings and Neoplatonism, and had produced a synthesis of his or their own from it together with other mystical and magical elements.

To the story of alchemy as an immediate precursor to the rise of modern science could be added the long story of astrology, because observation of the heavens had always had both astrological and astronomical interest for those who engaged in it. The key point is that as more responsible and disciplined approaches to the investigation of nature began to sift the genuine from the spurious, and as techniques and instruments progressed – not least the empirical and quantitative techniques and the rapid improvement of telescopes and microscopes – so the separation of real science from spurious science allowed the former to develop, with extraordinary rapidity in historical terms, into the mighty edifice that we see today.

See: BIOLOGY, SCIENTIFIC REVOLUTIONS, SOCIOBIOLOGY

SCIENTIFIC REVOLUTIONS

As noted in the foregoing, most histories of science date the beginning of 'the scientific revolution' – meaning the rise of modern science – to the publication in 1543 of Nicolaus Copernicus's *De Revolutionibus Orbium*

Coelestium (On the Revolutions of the Heavenly Spheres). This was also the year in which Andreas Vesalius published *De Humani Corporis Fabrica* (On the Structure of the Human Body), which revolutionized the understanding of human anatomy. Until then in Europe most proto-scientific and pre-scientific ideas about all aspects of nature were derived from the very often misleading authority of the ancients as contained in the works of Aristotle, Galen, Pliny the Elder's *Historia Naturalis* (Natural History), and others. Application of empirical methods and the use of the quantitative techniques of mathematics allowed the enquirers of the later Renaissance to challenge the hegemony over thought of both the ancients and religious orthodoxy, and to begin the process of understanding the world properly. The success of science from that day to this has been one of the greatest, the most outstanding, the most remarkable and admirable of all human achievements in history – and this despite the profoundly regrettable evil that science has sometimes been put to.

This is not to say that there had been no noteworthy scientific, mathematical and technological advances in the period from classical antiquity until 1543, for most certainly there had been – many of the most important in India, the Middle East, and notably in China. Ideas, techniques and discoveries in these places and times fed in, both positively and (by being discovered to be wrong: a useful advance) negatively, to the origins of the scientific revolutions in the sixteenth and seventeenth centuries. So too had the development of instruments like the telescope and magnifying lens, some of which began life as fairground curiosities until their potential was recognized.

But the quality and quantity of scientific advance from the mid-sixteenth century in Europe is of a different order from everything before it, and we have before our eyes the result: the transformation of the world and human experience that science has wrought. If anything deserved the name 'revolution' it is this; and true to the nature of science it is the work of many hands – not just Copernicus, Galileo, Newton, Priestley, Faraday, Maxwell, Einstein, Bohr, Heisenberg and others whose names are especially salient in the history books, but the collegial, critical, peer-reviewing, collaborative and competitive host of talented individuals who have put the building blocks of the house of science in place, one by one.

The idea of a 'scientific revolution' in this historical sense inevitably attracts the attention of theorists eager to understand how it happened. A well-known example is Thomas Kuhn's slender volume *The Structure of Scientific Revolutions* (1962) and the debate it generated. Kuhn's book has become a modern classic in more domains of thought than just the philosophy of science. It has sold over a million copies in twenty languages, and its central idea has become part of the wallpaper of thinking in many disciplines.

Kuhn's central idea is as follows. Science undergoes periods of 'normal' activity in which generally accepted methods and aims define what counts as appropriate areas of research and the right way of investigating them. But when difficulties accumulate, making the existing paradigm of enquiry unsustainable, a revolution occurs which introduces an entirely new paradigm that wholly replaces the old, constituting a new 'normal science' which operates until, in its turn, it is replaced by yet another 'paradigm shift', a phrase Kuhn made famous. Crucially, old and new paradigms are 'incommensurable'; the new is not an improvement on the old, it is just different, and the two cannot be compared.

Examples offered of paradigm shifts are the rise of seventeenth-century science, and the displacement of Newtonian science by relativity theory at the beginning of the twentieth century.

Kuhn claimed that he did not intend his thesis to be construed relativistically. The displacement of paradigms represents progress in his view, something that a relativist by definition cannot accept. An example of such a relativist would be Paul Feyerabend, who believed that what others thought of as development in science was in fact merely change in the meaning of scientific terms, so that later phases (in time) of science cannot be compared with earlier ones, rendering the idea of progress empty. Thus different ways of calibrating temperature, for example, involve a change in meaning of 'temperature', so that what is measured by dipping the fingertips into a liquid and what is measured by dipping the bulb of a mercury thermometer into it are two different things. By the same token, views of nature held by 'traditional' societies cannot be compared to modern science, and therefore have to be regarded as on an equal footing with it. It is an implication of Feyerabend's thesis in this respect that efforts to induce rainfall by Native American rain dances are therefore on a par with silver iodide seeding of clouds from an aeroplane.

Because Kuhn's view has an 'incommensurability' component as Feyerabend's does, it is hard to see how he can escape the charge of relativism. In any case his views have been gladly appropriated by postmodernists, creationists and the like, who aim to undermine science by impugning its claim to the special validity of scientific method.

Critics argue that Kuhn's picture of science is harmful, because it supports the way that the dominant social institutions which control science and its funding confer legitimacy on their own preferred science and scientists, while excluding people and ideas different from or opposed to them. This was particularly dangerous in the Cold War context, they say, when only those prepared to conform to the establishment view were able to have scientific careers. If one thinks about the difference between the views of Kuhn and Karl Popper, another great name in twentieth-century philosophy of science and originator of the falsifiability thesis, it is the latter's promotion of the critical spirit of scientific enquiry which in the view of these critics should be preferred.

See: FALSIFIABILITY, SCIENCE

SECULARISM

A secular dispensation is one in which matters of government, public policy and administration, and publicly funded provision of services, are kept distinct from any religious organizations or movements and their particular wishes for the form that society should take and how it should be run. More succinctly, the secular principle is often summarized as 'separation of Church and state' or 'separation of religion and public affairs'.

'Secular' does not imply 'anti-religious', it implies 'non-religious'. So there have been and are many religious people who are also secularists, because they take the view that religion and government should be kept apart. It has been argued that secularism in the Western tradition was an invention of the Christian Church, which wished to keep itself free of interference from the temporal powers whenever and wherever it found itself unable to govern the temporal powers.

Secularism should be distinguished from both atheism and humanism (on which there are separate entries in these pages). There is of course a natural connection between the three positions, but any one of them can be held without the other two, though it would for example be odd to find an atheist who was an anti-secularist.

In the natural way of these things, the word 'secular' has come to acquire additional connotations and extensions of meaning. So for a main example, a secular outlook is one that bases itself on reason and evidence, at the same time opposing acceptance of views on the basis of faith, tradition, authority or superstition. Secular values and principles are most illuminatingly associated with those of the Enlightenment, celebrating individual autonomy and enjoining the responsibility to think for oneself and to base one's life and outlook on rational and empirical grounds.

Commitment to science, humanist ethics and democratic institutions lies at the core of this outlook, and by its nature therefore secularism is pluralistic. Some secularists who are also atheists might argue against religion, but they would violate the concomitants of their own view if they sought to outlaw it; what they can ask for is that it should be a private matter and that if it conflicts with the broader common good it should be subordinated to it.

The United States of America is a constitutionally secular state; the First Amendment to the Constitution provides that there is to be no public interference in matters of religion and vice versa. Turkey under the reformist project of Mustapha Kemal Atatürk became a secular state after the fall of the Ottoman Empire. France is a secular state; the most populous part of the United Kingdom, England, is not a secular state, because it has an established Church which is deeply implicated in the constitutional fabric of the state, has a major unelected presence in the legislature, runs over a quarter of secondary schools and three-quarters of primary schools, and presides over most of the ritual functions of the state such as coronations of monarchs, royal weddings, and ceremonies of state including daily prayers in Parliament.

The idea of keeping religion out of other domains of activity is an old one, and in fact the origins of philosophy and its descendant science – traditionally assigned to Thales in the sixth century BCE – lie in the refusal to invoke traditional religious or indeed any supernaturalistic answers to questions about the origin and nature of the universe. That is a recurring theme in all traditions of thought; Indian philosophy's atheist schools and the demand for separation of theological and philosophical questions in the thought of Averroes (Ibn Rushd) are further examples.

The word 'secularism' itself was coined in 1846 by the atheist and Owenite socialist writer George Holyoake, who five years earlier had spent six months in prison for blasphemy. He was the last person to be convicted for this 'crime' in England. In a magazine founded for the purpose of promoting the idea of secularism, the *Reasoner*, Holyoake argued not merely for the separation of Church and state but for the development of a secular society, in which the influence of religion would be relegated to the private sphere and all public matters would be cooperatively decided on rational principles.

This suggests a distinction between constitutional and social secularism, an important distinction because a society can be functionally secular (as England and Norway are) although it exists in a state which has an established Church (as England and Norway do). And likewise, a state can be officially secular (as the United States and Turkey are) and yet have religion looming large in many social and political respects (as the United States and Turkey do).

In the United States and almost all parts of the Islamic world, the very idea of secularism is anathema. In the United States this is because the word rather mindlessly conjures ideas of atheism and its supposed horrors of immorality and even (paradoxically!) Satanism; in Islam the idea of separation of religion from public affairs is blankly unthinkable for all but the most educated and cosmopolitan: the religion is everywhere, and in the ideal for a devout Muslim it governs and interpenetrates everything. What meaning can 'separation of religion and public affairs' have for one who holds such a view?

In the view of some, the present writer included, the future safety and sanity of the world depend on secularism at least in the Church–state separation sense, and ideally in the more inclusive social sense too. The work of such organizations as the Secular Coalition for America and Americans United in the United States, and the National Secular Society in the United Kingdom, is vital in articulating the argument for secularism and opposing the continuous effort by religious organizations to increase their influence in the public domain. A notable achievement in secularist endeavour was its defeat of the Roman Catholic Church's efforts to have reference to Europe's Christian past inserted in the preamble to draft versions of a European Constitution. Europe is the most secular region of the world, being the home of the Enlightenment and all that this implies; for both sides of the debate about secularism that is a fact of singular importance, and illustrates the importance that secularism has for those who reflect on it.

See: AGNOSTICISM, ATHEISM, ENLIGHTENMENT, HUMANISM, HUMAN RIGHTS, RELIGION

SLAVERY

Slaves are human beings held against their will to perform labour and service; they cannot choose to leave or to withhold their labour, they are not paid a wage for the work they do though they are fed and housed, and they are typically forced into slavery by capture or purchase, or by being born to slave mothers. Their condition is analogous to animals such as oxen and dogs put to work on farms. Slaves who are owned by other human beings are known as 'chattel slaves'. The international

Slavery Convention of 1926 defined slavery as 'The status or condition of a person over whom any or all of the powers attaching to the right of ownership are exercised'. The International Labour Organization defines slavery as 'all work and service which is extracted from a person under the menace of any penalty and for which the said person has not offered himself voluntarily'. This latter definition allows that there can be slaves who are paid a wage; they are slaves because they are under compulsion, at risk of penalty, to perform the labour or service exacted from them.

Such is the very similar family of basic definitions; and they comprehend a number of different kinds of compelled, obligatory, unfree, bonded, indentured, debt etc. labour which are forms of slavery, and which remain scandalously prevalent in the world today.

No one capable of a moment's reflection can fail to be shocked by the enormity of slavery throughout history. Slavery was an essential part of the foundation of many societies from time immemorial right to the very recent history of all today's major economies. Without the millions of slaves who once toiled and died in the United States and in the imperial territories of Britain, France, Spain and Portugal, none of these countries would have grown rich and powerful in quite the way they did, if at all.

Because the trade in slaves and the use of slaves in West Indian plantations contributed to the British Empire's wealth, some descendants of slaves today demand an apology and reparations from Britain. The same demand is made in other countries with a slaving past, not least the United States. The claim is an understandable one, but it overlooks two significant facts.

The first is that everyone alive today is probably the descendant of a slave, for slavery has been ubiquitous in human history; and equally, everyone today is probably the descendant of a slave-owner too. One has only to do the arithmetic of world population in the past and now to see that, as we are all related to everyone else through our shared ancestries, so this must imply descent from both sides of the tragic story of slavery.

The second fact is that, as United Nations and International Labour Organzation figures persistently show, there is more slavery in the contemporary world than there ever was in the past. The UN calculates that more than 12 million people are in some form of slavery every year – whether as indentured labourers, trafficked prostitutes, chattel slaves, and the like – which compares to the 12 million Africans said to have been captured by other Africans and sold to white slavers in the three centuries of the Atlantic slave trade. The organization Free the Slaves claimed in 2006 that at a conservative estimate some 27 million people were in one or another form of slavery, the highest number of slaves in history, yet the smallest percentage of the world population as a whole.

Britain abolished its slave trade in 1807, and slavery itself in its imperial territories in 1833. France followed suit in 1848. A London court ruling in 1772 confirmed that slavery was illegal within England and Wales, and that any slave brought to these countries was free the moment his foot touched their soil. A court in Scotland in 1776 ruled that the same applied there. These jurisdictions lagged far behind Hungary, where slavery had been abolished in 1000 CE, and Sweden where it had been abolished in 1335. Japan abolished trade in slaves in 1587, though it did not outlaw slavery itself until the second half of the nineteenth century. Slavery was officially abolished in Iran in 1928 and (though here unofficially matters are different) in Saudi Arabia, the Yemen, and the United Arab Emirates in the early 1960s. Oman did the same in 1970. Slavery was finally made illegal in Niger in 2004. Most other countries abolished slavery in the nineteenth century after the British lead in 1833, the bulk of them in the second half of the century. Under colonial rule slavery was outlawed in African countries in the first decades of the twentieth century.

The slave trade had been abolished in a number of states of the United States by the end of the eighteenth century, and some abolished slavery outright; the first to do so was Vermont in 1774. But slavery itself was only finally abolished in the southern states in 1865, following the Union's victory over the Confederacy in the Civil War.

The movement to abolish slavery was known as Abolitionism, and its first proponent was Anthony Benezet, a Quaker immigrant to the United States from Britain (his family were originally French Huguenots who left France because of religious persecution), who persuaded his own brethren first, and through them the community of conscience at home in Britain, to oppose the slave trade and then slavery as such. Because the anti-slavery movement was championed mainly by people from the Dissenting religious communities who could not stand for parliament, William Wilberforce became their representative there, and has had more than his fair share of praise from history as a result.

Slavery today takes many forms and hides under many disguises, including forced labour in prison camps as in China, wage slavery, child labour in South Asia and Africa, human trafficking, indentured servitude, debt labour, and of course traditional forms of outright slavery.

Examples of the products of such slavery are commonplace. In the West every week people unknowingly touch something wholly or partly made by forced labour in China's huge gulag of prison camps where millions are incarcerated under 'administrative detention', which means without trial, for purposes of 're-education'. They make paper bags, plastic chopsticks, uncountable little components of toys and gadgets. The Chinese dissident Harry Wu, who was held in such a camp for twenty years, has with painful eloquence described the conditions under which the slave prisoners work and die in those camps. Despite the importance of forced labour to China's economy, the international community chooses to ignore its existence.

Millions of Aids orphans in Africa slave for a meagre living, suffering exploitation and abuse. Women in a number of traditional or theocratic societies are the property of men and are not permitted to live independently of them; in Saudi Arabia a woman cannot leave her house unless accompanied by a male relative, and functionally the condition of women in fundamentalist Christian communities in the southern United States is little different. Women in Saudi Arabia and the fundamentalist homes of the United States, like many others in similar dispensations, are slaves in a quite straightforward sense of the word: they are owned by, and lie at the disposal of, others.

Aristotle, despite being a great philosopher and one of the West's founding fathers, nevertheless approved of slavery, saying that some people are naturally born to be slaves. The founding fathers of the United States spoke eloquently about all men being born equal and having inalienable rights to life, liberty and the pursuit of happiness; yet some of them owned slaves, had children by them, and collectively they did not succeed in abolishing slavery itself when they wrote the Constitution – though some, to their credit, tried.

Serfs were never quite the same as slaves in feudal Europe, for they had certain rights as human beings which slaves proper were denied. But until the late nineteenth century Russian serfs were effectively slaves; they were tied to the noblemen's estates where they were born, and were bought and sold along with it. Serfdom was abolished by Tsar Alexander II in 1861.

Despite having been the norm in feudal Europe, serfdom was dismantled not for humanitarian considerations but to allow landowners to end ancient feudal rights of common grazing and gleaning that had once been among the few privileges enjoyed by serfs, and an important part of their livelihood. The enclosures caused terrible hardship among the rural poor.

Throughout history the amount of suffering caused by the enslavement of many by the relatively few has been a black mark against humanity. It is shocking to find how prevalent and widespread it remains in the contemporary world. Because every one of us is a descendant of slaves and almost certainly slave owners too, from some period in history even if far back in the most ancient times, and because almost every one of us unhesitatingly condemns slavery in all its forms, we have an obligation to work to eradicate it from our own times, and to prevent it returning in future. This is not an obligation many seem to take seriously.

See: EQUALITY, HUMAN RIGHTS

SOCIALISM

'Socialism' denotes a family of political theories sharing a common view that the most morally defensible economic system is one in which the means of production are publicly owned (by the state) or owned in common by the members of society (by the collective). In practice social-ist economies, or economies that have aspired to be socialist, have been characterized by centralized control of the means of production, or at the very least of the 'commanding heights of the economy', which means that decisions about the allocation of resources and the distribution of products have lain in the hands of a central party bureaucracy.

There are various forms of socialism, ranging from totalitarian and in practice harshly repressive 'Soviet' socialism and its Chinese equiv-alent, to the democratic socialism exemplified by mainstream left-wing political groupings in Western Europe. They share in common the view, held with different degrees of strength and preparedness to compromise, that private property, with its attendant evils of class division based on unfairly concentrated wealth and power, is inimical to general welfare.

Among the differences of opinion that have divided socialists is whether socialism can and should evolve out of a given current system, especially capitalism, or whether revolutionary overthrow of an existing order is required. Either way, the next question is whether socialism should be a system established by a grass-roots mass movement, or be led by a vanguard.

The principal motivation of socialism is the idea that in an economic order where a few grow rich by owning and controlling the means of production, with the many obliged to sell their labour for far less than the worth of what it produces, there is and always will be injustice, and the many will be denied the opportunities and social and cultural goods enjoyed by the rich. Common and cooperative ownership of the means of production empowers individual workers, and promotes a social order in which all are equal participants and benefit fully from their contributions to the common weal.

Socialist thinking began as a response to the individualism encouraged by such economic thinkers as Adam Smith during the Industrial Revolution. In nineteenth-century France the ideas of Pierre-Joseph Proudhon, Saint-Simon and Charles Fourier, and in Britain Robert Owen (founder of the cooperative movement), made significant contributions to socialist thought. They were moved by the poverty of the working class, and the manifest injustice of a system that depended on keeping them in poverty.

The single most significant contributor to socialism as an applied historical phenomenon is of course Karl Marx, who saw it as the transitional phase between capitalism and communism. During the socialist phase, so his theories have it, there would be central control of the means of production under the 'dictatorship of the proletariat', which would eventuate in a classless egalitarian dispensation in which the state itself would already have withered away – this being communism, in which each would give according to his ability, and get according to his need.

The first international working-class association, the IWA (known as the First International), was set up in 1864. It met in London, and Marx was one of its chief members. In succeeding decades socialist political parties were founded in Germany, Britain, the United States, and elsewhere. As a movement, though, socialism was riven with differences of opinion over whether efforts to introduce it should be revolutionary or gradualist, democratic or led in the first instance by a vanguard of activists. Through the Second International (founded 1889; Engels became its president in 1893) and the revolutions of 1917 onwards, that with varying success swept through Russia, Germany and, after the Second World War, China, there was a growing split between the revolutionists and the gradualists, with concomitant divergence in views about both theory and practice. The Russian and Chinese revolutions brought to fruition the revolutionary ideal, while in many European countries including Britain forms of democratic socialism succeeded at the polls, in the British case with transforming effect in the election of a Labour government in 1945.

But the economic models of the various socialist experiments have almost wholly proved a failure. The associated drive for social justice, inclusion, the widening of opportunity and the dismantling of the class society, has been more successful even if not completely so, showing that some of the ideals of socialism have in transmuted ways entered the consciousness of some of the more advanced European polities. Socialism's economic failure might be put down to many things, including the systematic opposition of those who have more to gain from a capitalist dispensation. Still, the jury remains out on what the right balance is between collective provision and the opportunities – and vagaries – of the market; which latter has shown itself to be a poisonous friend when insufficiently regulated, as shown by the meltdown of the financial markets in 2008, with parlous knock-on effects to the 'real economies' of affected countries.

Perhaps the fullest example of socialism in practice as a politically enforced model is Stalinism, the version of Soviet socialism practised under the dictatorship of Joseph Stalin (1879–1953). It is characterized by obligatory collectivization, the brutal suppression and wholesale murder of kulaks (the small farmers who resisted agricultural collectivization), savage measures of repression against dissent within and outside the Communist Party, sometimes accompanied by 'show trials' as a threatening example to the populace at large, massive industrialization, the pervasive use of secret police, intimidation, forced labour camps in the 'gulags' of Siberia, and strict policing of countries under Soviet influence in its 'bloc'.

After the death of Vladimir Ilyich Lenin in 1924 there was a struggle for the leadership of the Communist Party in which Stalin (born Joseph Vissarionovich Djugashvili) and Leon Trotsky (1879–1949, born Lev Davidovich Bronstein) were the chief contenders. Trotsky argued for 'permanent revolution' which had also to be universal; Stalin, more realistically, urged 'socialism in one country', and his view prevailed. This notion was one of Stalin's two principal additions to Communist theory; the other was 'aggravation of the class struggle', which in (terrible) effect meant violent suppression of political opposition and elimination of groups or classes who stood in the way of the 'development of socialism' – hence the fate of the kulaks.

Stalin was also responsible for the 'Great Turn', the radical restructuring of economic policy in the late 1920s. It reversed the near-capitalist policy that Lenin had perforce to adopt to keep the Soviet Union from bankruptcy after the war years before and following the revolution. As a result of the series of centrally managed Five Year Plans initiated by Stalin, the Soviet Union saw a massive increase in industrial productivity.

Stalin had Trotsky murdered in his Mexican exile in 1940. His own fate was to die naturally in 1953, but to undergo the famous revisionist attack on his leadership and personality cult by Nikita Khrushchev at the Twentieth Party Congress in 1956, and the dismantling of Stalinism in all the countries of the communist bloc save North Korea and Mao Zedong's China; and to have his name associated with bloodthirsty totalitarianism, so that along with the names of Hitler and Nazism, Stalin and Stalinism are names of horror.

See: CAPITALISM, COMMUNISM, MARXISM, POLITICS

SOCIOBIOLOGY

Sociobiology concerns the place of human nature in nature. It is a new and important field of enquiry prompted by evolutionary theory and palaeoanthropology among other disciplines, and it generates a considerable amount of controversy.

The discoveries and theories of Charles Darwin placed man firmly in nature, which was a shock for his contemporaries, almost all of whom accepted the long-prevailing orthodoxy that humanity is a divine insert among the flora and fauna of the world, which were provided by the deity for humanity's use and pleasure. Darwin himself had an uncannily simian look about him, like a patriarchal colobus monkey, a gift for cartoonists and a prompt for unpleasant reflections on the part of those who were deeply offended by the very idea of a 'descent of man'.

But whereas the physiological similarity between apes and humans was sufficient to make the former a symbol of the dark, degenerate and beastly side of the latter, the connection for a while was made almost entirely in the imaginative resource of such films as *King Kong, Planet of the Apes* and *Tarzan*, and stories in lurid magazines. Accumulating evidence from palaeoanthropology, whose serious beginnings lie in the nineteenth-century discovery of Neanderthal Man, fed the ape-man myth, and for a long time there was little connection between discoveries in palaeoanthropology and the earliest work in primate ethology, among them anecdotal efforts by the likes of Eugène Marais (*The Soul of the Ape*, 1919) and more systematically and carefully by biologists, chief among them Robert Yerkes of Yale University, whose main work was carried out in the years between the two world wars.

But with recognition of the close relationship between humans and other primates in so many startling respects – a recognition owing much to Jane Goodall's work with chimpanzees in Gombe, Tanzania; she was the first to witness chimpanzee tool-use, familial bonding, and tribal warfare – the idea was born that if the higher primate species have a common ancestor in the recent evolutionary past (a mere 5 million years in the case of chimpanzees and humans), and retain so many commonalities as revealed by ethology, the logical step is to accept that study of non-human primates can tell us much about our human selves. And as it has transpired, the locus of the commonalities between man and other apes lies as one would expect in shared genes, 98.4 per cent of them in the chimpanzee–human case.

Thus it was that in 1975 Edward O. Wilson could coin the word 'sociobiology' and describe it as a 'new synthesis' of biology, sociology, ethology, anthropology, population genetics and other pertinent disciplines. Sociobiology's persuasive premise is that social behaviour in animals has been selected under evolutionary pressures to enhance reproductive success. As applied to lemurs, dogs and the like, the idea is illuminating. As applied to human beings it is controversial, mainly because its critics see it as assuming genetic determinism, which overlooks the powerful influence of culture and intelligence in shaping the intricacies of human behaviour. One big question prompted by what Goodall observed in the way of tool-making, communal hunting, grooming behaviour and family ties among chimpanzees was: 'Which side of this debate do such observations favour?'

In particular, sociobiology's critics dislike the implication that if certain patterns of behaviour are genetically determined, we can do no other than accept them as givens. Consider male aggression, which might in certain circumstances enhance male reproductive success (by frequent rape, say). If this is hard-wired natural behaviour, does it mean that we can do nothing about it? Does sociobiology mean to suggest that because it is 'natural' it is good?

The natural reaction is to reassert the claim (though not for theological reasons this time) that humanity is special, and for the cited reason: the possession of intelligence and culture, which critics of sociobiology – among them Richard Lewontin and Stephen Jay Gould – have an easy time describing as a far greater influence on behaviour than can be explained by appeal to the biology of what makes for reproductive success alone. As this implies, the main sticking point for the critics is what they see as sociobiology's reductivist commitment to the idea that human behaviour is wholly a product of selfish genes.

It is readily obvious, in turn, why their critics should think that sociobiologists find such a reduction plausible. Mothers right across the mammalian world are jealously protective of their offspring, yet culture and intelligence have nothing to do with it: the behaviour is instinctive. Goodall's poignant descriptions of relations between chimpanzee mothers and their offspring, and her observations of separation anxiety and grief in response to death, accordingly hold a mirror to humankind's own deepest instinctual nature, and lend credence to the sociobiological view.

Some of sociobiology's defenders, in their turn, claim that one of their critics' motivations is a 'politically correct' distrust of anything that seems to imply a deterministic basis for differences between races and the sexes, in such respects as intelligence and other capacities. In opposing this implication, sociobiology's critics point out that 85 per cent of all genetic variation among humans exists within populations, that historical and cultural factors are largely responsible for community differences in 'intelligence' as measured by IQ tests, and likewise for in-equalities and hierarchies in human societies and for many alleged male and female differences.

In a review of the attack on sociobiology mounted by Lewontin and Steven Rose in their *Not In Our Genes* (1985), Richard Dawkins rejected the suggestion that sociobiology anywhere claims that human social arrangements are inevitable products of genes alone. Clearly, description of similar behaviours in chimpanzees and humans invites explanation at least in important part in terms of genetic factors, but – Dawkins insisted – the words 'in terms of' do not entail 'inevitably because of', especially in the human case where historical and cultural factors also play a very large part.

And it has to be remembered that historical and cultural factors are themselves evolutionary adaptations. In place of fur and claws, scaly skin, big teeth or wings, humans evolved self-reflexive consciousness and a high level of intelligence, which allows them to devise many different strategies for interacting successfully with the environments they encounter and can colonize. Even if the fundamental drive is a genetic imperative to reproduce so as to maximize the number of copies of one's genes in succeeding generations, and even if in all creatures other than humans the result is a relatively inflexible repertoire of strategies – chimpanzees do not write symphonies and use cosmetics as part of theirs – it does not follow that sociobiological explanation can be relegated to a minor or nugatory role only. On the contrary, it seems to offer deep insights into aspects of the creative variety of human behaviour, and into human nature itself.

See: ANIMAL RIGHTS, ANTHROPOCENTRISM, BIODIVERSITY, BIOLOGY, EVOLUTION

STANDARD MODEL

Since the late 1960s the best and most widely accepted scientific theory of the fundamental structure of matter and radiation has been the 'Standard Model' describing the elementary particles and the forces that bind them together into atoms. It has many contributors, but one can attribute its main formulation as a model to physicists Steven Weinberg, Abdus Salam and Sheldon Glashow in the 1960s, after the first of these had proposed a way of unifying the electromagnetic and weak force to constitute the electroweak force, and further combining this unification with a theory (most closely associated with the work of Peter Higgs, hypothesizer of the 'Higgs boson') explaining how the elementary particles acquire mass. For this seminal work Weinberg, Salam and Glashow jointly received the Nobel Prize for physics in 1979.

The importance of the Standard Model is that it advances the aim of attaining the simplest and most economical description possible of the basic constitution of matter. A powerful way of thinking of the structure of material reality is to see it as built out of elementary particles interacting and combining according to laws expressible in mathematical terms. Particles of matter interact by the mediation of force-bearing particles. Matter particles are called fermions and consist of two groups: the quarks, that is, the constituents of protons and neutrons forming the nucleus of the atom, and the leptons, which include the electrons and neutrinos.

These matter particles interact by passing force particles – the bosons – between them. The bosons are photons, gluons, and W and Z particles. Thus the electromagnetic force, mediated by photons, binds electrically charged particles together; the massive W and Z bosons mediate the weak force; and the massless gluons constitute the strong nuclear force that binds quarks together.

Among the charged leptons in the model, only electrons are stable, that is, retain the same charge; the others (the muon and tau leptons) decay extremely quickly, in fractions of a second.

A key element in the whole structure of matter thus hypothesized is the need for a particle that imparts mass to the matter particles. All the other elementary particles of the Standard Model have been experimentally observed, but this important and needed particle, named the 'Higgs boson' after one of the physicists who described what, if it exists, it must be like, has not at time of writing been observed because of the huge amount of energy required to produce one in laboratory conditions. The very high energy Large Hadron Collider at CERN in Switzerland is among other things concerned with settling the Higgs boson question.

The all-important role for the Higgs boson in the Standard Model is that it answers the question of where leptons and quarks get their masses, and how the difference arises between photons, which have no mass, and the massive W and Z bosons. Discovery of the Higgs boson gives the Standard Model further powerful confirmation to add to the half-century of successful experimental support it has received.

The Standard Model is still not complete, however, and that will remain true even with observation of the Higgs boson. Among the reasons are that the model does not offer a way of combining the electroweak and strong forces with the other fundamental force of nature, namely gravity; and the numerical parameters of the theory, of which there are about twenty, are not derived from physical principles but have to be ascertained experimentally. The effort to combine gravity with the atomic forces (in other words, to find a quantum theory of gravity) has been given a boost by 'string theory', which remains controversial.

The hope that the atomic forces operative at the microscopic level of nature can be unified with gravity which operates at the large – indeed universal – scale of nature, thus giving a Grand Unified Theory (inelegantly known, therefore, as GUT), turns on the assumption that nature is at its profoundest level simple, entailing that the four (or now, with the mathematical combination of the weak and electromagnetic forces into the 'electroweak force', three) forces of nature are in fact just versions of a single underlying force which we cannot yet grasp. This assumption is repeated for everything: there must ultimately be just one kind of stuff out of which the apparent variety of matter arises, and on which the one ultimate force operates in its apparently different ways.

This assumption harks back to the earliest Greek philosophers, the 'Pre-Socratic' thinkers who hypothesized a single underlying reality out of which the apparent diversity of nature comes. For example the Milesian thinker Thales, flourishing in the mid-sixth century BCE, took the view that the one underlying stuff is water, on the grounds that water is ubiquitous, necessary for life, and capable of taking all three forms of solid, liquid and gas (it freezes into ice, flows at normal temperatures, boils away into the air as steam). His pupil Anaximander called the underlying reality *apeiron*, denoting an undifferentiated, infinite, primordial stuff from which the variety of things can endlessly arise and be renewed. He was alone among the Pre-Socratic thinkers in nominating an unknown underlying substrate; for Anaximenes it was air and for Heraclitus it was fire. Later, for Democritus and Leucippus, it was atoms – by which is meant 'indivisibles'; they observed that if you crumble soil in your hand, it must eventually reduce to the smallest possible particle which cannot be further crumbled; this is *atomon* ('cannot be further divided'). Atoms fall in the void, combining and separating and by this means giving rise to the variety of nature.

We now know that atoms are not, alas, indivisible, but can be divided with a catastrophic explosion. But the idea that nature consists ultimately of atoms proved incorrect; atoms have structure – they can be described, as shown above, in terms of quarks, leptons and bosons – and given that the model has so many aspects and components, the natural supposition is that there are deeper levels of structure with fewer aspects and components – until eventually we arrive at the new *atomon*. Hence the belief, the desire, the hope, the goal, of a Single Stuff and a Single Force – and then perhaps just a Single.

Suppose you ask why there might not be seventeen and a half forces and eight and three-quarter stuffs, or any other arbitrary number – why the fetish for one of each, and even for just one that is both? Why the drive for ultimate simplicity? Part of the thought must be that complexity is unstable. If there were seventeen and a half forces and eight and three-quarter stuffs, they might keep on turning into each other and imploding or aggregating or swirling about. (Which, funnily enough, is what the world seems to do all the time.)

Another part of the thought is that by looking for the simplest ultimate explanation, even if you do not find that there is a simplest unified level, you will have expunged the ad hoc and the conceptually adventitious from your theories, and got closer to the truth thereby. This is a good point. It is allied to another, which owes itself to William of Ockham and is called 'Ockham's Razor', that the simplest theory is the most likely to be true (all other things being equal). This, however, is after all not such a good point; it certainly does not apply in the study of history, or of morality, or in politics. And these remarks ought to generate a bit of unease, because in suggesting that the truth might be complicated rather than simple, they hint that in the journey to oneness, the reason for the 'appearance' of complexity might be overlooked.

But that amateur thought cannot undermine either the beauty or the power of the Standard Model, which has proved so successful and resilient, so richly confirmed by experiment and application, and which looks as if it is at least a genuine staging-post on the way to the truth about the nature of material reality.

See: SCIENCE, SCIENTIFIC REVOLUTIONS, STRING THEORY

STRING THEORY

Physics, the enquiry into the fundamental structure of matter and the forces that act upon it, is a spectacular achievement of the human mind. With each succeeding increment of understanding of the nature of physical reality have come applications through technology, transforming the world and human life in it, sometimes unequivocally for ill as with the development of weapons of massive destructive power, but more often mainly for good, as with aeroplanes, computers, MRI scanners, laser surgery, and much besides.

The story of enquiry into the elementary structure of matter begins with Newton's discoveries about gravity and his invention of the calculus, which he used to describe motion. In the following two centuries scientists extended his discoveries into an understanding of electromagnetism, which they succeeded in describing fully in mathematical terms. At that point – the end of the nineteenth century – many physicists believed their work was done and their branch of science complete. But then the electron was discovered, and with it a whole new field of enquiry into the atom and the elementary particles composing it.

To begin with, the atom was pictured on a planetary model, with the nucleus, consisting of protons and neutrons, 'orbited' by electrons. Three forces were identified as holding atoms together: the strong and weak nuclear forces, and the electromagnetic force keeping electrons in their orbits. Finer understanding of the particles classified them into two kinds, known as quarks and leptons, the former being the constituents of the nuclear particles, and the latter consisting of electrons and neutrinos. Quarks have such properties as 'charm', 'colour' and 'upness' or 'downness', which determine the interactions between them.

A further classification divides all particles into fermions and bosons. The former are the constituents of matter, the latter are the particles that transmit forces between the matter particles. Whereas only one fermion can occupy one point at a time, many bosons can share the same point at the same time. This explains why matter is solid and why forces can be felt across and through solids.

The powerful theory that provides insights into the subatomic realm is quantum theory. A major puzzle is that the other powerful theory in physics, Einstein's General Theory of Relativity describing the nature of gravity, space and time, seems not to be consistent with quantum theory. One of the great challenges of physics, therefore, is to render these two major theories consistent, by finding a unifying theory that combines an understanding of the large-scale phenomenon of gravity with an understanding of the forces that bind elementary particles into atoms at the microscopic level. This has proved exceedingly difficult to do, but one of the most promising ways of achieving it is string theory, a first version of which was proposed in the early 1980s.

String theory postulates the existence of minuscule vibrating string-like strands and loops from whose vibrations the phenomena of gravity and the elementary particles alike arise. String theory succeeds in this remarkable unification firstly by proposing that there are nine spatial dimensions, six of them curled up so minutely as to be undetectable, and secondly by bringing certain other assumptions to bear, among them that there is an unchanging background geometry, and that the cosmological constant – the degree of energy in the universe hypothesized by Einstein as counteracting the gravitational pull of the universe's mass – is zero.

The mathematics describing strings and their behaviour is beautiful, and the laws required to govern string behaviour are elegant and simple. These facts, together with the power of the theory to achieve the grail of unification (in supersymmetric versions the theory unifies all the matter and force particles, the fermions and bosons), are strong reasons to think it must be true.

A little more detail explains why. Relativity theory offers powerful insights into the universe, and other theories – about the Big Bang, the evolution of galaxies, stars and planets, black holes, gravitational lensing effects, planetary orbits, and much besides – depend upon it. Quantum theory plays no part in this; the universe on the large scale is regarded as a purely classical domain. By the same token, quantum theory works very well as a description of the microscopic realm, where gravity is ignored. If a way were found of connecting the two theories, almost certainly into a third theory that embraces both, it would require that there be a particle to carry the gravitational force, a 'graviton', with a particular property, namely, zero mass and two units of spin. This idea was common property in physics for quite some time, but only as a flier, on the grounds that the mathematics of adding gravitons into the quantum mix simply did not work. Particles can interact at zero distance, but the effort to make gravitons do so – as they would need to – simply gave rise to mathematical nonsense.

Then in the early 1980s a happy coincidence suggested a way forward. Strings were proposed initially in an effort to explain the relationship between spin and mass in hadrons, a particle family which includes protons and neutrons. The idea did not work well, and an alternative called 'quantum chromodynamics' proved more successful. But viewing particles as excitations of strings allowed for a particle with zero mass and two units of spin, and further allowed that interactions between particles could be spread out in a way that unscrambled the mathematics of interactions between such a particle and others. This was a hallelujah discovery, and the accompanying hallelujah thought was that string theory might constitute the long-sought and vastly desired theory of quantum gravity at last.

Some theorists, however, express deep concerns about string theory, chief among them being that there is no complete formulation of it, that no one has proposed its basic principles, or specified what its main equations should be. Worst of all for a scientific theory, given that science lives and dies on this crucial point, string theory makes no directly testable predictions because the number of possible interpretations of it is so large. Indeed string theorists talk of a 'landscape' of many billions of possible string theories. To the great dismay of its critics this last fact has led some of string theory's senior proponents to claim that experimental verification of theory is not necessary – the sheer beauty of the mathematics in which the theory is expressed, they say, is convincing enough by itself.

Other defenders of string theory also appeal to the anthropic principle – the brute fact that the fundamental constants of physics and chemistry are fine-tuned in just such a way as to produce and sustain the life that exists on our planet – as a way out of the difficulty that otherwise no single version of the theory's many possible versions presents itself as uniquely right.

Because of the importance of fundamental physics and the apparent power of string theory within it, it matters that the question of testability should lie at the centre of debate about it. This is what gives critics like Lee Smolin (who is chief among the critics, having worked in string theory himself) their greatest concern, because it reaches beyond questions about the theory itself to the very basis of scientific culture. And this is so even if one accepts that there is no single correct methodology that applies across all branches of science, for the one thing that binds them together as sciences is answerability to test and conformity to nature. Together these are the sine qua non that anything properly describable as science must observe.

If there is something that might count as a test of string theory, it is the possibility that empirical work might show that the speed of light has varied during the universe's history. Anything that shows that general relativity might need adjustment would call string theory into question, for the theory assumes that general relativity is correct.

Another possibility is that very high energy particle colliders, such as the one at CERN in Switzerland, might discover the 'supersymmetric' partners of currently known particles, which would provide some experimental support for the family of string theories that hypothesize that every boson has a fermion partner (this pairing is known as 'supersymmetry'). The yet undetected supersymmetric partners of known particles are so massive that they cannot be detected by current experimental means; very high energy colliders might produce them.

So string theory might be indirectly testable after all, in that it could be undermined or supported by these means, even though by itself the theory says little that is subject to direct experimental assessment.

But to Lee Smolin and other sceptics about string theory it also matters that physics should welcome and encourage a variety of other approaches to the five fundamental problems facing physics, only one of which – the unification problem – is addressed by string theory. The other problems are, first, the need to make sense of quantum mechanics itself, which is full of unresolved puzzles and anomalies; the quantum world is a strange place, and its oddity is a hint that something more fundamental waits to be discovered. The second is the need to determine whether all the particles and forces of the Standard Model of subatomic physics can be understood in terms of a more inclusive theory that describes them as manifestations of a deeper reality. The third is to explain why the values of the free constants of nature – the numbers describing (for example) the masses of quarks and the strengths of the forces binding the atom – are as they are. And the fourth is to come up with an account of two profoundly puzzling phenomena that recent astronomical observations seem to reveal: the existence of dark matter, and the existence of dark energy.

The approaches that might help with some or all five of these major challenges include loop quantum gravity, 'doubly special relativity', and modified Newtonian dynamics. Unlike string theory they all make directly testable predictions, and if wrong can be shown to be so, itself always a positive advance in science.

Because the testability matter is the key question for critics of string theory, some of them contrast it unfavourably with these other possible approaches, and characterize string theory itself as metaphysics (in the pejorative sense of this term) rather than physics. The jury, as this shows, is out.

See: ANTHROPIC PRINCIPLE, FALSIFICATION, QUANTUM MECHANICS, RELATIVITY, SCIENCE, STANDARD MODEL

TECHNOLOGY

Strictly speaking, the word 'technology' should denote the *study* of practical or applied arts in all spheres of human activity, from industry to domestic labour; such is the meaning of the suffixed '-logy' from Greek *logos* (theory or discourse). But its primary meaning now is the equipment – such devices as machines and computers – by which science and inventive common sense are practically applied to the purposes and activities of mankind.

The word was coined in the early nineteenth century to fill a need of the then nascent industrial age, namely, a need to distinguish the new applied activities of manufacturing and engineering from just anything (including, e.g. painting and sculpture) done by hand rather than brain alone. But of course technology as such had existed for as long as mankind itself; the flint axe is a technology just as much as is a laptop computer.

It is easy to think that the increasingly rapid growth in technological expertise over the last two centuries, from steam power to nuclear power, from the train to the space rocket, from the muzzle-loading musket to the smart missile, from hot-metal printing presses to the Internet, marks a transformation of kind rather than mere degree in mankind's activities. That is to some extent true, because the technologies that have been most spectacular in every respect of their range, power and utility have been the result of equally marvellous growth in scientific understanding. Technology is the applied end of science; it is science put to work – not infrequently for ill, alas; but mainly for good.

But it has to be remembered that mankind's intelligence has always been at work meeting practical problems with inventiveness, even if for most of the last million years the technological progress made by mankind and its ancestors is as nothing to the last few thousand years, and these again are as nothing to the last few centuries, which again pale in comparison to the last century alone – to say nothing of the last few decades. The rate of innovatory change, and the increase in power, range and applicability of technologies, seem to be exponential. It is scarcely possible to imagine what we might see in the way of technology in the coming decades, though we do well to remember how many past prognostications and guesses have proved completely and sometimes magnificently wrong. No less a person than Wilbur Wright said to his brother Orville in 1901, after another failed attempt to get a heavier-than-air aircraft off the ground, 'Man will not fly for 50 years.'

Advances in technology can create new problems, which further advances are required to solve or diminish. In our own time climate change influenced by mankind's industrialization and the burning of fossil fuels is a stark case in point. As technologies make things possible which themselves rapidly mutate into necessities – travel by aircraft and motor vehicles, and the heating and lighting of buildings, are salient examples in the climate change case – so their costs undermine their benefits, and either new technological solutions have to be found or the seemingly impossible task of persuading the world back to early and less harmful technologies has to be undertaken.

The word 'technology', as noted, is not restricted in application only to devices such as machines, computers, trains, lasers and magnetic resonance imaging (MRI) scanners; it also applies to the techniques that such devices serve. But there is a close relationship between technology in general and engineering in particular, since the latter is the chief means by which instrumental control over some aspect of nature, or instrumental capability of some kind, is achieved.

The earliest known bits of technology, attributed to the ancestors of modern humans (modern humans emerged relatively recently, around 200,000 years ago), are stone tools found in Ethiopia and dating to 2.5 million years ago. The Acheulian era 1.5 million years ago saw the appearance of specialization in stone tools, with clear distinctions between the crafting of hammers, scrapers and choppers. Use of fire might have begun about the same time, but certainly *Homo erectus* was a regular fire-user by 1 million years ago. Then and during the following several hundred thousand years the ability to make clothing for warmth and to construct shelters – an important matter, for it freed our ancestors from relying on caves or other naturally occurring places of safety away from predators and the elements – meant that they could undertake or more effectively continue the travels that saw their descendants, *Homo sapiens*, colonize the entire world.

No doubt there was much skill and ingenuity in these early technologies, and the comparison between a beautifully crafted cutting flint and the stripped twigs used by one of today's chimpanzees for termite fishing is a speaking one. But it was when agriculture began that the graph of technological innovation really started its steep rise. This happened about 10,000 years ago, and not only involved agricultural technology itself – the domestication of cereal grasses – but was soon followed by settled urban life. Ancient city sites like Uruk (3500 BCE) and Mohenjo Daro (founded circa 2600 BCE) astonish by their sophistication, the latter with many appurtenances of advanced urbanism: permanent buildings, paved streets, sewers, public baths, and much else readily recognizable today. Equally impressive are the early irrigation systems, water reservoirs, dams and dykes, and likewise the technologies for mining, smelting and forging metals, and throwing and firing sophisticated pottery. In addition to fire humankind was also harnessing wind and water power as sources of energy, and by about 4000 BCE had invented the wheel, a revolutionary development because it not only facilitated transport and military capability, but provided a superb means of transferring energy from water and wind sources to needed points of application.

The screw, pulley, lever, the animal-drawn cart, writing, parchment and paper making, gunpowder, the use of the arch in building, brass and steel – and so impressively and copiously on for the long and varied list of human technological achievements, all the way to the computer and the spaceship – each played a vital part, as technology always did and does, in shaping societies and the nature of power and wealth structures within them.

Reflection on this fact prompts a variety of views. Some have what others think an overweeningly optimistic reliance on the capacity of technology to make the world a better place, and humans likewise, and correlatively to solve all problems, including those that it itself creates. Technology's true believers are sometimes called 'Technists', and their confidence in it 'Technism'.

On the opposite wing are those pessimists about technology – Luddites and others – who see technology as a threat, variously to jobs, freedom, the environment, intelligence, even human nature itself. Blake lamented the 'dark Satanic mills' of the Industrial Revolution, despoiling the countryside; the historical Luddites of the Industrial Revolution smashed the factory machines that deprived them of their piecework cottage industries; Herbert Marcuse and Martin Heidegger saw technology as a new kind of slave-master; Huxley and others created dystopian visions of technology's threat to human nature and relationships.

Both the optimistic and pessimistic views capture something right and respectively promising and threatening about technology. So it is plain common sense to see an intermediate position, surely possible, in which the disadvantages of technology are guarded against and profit taken from its advantages. The chief risks to this are the usual ones: the impulses to profit and power which see advantages in technology where others see disadvantages. The quarrel is an old and familiar one, between greed and the good.

See: CIVILIZATION, GLOBALIZATION, INTERNET, SCIENCE

TERRORISM

Terrorism is the deliberate use of violence to gain political ends, typically by mounting attacks on unsuspecting civilians or non-military institutions, or both, to coerce the outcome desired by their perpetrators. Bombings and shootings are standard among the means employed; the release of dangerous chemical or biological agents is among other means. In contrast to more or less conventional practices of war, the targets and methods of terrorists are unconventional, most often unannounced, directed usually at civilian populations, and as the label 'terrorism' implies, intended to create panic and anxiety among those attacked.

The term 'terrorist' is a pejorative, and accordingly those who carry out terrorist attacks invariably describe themselves in more positive terms as 'freedom fighters' or 'holy warriors' and the like. So for example Kurds in Turkey see themselves as struggling for an independent homeland, as do the Uighurs of Xinjiang in China. Both groups are regarded by the governing majorities in their regions as 'terrorists'.

The technique of gaining ends by terrorizing a target group is an old one, as old as history itself. In more recent times it was used – to take just a few random examples – not only by disaffected minorities, individuals or groups of fanatics, but by major organizations and even states: by the Christian Church in coercing heretical groups (for example the Cathars), by the revolutionaries in France in the early 1790s to enforce compliance with their new order, by the Nazis during the Second World War who sought to suppress resistance in occupied territories by killing the populations of whole villages.

The phrase 'state-sponsored terrorism' denotes the encouragement and funding of terrorists by governments. Iran, Syria and Libya among others have been accused of this; critics of covert United States activities in South America and the Middle East make the same charge.

The forms of terrorism we are alas too familiar with now are standardly employed by dissident or fanatical groups targeting a state apparatus.

More recent terrorism has taken the form of suicide bombings and car bombings carried out by (for a major example) Islamists in the United

States, Europe and the Middle East. The hijacking and then deliberate crashing of passenger aircraft into the World Trade Center buildings in New York and the Pentagon in Washington on 11 September 2001 are egregious paradigms of acts of terrorism. Suicide attacks were pioneered by the Tamils in Sri Lanka; at time of writing the attrition of willing suicide volunteers among the supporters of Al Qaeda has reportedly led that organization's leaders to discourage suicide attacks in favour of more conventional methods. The aims remain the same: to terrorize and disrupt, to hurt the perceived enemy even if there is no real prospect of ever defeating him.

It is easy to mislead oneself into thinking that terrorism is especially a feature of the asymmetrical power relations of the contemporary world, in which it represents the only way that objectively weak groups can confront and contest great military powers such as the United States. Although the point about terrorism as a response to asymmetries of power is true, it is not a phenomenon confined to the present. The caricature of the cloaked anarchist carrying a round bomb with a burning fuse sticking out of it dates from the late nineteenth century, and is a reminder by itself of the even longer history that terrorism and its related endeavour of insurgency have.

Resistance fighters in Nazi-occupied Europe carried out acts of what the Nazi authorities doubtless viewed as terrorism; but the fact that it is wrong to so describe those acts gives us the steer towards an important distinction. Blowing up railway lines and fuel depots, attacking military posts and airfields, cutting telegraph lines, and other such activities designed to disrupt the occupying force's effectiveness, are the classic examples of resistance activities against an enemy occupation. Mounting surprise attacks on unsuspecting civilians with a view to mass murder does not merit the dignity of description as resistance or asymmetrical warfare: it is murder, and all the worse for being mass murder. Nothing justifies it. If the French Resistance during the Second World War had pursued its aims by planting bombs among civilians in schools or concert halls, hoping to kill indiscriminately and numerously, that would have been terrorism, and unacceptable. In targeting the occupying forces they fought cleanly.

See: ACTIVISM, FUNDAMENTALISM, WAR

TOLERANCE

Tolerance is the act or state of allowing or indulging beliefs and practices that might not be preferred or even approved by oneself or the group to which one belongs. Toleration is the practice of tolerance; historically the main use of the term relates to the tolerance of religious beliefs and practices different from those of the majority, or from those established in a given political domain.

In this historical sense, toleration is an exceedingly important notion, for in its absence those who differ from a given orthodoxy might find themselves subject to discrimination, harsh treatment, and even execution; all were commonplace forms of intolerance in the past. Typically the orthodoxy in question was religious, but divergent sexual practices and novel scientific commitments might equally well put espousers at risk in the absence of toleration.

Toleration is not as rare a phenomenon historically as one might think. Persia's Cyrus the Great (c. 558–529 BCE) is applauded in Jewish scriptures for allowing the Jews to return to Jerusalem after their Babylonian captivity, and by Xenophon for promoting religious toleration in his empire. The Romans were generous to local cults and regional superstitions everywhere in their great empire, as a matter of policy allowing each region, city and even home to have its own peculiar gods. In its imperial phase Rome continued this policy under the proviso that its own public deities would be everywhere respected. The point of this was to ensure civic cohesion. Failure in this regard branded non-observers as 'atheists'; this is why Christians were widely persecuted up to the time of Constantine.

The great Buddhist emperor Ashoka is renowned for abjuring war and allowing other religions to flourish in his domains. Chinese emperors alternated periods of severe repression with highly tolerant epochs, in which many schools of thought and varieties of religion flourished. On the best reading, the Koran has passages urging peace with other religions, especially Christianity and Judaism as fellow 'religions of the book', and one practical consequence of this was the *convivencia* which allowed the three religious communities to live together in amity in medieval Spain.

In the early modern period in Europe, toleration became a burning issue first because of the attempt by the Roman Catholic Church to enforce conformity of belief and practice, and then, after the Reformation, because the various resulting major denominations sought to contain internal schisms and differences. As one of the first high principles of debate about civil liberties in the modern world, much was said and written about toleration in the seventeenth century in Europe, with the Protestant provinces of the Netherlands leading the way both in theory and practice.

In the nineteenth and twentieth centuries persecution of Jews has been by far the worst example of intolerance, and there have been too many other genocides and crimes against humanity premised on variously motivated ethnic, religious and political intolerances, from Bosnia and Kosovo to Darfur in the Sudan.

Although intolerance between religions and ethnicities seems to afford the paradigm, some of the most savage intolerance exists between different sects or factions of religions and other movements. In the terrible wars of religion that wracked Europe in the century and a half after the start of the Reformation, the hatred between Catholic and Protestant was literally murderous. No love was lost between Christian and Muslim, and even as religious controversy raged in Europe so the forces of the Christian and Ottoman powers were engaged in struggle, culminating in the victory of the former over the latter at the Battle of Lepanto (1571 – in which Cervantes lost the use of his left hand, earning him the proudly worn sobriquet *el manco de Lepanto*, the cripple of Lepanto). But the cruelty of Catholic to Catholic and Protestant to Protestant outweighed the mutual cruelties, showing that intolerance reaches its most exquisite pitch in attitudes towards those who should be one's fellows. One has only to read of the fates of Urbain Grandier in the scandal of the 'devils of Loudon' in 1632, or of Johan van Oldenbarnevelt, summarily executed in 1619 following the absurd quarrel between different factions of Calvinists in the Netherlands, to see how intrareligious hatred could burn with a phosphorescent ferocity greater than the generic hatred of one religion's votaries for those of another religion.

We tend to pride ourselves on being tolerant, but this is usually when we do not really care one way or the other about what others are doing. When we mind, and object, and dislike, but recognize the other's right to do what he does or to think what he thinks anyway, then the hard work of tolerance begins: for hard it can most certainly be.

See: ENLIGHTENMENT, HUMAN RIGHTS

TOTALITARIANISM

Any regime based upon strict authoritarian control over all aspects of life and the economy, and which therefore subordinates individual liberty to the regime's interests, is totalitarian. The purest forms of modern totalitarianism existed in Stalin's Soviet Union and Mao's China, but the Fascist regime in Nazi Germany and the many petty dictatorships that rose in the wake of departing colonialism after 1945 are close relatives.

The main characteristic of totalitarian regimes is their suppression, typically harsh, of free speech, dissent, and opposition; disregard for the rule of law, with government and the administration of justice effected by arbitrary fiat in its stead; and immunity and unaccountability for those in power.

Totalitarianism has been the commonest and most widespread form of government in world history, on the general model of absolute monarchy or so-called theocracy. The word itself was coined very recently – in fact in 1932, by Giovanni Amendola in his criticism of Italian Fascism's ambition to monopolize power and to bind together all the communal energies of Italy, with Fascist ideology as the new national religion. Mussolini regarded the term in a positive light, but although Germany's National Socialists (Nazis) spoke of the 'total state' and 'total mobilization of society' in the same way, they disliked the comparison with Bolshevism in the Soviet Union (in the lunatic Nazi view of the world, Bolshevism was part of a global 'Jewish conspiracy'), so they spoke instead of the *Volksgemeinschaft* or 'national community'. The underlying meaning was, however, in effect the same.

In what might be called the duolithic confrontation of the Cold War the term 'totalitarianism' served as a counter in the propaganda war waged by the Western alliance against the Soviet bloc. It was Churchill's famous speech given in March 1946 at Fulton, Missouri, in which he spoke of an 'Iron Curtain' coming down across Europe, that gave the term its currency in this usage. Since the end of the Cold War in 1989, the year in which the regimes of the Soviet bloc in Eastern Europe collapsed, and the Soviet Union with it – the iconic moment being the literal fall of the Berlin Wall – the term has been given a renewed and somewhat expanded life, for a chief example in application to Islamist aspirations for a revived global Caliphate.

See: AUTOCRACY, COMMUNISM, DEMOCRACY, FASCISM

TRUTH

Although we think we intuitively know what truth and falsehood are, it is not a simple task to define them. Aristotle said that to speak truly is 'to say of what is that it is, or of what is not that it is not', whereas to speak falsely is 'to say of what is that it is not, or of what is not that it is', thus capturing the idea that truth is the conformity of thought or speech to how things actually are. Problems arise the moment we try to define what that relation of 'conformity' is – and what two or more things are being related by it.

A further problem arises when we recognize that even if we had a good definition of truth, it does not necessarily help us to recognize truth when we have it; for this we need a criterion of truth, or a test of truth; and evidently there has to be an explanatory connection between the definition and the criterion.

Another complication is that before an adequate truth theory can be stated, one needs to know what is to count as that to which truth and falsity can be ascribed. Is it sentences, or is it what sentences express, namely, propositions? Is it beliefs, considered as something entertained in thought not necessarily in the form of a silent sentence or proposition, or is it theories, that is, sentences (or better, propositions) or sets of them jointly claiming to describe a fact or facts of some kind? There are difficulties about each of these possibilities, which it is not an easy matter to settle. For the time being one can talk of 'propositions' as the truth-bearers, meaning something minimal by this, to denote the 'what is said' by sentences of similar meaning (that is, the common content of English 'it is raining', French *il pleut*, German *es regnet*, Mandarin Chinese *xia yu*, and so on).

In the history of philosophical debate about truth a number of theories have been mooted. The most ancient is the one sketched above as Aristotle's theory, and which is more commonly known as the Correspondence Theory of Truth. It states that truth is a relation of correspondence between propositions and facts. Despite the seeming obviousness of this, the difficulty arises about all three concepts in play, 'propositions', 'facts' and 'correspondence'. The idea might seem to be that the correspondence is a match between elements of a proposition and elements of a fact. But what are propositions and facts, exactly, and what are their elements? Consider a cat sitting on a mat and someone asserting 'the cat is on the mat', and notice – just for a start – that the cat and the mat are a different sort of thing from the relation of the cat's being on the mat; 'on-ness' is not a thing on a par with a cat, and therefore the part of the proposition which 'corresponds' to the relation of on-ness does not function in the same way as the nouns 'cat' and 'mat' respectively used on the occasion to denote the cat and the mat in question.

In some sense the Correspondence Theory, or a better articulated version of it, seems to have the best chance of capturing our intuitions about truth. But because of the difficulties which, on further analysis, flow from the those already hinted, other theories have been suggested. One is the Coherence Theory, which says that a proposition is true if it coheres with others in a given set, false if it is inconsistent with them. The model for this view of truth is provided by geometry and logic, where the relation of coherence between propositions is logical entailment. But in talking about the world of everyday things and events, this is far too demanding a relation – and conversely, a relation of mere consistency is far too weak. In addition there is the problem that any internally 'coherent' set of propositions, such as (say) those constituting the system of astrology, cannot thereby be thought of as true merely because of that fact; some annexation to something external that roots them to fact, as the Correspondence Theory requires, is greatly more plausible.

In response to the inconclusiveness of debates about these two theories, some philosophers opt for what is called the Pragmatic Theory of Truth, which says that a proposition is true if holding it to be so works in practice. Philosopher and psychologist William James, brother of the more famous Henry, described the Pragmatic Theory of Truth as stating that those propositions are true that have 'cash value in experience'. The theory was opposed by Bertrand Russell and others on the ground that it makes truth into whatever it is expedient to believe – whereas, they pointed out, not a few truths are very inconvenient.

Such are the three main traditional theories of truth. In more recent philosophical debate a number of more sophisticated attempts have been made to capture the elusive deep structure of truth, or to show that in fact there is no such thing. The latter manoeuvre results in what are called 'minimalist' theories of truth, which say that the predicate expression 'is true' does not denote any substantial property of whatever the truth-bearers are, but simply has a functional role in the way we talk, serving as a device for iteration, or marking agreement, or giving a grammatical predicate where one is needed to form a complete sentence. Others (most notably the late American philosopher Donald Davidson) have argued that truth is indeed a substantial property of truth-bearers, but is indefinable.

One thing that might make unnecessary difficulty for this important region of philosophical debate is the assumption – often enough it is the desire – to think that truth is a univocal concept, that is, that there is one thing that truth is, in all the different kinds of discourse we engage in. Think instead that what we mean by 'is true' in mathematics might be different from what we mean when we say 'is true' in talking about the world of everyday objects and events; and that this might be different again from what we mean in talking about moral matters, as for example when we say 'what he did was wrong'. How truth is determined in each of these cases is very different from the way it is determined in the other cases, and suggests that we do well to find more precise concepts for what we mean in each case when we talk of truth. Perhaps, indeed, the predicate expression 'is true' is a kind of dummy or place-holder expression, like 'thing', into the place of which we should strive to put a more accurate term for what we mean in that case. On this view, truth is a substantial property of truth-bearers, but it is a different substantial property for different domains of discourse, that is, for different kinds of subject matter. This is most clearly seen in comparing the mathematical and everyday cases, in which the procedures for determining truth are completely different. Therein lies a clue.

But in the everyday case we certainly require that what we say or think about things can only be true if there is a match between what we say or think and how things actually are. In that sense the basic intuition of the Correspondence Theory relates to something essential, and no amount of difficulty over the exact deconstructing of elements and the precise meaning of 'corresponds' can undermine it wholly.

It matters in all discussion of truth to give full weight to the fact that truth matters, as a value in itself and as the target at which all our enquiry and thinking aims. Truth is sometimes described as 'an ideal of enquiry', the end-state on which the various endeavours of knowledge-acquisition hope to converge – like a distant point on which we fix our eyes as we travel, even if we never get there. Another perspective on the importance of truth is gained by examining the relation between it and 'truthfulness', and how they figure both in ethics and in domains of enquiry where objective fact is the focus. There can appear to be a tension between our desire not to be deceived – for truthfulness, in other words – and our scepticism about whether truth as such exists. Evidently both truth and truthfulness are intellectual and practical values, and understanding them involves understanding also the associated notions of accuracy and sincerity, the first a necessity of the search for truth, the second necessary to communicating it. What reflection on this shows is that whether or not anything genuinely objective answers to the notion of truth, the concept of it occupies a central and crucially regulative place in all our thinking and doing, and is therefore indispensable.

See: ETHICS, PHILOSOPHY

UTOPIA

'Utopia' of course means 'nowhere', though for historical reasons it has acquired the sense of what should more correctly be called 'eutopia', meaning 'good place' (the 'eu' prefix operating as it does in 'euphoria', 'euthanasia', 'eugenics'). The opposite of eutopia is dystopia, meaning 'bad place'. A utopia might be either eutopic, as many utopias in literature and philosophy have been, or dystopic as are Huxley's *Brave New World* and Orwell's *1984*. Some utopias intended as eutopias, such as the perfectly harmonious state envisaged in Plato's *Republic*, or the healthily blond all-conquering outdoor Third Reich envisioned by Hitler, are dystopias.

The majority of utopias offered as eutopias by their inventors fall into two kinds. Both kinds serve as commentaries on the actual situation of mankind, for from them one recognizes the all too familiar dystopian features of the real world.

The main kind of eutopia is blessed by perennial good weather (warm springtime is a favourite) and an abundance of easily gathered tasty – and usually vegetarian – food. There is no money, and in consequence there is no greed and therefore no strife, nor are there any distinctions of social position. Reason governs. In many eutopias (especially if devised by men) sex is freely available. Criminality, if any such exists, is treated as an illness, and subjected to pleasant cures. People wear charming clothing made on looms at their cottage doors. If machinery exists it is not such as to despoil the natural environment, and its presence frees people to the gentle avocations of leisure and culture.

Another kind of eutopia, the minority sort, is more austere. This sort is not untypically the product of feminist imaginations. Sex, or at very least heterosexuality, has ceased to exist in them; eutopia is all-female, its population parthenogenetically renewed. If men stray by chance amongst them they naturally fall desperately in love with one or more of the denizens, only to suffer some mortifying and humiliating comeuppance and to be expelled, with anathemas cast on their dystopic masculine instincts, so incongruent with the eutopian order.

It expresses the tragedy of humankind, and yet comes as no surprise, that in dreaming of better worlds so many writers have focused on remedies for the things that make the real world so often so dystopian – poverty, inequality, labour, pain, disease, hardship, sexual privation, the absence of love. There is in this way much poignancy in eutopian visions, so eloquently identifying – by imagining their absence – the opposites of the ills plaguing the reality.

Imagining eutopias has a long history, starting with the Golden Age myths in Hesiod and Homer. Later writers evidently came to think that it is depressing to place eutopia unreachably in the past, so they gave their imaginations to the future or alternative presents. Plato offered a picture of a rationally ordered society, his Republic, where philosophers rule, only the best are allowed to breed, and the resulting children are raised in state nurseries. The Roman historian Tacitus encouraged his readers to revive the austere republican virtues of Rome's earlier history by praising the hardy Germans who 'never weakened themselves by intermarriage with foreigners'. Christian authors, Tertullian chief among them, looked forward with glee to seeing non-Christians burn agonizingly in the flames of hell on Judgement Day. More peaceably and constructively, Tao Qian in early China dreamed of a perpetual springtime of peace and plenty, free from war and work.

The opening of modern times in Europe – the seventeenth and eighteenth centuries – imagined eutopias premised on the possibilities offered by the newly emerging sciences, or alternatively suggested by exploration's encounter with 'noble savages' whose simplicity of life seemed to reprimand European civilized decadence.

More recent and contemporary utopias are almost invariably dystopias. This is an interesting and in its way surprising development. It suggests that we have found technology more of a burden and a threat than a liberation and a help, as was promised. Some of the horrors that earlier utopiasts sought to avoid in their paradises, such as overpopulation and concentration of power in the hands of the irresponsible and wicked, have come to shape an image of a deeply troubled contemporary world in which science has extended man's capacity for savagery almost beyond belief. Imagine plotting a graph to illustrate the change from Golden Age myths to today's anticipations of hells created by climate change, nuclear war, globalized epidemics, and worse, and the downward line would curve in the opposite direction to the upward curve showing technological development, forming an 'X' suggesting – as we remember from schooldays – Wrong Answer!

Very few of the eutopias mooted in the world's literature have been the subject of efforts to apply them in practice, and only two have actually been put into practice, of which one worked and one did not. The one that did not work was the so-called 'communism' of Marxism–Leninism and its offspring in Stalinism and Maoism. The one that did work was Ebenezer Howard's Garden City idea; and in the flower-bedecked, green-grassed quiet suburbs of some British cities, all their amenities within walking distance and good transport links to places beyond, it works reasonably well still.

See: ANARCHY, CIVILIZATION, COMMUNISM, FASCISM

VEGETARIANISM

Three arguments are standardly advanced in support of vegetarianism. The weakest, though still compelling, is an economic argument, which turns on the consideration that an acre of land can feed two people if used as grazing for livestock, but can feed twenty if ploughed for grain. This is the weakest argument for vegetarianism because the food problem in the world is not one of insufficiency but inequitable distribution; some have far too much, most have too little, of an otherwise adequate amount overall.

Less weak, and therefore more compelling, is the health argument, which turns on the consideration that meat contains saturated fats and lots of bacteria, and if it is non-organically produced then it also contains antibiotics, vaccines and growth hormones, which with the fats and (despite the antibiotics) the bacteria find their way into the human mouth as it fulfils its function as a graveyard for the corpses of slaughtered beasts.

Strongest of all the arguments is the moral argument against creating and then killing sentient beings in order to eat them, when to live well enough we do not need to.

Prudence dictates taking the health argument seriously. What butchers call 'fresh meat' is nothing of the sort, but is in fact carrion, because meat is only soft enough to cut, cook and eat when it has begun to decay. That we eat rotten meat is a fact amazingly disguised in the case of game, hung for extra lengths of time to get even more rotten than other meats. Rotting is effected by millions of bacteria swarming in the meat; their task is to pre-digest it for us by eating it first; the gamey smell of hung venison comes from the excrement of the microbes smeared all over it –

everything that eats must excrete, and the meat is both dining room and toilet for the microbes.

To see how the microbes do their work in meat, put a dead mouse in your garden and watch it decompose. The process is all the more dramatic when seen on a speeded-up film. As a rapidly multiplying mass of microbes swarms all about and within it, the tiny corpse appears to writhe and wriggle as if trying to escape. Once the first wave of invaders has done its utmost on the proteins in the cadaver, and they have become cheesy, the 'cheese skippers' (*Piophila casei*) move in to work the same magic they perform on old cheese (and yes, on dirty feet – which is why the French call their best gorgonzola *les pieds de Dieu*). In ten hours bacteria multiply from 100 to 100 million, and in these numbers they swarm on the meat in the butcher's shop and in your kitchen, and they devour it and excrete on it just as they devoured and excreted on the corpse of the mouse.

But all the foregoing amounts to a prudential argument only. Perhaps you like filling your mouth with rotting flesh full of injected hormones and vaccines, pullulating with microbes and covered in microbe diarrhoea. All these things, plus a carcinogenic finish of heat-damage caused by the cooking process, add up to a tasty morsel, after all; and who can deny it?

The moral argument, by sharp contrast, is an argument of principle. Anyone who visited a factory farm, a livestock transport train and an abattoir on the same day would find it hard not to reflect a little on the treatment we mete out to our meat before we meet it on the plate in innocent and unrecognizable form as steak, chop or roast. Indeed the brutal facts of meat production should fill the normally reflective person with vastly more nausea than the rotten tale told above.

It is interesting to wonder how many regular meat-eaters would cut the throat of a cow themselves – over a drain, if they are wise, to carry away the litres of outpouring blood – and disembowel it and clear out the yards and yards of faeces-loaded intestines, and hack off its limbs and saw away big hunks of its muscles. Yet the tens of thousands of daily slaughterings of animals are hidden from view, an industrial process without senti- ment, electric saws whining all day long and severed corpses swinging up on huge meat-hooks every minute, dead staring eyes and heads bristling with hairs falling from necks as the saws slice through with an added momentary howl. It is a vision of hell to the unaccustomed gaze, and an admonition to the conscience once grasped in its full meaning.

How odd it is that we prosecute anyone who is cruel to an animal, even to a pig or a cow, yet no connection is made between that fact and what comes hot to the dinner table, all blood, guts, cruelty, injustice and health risk hidden below a veneer of succulence and a little gravy.

See: ANIMAL RIGHTS, ANTHROPOCENTRISM

VERIFICATIONISM

As noted in the entry on positivism and logical positivism, a key idea in that theory, and indeed in empirical approaches in the theory of knowledge (which includes the philosophy of science) in general, is 'verificationism'. I think this an important idea which merits fuller exploration, despite fashion in philosophy having moved on and the – incorrect – assumption made that the notion has mainly historical interest only.

According to the verification theory associated with the logical positivists and popularized by A.J. Ayer, a proposition is verifiable if and only if there are empirical means by which its truth-value can be determined. The logical positivists selected verification as the key concept for a theory of meaning because they wished to have a means of distinguishing genuinely significant propositions from those that are not genuinely significant. Significant propositions fall into two classes: formal propositions, such as those of logic and pure mathematics, which they regarded as tautological; and factual propositions, which are required to be empirically verifiable.

The idea of verification can be expressed in one of two slightly different ways. It can be regarded as specifying the nature of meaning, or as serving as a criterion of meaningfulness. It does the first in Schlick's claim 'the meaning of a proposition is its method of verification', while it does the second in A.J. Ayer's assertion that 'A sentence is factually significant to a given person if and only if he knows how to verify the proposition which it purports to express.' Note that if Schlick's definition of meaningfulness is correct, then Ayer's 'Verification Principle' is true; but the verification principle can be correct without Schlick's verificationist definition of meaning being correct, for even if it is right that a statement acquires factual significance for a given individual if he knows what observations would settle its truth or falsity, it does not follow that the method of verifying the proposition constitutes its meaning. Thus, 'the canary is in the cage' is verifiable by the verification principle, but 'the canary is in the cage' does not *mean* 'go into the drawing room and lift the cloth covering the cage [etc.]'.

The verification principle involves a distinction between sentences and propositions. A sentence is said to be 'factually significant' only if the proposition it purports to express is verifiable. A sentence which does not express a verifiable proposition expresses no proposition at all; it is nonsensical in the literal acceptation of this term. Consider the following two sentences: 1 'God is in his heaven' and 2 'The bird is in his nest.' Since there are means of verifying whether the bird is in the nest (one can go and look), 2 expresses a proposition, and is therefore meaningful; but there is no way of verifying whether what 1 says is either true or false, so it expresses no proposition, and is therefore meaningless – or, more correctly 'factually insignificant', for the verificationists allowed that 1 might have emotive meaning as expressing a particular non-cognitive attitude to the world. (This applies to all moral, aesthetic, and religious utterances: they are 'factually insignificant' because nothing counts as a method of verification for determining their truth-value; but they have emotive meaning for their utterers.)

So far the verification principle has been given in a restricted form, as stating that a sentence is factually insignificant if for a given person there is no means of verifying what the sentence states. But the principle can be generalized: if what a sentence says cannot be verified by anyone then the sentence is without qualification factually insignificant. In this form the principle itself requires qualification: sentences which are factually insignificant are those for which there is no means of verification *in principle*. If one did not thus qualify the view, a particular sentence might count as meaningless in virtue of the merely contingent fact that no one had so far verified it, but would become meaningful once someone did so.

There seem to be obvious problems with this view. For one thing, the general laws of science are not, even in principle, verifiable, if 'verifying' means furnishing conclusive proof of their truth. They can be strongly supported by repeated experiment and accumulated evidence, but they cannot be verified completely. Another victim is history: in what way can the truth of assertions about the past be verified by present or future observations? Yet both science and history are bodies of factually significant sentences. Worse still is the consideration that not even an assertion about some currently observed physical object can be conclusively verified, because the number of observations relevant to its verification might be infinite; and while there remains the possibility of a single future observation refuting what one says about the object, that statement is not and cannot be counted as verified.

The verificationists' response is to suggest a liberalization of the principle, so that it admits of cases where all that is possible is evidence relevant to the truth of a statement. A sentence is on this view factually significant if empirical procedures are relevant to determining its truth-value.

A critic would say that this merely causes the problem to reappear in another quarter – specifically, to do with the nature of 'relevance'. What is 'relevant' evidence for or against an assertion about empirical matters of fact is to a large extent a matter of policy. What counts as relevant evidence might vary widely according to the conceptual strategy of observers, but only on a relativist view would the meaning of terms vary with the relevant verifying context. For example: suppose that in some remote country during a drought it is made to rain. According to the scientists involved, the immediate cause of rain was chemical seeding of clouds from an aeroplane. According to the local community, rain was brought on by a witchdoctor's rain-dance. Each school of thought has different views as to what counts as relevant evidence in verifying what each has asserted.

An answer to this is that if anyone seriously proposed that chemical seeding and witchdoctor-dancing are genuinely alternative hypotheses, or have equal explanatory potency, there is a definitive way of showing why this is not so – by showing which is the more reliably successful of the two while simultaneously conforming better with much else that we know and can do. And that would soothe any qualms about what counts as relevant evidence too.

This does not quite settle matters, alas, for the sceptic about verification. More sophisticated versions of verificationism turn on the idea that a sentence is verifiable if it entails statements about what can be observed. An objection to this is that the truth of a sentence about some physical state of affairs is consistent with the falsity of any observational report associated with it. Suppose someone says 'Jones is on the other side of the street', and I look but fail to see Jones – perhaps because he has just gone into a shop or has been obscured by a passing bus. My failing to see Jones – that is, the truth of the statement 'I do not see Jones on the other side of the street' – is consistent with the truth of 'Jones is on the other side of the street'. It would be absurd to take it that the failure of the observation cancels the latter statement's truth. If what a sentence says is true and the observation statement it is supposed to entail false, we would have a contradiction on our hands; but there is nothing contradictory in the example.

This criticism of the verificationist proposal is of course artificial.

The entailment of observation sentences carries a *ceteris paribus* clause – 'other things being equal' – meaning that 'Jones is across the street' entails 'you can see Jones there if you look providing your line of vision is not obstructed by a bus etc.' – so the failure of the statement under verification to entail the immediate success of every observation relevant to its verification is not a refutation of the verification principle.

Another objection that opponents of verificationism were quick to make is that the principle itself falls into neither of the categories of significant propositions which it is used to demarcate. It is not a tautology, nor is it empirically verifiable. What status, its critics asked, is it supposed to have? One suggestion is that it is a convention, in the sense that it offers a definition of meaningfulness which accords with the conditions that are in practice satisfied by empirically informative propositions. Add the idea that the a priori propositions of logic and mathematics have meaning by definition, and a prescriptive element saying that only statements of these two classes should be regarded as having truth-value, and then stipulate that only statements having truth-value can be regarded as literally meaningful – and there you have the verification principle.

The difficulty with this is twofold. The prescriptive element can be challenged as merely arbitrary legislation; and the descriptive element can be challenged as at most showing that the statements of metaphysics, ethics, aesthetics and theology do not fall into the classes of statements preferred by the logical positivists, from which it does not follow that they lack truth-value or fail to be meaningful. At most, the descriptive element affirms what is already recognized, that an account of the meaning and – if the notion is applicable – truth-value of statements, or extremely general statements about the nature of the world or human experience, requires a treatment different both from that which accounts for assertions about observable phenomena, and that which characterizes formal languages. This of itself gives no grounds for excluding metaphysics, or any of the other enquiries, in sole favour of what can be of use to natural science.

I think a better answer is to note that there are different ways in which statements can be empirically supported, including their utility and efficacy in experience in 'the long run'. On this view, the verification principle is empirically supported by its general success in differentiating empirically successful statements from others in the course of science and ordinary experience. One can suggest that a test of the principle is analogous to the test of a regulation or law: what is tested in the latter case is effectiveness relative to an aim, and the same surely applies to verification as a principle of demarcation for statements of science and common sense.

The objections to verificationism canvassed in the foregoing have been taken to undermine it to such an extent that in its original logical positivist form, at least, it is no longer widely held. In the modified form suggested by some of these remarks in response, I take it to have a continuing validity in the economy of our thought.

See: PHILOSOPHY, POSITIVISM AND LOGICAL POSITIVISM

VIRTUE ETHICS

The idea that ethics is about character, about the education of moral sensibility and virtues, the government of emotions, the fostering of good relationships, the achievement of valuable goals including happiness, and the development of moral wisdom, was central to ethical debate in antiquity, and was part of the revival of interest in the foundational questions of ethics in the eighteenth century, when the hegemony of religion over morality had been broken. In more recent philosophy the main contending ethical theories have been very different: they have been reduced to two principal outlooks, deontology and consequentialism in its chief form of utilitarianism. But increasingly in the second half of the twentieth century and since, the focus has returned to 'virtue ethics', describable in the terms that open this paragraph. In large part this is a result of dissatisfaction with the failure of deontology and consequentialism to answer the fundamental questions, 'What sort of person should I be? What sort of life is the best?' for they focus almost exclusively on the supposed intrinsic rightness of acts or their consequences, and if they allude to agents and patients in moral circumstances, they do so merely as factors in the calculation of the moral worth of acts themselves.

The philosophers of classical antiquity took character traits as the main target of attention, seeking to identify those that are good and accordingly merit the name of 'virtues'. The intimate connection between political and ethical considerations – the idea being that the good society is one in which individual good can best be achieved – led Plato in his *Republic* to consider which form of political organization, whether democracy, aristocracy, tyranny or oligarchy, best encourages the virtues. Both Plato and Aristotle, and particularly the latter in his *Nicomachean Ethics*, discussed the virtues of wisdom, temperance, courage and justice, and the types of human being – ranging from the great-souled individual to the moral monster – distinguished by the presence or absence of these and other virtues.

The presence of Aristotle in discussion of virtue ethics is nigh indispensable. In his view, a virtue (*arete*, sometimes translated as 'excellence') is a character trait or disposition which manifests itself in a variety of situations and actions, rather like a habit and indeed just as learnable as a habit. Accordingly a moral education has as its aim the inculcation of habits of virtue so that the individual becomes a virtuous person. This is the same thing in Aristotle's view as cultivating 'practical wisdom' (*phronesis*), which is the kind of wisdom required to determine the best course of action whenever a moral decision has to be made. Since reason is the highest endowment of humankind, life lived in accordance with reason is the best kind of life; the reasoning required in circumstances of moral choice is practical reason, and its employment will lead to its possessor experiencing *eudaimonia*, usually translated as 'happiness' but actually meaning something richer and deeper than that – in fact meaning a strong and satisfying sense of well-being and well-doing, of flourishing as only a rational and feeling human individual can flourish when his life and relationships are good.

As this sketch of Aristotle's view shows, a virtue ethics combines normative considerations about what is good and right with considerations in moral psychology about the experience of being the sort of person who does what is good and right, and who does this because of the kind of person he is – that is, because of his character, morally educated or self-educated to be virtuous (to be brave, kind, considerate, honest, enduring, truthful, realistic, consistent, loving, hard-working, friendly, noble, aspirational, resolute, self-contained, reasonable ...).

Renewed discussion of virtue ethics was prompted by Elizabeth Anscombe's paper 'Modern Moral Philosophy' (1958), and further promoted by Alasdair MacIntyre in an important book called *After Virtue* (1981). This was a valuable turn, because the technical debates about deontology and consequentialism in academic philosophy had all but severed the connection between ethical theory and life – although in characteristic fashion academic philosophy has sequestered debate about virtue ethics in the same way too, so that one would not think there had been an attempt from that direction to restore ethical discussion to the practicalities of life. An interesting fact about virtue ethics' two revivers is that both were Catholics, and both had religious motivations for challenging the terms of academic moral debate. This reprises the fact that when, after some centuries, the early Christian Church realized that the Second Coming had been delayed *sine die*, it had to import ethics from the Greek tradition to flesh out the thin and impractical code in the New Testament, whose ethical injunctions are liveable only by anchorites, monks and nuns (give away all you have, repudiate your family if they do not agree, be wholly passive, love everyone and especially your enemies, avoid sex if possible, do not value learning and wisdom but embrace ignorance, poverty and social marginalization – and so forth: what Nietzsche called 'slave morality', the turning into virtues of the downtrodden quality of life experienced by the Jews in bondage in Egypt). The Church imported a lot of its ethics from the richer and deeper traditions of Aristotelianism and Stoicism, and functionally what for many centuries was known as a 'Christian gentleman' was Aristotle's *megalopsychos* or magnanimous man.

One reason why virtue ethics fell out of favour with moral philosophers for a time was that it is (so critics claimed) unable to provide guidance on how one is to act in concrete situations. The idea that ethics is all about what sort of people we should be, with its focus therefore on agents and their character rather than their actions and what they cause, seems to detach ethics from actual situations where moral choices have to be made. Both deontology and consequentialism sought to specify a decision procedure for judging what the right action is in a given case, and moreover one that anyone (including someone who is not virtuous) could recognize as such and be able to apply. Proponents of virtue ethics respond by saying that it is precisely *phronesis* – the knowledge, insight, moral sensitivity and experience-informed capacity for sound judgement – that is required to recognize what rule applies (if rules are the point), or what should be done, in given cases. Moreover, the very concept of virtue is itself implicitly action-guiding: think what it means to list such traits as honesty, friendliness, helpfulness, courage, and the others, as virtues; they directly imply the types of behaviour required in situations which call them forth. The same is true of any list of vices – lack of sympathy, tactlessness, selfishness, cowardice, rashness, profligacy, disloyalty, laziness, uncooperativeness, rudeness, dishonesty, hypocrisy, ingratitude, vindictiveness, brutality, shamelessness, harshness, cruelty, and more – merely contemplating them indicates what not to do in concrete situations as well as what not to be generally.

This is not to say that virtue ethics escapes all the difficulties faced by reflection on morality. One still has to determine how to resolve conflicts between competing goods, and there is still the task of providing ultimate foundations for the virtues, that is, explaining why they are virtues (why are honesty, kindness, courage, fortitude, lovingness, resolution and the rest good? The answers are surely not hard to find). But virtue ethics has much to recommend it – not least because of the support it receives, and not all that indirectly, from our increasing neuroscientific and socio-biological awareness of humanity's essentially social nature, and all that this means for the flourishing of individuals and societies alike.

See: CONSEQUENTIALISM, DEONTOLOGY, ETHICS

WAR

It is not easy to define war, because the nature of violent conflict has changed dramatically in recent times, so that the clarity of meaning once attached to 'war' to denote armed conflict between organized entities such as states has blurred into ambiguity and – in such phrases as 'war on drugs' and 'war on terror' – outright propagandistic misuse. Terrorists and guerrillas attack states and one another, countries fight powerful and heavily armed criminal organizations such as drug cartels within their own borders, insurgencies pullulate like inflamed acne on the face of humanity. All this merits being described as strife, conflict, battle; it is no longer so easy to say which of them are wars as such. Perhaps all shooting and bombing to kill above what the police call 'murder' should qualify.

Carl von Clausewitz defined war as 'an act of force to compel our enemy to do our will'. This definition invites reflection on who the 'we' are in it; for von Clausewitz himself it was Prussia, and by implication therefore it was a state. This accords with official definitions of war as organized violence between identifiable political units or groupings. An important addition made in some definitions is that the organized violence in question has to be explicitly or at very least implicitly sanctioned by international law in order for it to count as war proper – for otherwise it is merely terrorism or large-scale gangsterism, as with the fighting induced by drug barons' armies in South America, or the inter-necine violence involving different religious or political factions within a society, short of outright civil war. To those who die in any of these conflicts these distinctions would no doubt seem academic.

'Civil war' legitimately contains the word 'war', because what is con-noted is at least two opposing sides with sufficiently clear identities and aims, fighting each other in pursuance of realizing those aims.

Violence is not the only feature of real war. The parties additionally use espionage, deceit, propaganda, and economic and psychological pressures of various kinds in order to gain advantage, and they make intensive diplomatic efforts to gain allies or to disengage the other side's allies. When all these features are present, but with armed forces in stand-off mode and not actually firing live ammunition at each other, the situation is well described as 'cold war'.

One of the ironic pleasantries of cold war is that it tends to kill only civilians, whereas in hot war soldiers also get killed. This is because economic embargoes and sanctions preventing food and medicines reaching a civilian population have their worst effect on those least likely to be involved in any branch of the military – namely, babies, pregnant women, and the elderly.

Hot shooting wars once mainly killed combatant young men, though in the wake of battles civilian populations often suffered pillage, rape, enslavement and other examples of war's charming consequences. But hot shooting wars in the later part of modern times have put civilians right on the front line, with aerial bombing and even atomic weapons brought into play against them as a means of attempting to coerce their surrender and disrupt the home front in order to make the fighting front untenable. The Second World War is the classic modern example of organized indiscriminate assault on civilian populations as a weapon of war.

That war is a fertile ground for the flourishing of gross injustice goes without saying. It seems odd therefore that there should be such a lot of debate over the concept of 'just war'. But the concept is an important one, given the way the world is; and merits examination.

The first thought is that although war is always an evil, it is sometimes the lesser of two evils; and when it is so, it can be justified. Immediately one says this, though, one has to remember that even though a war can be justified, this does not entail that everything done in the conduct of it is thereby also justified. For example, the Allies' war against Nazi Germany was certainly justified once all hopes of peace had been lost; but it does not follow that everything the Allies did in fighting the war was justified. For a salient example, the indiscriminate attacks on civilian populations by aerial bombing at very least invite moral audit. This rightly implies that there are ethical limits to behaviour in war, contradicting at least some of the implications of Churchill's remark that 'There is no middle course in wartime.'

The briefest reflection shows that there indeed have to be moral limits to behaviour in war. Debate about the question can be traced first to St Thomas Aquinas. In Part Two of his *Summa Theologica* he examines the proposition 'that it is always sinful to wage war', and argues to the contrary that war can be just if the following three conditions are satisfied: first, that there is a just cause of war, second, that it is begun on proper authority, and third, that it aims at 'the advancement of good, or the avoidance of evil', which he summarized as 'having the right intention'.

These conditions have been supplemented by two others in the work of more recent theoreticians, who argue that a war must also have a reasonable chance of success, and that the means used in its conduct must be proportional to the ends sought. The first supplement seems doubtful to some critics, who argue that it might be immoral to avoid engaging in what is otherwise a just war because one is not guaranteed victory.

The second supplementary condition is also a controversial one, for the indirectly connected reason that it seems simply obvious that once engaged in war it is wrong to fight with (as the phrase has it) one hand tied behind one's back. One of the wrongs one can commit in fighting a just war is to lose it by half-heartedness, bad planning, poor equipment, disorganization or incompetence.

But does this in turn justify using nuclear weapons or poison gas? This point raises the separate but profoundly important question of what counts as acting justly once one is engaged in fighting a just war. The difference is standardly captured by speaking of a *justum bellum* – just war – and the *jus in bello* – just action in the conduct of the war.

Aquinas's three conditions seem clear and persuasive. Matters get difficult with the nitty-gritty. What really counts as a just cause for starting a war? Can we always be certain that we are right in claiming to seek 'the advancement of good, or the avoidance of evil'?

One good example of a just cause for war is defence against aggression; another is going to the aid of victims of aggression. Does this mean it is also just to launch pre-emptive military action against a potential aggressor? When Aquinas spoke of promoting good or abating evil he thereby implied that wars for what the Nazi's called *Lebensraum,* or for oilfields or other economic resources, or merely for aggrandizement, are not justified. Those seeking to prevent a hostile power from invading them or causing them other forms of harm might invoke 'avoidance of evil' as their justification, and sometimes no doubt with justification. Equally open to question as a justification is the claimed positive aim of promoting good, which only holds water if it is genuinely about restoring peace, ensuring stability, helping the eventual growth of democracy and prosperity, and by all these means ensuring that the parties to the conflict cease to be enemies. Alas, many wars, even just ones, fail in these respects because the much harder task of 'winning the peace' defeats all parties.

Satisfaction of the Aquinas conditions can be regarded as minimally necessary for going to war, but they cannot by themselves count as sufficient for doing so. Other questions have to be answered first. Has every diplomatic effort been made? Is there consensus that the cause is just and intentions are right? Is military action really the only way to achieve the intended aims? In most international affairs diplomacy and such forms of pressure as sanctions are better first steps than the use of military force, which should surely only ever be a last resort. Any war that was not a last resort would have to have very compelling motivations to be just.

However just a war, the hard truth is that it diminishes the stock of human good, and injures civilization, all too typically destroying in mere seconds what it took centuries to build.

Wars caused by religious feeling and differences, even if the causal link is indirect, are never justifiable. Whatever the excuse given for such wars, they share the same root cause: divisions generated by differences in belief systems which, because they are not about matters of verifiable or even rationally plausible fact, are all the more passionately – hotheadedly, unreasoningly, violently – espoused.

It is hard to answer the question why wars happen, not least because they happen for so many reasons. In 1931, the centenary of Carl von Clausewitz's death, and therefore an occasion for meditation on his famous treatise *On War* in the light of the carnage of the First World War, Albert Einstein wrote to Sigmund Freud to ask, 'Why war?' Einstein had concluded that science cannot explain why humans, in a manner shared by very few other animals, kill their own kind in highly organized ways, dedicating vast resources to the task. Like Bertrand Russell he had come to think that world government was the only defence against future wars. At the invitation of the League of Nations, who asked him to choose someone to discuss the matter with, he wrote to Freud for his opinion. He hoped that Freud's new and then fashionable theory of psychoanalysis could offer both a diagnosis and a cure.

Freud's answer – dedicated, as it turned out aptly enough, to Mussolini – was pessimistic. He replied that violence and inequality are natural to man. History shows that the weak combine to oppose the strong, by their collective strength eventually fashioning a legal order. 'The eagerly desired reign of "everlasting" peace' might, Freud wrote, be achieved by this means, but only through the paradox of the collective's power to make war on warmongers. But the operative word is 'might'; Freud confessed that it was highly unlikely because aggression, inequality and strife are endemic features of the human condition.

This is not a very compelling answer, for it contains neither real diagnosis nor real cure. It assumes a natural human propensity to aggression and further assumes that collective aggression is the sum of individual aggressions. Neither assumption, and especially the latter, is convincing by itself. People might occasionally feel aggressive, and hormonal reasons might explain a spike in aggressiveness among some adolescent and young adult males. Other animals are aggressive, but in specific, self-limiting ways: males contest each other for mates, females protect their young, all compete for food when it is scarce. But fights invariably end when one combatant flees or submits. Apart from humans and chimpanzees, animals do not typically prey on their own kind (though a lion taking control of a pride might kill the cubs in order to bring its lionesses into heat so that he can mate with them). A troop of baboons will drive off invaders of its territory, but will not kill or enslave them. Social animals move to new territory in search of water and food resources, but they do not try to enlarge existing territory by conquest. Only humans do such things.

Explanations for war therefore have to be sought in other places, not just in psychology; and one suspects that they will mainly be found in the complicated nexus of economic, political and cultural aspects of human societies. One view has it that wars are problem-solving devices in periods when the international order is destabilized by economic and political difficulties. It can also be a problem-solving device for difficulties on the home front; when a state goes to war it has to redirect major resources in personnel, manufacturing, and other pillars of the economy, by this means overcoming or avoiding, even if only for a time, those difficulties.

Technology receives a major boost in wartime, and the rate of technological change speeds up dramatically. At the beginning of the Second World War the air forces of the world still had biplanes in service; by the end, jet fighters and missiles were in use. And this is not the only arena of accelerated development, for by posing huge logistical challenges, war can radically alter administrative practices and techniques.

Marxist theory offers a somewhat similar analysis, seeing war as itself a weapon in the competition between capitalist economies. It shares with other historical analyses the view that states do not stumble into war, but choose it, in the endless quest for greater influence and enlarged control over raw materials and other productive resources. On this view war is about wealth and power; it is a tool wielded by the political and commercial agencies in control of the state, and thus is what our leaders deliberately get us into. Happily for these leaders, demagoguery on simple-minded nationalistic and patriotic themes reliably rouses enough young men for death and destruction to follow.

The major wars of the twentieth century had the overall effect of shifting power and redistributing wealth in major ways. The chief beneficiary was the United States, giving it international dominance economically and militarily. The other major beneficiaries, paradoxically, were the defeated of the Second World War, who could restructure from scratch, and experienced economic miracles as a result: Germany and Japan. And these wars were as usual revolutionary in some of their consequences too: they gave birth to the Soviet Union after the First World War and Maoist China after the Second World War.

See: POLITICS, WAR CRIMES

WAR CRIMES

War crimes have existed as long as war has existed, but the moral and legal concept of a war crime was devised, along with that of 'crimes against humanity', by the drafters of the charter which instituted the War Crimes Tribunal that met at Nuremberg in 1945 to prosecute Nazi leaders, among them Hermann Göring, Albert Speer and Admiral Dönitz.

When the Allies decided to try Nazis before a court, they were faced with an immediate difficulty: there was no body of law to serve as a basis for doing so. The tribunal's charter was drafted to remedy this lack. Some jurisprudents were worried that the accused Nazis were being tried according to laws devised after their crimes were committed, which is a breach of a fundamental notion of legality. There was also the difficulty that all the prosecuting nations were in various ways and to various degrees themselves guilty of some of the same crimes.

The first of these problems was overcome by an act of international will on the Allies' part, and the second was overcome by ruling out the possibility of the defendants using a *tu quoque* ('you too') argument in defence. The sheer scale of the atrocities committed by the Nazis, and the need for an emphatic gesture by the international community condemning military aggression and the Holocaust, made Nuremberg necessary. One thing thereby shown is the difference between law and justice, for Nuremberg was a case of justice being done even in the absence of law. It received retrospective endorsement in the creation of the United Nations Universal Declaration of Human Rights and the two more detailed human rights Covenants that followed, to say nothing of the various national human rights conventions adopted by many countries, and the postwar debate on the laws of war.

The Nuremberg tribunal's charter defined a war crime as follows: 'Article 6(b) War Crimes: namely, violations of the laws or customs of war. Such violations shall include, but not be limited to, murder, ill-treatment or deportation to slave labour or for any other purpose of civilian populations of or in occupied territory, murder or ill-treatment of prisoners of war or persons on the seas, killing of hostages, plunder of public or private property, wanton destruction of cities, towns, or villages, or devastation not justified by military necessity.'

The crimes listed here were those committed by the Nazi regime in its conduct of war. It happens that some of them were also committed by the Allies, especially in their 'area bombing' campaigns over Germany and Japan, in which entire civilian populations were subjected to massive indiscriminate aerial bombardment. When the definition of 'war crime' was drafted by the charter writers, this application of the term was not in their minds; but a retrospective application of them is hard to resist.

One of the most optimistic developments in the world since 1945 is the growth in awareness of human rights, and invocation of them as a way of protecting vulnerable individuals and groups in countries with irresponsible regimes. The main problem with human rights instruments is the lack of effective means to enforce them. The same problem, and for the same reasons, infects the task of enforcing respect for the laws of war. Until recently there was not even an international court before which violations of human rights and war crimes could be tried, with the result that ad hoc tribunals had to be set up to deal with such matters, as with the Bosnian tribunal that tried Slobodan Milošević in The Hague. Such a body now happily exists, in an infant and as yet weak state: it is the International Criminal Court instituted by the UN Treaty of Rome in 1999. It should perhaps be regarded as a scandal that it took until the penultimate year of history's bloodiest, most violent, and most atrocity-ridden century for such a thing to begin to exist.

See: JUSTICE, LAW, WAR

WEALTH

Wealth is a more than sufficient quantity of resources, whether in the form of goods and property or credit. In some dispensations access to social goods and services such as education and health care is counted as part of wealth too. In their usual reductive way, economists define wealth as the balance of assets over liabilities at a given point in time.

It might come as a mild surprise to find that Aristotle's definition of wealth is: 'whatever money can buy'. It is commonplace now for wealth to be measured in terms of money, even though the value of money is itself measured in terms of what it has the power to purchase. But there is an implication of Aristotle's definition which is worth drawing out. If wealth is measured by quantity of money, then a man with a million in the bank and liabilities far less than a million is a wealthy man. But suppose he buys nothing with it, neither goods nor services, neither pleasures nor pastimes. He is in that respect in exactly the same situation as a man who has no money at all. He who will not spend is on a par with he who has not the wherewithal to spend: they are both poor.

By contrast, a man with a few thousand to spare over his liabilities, who spends them on the amenities and grace notes of life, is a richer man by far. As this suggests, the true measure of wealth is not what you have but what you spend.

In this respect, then, Aristotle is surely in the right, for his definition in effect says that to spend is to gain. But even this satisfactory thought requires a qualification, because if the spending is devoted to empty ostentation, to self-destructive habits, to what makes people stupid and harmful, then it is the worst of its kind: it is expense merely, and waste, and shame.

But Aristotle's definition omits the well-known and obvious fact that there are kinds of wealth, and many of them, that cannot be bought with money. Education can be bought, but not intelligence; clothes, but not style; cosmetics, but not beauty; sex, but not love. Money can of course buy help towards love and beauty. But it is the things themselves that are the real wealth. And it is the things most taken for granted before they are lost or compromised in which the profoundest wealth consists: eyesight, hearing, mobility, health in general, friends, the beloved.

Historically and culturally wealth has been understood in remarkably similar ways. One common thread is abundance in such economically significant factors as (variously) cows, land, accumulated income, or equities. Another is possession of inessentials such as works of art, large houses, numbers of wives, concubines or mistresses, surplus in general being a signifier of wealth, advertising its possession and conferring grandeur on its possessor.

More technical conceptions of wealth began to be formulated in the eighteenth century in the work of Adam Smith and his successors among economists, including Karl Marx. The more thoughtful among them were concerned by the fact that wealth tends to accumulate in fewer and fewer hands as the processes of its creation unfold, unless there is a redistributive mechanism in place or unless more equitable means of participating in the wealth creation process exist. Capitalism does not naturally lend itself to either, and requires regulation to limit excessive accumulation by the few. Nowhere in capitalist economies is such accumulation a rarity.

A danger in money wealth is that unless it is superabundant to the degree that no thought need ever be given to it, the appetite for it feeds upon itself, growing continually greater. It is a puzzle to some why a rich person goes on seeking to get richer, if it is not the satisfaction of the work, or its excitement and challenge, which are the real motivation. Surely there is a point when a given degree of wealth is sufficient. According to the wise, matters are the other way round: it is a sufficiency that is wealth: and that sufficiency might be very little. A contented poor man is among the richest of all men.

The key point about wealth is its relationship to power, and that means power of all kinds and not just political power – although the connection here goes without saying, especially in plutocracies like the United States of America where the endeavour to get into political office is a highly expensive business. The power to gain access to the goods of life, among them education, health, safety, prestige, convenience, social position, pleasure, and much else, is immensely facilitated by money. This does not mean that there are no routes to some of these things aside from a fat bank account, but the latter is certainly the easiest way. That is why it is so desirable.

See: BUSINESS ETHICS, CAPITALISM, CONSUMERISM, ECONOMICS

WESTERNIZATION

In the centuries since the beginning of modern times – that is, since the beginning of the seventeenth century CE – the wealth, power and therefore influence of Europe and its descendent nations in North America and elsewhere (for short, 'the West') have transformed the world, in varying degrees bringing to bear the effects of science, industrial development and capitalism, and in some places forms of government and law, that are distinctive of the Western achievement.

To some, this spread of influence has been tantamount to the spread of enlightenment and 'modernization'. To others, Western values and practices appear inimical to domestic values; the coercive accompaniment of Western religious beliefs and practices has been a negative feature, but even more so has been the apparent moral laxness of the Western lifestyle, with scantily clad women and sexually explicit art and cinema. To many, therefore, the Western influence has been felt either or both as an imposition, or as an undermining of traditional values. The first was one of the mainsprings of nationalistic rejection of Western colonialism, the second continues to be a source of animosity to the West especially among Muslims.

There is a very schizoid attitude to Westernization in many non-Western parts of the world. Consider China, which has made urgent efforts to ape the West in industrialization, in building high-rise cities on the American model, and in adopting wholesale the civil and military technology of the West. This would seem to be a case of the sincerest form of flattery. Yet at the same time China's rulers repudiate Western political and social models, and complain bitterly when accused by Western governments and non-governmental organizations of (for example) lack of democracy and widespread human rights violations. In this connection the Chinese complain about the West's efforts to impose alien Western values on China. The contradiction is stark.

It is all the starker when one considers that (for an associated example) the United Nations Universal Declaration of Human Rights, now regarded by China and by Third World countries as an unwarranted and provocative Western Enlightenment imposition, was drawn up by people from all over the world (including Lebanon and China), and was at first more gleefully welcomed by what were once called Third World countries than by the great Western powers, for the latter regarded the Universal Declaration as a stumbling block to activity in their colonies and spheres of influence.

It remains that while many aspects of Western influence in the non-Western world are welcomed, to the extent that the net flow of global migration is towards Western countries – regarded as desirable, exciting, full of opportunity, and offering vastly better lives than most non-Western countries – there is also legitimate cause for concern about the effect of Western power and its less savoury values in causing harm, environmental degradation, and resentment elsewhere in the world.

There was good reason for such resentment. The colonization of non-American high streets by McDonald's hamburger outlets and Coca-Cola advertisements was the outward and visible manifestation of even deeper inroads by American money and might, implying dependence on American say-so and know-how, and adoption of American models of capitalism and political structure as the cost of receiving aid, protection, military hardware, and associated benefits.

Among other visible manifestations of Westernization that prompted resentment were the consequences of activity by global Western companies seeking cheap labour and natural resources to exploit, sometimes with open-cast mining and other environmentally damaging activities. To some extent anyway, international companies have since begun to behave more responsibly and sensitively in all these connections – but only after a high cost in lost hearts and angered minds.

Western medicine, education, technology, communications and expertise constitute the positive side of the Westernization story. Clean water, treatments for remediable blindness and parasitic diseases, the combating of malaria, the donation of food and financial aid in times of crisis, and other ways in which the resources of the West yield help and fresh possibilities to parts of the world still developing towards their better potentialities, all constitute a success story for the ideal of progress. In the world as the history of the last few centuries has made it, and taking into account the violent setbacks that have been involved too, the spread of things Western to other points of the compass has done much good as well as harm – and almost certainly more good than harm.

See: CAPITALISM, CONSUMERISM, GLOBALIZATION

XENOPHOBIA

Medical dictionaries define xenophobia as a morbid or abnormal fear, distrust and dislike of strangers and foreigners, but in strict truth there is no connotation of the morbid or the abnormal about xenophobia; rather the contrary, it is all too common and ordinary an attitude. In strict etymology it means 'fear of strangers' (or 'outsiders'), derived from the Greek words *xenos* meaning 'stranger, foreigner, outsider' and *phobos* meaning 'fear' or 'aversion'.

Obviously enough xenophobia easily associates with racism, but it is not automatically the same thing. In living memory villagers in rural England would take a very long time indeed – quite literally, decades – to accept as one of their own someone who had moved into their neighbourhood from another village in the same county. Immigrants from the next village might typically be called 'foreigners'; in such circumstances what chance of assimilation did a Jamaican or Pakistani immigrant have?

If there is a country where xenophobia was ever officially lacking, though in recent times this has changed, it is the United States of America, which in the last decades of the nineteenth century and the early part of the twentieth century saw such a volume of mass immigration, needed for the geographical and economic expansion of the country, that one might be tempted to describe the official attitude as 'xenophilia'.

Some states have adopted exclusionist policies opposite to that of the United States in its great days of encouraged immigration. Japan, for a major example, was closed to foreigners for two hundred years from the mid-seventeenth century – that is, from the time that Japan began to experience increasing nibbles from Europe's worldwide expansion in trade and colonization. This policy of *sakoku* or 'national closure' not only kept non-Japanese out of the country, but involved a refusal to engage in relations with foreign governments. The problem of what many see as excessive immigration into the wealthy countries of Europe from Africa, South Asia and the Middle East makes some wish for policies that, if not quite as extreme as *sakoku*, nevertheless have something of the same effect.

What xenophobia and racism have in common is prejudice and suspicion generated by ignorance, dislike or anxiety about the difference, real or supposed, of the 'other'. Both therefore result in discrimination, and at the extreme in expulsions and pogroms, a common experience of Jewry throughout history. Xenophobia can be felt both towards immigrant populations near at hand, and towards the people of other countries. Governments play on the readiness of the latter kind of xenophobic tendency in time of war to encourage patriotism and unity of purpose.

Sociobiological theories hypothesize innate grounds for members of human groups to prefer their own, and for sentiments of kinship and acceptance to decrease as distance, in all respects of ethnicity, culture and geography, increases between the home group and others. Experiments have supported this view.

The fallacy that what is natural is therefore automatically good has led some to say that because ethnocentrism is an objective fact, it is acceptable. But ethnocentrism, even though it is not by itself the same thing as xenophobia, though of course it all too easily becomes xenophobia, is not acceptable in an integrated, globalized world. And given its propensity to manifest as xenophobia, the greatly more important point is that there is nothing acceptable about xenophobia, which, in expressing itself not merely as preference for one's own but as rejection of those who are not one's own, gives rise to anti-Semitism, racism, unfriendliness and even hostility to individuals who do not look, speak or dress in ways that, by a narrow definition, are acceptable or familiar. It is a sentiment of divisiveness which makes the ground of human affairs always fertile for conflict. And that is unequivocally a bad thing.

See: ANTI-SEMITISM, RACISM, SOCIOBIOLOGY

ZEITGEIST

It would be quite an achievement to choose three dozen people in today's world whose names will still resonate in two hundred years' time. That is what William Hazlitt succeeded in doing in a collection of essays about those of his contemporaries he thought significant. He gave the title *The Spirit of the Age* (1826) to the volume in which the essays appeared, suggesting that the similarities and differences among the people of genius he had written about expressed the essence of the time. The phrase was a translation of a term that Johann Gottfried von Herder had coined half a century before to translate the title of C.A. Adolph's *Genius Specula*, 'the guardian spirit of the century'. The term was *Zeitgeist*, and it quickly entered literary usage among the German Romantics, and had become a term of art in Hegel's philosophy.

In its early use, as Hazlitt's adaptation of the idea behind the term shows, 'Zeitgeist' connoted the dominating influence of a group of writers, thinkers and artists whose experience and attitudes gave their age its distinctive character. There was no suggestion that they collaborated in doing this, but it was taken as read that their shared experience resulted in something identifiable and characteristic that retrospect could recognize. And indeed in the usage of the German Romantics, Zeitgeist was a term chiefly of historical application.

The term now has less to do with the atmosphere created by what is common to the (retrospectively) understood sensibility of creative groups, than with what, much more loosely, is taken to be a prevailing current set of trends, fashions, attitudes and feelings in a society, especially in its culturally most influential domains – for example, among the smart sets in Paris, London and New York.

In neither the originating German Romantic sense nor in its contemporary looser sense is the term especially helpful. Think, for example, how one would attempt to characterize the Zeitgeist of the late Elizabethan and early Jacobean period in England, when Marlowe, Shakespeare, Ben Jonson, Beaumont and Fletcher and Donne were writing, which saw religious conflict and the rise of Puritanism, the discovery of new worlds through maritime exploration, and the beginnings of the scientific revolution. It is hard to think what to describe as the Zeitgeist of so various and multiple an epoch; and perhaps to try to do so would be to miss the essential contradictions that have to be grasped for an adequate understanding of it. If a term were needed, then, to denote a summarization of the trends and characteristics of a time, a better alternative might be the plural: *Zeitgeisten.*

Appendix

Entries in the body of the book are alphabetically arranged. Below are the main entry headings grouped according to relations of subject matter, with 'Politics and Society' being subdivided into 'Politics and Law' and 'Society and Social Questions' – this last a more heterogeneous category than the others – followed by 'Philosophy', 'Religion' and 'Science'. Because of the inevitable problem of 'lumping and splitting' – the question of whether to subsume certain ideas under certain others, or to give each a separate entry – the main headings disguise the fact that a larger number of ideas are discussed than the heading words by themselves suggest; so the index is the key resource and true guide to the contents of this book.

Attentive conning of the lists below will show that a number of headings figure in more than one category – the reasons are obvious enough, and the fact that there is some repetition and overlap in the entries anyway is useful in showing how ideas figure in different settings and conceptual relationships. But each entry is self-standing, and aims to be informative on its own.

The bibliography consists of short indicative lists for each of the entries, intended merely as prompts or starting points for further enquiry.

POLITICS AND
SOCIETY

Politics and Law

absolutism
activism
anarchism
aristocracy
black consciousness
Black Power
capitalism
class
communism
democracy
economics
equality
Fascism
feminism
freedom of speech
globalization
human rights
identity
justice
law
liberalism
liberty
Marxism
nationalism
neoconservatism
politics
privacy
punishment
socialism

A Short Indicative Bibliography

ABSOLUTISM

Filmer, R., *'Patriarcha' and Other Writings* (Cambridge University Press, 2008)

Hobbes, T., *Leviathan* (Longman, 2008)

Kelsey, H., *Absolutism and Relativism in Philosophy and Politics* (Irvington, 1993)

ACCOMMODATION THEORY

Giles, H., Coupland, N., and Coupland, J., 'Accommodation Theory: Communication, Context, and Consequence', in H. Giles, N. Coupland and J. Coupland (eds.), *Contexts of Accommodation: Developments in Applied Linguistics* (Cambridge University Press, 1991)

ACTIVISM

Carson, R., *Silent Spring* (Penguin Classics, 2000)

Shaw, R., *The Activists' Handbook* (University of California Press, 2001)

Tarrow, S., *The New Transnational Activism* (Cambridge University Press, 2005)

ADVERTISING

Conrad Levinson, J., and Rubin, C., *Guerrilla Advertising* (Houghton Mifflin, 1994)

Packard, V., *The Hidden Persuaders* (Ig Publishing, 2007)

Steel, J., *Truth, Lies and Advertising: The Art of Account Planning* (John Wiley & Sons, 1998)

AESTHETICS

Bourriaud, N., *Relational Aesthetics* (Les Presses du Réel, 1998)

Danto, A.C., *The Abuse of Beauty (Paul Carus Lectures)* (Open Court Publishing Co., 2003)

Dickie, G., *Introduction to Aesthetics: An Analytic Approach* (Oxford University Press, USA, 1997)

AFTERLIFE

The Bible: Authorized King James Version (Oxford Paperbacks, 2008, Matthew 27: 50–4)

Browne, S., and Harrison, L., *Life on the Other Side: A Psychic's Tour of the Afterlife* (Signet, 2001)

Fry, C., *Secrets From the Afterlife* (Ebury Press, 2008)

Plato, *Republic* (Oxford Paperbacks, 2008, 10.614–10.621)

AGNOSTICISM

Joshi, S.T. (ed.), *The Agnostic Reader* (Prometheus Books, 2007)

Spencer, H., *First Principles* (University Press of the Pacific, 2002)

ALTRUISM

Aristotle, *Nicomachean Ethics* (Penguin Classics, 2004, Books 8 and 9)

Cronin, H., *The Ant and the Peacock: Altruism and Sexual Selection from Darwin to Today* (Cambridge University Press, 1993)

Nagel, T., *The Possibility of Altruism* (Princeton University Press, 1979)

ANARCHISM

Berkman, A., *What Is Anarchism?* (AK Press, 2003)

Goldman, E., *Anarchism and Other Essays* (Bastian Books, 2008)

Proudhon, P., *Selected Writings*, tr. E. Fraser (Macmillan, 1970)

ANIMAL RIGHTS

Regan, T., *The Case for Animal Rights* (University of California Press, 1992)

Singer, P., *Animal Liberation* (Ecco, 2001)

ANTHROPIC PRINCIPLE

Barrow, J.D., and Tipler, Frank J., *The Anthropic Cosmological Principle* (Oxford University Press, 1990)

Bostrom, N., *Anthropic Bias: Observation Selection Effects in Science and Philosophy* (Routledge, 2002, Introduction)

Penrose, R., *The Emperor's New Mind: Concerning Computers, Minds and the Laws of Physics* (Oxford Paperbacks, 1999, pp. 560–2)

ANTHROPOCENTRISM

Foreman, D., *Confessions of an Eco-Warrior* (Crown Publications, 1993)

Passmore, J., *Man's Responsibility for Nature* (Gerald Duckworth & Co. Ltd, 1980)

ANTI-SEMITISM

The Bible: Authorized King James Version (Oxford Paperbacks, 2008, I Thess. 2: 14–16, John 18: 20–2, Matthew 27: 24–5, Acts 7: 51–3)

Flannery, E.H., *The Anguish of the Jews: Twenty-Three Centuries of Anti-Semitism* (Macmillan Company, 1965)

MacDonald, K., *Separation and its Discontents: Toward an Evolutionary Theory of Anti-Semitism* (1st Books Library, 2003)

ARISTOCRACY

Cannadine, D., *Aspects of Aristocracy: Grandeur and Decline in Modern Britain* (Penguin Books, 1995)

Marriott, J., *This Realm of England: Monarchy, Aristocracy, Democracy* (Blackie & Son, 1938)

Waugh, E., *Brideshead Revisited: The Sacred and Profane Memories of Captain Charles Ryder* (Penguin Classics, 2008)

ARTIFICIAL INTELLIGENCE

Finlay, J., and Dix, A., *An Introduction to Artificial Intelligence* (UCL Press Ltd, 1999)

Haugeland, J., *Artificial Intelligence: The Very Idea* (MIT Press, 1989)

Russell, S., and Norvig, P., *Artificial Intelligence: A Modern Approach* (Pearson Education, 2003)

ATHEISM

Dawkins, R., *The God Delusion* (Mariner Books, 2008)

Joshi, S.T., *Atheism: A Reader* (Prometheus Books, 2000)

Martin, M., *Atheism: A Philosophical Justification* (Temple University Press, 1992)

AUTONOMY

Dworkin, G., *The Theory and Practice of Autonomy* (Cambridge University Press, 1988)

Kant, I., *Groundwork of the Metaphysic of Morals* (Wilder Publications, 2008)

Mitchell, S.A., *Influence and Autonomy in Psychoanalysis* (Routledge, 2005)

BIG BANG COSMOLOGY

Singh, S., *Big Bang: The Most Important Scientific Discovery of All Time and Why You Need to Know About It* (HarperPerennial, 2005)

Steinhardt, P.J., and Turok, N., *Endless Universe: Beyond the Big Bang* (Phoenix, 2008)

BIODIVERSITY

Leakey, R., and Lewin, R., *The Sixth Extinction: Biodiversity and its Survival* (Weidenfeld & Nicolson, 1996)

Wilson, E.O., *Biodiversity* (National Academy Press, 1988)

BIOETHICS

Bryant, J., Baggott la Velle, L., and Searle, J., *Introduction to Bioethics* (Wiley, 2005)

Kuhse, H., and Singer, P., *Bioethics: An Anthology* (WileyBlackwell, 2006)

O'Neill, O., *Autonomy and Trust in Bioethics* (Cambridge University Press, 2008)

BIOLOGY

Alberts, B., Bray, D., Hopkin, K., Johnson, A., Lewis, J., Roberts, K., Raff, M., and Walter, P., *Essential Cell Biology* (Garland Science, 2003)

Campbell, N., and Reece, J., *Biology (with Mastering Biology)*™ (Pearson, 2008)

Sterelny, K., and Griffiths, P.E., *Sex and Death: An Introduction to the Philosophy of Biology* (University of Chicago Press, 1999)

BIOPOIESIS

Bryson, B., *A Short History of Nearly Everything* (Broadway Books, 2003, pp. 300–2)

Grossinger, R., *Biopoiesis* (North Atlantic Books, 1984)

BLACK CONSCIOUSNESS

Biko, S., and Arnold, M., *Steve Biko: Black Consciousness in South Africa* (Random House, USA, 1988)

Branch, T., *At Canaan's Edge: America in the King Years, 1965–68* (Simon & Schuster Ltd, 2007)

Brodber, E., *The Continent of Black Consciousness: On the History of the African Diaspora from Slavery to the Present Day* (New Beacon Books, 2003)

BLACK HOLES

Ferguson, K., *Prisons of Light – Black Holes* (Cambridge University Press, 1998)

Susskind, L., Lindsay, J., *An Introduction to Black Holes, Information and the String Theory Revolution: The Holographic Universe* (World Scientific Publishing Company, 2004)

Taylor, J., *Black Holes: The End of the Universe?* (Souvenir Press, 1998)

BLACK POWER

Hamilton, C.V., and Ture, K., *Black Power: The Politics of Liberation* (Vintage, 1992)

Wright, R.A., and West, C., *Black Power: Three Books from Exile: Black Power/ The Color Curtain/And White Man, Listen! (P.S.)* (HarperPerennial Modern Classics, 2008)

BUDDHISM

Dalai Lama, *The Little Book of Buddhism* (Rider & Co., 2000)

Gyatso, G.K., *Introduction to Buddhism: An Explanation of the Buddhist Way of Life* (Tharpa Publications, 2008)

Harvey, P., *An Introduction to Buddhism* (Cambridge University Press, 1993)

BUSINESS ETHICS

Chryssides, G., and Kaler, J.H., *An Introduction to Business Ethics* (Thomson Learning, 1993)

Solomon, R.C., Hanson, K., and Martin, C., *Above the Bottom Line: An Introduction to Business Ethics* (Wadsworth Publishing, 2003)

CAPITALISM

Bowles, S., Edwards, R., and Roosevelt, F., *Understanding Capitalism: Competition, Command and Change* (Oxford University Press, USA, 2005)

Ricardo, D., *Principles of Political Economy and Taxation* (Frederick Ellis, 2007)

Rodinson, M., *Islam and Capitalism* (University of Texas Press, 1979)

CATHOLICISM

Hahn, S., and Hahn, K., *Rome Sweet Home: Our Journey to Catholicism* (Ignatius Press, 1993)

Pollard, J., *Catholicism in Modern Italy: Religion, Science and Politics, 1861 to the Present* (Routledge, 2008)

CHRISTIANITY

The Bible: Authorized King James Version

Pope Benedict XVI, *Introduction to Christianity* (Ignatius Press, 2004)

Ward, K., *Christianity: A Beginner's Guide* (Oneworld Publications, 2008)

CIVILIZATION

Clark, K., *Civilisation: A Personal View* (HarperCollins, 1990)

Durant, W., *Heroes of History: A Brief History of Civilisation* (Simon & Schuster, 2001)

Huntington, S.P., *The Clash of Civilizations and the Remaking of World Order* (Simon & Schuster, New York, 1996)

CLASS

James, L., *The Middle Class* (Abacus, 2008)

Marshall, G., et al., *Social Class in Modern Britain* (Routledge, 1989)

Marx, K., and Engels, F., *The Communist Manifesto: Complete With Seven Rarely Published Prefaces* (Filiquarian Publishing, 2005)

CLONING

Huxley, A., *Brave New World* (Vintage Classics, 2007)

Pence, G.E., *Who's Afraid of Human Cloning?* (Rowman & Littlefield Publishers, 1998)

Pence, G.E., *Cloning After Dolly: Who's Still Afraid?* (Rowman & Littlefield Publishers, 2005)

COGNITIVE SCIENCE

Bechtel, W., *A Companion to Cognitive Science* (WileyBlackwell, 1999)

Stein, D.J., *Cognitive Science and the Unconscious (Progress in Psychiatry)* (American Psychiatric Publishing, 1997)

Thagard, P., *Mind: Introduction to Cognitive Science* (MIT Press, 2005)

COGNITIVE THERAPY

Beck, A.T., Rush, A.J., Shaw, B.F., and Emery, G., *Cognitive Therapy of Depression* (Guilford Press, 1979)

Beck, A.T., and Beck, J.S., *Cognitive Therapy: Basics and Beyond* (Guilford Press, 1995)

COMMUNISM

Furet, F., Nolte, E., and Golsan, K., *Fascism and Communism* (University of Nebraska Press, 2005)

Marx, K., and Engels, F., *The Communist Manifesto: Complete With Seven Rarely Published Prefaces* (Filiquarian Publishing, 2005)

Samuel, R., *The Lost World of British Communism* (Verso Books, 2006)

CONSEQUENTIALISM

Bentham, J., *Principles of Morals and Legislation* (Prometheus Books, 1988, Chapter 1)

Pettit, P., *Consequentialism* (Dartmouth Publishing, 1993)

Slote, M.A., *Common-sense Morality and Consequentialism* (Routledge & Kegan Paul, 1985)

CONSUMERISM

Bauman, Z., *Work, Consumerism and the New Poor* (Open University Press, 1998)

Frank, T., *The Conquest of Cool: Business Culture, Counterculture and the Rise of Hip Consumerism* (Chicago University Press, 1998)

Twitchell, J.B., *Lead Us Into Temptation* (Columbia University Press 1999)

Veblen, T., *The Theory of the Leisure Class* (Arc Manor, 2008)

CREATIONISM

The Bible: Authorized King James Version

Eldredge, N., *The Monkey Business: A Scientist Looks at Creationism* (Washington Square Press, 1982)

Eldredge, N., *The Triumph of Evolution: And the Failure of Creationism* (W.H. Freeman, 2001)

DAOISM (TAOISM)

Blofeld, J., *Taoism: The Road to Immortality* (Shambhala Publications, 1978)

Creel, H.G., *What is Taoism? And Other Studies in Chinese Cultural History* (University of Chicago Press, 1982)

Zhuangzi, *Zhuangzi* (Prentice Hall, 2007)

DEMOCRACY

Birch A.H., *The Concepts and Theories of Modern Democracy* (Routledge, 1993)

Diamond, L., and Plattner, M.F., *Electoral Systems and Democracy* (Johns Hopkins University Press, 2006)

Plato, *Gorgias* (Penguin Classics, 2004, 515E)

DEONTOLOGY

Bentham, J., *Deontology; or, the Science of Morality* (BookSurge, 2000)

Kant, I., *Groundwork of the Metaphysic of Morals* (Wilder Publications, 2008)

Rawls, J., *Lectures on the History of Moral Philosophy* (with Barbara Hermann) (Harvard University Press, 2000)

Rickaby, J., *Moral Philosophy: Ethics, Deontology and Natural Law* (Longmans, Green & Co., 1923)

ECONOMICS

Basu, K., *Prelude to Political Economy: A Study of the Social and Political Foundations of Economics* (Oxford University Press, 2003)

Dasgupta, P., *Economics* (Oxford University Press, 2007)

Smith, A., *Wealth of Nations* (Harriman House Publishing, 2007)

EDUCATION

Aristotle, *Politics* (Dover Publications, 2000, 1313a34)

Dewey, J., *Democracy and Education: An Introduction to the Philosophy of Education* (NuVision Publications, 2007)

Noddings, N., *Philosophy of Education* (Westview Press, 2006)

EGOISM

Broad, C.D., *Critical Essays in Moral Philosophy*, 'Egoism as a Theory of Human Motives' (Branch Line, 1979)

Rand, A., *The Virtue of Selfishness: A New Concept of Egoism* (Quality Paperback Book Club, 1998)

ENLIGHTENMENT

Gay, P., *The Enlightenment: An Interpretation* (W.W. Norton, 1996)

Jefferson, T., *The Declaration of Independence* (Verso, 2007)

Kant, I., *Foundations of the Metaphysics of Morals and What is Enlightenment?* (Bobbs-Merrill, 1959)

Kors, A.C., *Encyclopedia of the Enlightenment* (Oxford University Press, USA, 2003)

EPISTEMOLOGY

Norris, C., *Epistemology* (Continuum International Publishing Group, 2005)

Plato, *Theaetetus* (Penguin Classics, 2004)

Williams, M., *Problems of Knowledge: A Critical Introduction to Epistemology* (Oxford University Press, 2001)

EQUALITY

Callinicos, A., *Equality* (Polity Press, 2000)

Cohen, G.A., *Self-ownership, Freedom, and Equality* (Cambridge University Press, 1995)

Hayek, F., *Constitution of Liberty* (Routledge, 2006)

ETHICS

Blackburn, S., *Being Good: A Short Introduction to Ethics* (Oxford Paperbacks, 2002)

Mackie, J.L., *Ethics: Inventing Right and Wrong* (Penguin, 1991)

Wiggins, D., *Twelve Lectures on the Philosophy of Morality* (Penguin 2006)

Williams, B., *Morality: An Introduction to Ethics* (Cambridge University Press, 1993)

ETHICS, HISTORY OF

MacIntyre, A.C., *A Short History of Ethics: A History of Moral Philosophy from the Homeric Age to the Twentieth Century* (University of Notre Dame Press, 1998)

Reath, A., Hermann, B., and Korsgaard, C.M., *Reclaiming the History of Ethics: Essays for John Rawls* (Cambridge University Press, 2008)

Sidgwick, H., *Outlines of the History of Ethics for English Readers* (Thoemmes Continuum, 1995)

ETHNOCENTRISM

Fuglestad, F., *The Ambiguities of History: The Problem of Ethnocentrism in Historical Writing* (Oslo Academic Press, 2005)

Sumner, W.G., *Folkways: A Study of the Sociological Importance of Usages, Manners, Customs, Mores and Morals* (Dover, 1959)

EUTHANASIA

Dworkin, G., Frey, R.G., and Bok, S., *Euthanasia and Physician-Assisted Suicide* (Cambridge University Press, 2008)

Hippocrates, *Hippocrates the Oath or the Hippocratic Oath* (Ares Publishers, 1997)

EVOLUTION

Dawkins, R., *The Blind Watchmaker: Why the Evidence of Evolution Reveals a Universe Without Design* (Topeka Bindery, 2008)

Gould, S.J., *Punctuated Equilibrium* (Harvard University Press, 2007)

Huxley, J., *Evolution: The Modern Synthesis* (Allen & Unwin, 1974)

EXISTENTIALISM

Camus, A., *The Myth of Sisyphus* (Penguin Classics, 2006)

Kaufmann, W., *Existentialism from Dostoevsky to Sartre* (Plume, 1975)

Macquarrie, J., *Existentialism* (Penguin Books, 1991)

EXPERIMENTAL PHILOSOPHY

Knobe, J., and Nichols, S., *Experimental Philosophy* (Oxford University Press, 2008)

Sinnot-Armstrong, W., *Moral Psychology* (MIT Press, 2007)

FALSIFIABILITY

Popper, K., *Conjectures and Refutations* (Routledge, 1963)

Popper, K., *The Logic of Scientific Discovery* (Routledge, 2002)

FASCISM

Bolton, K., *An Introduction to Fascism* (Steven Books, 2004)

Paxton, R.O., *The Anatomy of Fascism* (Penguin, 2005)

FEMINISM

Aristophanes, *Four Plays: Lysistrata, The Frogs, A Parliament of Women, Plutus* (Signet Classics, 2004)

Mill, J.S., *On Liberty and The Subjection of Women* (Penguin Classics, 2006)

Valenti, J., *Full Frontal Feminism: A Young Woman's Guide to Why Feminism Matters* (Seal Press, 2007)

Watkins, S., *Introducing Feminism* (Icon Books, 1999)

FREEDOM OF SPEECH

Amar, V.D., *Freedom of Speech: First Amendment* (Prometheus Books, 2008)

Mill, J.S., *On Liberty and The Subjection of Women* (Penguin Classics, 2006)

FUNDAMENTALISM

Packer, J.I., *Fundamentalism and the Word of God: Some Evangelical Principles* (Inter-Varsity Press, 1996)

Ruthvcn, M., *Fundamentalism: A Very Short Introduction* (Oxford University Press, 2007)

FUTURE, THE

Cornish, E., *Futuring: The Exploration of the Future* (World Future Society, 2005)

GAME THEORY

Binmore, K.G., *Fun and Games: A Text on Game Theory* (Houghton Mifflin, 1992)

Poundstone, W., *Prisoner's Dilemma: John Von Neumann, Game Theory and the Puzzle of the Bomb* (Anchor Books, USA, 1993)

Von Neumann, J., and Morgenstern, O., *Theory of Games and Economic Behavior* (Princeton University Press, 1992)

GLOBALIZATION

Legrain, P., *Open World: The Truth About Globalisation* (Abacus, 2003)

Micklethwait, J., and Wooldridge, A., *A Future Perfect: The Challenge and Hidden Promise of Globalization* (Crown Business, 2000)

HINDUISM AND BRAHMANISM

Monier-Williams, M., *Brahmanism and Hinduism: Or Religious Thought and Life in India as Based on the Veda and Other Sacred Books of the Hindus* (Kessinger Publishing, 2005)

The Upanishads (Penguin Classics, 2005)

HISTORY

Elton, G., *The Practice of History* (2nd edn.) (Blackwell, 2002)

Jenkins, K., *On 'What Is History?'* (London, 1995)

HUMANISM

Herrick, J., *Humanism: An Introduction* (Prometheus Books, 2005)

Sartre, J.-P., *Existentialism and Humanism* (Methuen Publishing, 2007)

HUMAN RIGHTS

Alston, P., and Goodman, R., *International Human Rights in Context: Law, Politics, Morals* (Oxford University Press, 2007)

Hunt, L., *Inventing Human Rights: A History* (W.W. Norton, 2008)

IDENTITY

Sen, A., *Identity and Violence* (Penguin, 2007)

INTERNET

Crystal, D., *Language and the Internet* (Cambridge University Press, 2006)

Turkle, S., *Life on the Screen: Identity in the Age of the Internet* (Simon & Schuster, 1997)

Zittrain, J., *The Future of the Internet: and How to Stop It* (Allen Lane, 2008)

INTUITIONISM, MATHEMATICAL AND LOGICAL

Dummett, M., *Elements of Intuitionism* (Clarendon Press, 2000)

Heyting, A., *Intuitionism: An Introduction* (North-Holland Publishing, 1956)

IRRATIONALISM

Berlin, I., and Hardy, H., *The Magus of the North: J.G. Hamann and the Origins of Modern Irrationalism* (Farrar Straus & Giroux, 1994)

Stove, D., *Scientific Irrationalism: Origins of a Postmodern Cult* (Transaction Publishers, USA, 2007)

ISLAM

Lewis, B., *The Jews of Islam* (Routledge, 2007)

The Qur'an (Oxford University Press, 2008)

Ruthven, M., *Islam: A Very Short Introduction* (Oxford Paperbacks, 2000)

JUDAISM

De Lange, N., *An Introduction to Judaism* (Cambridge University Press, 2000)

Diamant, A., *Choosing a Jewish Life: A Handbook for People Converting to Judaism and for Their Family and Friends* (Schocken, 1998)

JUSTICE

Barry, B., *Why Social Justice Matters* (Polity Press, 2005)

Nozick, R., *Anarchy, State and Utopia* (Blackwell Publishers, 1978)

Rawls, J., *A Theory of Justice* (Harvard University Press, 2005)

LAW

Austin, J., *The Providence of Jurisprudence Determined* (Prometheus Books, 2000)

Harris, P., *An Introduction to Law* (7th edn) (Cambridge University Press, 2006)

LIBERALISM

Locke, J., *Of Civil Government: The Second Treatise* (Wildside Press, 2008)

Manent, P., *An Intellectual History of Liberalism* (Princeton University Press, 1996)

Rawls, J., *Political Liberalism* (Columbia University Press, 2005)

LIBERTY

Berlin, I., *Liberty: Incorporating Four Essays on Liberty* (Oxford University Press, USA, 2002, 'Two Concepts of Liberty')

Keillor, G., *Liberty* (Viking Books, 2008)

Mill, J.S., *On Liberty and The Subjection of Women* (Penguin Classics, 2006)

LOGIC

Copi, I. M., and Cohen, C., *Introduction to Logic* (Prentice Hall College Division, 1998)

Haack, S., *Philosophy of Logics* (Cambridge University Press, 1978)

Hodges, W., *Logic* (Penguin, 2001)

LOGIC, FALLACIES OF INFORMAL

Walton, D. N., *Informal Logic* (Cambridge University Press, 1989)

LOVE

Ackerman, D., *A Natural History of Love* (Vintage, 1995)

Stendhal, *On Love* (1822)

MARXISM

Callinicos, A., *The Revolutionary Ideas of Karl Marx* (London, 1996)

Marx, K., and Engels, F., *Historical Materialism: Preface to 'A Contribution to the Critique of Political Economy'* (Pluto Press, 1971)

Woods, A., *Reformism or Revolution: Marxism and Socialism of the 21st Century* (Well Red Publications, 2008)

MEANING, THEORY OF

Horwich, P., *Meaning* (Clarendon Press, 1998)

Lehrer, A., and Lehrer, K., *Theory of Meaning* (Prentice Hall, 1970)

METAPHYSICS
Aristotle, *The Metaphysics* (Penguin Classics, 2004)
Lowe, E.J., *A Survey of Metaphysics* (Oxford University Press, 2002)
Strawson, P.F., *Identity: an Essay in Descriptive Metaphysics* (University Paperbacks, 1977)

MIND, PHILOSOPHY OF
Gallagher, S., and Zahavi, D., *The Phenomenological Mind: An Introduction to the Philosophy of Mind and Cognitive Science* (Routledge, 2007)
Rey, G., *Contemporary Philosophy of Mind* (WileyBlackwell, 1996)

MULTICULTURALISM
James, W., *A Pluralistic Universe* (Wildside Press, 2008)
Modood, T., *Multiculturalism* (Polity Press, 2007)
West, P., *The Poverty of Multiculturalism* (Civitas: Institute for the Study of Civil Society, 2005)

NATIONALISM
Gellner, E., *Nations and Nationalism* (Cornell University Press, 1983)
Grosby, S., *Nationalism: A Very Short Introduction* (Oxford University Press, 2005)
Miller, D.I., *Citizenship and National Identity* (Polity Press, 2000)

NEOCONSERVATISM
Heilbrunn, J., *They Knew They Were Right: The Rise of the Neocons* (Doubleday Books, 2008)
Murray, D., *Neoconservatism: Why We Need It* (Social Affairs Unit, 2005)
Stelzer, I., *Neoconservatism* (Atlantic Books, 2005)

NEUROPHILOSOPHY
Churchland, P.S., *Neurophilosophy: Towards a Unified Science of the Mind/ Brain* (MIT Press, 1989)
Churchland, P., *Neurophilosophy at Work* (Cambridge University Press, 2007)

NEUROSCIENCE
Bechtel, W., *Mental Mechanisms: Philosophical Perspectives on Cognitive Neuroscience* (Psychology Press, 2007)
Johnson, M.H., *Developmental Cognitive Neuroscience* (WileyBlackwell, 2004)
Zeman, A., *A Portrait of the Brain* (Yale University Press, 2006)

ORTHODOX CHRISTIANITY

Ware, T., *The Orthodox Church* (Penguin, 1993)

PHILOSOPHY

Blackburn, S., *Think: A Compelling Introduction to Philosophy* (Oxford Paperbacks, 2001)

Perry, J., and Bratman, M., *Introduction to Philosophy: Classical and Contemporary Readings* (Oxford University Press, USA, 1998)

Russell, B., *The Problems of Philosophy* (Standard Publications, 2008)

POLITICS

Aristotle, *Politics* (Dover Publications, 2000, 1252b30–1253a3)

Jones, B., Kavanagh, D., Moran, M., and Norton, P., *Politics UK* (Longman, 2006)

Plato, *Republic* (Oxford Paperbacks, 2008)

POSITIVISM AND LOGICAL POSITIVISM

Ayer, A. J., *Logical Positivism* (Greenwood Press reprint, 1978)

Friedman, M., *Reconsidering Logical Positivism* (Cambridge University Press, 1999)

Hume, D., *An Enquiry Concerning Human Understanding* (Oxford University Press, 2008)

POSTMODERNISM

Jameson, F., *Postmodernism: Or, the Cultural Logic of Late Capitalism* (Verso Books, 1992)

Ruland, R., and Bradbury, M., *From Puritanism to Postmodernism: A History of American Literature* (Penguin, 1993)

PRIVACY

Alderman, E., and Kennedy, C., *The Right to Privacy* (Vintage, 1997)

Gavison, R., 'Privacy and the Limits of the Law', in Gorr, M.J., and Harwood, S. (eds.), *Crime and Punishment: Philosophic Investigations* (Wadsworth Publishing, 2000, pp. 46–68)

Solove, D.J., *Understanding Privacy* (Harvard University Press, 2008)

PROTESTANTISM

McGrath, A.E., and Marks, D.C., *The Blackwell Companion to Protestantism* (WileyBlackwell, 2006)

Wylie, J.A., *The History of Protestantism*, 4-vol. set (Hartland Publications, 2002)

PSYCHOANALYSIS

Freud, S., *The Complete Psychological Works of Sigmund Freud: 'New Introductory Lectures on Psychoanalysis' and Other Works*, vol. 22 (Vintage, 2001)

Rycroft, C., *A Critical Dictionary of Psychoanalysis* (Penguin, 2005)

Sharpe, M., *Understanding Psychoanalysis* (Acumen Publishing, 2008)

PSYCHOLOGY

James, W., *The Principles of Psychology*, vols 1 and 2 in one volume (Harvard University Press, 1983)

Smith, E., Nolen-Hoeksema, S., and Fredrickson, B., *Atkinson and Hilgard's Introduction to Psychology* (Wadsworth Publishing, 2003)

Wundt, W., *An Introduction to Psychology* (Read Books, 2007)

PUNISHMENT

Foucault, M., *Discipline and Punish: The Birth of the Prison* (Penguin, 1991)

Hart, H.L.A., and Gardner, J., *Punishment and Responsibility: Essays in the Philosophy of Law* (Oxford University Press, USA, 2008)

QUANTUM MECHANICS

Griffiths, D.J., *An Introduction to Quantum Mechanics* (Addison Wesley, 2004)

Pauling, L., and Wilson, E.B., *Introduction to Quantum Mechanics* (Courier Dover Publications, 1963)

Sakurai, J.J., *Modern Quantum Mechanics*, reissued 2nd edn (Addison Wesley, 1993)

RACISM

Malik, K., *The Meaning of Race* (New York University Press, 1996)

UNESCO, *The Race Question in Modern Science* (UNESCO, 1959)

REALISM

Putnam, H., *Realism With a Human Face*, edited and introduced by James Conant (Harvard University Press, 1990)

Wright, C., *Realism, Meaning and Truth* (Oxford University Press, 1993)

RELATIVISM

Boghossian, P., *Fear of Knowledge: Against Relativism and Constructivism* (Clarendon Press, 2007)

Meiland, J., *Relativism: Cognitive and Moral* (University of Notre Dame Press, 1992)

RELATIVITY

Geroch, R., *General Relativity From A to B* (University of Chicago Press, 1978)

Rindler, W., *Introduction to Special Relativity* (Oxford University Press, 1991)

Schutz, B.F., *A First Course in General Relativity* (Cambridge University Press, 1985)

RELIGION

Firth, R., *Religion: A Humanist Interpretation* (Routledge, 1995)

Hume, D., *Hume – Dialogues Concerning Natural Religion: And Other Writings* (Cambridge University Press, 2007)

Morris, B., *Anthropological Studies of Religion: An Introductory Text* (Cambridge University Press, 1987)

ROMANTICISM

Rousseau, J., *Collected Writings of Rousseau* (Dartmouth College, 1997)

Wu, D., *A Companion to Romanticism* (WileyBlackwell, 1999)

Wu, D., *Romanticism: An Anthology* (WileyBlackwell, 2005)

SCEPTICISM

Luper, S., *The Skeptics* (Ashgate, 2003)

Stroud, B., *The Significance of Philosophical Scepticism* (Oxford University Press, 1984)

Williams, M., *Unnatural Doubts* (Blackwell, 1991)

SCIENCE

Dawkins, R. (ed.), *The Oxford Book of Modern Science Writing* (Oxford University Press, 2008)

Goldacre, B., *Bad Science* (Fourth Estate, 2008)

Trefil, J.S., *101 Things You Don't Know About Science and No One Else Does Either* (Houghton Mifflin, 1998)

SCIENTIFIC REVOLUTIONS

Hacking, I. (ed.), *Scientific Revolutions* (Oxford University Press, 1981)

Henry, J., *The Scientific Revolution and the Origins of Modern Science* (Palgrave Macmillan, 2001)

Kuhn, T., *The Structure of Scientific Revolutions* (Books on Demand, 1970)

SECULARISM

Bhargava, R., *Secularism and its Critics* (Oxford University Press, 2004)

Jakobsen, J., and Pellegrini, A. (eds.), *Secularisms* (Duke University Press, 2008)

SLAVERY

Walvin, J., *A Short History of Slavery* (Penguin 2007)

Washington, B., *Up From Slavery: An Autobiography* (Penguin Classics, 2007)

Williams, E.E., *Capitalism and Slavery* (University of North Carolina Press, 1994)

SOCIALISM

Huberman, L., and Sweezy, P.M., *Introduction to Socialism* (Monthly Review Press, 1968)

Marx, K., and Engels, F., *The Communist Manifesto: Complete With Seven Rarely Published Prefaces* (Filiquarian Publishing, 2005)

Schumpeter, J.A., *Capitalism, Socialism and Democracy* (HarperPerennial, 1962)

SOCIOBIOLOGY

Alcock, J., *The Triumph of Sociobiology* (Oxford University Press, USA, 2003)

Lewontin, R.C., Rose, S., and Kamin, L.J., *Not In Our Genes: Biology, Ideology and Human Nature* (Penguin Books, 1990)

Wilson, E.O., *Sociobiology: The New Synthesis*, 25th anniversary edition (Belknap Press, 2000)

STANDARD MODEL

Close, F., *Particle Physics: A Very Short Introduction* (Oxford University Press, 2004)

Griffiths, D.J., *Introduction to Elementary Particles* (Wiley, 1987)

Ramond, P., *Journeys Beyond the Standard Model* (Westview Press, 2003)

STRING THEORY

Musser, G., *The Complete Idiot's Guide to String Theory* (Alpha, 2008)

Smolin, L., *The Trouble with Physics* (Houghton Mifflin, 2006)

Zwiebach, B., *A First Course in String Theory* (Cambridge University Press, 2004)

TECHNOLOGY

Goldin, C., and Katz, L.F., *The Race Between Education and Technology* (Belknap Press, 2008)

Ihde, D., *The Philosophy of Technology: An Introduction* (Paragon House Publishers, 1993)

TERRORISM

Köchler, H., *Manila Lectures 2002: Terrorism and the Quest for a Just World Order* (Foundation for Social Justice, 2002)

Laqueur, W., *No End to War: Terrorism in the Twenty-First Century* (Continuum International Publishing Group Ltd, 2004)

Townshend, C., *Terrorism: A Very Short Introduction* (Oxford Paperbacks, 2002)

TOLERANCE

Kraft, J., and Basinger, D., *Religious Tolerance Through Humility: Thinking with Philip Quinn* (Ashgate, 2008)

Scanlon, T.M., *The Difficulty of Tolerance: Essays in Political Philosophy* (Cambridge University Press, 2003)

TOTALITARIANISM

Arendt, H., *The Origins of Totalitarianism* (Schocken Books, 2004)

Howe, I., *1984 Revisited: Totalitarianism in Our Century* (Joanna Cotler Books, 1983)

Popper, K., *The Open Society and its Enemies* (Routledge, 2002)

Zizek, S., *Did Somebody Say Totalitarianism? Four Interventions in the (Mis) use of a Notion* (Verso Books, 2001)

TRUTH

Blackburn, S., *Truth: A Guide for the Perplexed* (Penguin, 2006)

Dummett, M., *Truth and Other Enigmas* (Harvard University Press, 1978)

Fernández-Armesto, F., *Truth: A History and Guide for the Perplexed* (St Martin's Press, 1997)

UTOPIA

Carey, J. (ed.), *The Faber Book of Utopias* (Faber and Faber, 2000)

Huxley, A., *Brave New World* (Vintage Classics, 2007)

More, T., Bacon, F., and Neville, H., *Three Early Modern Utopias: Sir Thomas More's 'Utopia', Francis Bacon's 'New Atlantis', Henry Neville's 'Isle of Pines'* (Oxford Paperbacks, 1999)

VEGETARIANISM

Bodhipaksa, *Vegetarianism* (Windhorse Publications, 2006)

Singer, P., *Animal Liberation* (Ecco, 2001)

VERIFICATIONISM

Ayer, A.J., *Language, Truth and Logic* (Penguin Classics, 2001)

Quine, W.V.O., *From a Logical Point of View* (Harvard University Press, 1980, 'Two Dogmas of Empiricism')

VIRTUE ETHICS

Aristotle, *Nicomachean Ethics* (Penguin Classics, 2004)

Crisp, R., and Slote, M. (eds.), *Virtue Ethics* (Oxford University Press, 1997)

Foot, P., *Virtues and Vices: And Other Essays in Moral Philosophy* (Clarendon Press, 2002)

Oakley, J., and Cocking, D., *Virtue Ethics and Professional Roles* (Cambridge University Press, 2008)

WAR

von Clausewitz, C., *On War* (Oxford University Press, 2008)

Zi, S., *The Art of War* (Filiquarian Publishing, 2006)

WAR CRIMES

Conot, Robert E., *Justice at Nuremberg* (Harper & Row, 1983)

Gutman, R., *Crimes of War* (W.W. Norton, 1999)

WEALTH

Beinhocker, E., *The Origin of Wealth: Evolution, Complexity, and the Radical Remaking of Economics* (Random House Business Books, 2007)

Smith, A., *Wealth of Nations* (Harriman House Publishing, 2007)

WESTERNIZATION

Latouche, S., *The Westernization of the World: Significance, Scope and Limits of the Drive Towards Global Uniformity* (Polity Press, 1996)

Stearns, P.N., *Western Civilisation in World History* (Routledge, 2003)

XENOPHOBIA

Report drawn up on behalf of the Committee of Inquiry into Racism and Xenophobia on the Findings of the Committee of Inquiry (European Parliament, 1991)

Wistrich, R.S., *Demonizing the Other: Antisemitism, Racism and Xenophobia* (Routledge, 1999)

ZEITGEIST

Hazlitt, W., *The Spirit of the Age, Or, Contemporary Portraits* (New Leaf Health and Fitness, 2008)

Jaspars, K., *Man in the Modern Age* (London, 1933)

Index